THE LETTERS OF

Charles and Mary Anne Lamb

Volume II • 1801–1809

CHARLES LAMB AT TWENTY-NINE IN THE DRESS OF A VENETIAN SENATOR.
From an oil painting by William Hazlitt. Courtesy of the National Portrait
Gallery, London.

THE LETTERS OF

Charles and Mary Anne Lamb

Volume II • 1801–1809

EDITED BY EDWIN W. MARRS, Jr.

CORNELL UNIVERSITY PRESS

ITHACA AND LONDON

1976

First published 1976 by Cornell University Press.
Published in the United Kingdom by Cornell University Press Ltd.,
2-4 Brook Street, London W1Y 1AA.

International Standard Book Number 0-8014-0977-2
Library of Congress Catalog Card Number 75-8436
Printed in the United States of America by York Composition Co., Inc.

CONTENTS

ILLUSTRATIONS

ABBREVIATIONS

Ainger (1888) Alfred Ainger, ed. *The Letters of Charles Lamb: Newly Arranged, with Additions*. 2 vols. London and New York: Macmillan, 1888.

Ainger (1900) Alfred Ainger, ed. *The Letters of Charles Lamb: Newly Arranged, with Additions*, Vols. I–IV. Vols. IX–XII of *The Life and Works of Charles Lamb*. 12 vols. London: Macmillan, 1899–1900.

Ainger (1904) Alfred Ainger, ed. *The Letters of Charles Lamb: Newly Arranged, with Additions*. 2 vols. London and New York: Macmillan, 1904.

C. L. Charles Lamb.

CLSB *Charles Lamb Society Bulletin*. Retitled *Charles Lamb Bulletin* January 1973.

Coleridge's Letters Earl Leslie Griggs, ed. *Collected Letters of Samuel Taylor Coleridge*. 6 vols. Oxford: Clarendon Press, 1956–1971.

Coleridge's Poetical Works (1912) Ernest Hartley Coleridge, ed. *The Complete Poetical Works of Samuel Taylor Coleridge, Including Poems and Versions of Poems Now Published for the First Time*. 2 vols. Oxford: Clarendon Press, 1912.

Coleridge's Shakespearean Criticism Thomas Middleton Raysor, ed. *Samuel Taylor Coleridge: Shakespearean Criticism*. 2d ed. 2 vols. 1960. Rpt. London: Dent; New York: Dutton, 1967.

De Quincey's Writings David Masson, ed. *The Collected Writings of Thomas De Quincey*. 14 vols. London: Black, 1896–1897.

Fate of the Fenwicks, The A. F. Wedd, ed. *The Fate of the Fenwicks: Letters to Mary Hays (1798–1828)*. London: Methuen, 1927.

Fitzgerald Percy Fitzgerald, ed. *The Life, Letters and Writings of Charles Lamb*. 6 vols. London: Moxon, 1876.

Friend, The, ed. Barbara Rooke Barbara E. Rooke, ed. *The Friend, I [and II]*, in *The Collected Works of Samuel Taylor Coleridge*, ed. Kathleen Coburn and Bart Winer. Vol. IV, Parts 1 and 2. London: Routledge & Kegan Paul; Princeton: Princeton University Press, 1969.

Godwin C. Kegan Paul. *William Godwin: His Friends and Contemporaries.* 2 vols. London: King, 1876.

Harper Henry H. Harper [and Richard Garnett], eds. *The Letters of Charles Lamb: In Which Many Mutilated Words and Passages Have Been Restored to Their Original Form; with Letters Never before Published and Facsimiles of Original MS Letters and Poems.* 5 vols. Boston: Bibliophile Society, 1905.

Hazlitt W[illiam] Carew Hazlitt, ed. *Letters of Charles Lamb: With Some Account of the Writer, His Friends and Correspondents, and Explanatory Notes. By the Late Thomas Noon Talfourd, D.C.L., One of his Executors. An Entirely New Edition, Carefully Revised and Greatly Enlarged.* 2 vols. London: Bell, 1886.

Hazlitt Herschel Baker. *William Hazlitt.* Cambridge, Mass.: Harvard University Press, 1962.

Hazlitts, The W[illiam] Carew Hazlitt. *The Hazlitts: An Account of Their Origin and Descent.* Edinburgh: Ballantyne, Hanson, 1911.

Hazlitt's Works P. P. Howe, ed. *The Complete Works of William Hazlitt. After the Edition of A. R. Waller and Arnold Glover.* 21 vols. London and Toronto: Dent, 1930–1934.

H. C. R. on Books and Writers Edith J. Morley, ed. *Henry Crabb Robinson on Books and Their Writers.* 3 vols. London: Dent, 1938.

H. C. R.'s Diary Thomas Sadler, ed. *Diary, Reminiscences, and Correspondence of Henry Crabb Robinson, Barrister-at-Law, F.S.A.* 2 vols. Boston: Fields, Osgood, 1870.

Holcroft Elbridge Colby, ed. *The Life of Thomas Holcroft: Written by Himself, Continued to the Time of His Death from His Diary Notes & Other Papers by William Hazlitt, and Now Newly Edited with Introduction and Notes.* 2 vols. London: Constable, 1925.

Hunt's Autobiography Roger Ingpen, ed. *The Autobiography of Leigh Hunt: With Reminiscences of Friends and Contemporaries, and with Thornton Hunt's Introduction and Postscript.* 2 vols. New York: Dutton, 1903.

Lamb and Hazlitt William Carew Hazlitt, ed. *Lamb and Hazlitt: Further Letters and Records Hitherto Unpublished.* New York: Dodd, Mead, 1899.

Lamb and the Lloyds E. V. Lucas, ed. *Charles Lamb and the Lloyds.* London: Smith, Elder, 1898.

Lambs, The William Carew Hazlitt. *The Lambs: Their Lives, Their Friends, and Their Correspondence. New Particulars and New Material.* London: Mathews; New York: Scribner's, 1897.

Lives of the English Poets George Birkbeck Hill, ed. *Lives of the*

English Poets by Samuel Johnson, LL.D. 3 vols. 1905. Rpt. New York: Octagon Books, 1967.

Lloyd-Manning Letters Frederick L. Beaty, ed. *The Lloyd-Manning Letters.* Bloomington: Indiana University Press, 1957.

Lucas (1905) E. V. Lucas, ed. *The Works of Charles and Mary Lamb.* 7 vols. New York: Putnam's; London: Methuen, 1903–1905.

Lucas (1912) E. V. Lucas, ed. *The Letters of Charles and Mary Lamb, 1796–1820* [and *1821–1842*]. Vols. V–VI of *The Works of Charles and Mary Lamb;* 6 vols. London: Methuen, 1912.

Lucas (1935) E. V. Lucas, ed. *The Letters of Charles Lamb: To Which Are Added Those of His Sister, Mary Lamb.* 3 vols. London: Dent and Methuen (copublishers), 1935.

Macdonald William Macdonald, ed. *Letters of Charles Lamb,* Vols. I–II. Vols. XI–XII of *The Works of Charles Lamb.* Large-paper Edition. 12 vols. London: Dent; New York: Dutton, 1903.

M. A. L. Mary Anne Lamb.

Manning-Lamb Letters G. A. Anderson [and P. P. Howe], eds. *The Letters of Thomas Manning to Charles Lamb.* London: Secker, 1925.

Mary and Charles Lamb W[illiam] Carew Hazlitt, ed. *Mary and Charles Lamb: Poems, Letters, and Remains: Now First Collected, with Reminiscences and Notes.* London: Chatto and Windus, 1874.

New Southey Letters Kenneth Curry, ed. *New Letters of Robert Southey.* 2 vols. New York and London: Columbia University Press, 1965.

Purnell Thomas Purnell, ed. *The Complete Correspondence and Works of Charles Lamb.* 4 vols. London: Moxon, 1870.

Rickman Orlo Williams. *Lamb's Friend the Census-taker: Life and Letters of John Rickman.* London: Constable, 1911.

Sala George Augustus Sala, ed. *The Complete Correspondence and Works of Charles Lamb.* London: Moxon, 1868.

Shelley and His Circle Kenneth Neill Cameron and Donald H. Reiman, eds. *Shelley and His Circle: 1773–1822.* 6 vols. Cambridge, Mass.: Harvard University Press, 1961–1973.

Southey's Correspondence Charles Cuthbert Southey, ed. *The Life and Correspondence of Robert Southey.* 6 vols. 1849–1850. Rpt. St. Clair Shores, Mich.: Scholarly Press [1968].

Talfourd (1837) Thomas Noon Talfourd, ed. *The Letters of Charles Lamb, with a Sketch of His Life.* 2 vols. London: Moxon, 1837.

Talfourd (1848) Thomas Noon Talfourd, ed. *Final Memorials of Charles Lamb; Consisting Chiefly of His Letters Not before Pub-*

lished, with Sketches of Some of His Companions. 2 vols. London: Moxon, 1848.

Wordworths' Letters Ernest de Selincourt, ed. *The Letters of William and Dorothy Wordsworth.* 6 vols. Oxford: Clarendon Press, 1935–1939. 2d ed.: Vol. I, rev. Chester L. Shaver (1967); Vol. II, rev. Mary Moorman (1969); Vol. III, rev. Mary Moorman and Alan G. Hill (1970).

Works E. V. Lucas, ed. *The Works of Charles and Mary Lamb.* 7 vols. New York: Putnam's; London: Methuen, 1903–1905.

The act, scene, and line numbers locating the passages from Shakespeare correspond to those in *The Riverside Shakespeare,* ed. G. Blakemore Evans *et al.* (Boston: Houghton Mifflin, 1974).

LIST OF LETTERS

PART IV

Letters 103–140
16 Mitre Court Buildings, Inner Temple
April 1801 — December 1, 1802

103. *Charles Lamb to Thomas Manning*

April 1801

I was not aware that you owed me anything beside that guinea;[1] but I dare say you are right. I live at No. 16 Mitre-court Buildings, a pistol-shot off Baron Maseres'. You must introduce me to the Baron. I think we should suit one another mainly. He lives on the ground floor for convenience of the gout; I prefer the attic story for the air! He keeps three footmen and two maids; I have neither maid nor laundress, not caring to be troubled with them! His forte, I understand, is the higher mathematics; my turn, I confess, is more to poetry and the belles lettres. The very antithesis of our characters would make up a harmony. You must bring the baron and me together.—N. B. when you come to see me, mount up to the top of the stairs—I hope you are not asthmatical—and come in flannel, for it's pure airy up there. And bring your glass, and I will shew you the Surrey Hills. My bed faces the river so as by perking up upon my haunches, and supporting my carcase with my elbows, without much wrying my neck, I can see the white sails glide by the bottom of the King's Bench walks as I lie in my bed. An excellent tiptoe prospect in the best room: casement windows with small panes, to look more like a cottage. Mind, I have got no bed for you, that's flat; sold it to pay expenses of moving. The very bed on which Manning lay—the friendly, the mathematical Manning! How forcibly does it remind me of the interesting Otway! 'The very bed which on thy marriage night gave thee into the arms of Belvidera, by the coarse hands of ruffians—'[2] (upholsterers' men,) &c. My tears will not give me leave to go on. But a bed I will get you, Manning, on condition you will be my day-guest.

I have been ill more than [a] month, with a bad cold, which comes upon me (like a murderer's conscience) about midnight, and vexes me for many hours. I have successively been drugged with Spanish licorice, opium, ipecacuanha, paregoric, and tincture of foxglove (tinctura purpuræ digitalis of the ancients). I am afraid I must leave off drinking.

MS: unrecovered. Text: Lucas (1935), I, 254. Also pub.: Talfourd (1837), I, 174–175; Sala, I, 350–352; Purnell, I, 350–352; Fitzgerald, II, 184–186; Hazlitt, I, 297–298; Ainger (1888), I, 169–170; Ainger (1900), II, 38–40; Macdonald, I, 199–200; Ainger (1904), I, 189–190; Harper, III, 13–14; Lucas (1905), VI, 217–218; Lucas (1912), V, 221.

1. How Manning had incurred the debt is not known. Manning's letters to Lamb written between March 14, 1801, and January 28, 1802, have not been recovered. Lamb's neighbor, mentioned below, who lived at 5 King's Bench Walk, Inner Temple, was Francis Maseres (1731–1824), the author of several books on mathematics and the author, editor, and translator of a number of social, political, and historical studies, especially on Quebec. In 1750 he became a barrister, in 1774 a bencher, and later the treasurer of the Inner Temple. From 1766 to 1769 he was the attorney general of Quebec and from 1773 to 1824 the cursitor baron of the exchequer (a title not of noble order). He was in 1780 appointed the senior judge of the London sheriff's court. Lamb recalled him in "The Old Benchers of the Inner Temple" (*Works*, II, 90).

2. Thomas Otway, *Venice Preserv'd*, I, i, 245–246 and 248.

104. *C. L. to Robert Lloyd*

[April 16, 1801]

Fletcher's Purple Island[1] is a tedious Allegory of the Parts of the Human body. I would not advise you to lay out six *pence* upon it. It is not the work of Fletcher, the Coadjutor of Beaumont, but one Phineas a kinsman of his.— If by the work of Bishop Taylor, whose Title you have not given correctly, you mean his **Contemplations** on the State of Man in this Life and that which is to come;[2] I dare hope you will join with me in believing it to be spurious. The suspicious circumstance of its being a posthumous work, with the total dissimilarity in style to the genuine works, I think evince that it never was the work of **Doctor Jeremy Taylor** Late Lord Bishop of **Down & Connor** in Ireland and Administrator of the **See** of **Dromore;** such are the Titles which his Sounding title pages give him, & I love the man, and I love his paraphernalia, and I like to name him with all his attributions and additions—. If you are yet but lightly acquainted with his real manner, take up and read the whole first chapter of the Holy **Dying;**[3] in particular turn to the first paragraph of the 2 sect. of that chapter for a simile of a rose, or more truly many similes within simile, for such were the riches of his fancy, that when a beauteous image offered, before he could stay to expand it into all its capacities, throngs of new coming images came up, and justled out the first, or blended in disorder with it, which imitates the order

of every rapid mind. But read all the first chapter by my advice; & I know I need not advise you, when you have read it, to read the second. .— **or** for another specimen, (where so many beauties crowd, the judgment has yet vanity enough to think it can discern a handsomest, till a second judgment and a third ad infinitum start up to disallow their elder brother's pretensions) turn to the Story of the Ephesian Matron in the second[4] section of the 5th Chapter of the same Holy *Dying* (I still refer to the *Dying* part, because it contains better matter than the Holy Living, which deals more in **rules** than **illustrations,** I mean in comparison with the other only, else it has more & more beautiful illustrations than any prose book besides)— read it yourself and shew it to Plumstead (with my **Love,** & bid him write to me) and ask him if **Willy** himself has ever told a story with more circumstances of **fancy & humour.** The paragraph begins "But that which is to be faulted," & the story not long after follows.— — Make these references, while P. is with you, that you may stir him up to the Love of Jeremy Taylor, & make a convertite of him.— — Coleridge was the man who first solemnly exhorted me to **"study"** the works of Dr. Jeremy Taylor, and I have had reason to bless the hour in which he did it.— Read as many of his works as you can get. I will assist you in getting them, when we go a stall hunting together in **London,** and its odds if we dont get a good Beaumt. & Fletcher cheap. .—

Bp. Taylor has more, & more beautiful, imagery, and (what is more to a Lover of Willy) more knowledge & description of **human life** and manners, than any prose book in the language.:— he has more **delicacy, & sweetness,** than any mortal, the "gentle"[5] Shakespear hardly excepted,—his similes and allusions are taken, as the bees take honey, from all the youngest, greenest, exquisitest parts of nature, from plants, & flowers, & fruit, young boys & **virgins,** from little children perpetually, from sucking infants, babies' smiles, roses, gardens,—his imagination was a spatious Garden where no vile insectœ could crawl in, his apprehension a **"Court"** where no foul thoughts kept "leets & holydays."—[6]

Snail & worm give no offence,—
　　Newt nor blind worm be not seen,—
　Come not near our fairy queen——

You must read Bishop Taylor with allowances for the subjects on which he wrote, and the age *in* which.— You may skip or patiently endure his tedious discourses on rites & ceremonies, Baptism & the Eucharist, the Clerical function, and the antiquity of Episcopacy, a good deal of which are inserted in works not purely controversial—his polemical works you may skip altogether, unless you have a taste for the exertions of **vigorous reason** & subtle distinguishing on uninteresting topics.— Such of his works as you should begin with, to get a taste for him (after which your **Love** will lead you to his Polemical and drier works, as Love led Leander "over boots"⁷ knee-deep thro' the Hellespont,)—but read first the Holy Living & Dying, his Life of Christ & *Sermons* both in folio.— And above all try to get a beautiful little tract on **the measures** and **offices** of **Friendship**, printed with his *opuscula* duodecimo, & also at the end of his Polemical Discourses in folio.— — Another thing you will observe in Bp. Taylor, without which consideration you will do him injustice. He wrote to different classes of people. His Holy Living & Dying & Life of X't were designed and have been used as popular books of family Devotion, and have been thumbed by old women, and laid about in the window seats of old houses in great families, like the Bible, and the "**Queene-like-Closet** or rare boke of Recipes in medicine & cookery, fitted to all capacities"— —.⁸ Accordingly in these *the fancy* is perpetually applied to; any slight conceit, allusion, or analogy, any "prettiness," a story true or false, serves for an argument, adapted to women & young persons & "incompetent judgments"—whereas the Liberty of Prophecy (a book in your father's book-case) is a series of **severe** & masterly **reasoning,** fitted to great Clerks & learned Fathers, with no more of **Fancy,** than is subordinate & ornamental.— Such various powers had the Bishop of Down & Connor, Administrator of the See of Dromore! My theme and my glory!—

<div align="right">farewell—
C Lamb</div>

MS: Henry E. Huntington Library; by permission of The Huntington Library, San Marino, Calif. Pub.: Ainger (1900), II, 34–38; Macdonald, I, 200–203; Ainger (1904), I, 186–189; Harper, I, facsimile, and III, 14–18; Lucas (1935), I, 255–258. Address: Robert Lloyd/Charles Lloyd's/Birmingham. Postmark: April 16, 1801.
 1. *The Purple Island, or the Isle of Man* (1633), by the poet Phineas Fletcher (1582–1650), a cousin of the dramatist John Fletcher.

2. *Contemplations of the State of Man in This Life, and in That Which Is to Come* (1684) may have been written by Jeremy Taylor. But it may be Taylor's compilations of extracts from Sir Vivian Mullineux's *A Treatise of the Difference betwixt the Temporal and the Eternal* (1672), a translation of *Diferencia de lo temporal y eterno*, by the Spanish Jesuit Juan Eusebio Nieremberg (1595–1658). Or it may be Taylor's translation from a Latin or an Italian translation of Nieremberg's work. See *The Golden Grove: Selected Passages from the Writings of Jeremy Taylor, with a Bibliography of the Works of Jeremy Taylor,* ed. Logan Pearsall Smith and Robert Gathorne-Hardy (Oxford: Oxford University Press, 1930), pp. 327–328.

3. Underscored twice. *The Rule and Exercises of Holy Dying* was published in 1651.

4. Properly, eighth. The first *"Dying"* in this sentence is also underscored twice. *The Rule and Exercises of Holy Living* was published in 1650. Plumstead Lloyd (1780–1836), another of the Lloyd brothers, was at about this time living in Ipswich. In 1804 he was married to Frances Isabella Bettenson of Ipswich and afterward moved to London. (See the *Lloyd-Manning Letters,* pp. 55 and 76.) Willy is Shakespeare.

5. Ben Jonson, "On the Portrait of Shakespeare. To the Reader," line 2, and "To the Memory of My Beloved Master William Shakespeare, and What He Hath Left Us," line 56.

6. *Othello,* III, iii, 140. Next is an inexact quotation from *A Midsummer Night's Dream,* II, ii, 23 and 11–12.

7. *The Two Gentlemen of Verona,* I, i, 25. Besides Taylor's *Holy Living, Holy Dying,* and one of the many collections of Taylor's sermons, mentioned below are *The Great Exemplar of Sanctity and Holy Life According to Christian Institution. Described in the History of the Life and Death of the Ever Blessed Jesus Christ the Saviour of the World* (1649); *A Discourse of the Nature, Offices and Measures of Friendship, with Rules of Conducting It* (1657), which was republished with additions as *Opuscula* (1678); and ΣΥΜΒΟΛΟΝ ΗΘΙΚΟΠΟΛΕΜΙΚΟΝ. *Or a Collection of Polemical and Moral Discourses* (1657).

8. *A Queen-like Closet; or, Rich Cabinet; Stored with All Manner of Rare Receipts for Preserving, Candying, and Cookery* (1670), by Mrs. Hannah Woolley, or Wolley, afterward Mrs. Challinor (fl. 1670). Lamb wrote in "The Months" (*Works,* I, 308) that its fourth (1681) edition "had been the strange delight of my infancy." To "incompetent judgments," below, cf. Alexander Pope's *An Essay on Criticism,* II, 2. Taylor's ΘΕΟΛΟΓΙΑ 'ΕΚΛΕΚΤΙΚΗ. *A Discourse of the Liberty of Prophesying. Shewing the Unreasonablenes of Prescribing to Other Mens Faiths, and the Iniquity of Persecuting Differing Opinions* was published in 1647.

105. *C. L. to Robert Lloyd*

[June 26, 1801]

Cooke[1] in Richard the Third is a perfect caricature. He gives you the *monster* Richard, but not the *man* Richard. Shakespear's bloody character impresses you with awe and deep admiration of his witty parts, his consumate hypocrisy, and indefatigable prosecution of purpose. You despise, detest, and loath the cunning, vulgar, low and fierce Richard, which Cooke substitutes in his place. He gives you no other

idea, than of a vulgar villain, rejoycing in his being able to over reach, and not possessing that joy in *silent* consciousness, but betraying it, like a *poor* villain in sneers and distortions of the face, like a droll at a country fair: not to add that cunning so self-betraying and manner so vulgar could never have deceived the politic Buckingham, nor the soft Lady Anne: *both,* bred in courts, would have turned with disgust from such a fellow.— Not but Cooke has *powers;* but not of discrimination. His manner is strong, coarse & vigorous, and well adapted to some characters.— But the lofty imagery and high sentiments and high passions of *Poetry* come black & prose-smoked from his prose Lips.— I have not seen him in *Over Reach,*[2] but from what I remember of the character, I think he could not have chosen one more fit! I thought the play a highly finished one, when I read it sometime back. I *remember* a most noble image. Sir Giles drawing his sword in the last scene, says

> Some undone widow sits upon mine arm,
> And takes away the use on't.

This is horribly fine, and I am not sure, that it did not suggest to me my conclusion of Pride's Cure; but my imitation is miserably inferior.

> This arm was busy in the day of **Naseby:**
> Tis paralytic now, & knows no use of weapons——[3]

Pierre & Jaffier are the best things in Otway.— Belvidere is a poor Creature; and has had more than her due fame—Monimia is a little better, but she *whines.*— I like Calista in the Fair Penitent better than either of Otway's women— —. **Lee's** Massacre of Paris is a noble play, very chastely & finely written. His Alexander is full of that madness, "which rightly should possess a poet's brain." Œdipus is also a fine play, but less so than these two. It is a joint production of **Lee & Dryden.** All for **Love** begins with uncommon Spirit, but soon flags, and is of no worth upon the whole—. The last scene of Young's Revenge is sublime: the rest of it not worth 1*d* ——

I want to have your opinion & Plumstead's on **Cooke's** Richard the Third. . I am possessed with an Admiration of the genuine Richard, his genius, and his mounting spirit, which no consideration of his cruelties can depress. . Shakespear has not made Richard so black a **Monster,** as is supposed. Whereever he is monstrous, it was to conform to vulgar opinion. But he is generally a **Man.** Read his most exquisite

address to the Widowed Queen to court her daughter for him,[4] the topics of maternal feeling, of a deep knowledge of the heart, are such as no monster could have supplied. Richard must have *felt*, before he could feign so well; tho' ambition choked the good seed. I think it the most finished piece of Eloquence in the world; of *persuasive* Oratory, far above Demosthenes, Burke, or any man.— Far exceeding the courtship of Lady **Anne.**— *Her* relenting is barely natural after all; the more perhaps S's merit to make *impossible* appear *probable,* but the *Queen's consent* (taking in all the circumstances & topics, *private* and *public,* with his angelic address, able to draw the host of [. . .]e[5] Lucifer,) is *probable;* and [. . .]e **resisted it.— — This** observation applies to many other parts. All the inconsistency is, that Shakespeares better Genius was forced to struggle against the prejudices, which made a monster of Richard. He set out to paint a *monster,* but his human sympathies produced a *Man—*

Are you not **tired** with this *ingenious* criticism? **I am.**

God bless you

[. . .]

Richard itself is wholly metamorphosed in the wretched *Acting play* of that name, which you will see: altered by *Cibber.*——

MS: Huntington Library. Pub.: Ainger (1900), II, 43–46; Macdonald, I, 204–206; Ainger (1904), I, 192–194; Harper, III, 20–22; Lucas (1935), I, 259–261. Address: Mr. Robt. Lloyd/Ch. Lloyd Esqr/Birmingham. Postmark: June 26, 1801.

1. George Frederick Cooke (1756–1811), of whom Lamb wrote as he writes here in "G. F. Cooke in 'Richard the Third'" and "On the Tragedies of Shakspeare, Considered with Reference to Their Fitness for Stage Representation" (*Works,* I, 36–38 and 105–106). Lamb may also have written "Theatre: Covent Garden," in the *Morning Post* of January 9, 1802 (*Works,* I, 399–400), critical of Cooke's performance as Lear. See Letter 120, note 7.

2. Sir Giles Overreach, in Philip Massinger's *A New Way to Pay Old Debts,* from which Lamb, below, quotes V, i, 363–364.

3. Later deleted from "Pride's Cure." See *Works,* V, 366, for the original placement of the lines. Judged below are Pierre, Jaffeir, and Belvidera of *Venice Preserv'd;* Monimia of Otway's *The Orphan;* Calista of Nicholas Rowe's *The Fair Penitent;* and Alexander of Nathaniel Lee's *The Rival Queens.* The quotation is from Michael Drayton's "To My Most Dearly-loved Friend Henry Reynolds Esquire, of Poets and Poesie," line 110. *All for Love, or the World Well Lost* is by John Dryden. Edward Young wrote *The Revenge.*

4. *Richard III,* IV, iv, 291–336.

5. The first halves of two lines went when the signature on the verso was clipped from the letter. Lamb in his postscript refers to Colley Cibber's *Richard III* (1700), an adaptation of Shakespeare regarded as the acting version of the play from 1700 to 1821.

106. *C. L. to William Godwin*

[Monday, June 29, 1801]

Dear Sir,

Doctor **Christy's** Brother and Sister[1] are come to town, and have shewn me great civilities. I in return wish to requite them, having by *God's grace* principles of generosity *implanted* (as the moralists say) in my nature, which have been duly cultivated and watered by good and religious friends and a pious education. They have picked up in the northern parts of the island an astonishing admiration of the great Author of the New Philosophy in England, and I have ventured to promise their *taste* an evening's gratification by seeing Mr. Godwin *face* to *face*! ! ! ! ! Will you do them, & me *in* them, the pleasure of drinking tea and supping with me, at the *old* number 16,[2] on Friday or Saturday next? An early nomination of the day will very much oblige

Yours sincerely

Ch Lamb

MS: Lord Abinger, Bures, Suffolk; transcribed from the microfilm of the Abinger Collection in the William R. Perkins Library, Duke University, Durham, N.C. Pub.: Hazlitt, I, 298; Ainger (1888), I, 170; Ainger (1900), II, 42–43; Macdonald, I, 206; Ainger (1904), I, 192; Harper, III, 23; Lucas (1905), VI, 219; Lucas (1912), V, 223; Lucas (1935), I, 258–259. Date, by Godwin: June 29, 1801.

1. Probably the brother and sister (who have not been identified) of Dougall Christie (1777–1857) of the Indian Medical Service, the father of the diplomatist and man of letters William Dougal, or Dougall, Christie (1816–1874). Dr. Christie received the certificate of the corporation of surgeons in 1798, became an assistant surgeon of the Bombay establishment in 1799, and surgeon in 1808. He was its agent for the manufacture of gunpowder from 1818 to 1821, was furloughed in 1821, and was retired in 1824. His residence by 1832 was 37 Montagu Square, London. He died in Freshwater, Isle of Wight.

2. Perhaps the numbering in Mitre Court Buildings repeated on a new set of apartments.

107. *C. L. to Walter Wilson*

August 14, 1801

Dear Wilson,

I am extremely sorry that any serious difference should subsist be-

tween us on account of some foolish behaviour of mine at Richmond; you knew me well enough before—that a very little liquor will cause a considerable alteration in me.

I beg you to impute my conduct solely to that, and not to any deliberate intention of offending you, from whom I have received so many friendly attentions. I know that you think a very important difference in opinion with respect to some more serious subjects between us makes me a dangerous companion; but do not rashly infer, from some slight and light expressions which I may have made use of in a moment of levity in your presence, without sufficient regard to your feelings—do not conclude that I am an inveterate enemy to all religion. I have had a time of seriousness, and I have known the importance and reality of a religious belief. Latterly, I acknowledge, much of my seriousness has gone off, whether from new company or some other new associations; but I still retain at bottom a conviction of the truth, and a certainty of the usefulness of religion. I will not pretend to more gravity or feeling than I at present possess; my intention is not to persuade you that any great alteration is probable in me; sudden converts are superficial and transitory; I only want you to believe that I have *stamina* of seriousness within me, and that I desire nothing more than a return of that friendly intercourse which used to subsist between us, but which my folly has suspended.

<div style="text-align: right">

Believe me, very affectionately yours,

C. Lamb

</div>

MS: unrecovered. Text: Lucas (1935), I, 261. Also pub.: Talfourd (1848), I, 132–133; Purnell, II, 62–63; Fitzgerald, II, 421–422; Hazlitt, I, 301–302; Ainger (1888), I, 170–171; Ainger (1900), II, 46–47; Macdonald, I, 207; Ainger (1904), I, 194–195; Harper, III, 23–24; Lucas (1905), VI, 219–220; Lucas (1912), V, 223–224. Walter Wilson (1781–1847), a relative of John Walter (1776–1847)—John Walter was the chief proprietor of the *Times*—had since 1798 worked as a clerk with Lamb. Wilson left the East India House in 1803 to become a bookseller, in the beginning with one Maxwell of Bell Yard, Temple, and in 1806 on his own at Mewsgate, Charing Cross, in the quarters vacated by the bookseller Thomas Payne, the younger (1752–1831). The title page of the younger John Lamb's pamphlet on the prevention of cruelty to animals, however (a pamphlet discussed in Vol. III, Letter 246, notes), shows Wilson and Maxwell associated as publishers at 17 Skinner Street, Snow Hill, in 1810. In about 1806 Wilson began *The History and Antiquities of Dissenting Churches and Meeting Houses in London, Westminster, and Southwark: Including the Lives of Their Ministers, from the Rise of Nonconformity to the Present Time* (1808–1814), inherited a considerable income, and entered the Inner Temple. But he seems never to have practiced law. In 1811 he was living at 29 Strand and by 1814

in Camden Town. He retired first to Dorset; to Lufton, Somersetshire, by 1822; and by 1829 to Burnet House, near Bath. There he wrote *Memoirs of the Life and Times of Daniel de Foe* (1830), to which Lamb contributed an "Estimate of de Foe's Secondary Novels" (*Works*, I, 325–327). In about 1834 Wilson moved into Bath. By the time of his death he was listed as one of the eight registered owners of the *Times*. Lucas had access to a recollection of Lamb that Wilson wrote in 1836, in which Wilson explains the incident for which Lamb apologizes here and commends the apology itself:

> Some of his frolics, however, were of a more dangerous description. I remember going with him by water upon a party of pleasure to Richmond, accompanied by some of our mutual acquaintances. Upon our return to town, after roaming about the delightful scenery of the neighbourhood, those in the boat found the utmost difficulty in restraining him from the performance of some of his accustomed gambols. Not satisfied with sporting his wit, he was for giving it [vent (?)] by those bodily movements that were quite unsuited to so unsteady a conveyance in the watery element. The consequence was that the boat was within a hair's-breadth of being upset; and if none of us had received any other injury than a ducking I believe he was the only one who would have viewed it in the nature of a sport. He had placed us all, however, in imminent peril; and the contemplation of it after our escape was anything but satisfactory. Availing myself of the privilege of a friend, I wrote to him a letter of remonstrance upon his conduct, descanting at the same time upon some other matters in amicable debate between us. Like the late Rowland Hill [1744–1833; a preacher], he could not restrain his wit, even upon the most solemn subjects. This I considered offensive, and expressed myself accordingly. His reply, which I have still by me, was just such as might be expected from a right-minded person, whose heart also was in its right place. Characterized by simplicity, by good feeling, and by an excellent judgment, it was calculated to produce all the effect he could desire, and which it did produce. Our friendship did not suffer a momentary interruption; nor am I conscious that so much as an angry word ever passed between us. I always found him the same kind single-hearted creature, and now look back upon our early intercourse with unmixed pleasure and satisfaction. [Lucas (1935), I, 262–263]

Hazlitt may have been referring to the same incident when he wrote, in "On Coffee-house Politicians," that someone believed Lamb "could not be an excellent companion, because he was seen walking down the side of the Thames, *passibus iniquis* [with uneven steps], after dining at Richmond" (*Hazlitt's Works*, VIII, 202).

108. *C. L. to Manning*

[?Saturday, August ?22, 1801]

Dear Manning,

I have forborne writing so long (and so have you for the matter of that) until I am almost ashamed either to write or to forbear any longer. But as your silence may proceed from some worse cause than neglect, from illness or some mishap which may have befallen you, I begin to be anxious. You may have been burnt out, or you may have

married, or you may have broke a Limb, or turned Country Parson, any of these would be excuse sufficient for not coming to my Supper: I am not so unforgiving as the nobleman in Saint Mark.—[1] For me nothing new has happened to me, unless that the poor Albion died last Saturday of the world's neglect: & with it the fountain of my puns is choked up forever.—

All the Lloyds wonder that you do not write to them. They apply to me for the cause. Relieve me from this weight of ignorance, & enable me to give a truly oracular response.—

I have been confined some days with swelled cheek & rheumatism: they divide and govern me with a vice-roy headache in the middle.— I can neither write nor read without great pain. It must be something like obstinacy, that I chuse this time to write to you in after many months interruption—.

I will close my **Letter** of simple Enquiry with an Epigram on Mackintosh[2] the Vindeciæ Gallicæ man, who has got a place at last; one of the last I *did* for the Albion.—

Tho thou'rt like Judas an apostate black,
In the resemblance one thing thou dost lack;
When he had gotten his ill-purchas'd pelf,
He went away, & wisely hang'd himself:
This thou may do at last; yet much I doubt,
If thou hast any **Bowels** to gush out!—

Yours as ever
C L

MS: Huntington Library. Pub.: Talfourd (1848), I, 130–132; Sala, I, 366–367; Purnell, I, 366–367; Fitzgerald, II, 199–200; Hazlitt, I, 299–300; Ainger (1888), I, 171–172; Ainger (1900), II, 47–49; Macdonald, I, 208; Ainger (1904), I, 195–196; Harper, III, 25–26; Lucas (1905), VI, 220–221; Lucas (1912), V, 224–225; Lucas (1935), I, 263–264. Address: Mr Manning/Mr. Crisp's/Opposite St. Mary's Church/Cambridge. Postmark: August 18[01]. The comment in the first paragraph on the *Albion and Evening Advertiser* suggests a more specific date for the letter than is provided by what remains of the postmark. The letter is dated the twenty-second without question in Lucas (1935), I, 263.

1. It is in Luke 14 : 21–27 where is told of the man who would not forgive those who excused themselves from attending his great supper. The *Albion and Evening Advertiser,* referred to in the following sentence, was a republican daily started in 1799 and ordered to die by the courts on about August 15, 1801, because, according to Lamb in "Newspapers Thirty-five Years Ago" (*Works,* II, 225), he had offended Charles Stanhope, third Earl Stanhope, with the epigram

published in it quoted at the end of this letter. The paper was owned at the time of its demise by John Fenwick (d. 1820?), who figures in "Newspapers Thirty-five Years Ago" and, as Ralph Bigod, Esq., in "The Two Races of Men" and "The Praise of Chimney-sweepers" (*Works*, II, 23–25 and 113). With his wife and children Fenwick also figures in the Lambs' letters. He first appears elsewhere—in a letter from Godwin to him of February 15, 1793 (*Shelley and His Circle*, I, 117), when Fenwick was in France, presumably gathering material for his translation of *The Memoirs of General [Charles François (1739–1823)] Dumouriez* (1794). In 1797 Fenwick and his wife attended Mrs. Mary Wollstonecraft Godwin in her final illness. In 1799 he left his family to shift for itself and fled from his creditors to Dublin. By August he was back in London working on translations and perhaps on *The Indian: A Farce* (1800). In about June 1801 he somehow purchased *The Albion* from Daniel Lovel (d. 1818), who later owned and edited *The Statesman*. Near the end of 1801 Fenwick bought *The Plough*, or *Plow* (which has not otherwise been identified), with money lent to him by Sir Hugh Percy, second Duke of Northumberland (1742–1817). By September 1802 Fenwick was again hiding from creditors and had sent his wife and children to the home of his brother, Thomas, a tradesman of Penzance who in 1803 went bankrupt himself. In July John Fenwick was in Portsmouth, in 1806 he returned to London to surrender himself to the authorities, and between then and 1808 he was committed to the Rules of the Fleet, that is, made to live within the area prescribed for those debtors assigned to Fleet Prison. In 1812 he and his brother attempted to establish a newspaper; in 1817 he was editing *The Statesman*. After Lamb's mentions of him to Barron Field in a letter of August 31, 1817, Fenwick disappears. The conjecture in *The Fate of the Fenwicks* that he probably went to Australia seems derived from a misreading of that letter. It is stated in Lucas (1935), I, 418, that he settled in America. Eliza (d. 1840?), his wife, was the author of the novel *Secrecy* (n.d.) and such children's books as *The Class Book: Or, Three Hundred and Sixty-five Reading Lessons Adapted to the Use of the Schools* (1806), *Infantine Stories, Composed Progressively, in Words of One, Two, and Three Syllables* (1810), *Lessons for Children . . . : A New Edition* (1811; tr. into French in 1820), *Rays from the Window. Being an Easy Method for Perfecting Children in the First Principles of Grammar* (2d ed.; 1812), and *The Bad Family; and Other Stories* (1898). In 1798 she wrote Mary Hays (see Vol. I, Letter 58, note 1) of Fenwick's failure to provide for her and their two children—Eliza Anne, later a Mrs. Rutherford (1789?–1827?); and Orlando (1798–1816)—and of her determination to relieve their want by starting a school. She had opened one by the beginning of 1799, possibly with the assistance of Thomas Holcroft, but it soon closed. She and her children were forced to live off and on with friends in or near London for the next two or three years. She earned a living during her years in Penzance by working in her brother-in-law's shop and by coloring prints. By 1806 she and her children were back in London, where Eliza Anne was beginning a career as an actress. From November 1807 to January 1808 Mrs. Fenwick managed the Godwins' Juvenile Library at 41 Skinner Street. Her daughter's interest in the stage then took Mrs. Fenwick and her children to Belfast. In 1811 Mrs. Fenwick became a governess in the Mocatta family of London, and in 1812 she went in a like capacity to the Honnor family of Lee Mount, near Cork. She left it in 1814 for Barbados, where her daughter had gone in 1811 with the acting company of a Mr. Dyke and in 1812 had married the irresponsible Rutherford, an actor who in 1818 deserted her and their children for London. In 1822 Mrs. Fenwick, her daughter, and her four grandchildren left the island (and the grave of her son, who had died of yellow fever), first for New Haven, Connecticut, and in 1825 for New York. Following the death of Mrs. Rutherford she took the children to Niagara Falls, where she established a school for girls, and then to Toronto, where she ran a boardinghouse

for college students. In about 1834 her grandsons William (b. 1813) and Thomas (b. 1815) were drowned in Lake Ontario. In 1837 her grandson Rowland (b. 1818) was married against her wishes. Mrs. Fenwick afterward lived out her life in Providence, Rhode Island, with her granddaughter, Elizabeth (1817?–1899), who in 1844 became the second wife of the American naturalist and missionary to West Africa the Reverend Dr. Thomas Staughton Savage (1804–1880). Lucas saw a copy of *Elia. Essays Which Have Appeared under That Signature in the London Magazine* (1823) inscribed "Elia to his old and best friends, Mrs. Fenwick and her good daughter" (Lucas [1935], I, 265), which, with the Lambs' many comments about various members of the family, more than hints of letters to them. But not a note has surfaced.

2. Sir James Mackintosh (1765–1832), philosopher, physician, barrister, brother-in-law of Daniel Stuart, and the author of *Vindiciæ Gallicæ* (1791), in which Mackintosh answered Edmund Burke's *Reflections on the French Revolution* (1790). Lamb could have thought that Mackintosh had agreed to become a judge in Trinidad, an advocate general in Bengal, the master of a college in Calcutta, or, as Lamb incorrectly stated in "Newspapers Thirty-five Years Ago" (*Works,* II, 225), the recorder of Bombay. But he was unsuccessful in his applications for the first two, refused the third, and was not appointed to the fourth until 1804. The apostasy that Lamb condemns him for in the epigram (called "To Sir James Mackintosh" in *Works,* V, 102, but whose title and precise date of publication in the *Albion and Evening Advertiser* cannot be cited because a copy of the paper cannot be found) was his adoption of Burke's severe judgment of the French Revolution soon after he and Burke met and his publication of *A Discourse on the Study of the Law of Nature and Nations* (1799), in which Mackintosh repudiated the doctrines, philosophically and politically liberal, of *Vindiciæ Gallicæ.*

109. *C. L. to Manning*

[August 31, 1801]

I *heard* that you were going to China, with a commission from the Wedgewoods to collect hints for their pottery, and to teach the Chinese *perspective.*[1] But I did *not* know that *London* lay in your way to Pekin. I am seriously glad of it, for I shall trouble you with a small present for the Emperor of Usbeck Tartary, as you go by his territories: it is a fragment of a dissertation on the "state of political parties in England at the end of the 18th Century," which will no doubt be very interesting to his Imperial Majesty. It was written originally in English for the use of the *two* and *twenty* readers of the Albion (this *calculation includes* a printer, four pressmen, and a devil,) but becoming of no use, when the albion stopt, I got it translated into Usbeck Tartar by my good friend Tibet Kulm, who is come to London with a *civil* invitation from the Cham to the English Nation to go over to the worship of the Lama.

The Albion is dead, dead as nail in door,[2] and my revenues have died with it, but I am not as a man without hope. I have got a sort of an opening to the Morning Chronicle ! ! ! Mr. Manning, by means of that Common Lyar of Benevolence **Mister Dyer.** I have not seen Perry[3] the Editor yet, but I am preparing a specimen: I shall have a difficult job to manage, for you must know, that Mister Perry, in common with the Great body of the Whigs ! ! thinks the Albion *very low.* I find I must rise a peg or so, be a little more decent and less abusive: for to confess the truth, I had arrived to an abominable pitch, I spared neither age nor sex, when my cue was given me.— **Ni'm'port** (as they say in French) any climate will suit me.

So you are about to bring your old face-making face to London. You could not come in a better time for my purposes: for I have just lost **Rickman,** a faint idea of whose character I sent you—he is gone to Ireland for a year or two to make his fortune—& I have lost by his going what seems to me I can never recover: *a finished man.*[4] His memory will be to me as the Brazen Serpent to the Israelites: I shall look up to it, to keep me upright and honest.— But he may yet bring back his honest face to England one day—. I wish Your affairs with the Emperor of China had not been *so* **urgent,** that you might have stay'd in Great Britain a year or two longer, to have **seen** him— for, judging from *my own* experience, I almost dare pronounce you never saw his equal: I never saw a man, that could be at all a second or substitute for him in any sort.[5]

Imagine that what is here erased, was an apology & explanation, perfectly satisfactory you may be sure! ! for rating this man so highly at the expence of —— & —— & —— & M—— & —— & —— & ——. But **Mister Burke** has explained this phenomenon of our nature very prettily in his letter to a Member of the National assembly, or else in appeal to the Old Whigs, I forget which—.[6] do you remem[ber an] instance from **Homer** (who understood these matters to[lerably w]ell) of Priam driving away his **other Sons** with expressions of wrath & bitter reproach, when Hector was just dead, not that—&c.—

I live where I did in a *private* manner, because I do'nt like *state.* Nothing is so disagreeabl[e] to me as the clamours and applauses of the mob. For this reason I live in an *obscure* situation in one of the courts of the Temple.——

C L

MS: Huntington Library. Pub.: Talfourd (1837), I, 208–211; Sala, I, 369–371; Purnell, I, 369–371; Fitzgerald, II, 202–204; Hazlitt, I, 302–304; Ainger (1888), I, 172–174; Ainger (1900), II, 49–51; Macdonald, I, 209–210; Ainger (1904), I, 196–198; Harper, III, 26–28; Lucas (1905), VI, 223–224; Lucas (1912), V, 227–228; Lucas (1935), I, 265–267. Address: Mr. Thos. Manning/ Diss/Norfolk. Postmark: August 31, 1801.

1. This is as much a joke as the rest of the paragraph.

2. *II Henry IV,* V, iii, 120–121.

3. James Perry (see Vol. I, Letter 5, note 5), whose rejection of more than three-fourths of what Lamb wrote for the *Morning Chronicle* (see Letter 111, first paragraph) may have discouraged Lamb from trying to publish anything in the paper. Nothing in it during this period is at any rate identifiably his.

4. For John Rickman's move to Dublin Castle and for what Lamb in Letter 111 calls Rickman's "new dignities" see Vol. I, Letter 86, note 4. For the brazen serpent and the Israelites (mentioned following), who believed such a serpent served as a counterspell to malignant demons, see Numbers 21:6–9 and 2 Kings 18:4.

5. A canceled line follows.

6. Not in *A Letter to a Member of the National Assembly, in Answer to Some Objections to His Book on French Affairs* (1791) but in *An Appeal from the New to the Old Whigs, in Consequence of Some Late Discussions in Parliament Relative to the Reflections on the French Revolution* (1791) did Burke defend his especial concern for the monarchy as a member of the British constitution on the grounds that that was the member in danger and not because he valued that member above the other members—democracy and the aristocracy. Burke incorporated in his defense the episode (in the *Iliad,* tr. George Chapman, XXIV, 243–249) of Priam driving off his nine other sons while intent on the body of Hector. See *The Works of the Right Honorable Edmund Burke* (Boston: Little, Brown, 1904), IV, esp. 93–95.

110. *C. L. to Godwin*

[Margate
September 16, 1801]

Dear Sir,

Nothing runs in my head, when I think of yo[ur] story,[1] but that you should make it as like the Life of Savage as possible. That is a known & familiar tale, and its effect upon the public mind has been very great. Many of the incidents in the true History are easily made dramatical. For instance, **Savage** used to walk backwards & forwards a nights by his mother's window, to catch a glimpse of her, as she passed with a candle. With some such situation the play might happily open.— I would plunge my **Hero,** exactly like Savage, into difficulties & embarrassments, the consequences of an **Unsettled mind;** out of which he may be extricated by the unknown interference of his mother. He should be attended from the beginning by a **friend,** who

should stand in much the same relation towards him, as **Horatio** to **Altamont** in the play of the **Fair Penitent**. A character of this sort seems indispensible. This friend might gain interviews with the mother, when the son was refused sight of her— —like Horatio with Calista, he might wring her soul[2]— —like Horatio, he might learn the secret *first*—. he might be exactly in the same perplexing situation, when he learned it, whether to tell it or conceal it from the **Son**—. **at last** (excuse me for hinting a crude ending, I can do no better) he might be driven to extremities in some such way as this— the **Son** (I have still Savage in my head) might **kill** a man (as he did) in an affray.— he should receive a pardon, as Savage did—& the **Mother** might interfere to have him *banished*—. this should provoke the **Friend** to demand an interview with **her Husband**, & disclose the whole secret— —the husband refusing to believe any thing to her dishonor should fight with him—. the H[usband repents][3] before he dies, the Mother explains & [confess]es every thing in his presence.— **The Son** is admitted to an interview with his now acknowledged mother—. instead of embraces, she resolves to abstract herself from all pleasure, even from his sight, in voluntary penance all her days after.—

This is crude indeed! ! but I am totally unable to suggest a better.— I am the worst hand in the world at a plot. But I understand enough of passion, to predict that your story, with some of Savage's, which has no repugnance but a natural alliance with it, cannot fail. The mystery of the suspected relationship—the suspicion, generated from slight & forgotten circumstances, coming at last to act as Instinct, & so to be mistaken for Instinct—the Sons unceasing pursuit and throwing of himself in his mother's way, something like **Falkland's** eternal persecution of **Williams**[4]— —the high & intricate passion in the mother, the being obliged to shun and keep at distance the thing nearest to her heart—to be cruel, where her heart yearns to be kind, without a possibility of explanation——. You have the power of life and death & the hearts of your **Auditors** in your hands— —. Still **Harris** will want a skeleton, and he must have it.— I can only put in some sorry hints— —. The discovery to the **Son's friend** may take place not before the 3d act—it[5] some such way as this—the mother may cross the street—he may point her out to some gay companion of his as the **Beauty** of **Leghorn**—the pattern for wives &c. &c.——his

companion, who is an Englishman, **laughs** at his mistake, and knows **her** to have been the famous **Nancy Dawson**,[6] or any one **else,** who captivated the **English King**—. Some such way seems dramatic, and speaks to the **Eye**—the Audience will enter into the **Friend's** surprize, and into the perplexity of his situation— —. These **ocular Scenes** are so many great Landmarks, rememberable headlands and light-houses in the voyage. Macbeth's witch has a good advice to a Tragic writer, what to do with his Spectator,

> *"Shew* **his** *eyes* **and grieve his heart"**————[7]

The most difficult thing seems to be, **What to do with the Husband?**— You will not make him jealous of his own Son? that is a stale & an unpleasant trick in **Douglas** &c. Cant you keep him out of the way till you want him, as the Husband of **Isabella** is conveniently sent off, till his cue comes? there will be story enough without him, and he will only puzzle all. Catastrophes are worst of all. **Mine** is most stupid. I only propose it, to **fulfill** my engagement, not in hopes to convert you. It is always difficult to get rid of a **Woman** at the end of a Tragedy. *Men* may fight & die. A woman must either take poison, *which is a nasty trick,* or go mad, *which is not fit to be shewn,* or **retire,** *which is* ***poor:*** only **retiring** is most *reputable.* .

I am sorry I can furnish you no better; but I find it extremely difficult to settle my thoughts upon any thing but the scene before me, when I am from home, I am from home so seldom. If any the least hint crosses me, I will write again. And I very much wish to **read** your **plan,** if you could abridge it & send it.— In this little scrawl, you must take the will for the **deed,** for I most sincerely wish success to your play.—

<div align="right">farewell
C L</div>

if you write direct to be left at [. . .][8]

MS: Lord Abinger. Pub.: Hazlitt, I, 305–307; Ainger (1888), I, 175–177; Ainger (1900), II, 52–53; Macdonald, I, 211–213; Ainger (1904), I, 199–201; Harper, III, 29–32; Lucas (1905), VI, 225–227; Lucas (1912), V, 229–231; Lucas (1935), I, 268–270. Address: Mr Godwin/the Polygon/Somer's Town/near London. Postmark: Margate, September 16, 1801. Lamb wrote of Margate, where he and Mary are vacationing, in "The Old Margate Hoy" (*Works,* II, 177–183).
1. "Faulkener, a Tragedy in Prose." Lamb contributed its Prologue (*Works,*

V, 123), in praise of Daniel Defoe because Godwin, substituting a son for a daughter, founded the tragedy upon an incident in the second (1745) edition of Defoe's *Roxana.* Here Lamb asks Godwin to consider additionally the life of the poet Richard Savage (1697?–1743), which Dr. Johnson especially made familiar in his *Life of Savage* (1744) and in the *Lives of the English Poets.* Savage had claimed to be the illegitimate son of Richard Savage, fourth Earl Rivers (1660?–1712), and Anne, the daughter of Sir Richard Mason and the wife first of Charles Gerard, second Earl of Macclesfield (1659?–1701), and then of Colonel Henry Brett (d. 1724). Savage was condemned to death in 1727 for the murder of James Sinclair in a tavern quarrel, was pardoned in 1728 on the intercession of Frances Thynne, Countess of Hertford (d. 1754), and died a debtor imprisoned in Bristol.

2. Cf. Rowe, *The Fair Penitent,* III, 92.

3. This and the bracketed locution following either have been torn away or are illegible. They have been supplied from Lucas (1935), I 268.

4. In Godwin's *The Adventures of Caleb Williams, or Things as They Are* (1794), which the younger George Colman (see Vol. I, Letter 101, note 7) dramatized as *The Iron Chest* and had presented at Drury Lane on March 12, 1796. Lamb's "to be cruel, where her heart yearns to be kind," below, is a paraphrase of *Hamlet,* III, iv, 178.

5. For "in."

6. Nancy Dawson (1730?–1767) was a dancer first at Sadler's Wells and then at Covent Garden, where she became famous for dancing the hornpipe in John Gay's *The Beggar's Opera* in 1759.

7. *Macbeth,* IV, i, 110. Isabella and her husband, Biron, mentioned below and in Letter 112, are in Thomas Southerne's *The Fatal Marriage.*

8. Three or four words are either illegible or have been torn away.

111. *C. L. to John Rickman*

<div align="right">

Margate
Wednesday 16th Sept. [1801]
Where I stay a week longer

</div>

Dear Rickman,

Your Letter has found me at Margate, where I am come with Mary to drink sea water and pick up shells—. I am glad to hear that your new dignities sit so easy upon you. No doubt you are one of those easy "well dressed" Gentlemen, that we may know at first sight to belong to the "Castle," when we meet them in the Park. .—Your Letter contains a very fair offer about my Play, which I must first dispatch. I seriously feel very much obliged to you, *and all that,* but I have a scheme in my head to print it about Xmas time, when the Town is fuller! ! about that time I expect the repayment of a Loan, which was bigger than I ought to have trusted, but I hope not bigger than my borrowing friend will then be able to repay. If he should disappoint

me, I ⟨will⟩ may! throw myself upon you: meantime I am too proud ever to &c.—.—.— — I do not write in *any* paper. George Dyer, that common Lyar of Benevolence, has taken some pains to introduce me to the Morning Chronicle, and I did something for them, but I soon found that it was a different thing writing for the Lordly Editor of the Great Whig Paper to what it was scribbling for the poor Albion. More than 3.4ths of what I [di]d was superciliously rejected; whereas in the old Albion the [seal]¹ of my wellknown hand-writing was enough to drive any nons[en]se current. I believe I shall give up this way of writing, and turn honest, scramble on as well as I can for a year, and make a Book, for why should every creature make books but I?— —

G. Burnett had just finished his Essay when I came away. Mushrooms scramble up in a night; but diamonds, you know, lie a long while ripening in the bed. The purport of it is to persuade the world, that Opinions tending to the subversion of Established Religions & Governments, Systems of Medicine &c. should not be rashly vented in every company: a good orthodox doctrine, which has been preached up with the "holy text of Pike and Gun"² with you in Ireland, and is pretty familiar in England, but it is novel to George; at least he never wrote an Essay upon the Subject before. Critics should think of this, before they loosely cry out This is Commonplace, What is there new in it? it may be all new to the Author, *he* may never have thought of it before; & it may have cost him as much brain-sweat as a piece of the most inveterate originality.— — However George is in pretty good keeping, while the merits of his Essay lie under consideration. He has got into joint rooms with a young Surgeon,³ whose Uncle is an eminent Winemerchant, and gives his Nephew **long tick,** so they drink two sorts of wine, and live happy. George was turned out of his White Friars Lodging because he wanted too much attendance. He used to call up the girl, and send her down again, because he had forgot what he wanted; and then call her again, when his thought came back, to ask what a Clock it was. Fenwick has been urgent with me to write to you about his plan,⁴ and I gave him a drunken promise that I would, but you have saved me a disagreeable topic, for I know you have enough to do, and must serve him at your leisure. **The Welfare of Ireland,** perhaps of the whole World, must not stand still, while the interests of a newspaper are debating! !— He is very sanguine, and if he tells true, he has had very important encouragement; but he always **said &**

thought, that the Albion had very sufficient patronage. Some people can *see any thing* but their own interest, and they chuse to look at that through glasses.— — Dr. Christie has transported his solemn physiognomy to Portsmouth in his way to India. He departed without calling upon me, tho' he never could have called upon a more welcome occasion; consequently he did not get your Letter, but I imparted its contents to his brother.— — I know no more news from here, except that the **Professor** (Godwin) is *Courting.*[5] The Lady is a Widow* with green spectacles & one child, and the Professor is grown quite juvenile. He bows when he is spoke to, and smiles without occasion, and wriggles as fantastically as Malvolio, and has more affectation than a canary bird pluming his feathers when he thinks somebody looks at him. He lays down his spectacles, as if in scorn, & takes 'em up again from necessity, and winks that she may'nt see he gets sleepy about eleven oClock. You never saw such a philosophic coxcomb, nor any one play the Romeo so unnaturally.— His second play, my God-son, is flatly rejected by **Harris,**[6] because it is a Persian Story about Shaw Abbas & the valiant Sefi his son: but Harris has offered to pay him at all events, if he will take a domestic plain story, **not heroic** nor **foreign;** so, after many indignant declarations that he could not hear such a *creeping way* (his expression) his proud heart has come down to Harris's proposals; so he is filching a tale out of one of Defoe's novels, & has made me write him hints. **Floreat Tertia!**———[7]

And now

farewell, Master Secretary!—

and if your Diplomatic Majesty has any commissions for tape or bone lace &c. in London, depend upon a faithful performance of the same. I could find Matter for a longer Letter, and will another day, if you will find time to read it. Meantime believe me Yours sincerely. . Mary sends her kindest remembrances—. **No hurry for the Pork**——

C Lamb

*a very disgusting woman.—

MS: Huntington Library. Pub.: Ainger (1904), I, 201–204; Harper, III, 32–36; Lucas (1935), I, 272–274. Address: John Rickman Esqr/Dublin Castle.

1. Supplied from Lucas (1935), I, 272. George Burnett's essay described in the next paragraph has not been identified. Southey described it as metaphysical, some-

thing that could be titled "Much Ado About Nothing," and "not saleable" (*Rickman*, p. 61).

2. Samuel Butler, *Hudibras*, I, i, 194.

3. Unidentified, as is his uncle.

4. Apparently to purchase *The Plough*.

5. Underscored twice. On May 5 Godwin had met and on December 21, 1801, was married to Mary Jane Clairmont (1768–1841). She was possibly the daughter of Andrew Peter Devereaux and the widow of Charles Gaulis Clairmont (d. 1796). She was the mother of Charles Gaulis Clairmont (1794–1850) and Claire, or "Clara Mary Jane," Clairmont (1798–1879), who in 1817 bore Clara Allegra, or "Alba," Biron (d. 1822), reputedly to Byron. Lamb below likens Godwin's behavior to Malvolio's in *Twelfth Night*, III, iv, esp. 11–56.

6. Thomas Harris of Covent Garden. See Vol. I, Letter 96, note 2.

7. "Let the Third Flourish!"

112. *C. L. to Godwin*

Somers Town [Margate]
18 Septr. 1801

I have read your scheme very attentively. Some strong objections lie against it.— That Arabella[1] has been mistress to King Charles, is sufficient to all the purposes of the story. It can only diminish that respect we feel for her, to make her turn whore to one of the Lords of his Bedchamber.— Her **Son** must not know that she has been a whore; it matters not that she has been whore to a *King*, equally in both cases it is against **decorum** and against the delicacy of a son's respect, that he should be privy to it. No doubt, many sons might feel a wayward pleasure in the honorable guilt of their mothers, but is it a true feeling? is it the *best* sort of feeling? is it a feeling to be exposed on theatres to mothers and daughters?— Your conclusion (or rather **Defoe's**) comes far short of the *tragic ending,* which is always expected; and it is not safe to disappoint. A tragic auditory wants *blood.* They care but little about a man and his wife parting.—[2] Besides, what will you do with the **Son,** after all his pursuits and adventures? even quietly leave him to take guinea and a half lodgings with Mama in Leghorn! O impotent and pacific measures!— — — I am certain that you must mix up some strong ingredients of distress to give a savor to your pottage. I still think, that you may & must graft the story of Savage upon **Defoe.** Your hero must *kill* a **man, or do something.**— Cant you bring him to the gallows or some great mischief, **out** of which **She** *must* have recourse to an explanation with her husband to save him? ? Think **on**

this— —. The Husband for instance has Great friends in Court at Leghorn. The Son is condemned to death. **She** cannot teaze him for a stranger. **She** must **tell** the whole truth. or she *may* teaze him, *as for a stranger,* till (like othello in Cassio's case) he begins to suspect her for her importunity.[3] or, *being pardoned,* can she not teaze her husband to get him banish'd?— something of this I suggested before. *Both* is best. The murder & the pardon will make business for the 4th Act, & the banishment and the explanation (by means of the ***Friend,*** I want you to draw) the 5th— —— ——. You must not open any of the truth to Dawley by means of a Letter. A Letter is a feeble messenger on the stage. **Somebody,** the **Son** or his friend must, as a coup de main, be exasperated & obliged to **tell** the husband. **Damn** the Husband, & his "Gentleman like qualities." Keep him [ou]t of sight, or he will trouble all. [Le]t him be in England on trade, & come home, as **Biron** does in Isabella,[4] in the 4th Act, when he is wanted. I am for introducing situations, sort of counterparts to situations, which have had their effect *tried* in other plays, *like* but not the *same.* On this principle I recommended a friend like Horatio in the Fair Penitent, & on this principle I recommend a situation like othello's with relation to Desdemona's intercession for Cassio.—

By-scenes may likewise receive hints. The Son may see his mother at a *feast* or *mask,* as Romeo Juliet. The Festivity of the company contrasts with the strong pertarbations of the individuals—. **Dawley** may be told his wife's past unchastity at a mask by some witch-character— as Macbeth upon the heath in dark sentences—. this may stir his brain & be forgot—but will come in aid of stronger proof hereafter.— From this what you will perhaps call whimsical way of counterparting, this honest stealing, & original mode of plagiarism, much yet I think remains to be **sucked.**— — Excuse these abortions—I thought you would want the draught soon again, & I could not send it empty away.

Yours truly——

Willm. Godwin! ! ![5]

I shall be glad to come *home* and talk these matters with you.

MS: Lord Abinger. Pub.: Hazlitt, I, 308–309; Ainger (1888), I, 177–179; Ainger (1900), II, 56–58; Macdonald, I, 214–216; Ainger (1904), I, 204–206; Harper, III, 36–39; Lucas (1905), VI, 228–229; Lucas (1912), V, 232–234; Lucas (1935), I, 275–277. Address: Mr. Godwin/Polygon/Somers Town/near London. Postmark: Margate, September 19, 1801. The letter appears not to be

a fragment, the notations in *Godwin*, p. 87, and in the editions listed above to the contrary. It is stated in Lucas (1935), I, 277, that Lamb's reasons "for humorously signing this letter with Godwin's name and adding his address (Lamb, it will be noticed, was then at Margate) is that Godwin had (1) recently addressed to Lamb an unsigned letter, and (2) that he was exceedingly anxious that his name should not be mentioned as the author of the play ['Faulkener']."

1. She and King Charles, and Dawley, below, are in "Faulkener."
2. A canceled line follows.
3. *Othello*, III, iii, 251.
4. See Letter 110, note 7. Below are specific references to *Othello*, III, iii, 45–83, and iv, 92–95; *Romeo and Juliet*, I, v, 41–53; and *Macbeth*, I, iii, 38–78.
5. Written, in part, over "C Lamb." Lamb, obviously, was doing more than canceling his name by signing Godwin's over it.

113. *C. L. to Manning*

[Late September or early October 1801]

Pray what maps do you use, when you travel? Perhaps you have hit upon one that leaves London *out*.— Do let me send you down a complete set of Mercator's Charts, or Carrington Bowles's Survey of England,[1] against you travel next. You certainly *imagined* that London had been in your road; and *misled me*.

White writes me word from the country, where he is gone to recruit his strength, that he goes groping in all the hedges and copses about Oxford among daisies, Kingcups, and pissabeds, for the seeds of poetry, which George Dyer will still have it are to be found there!— [. . .]

He says that Sam. Taylor Coleridge appears to him as much as ever under the influence of a cold vanity, and does not spare absentem rodere amicum.[2] Is my Latin correct? Pity, that such human frailties should perch upon the margin of Ulswater Lake. 'Pity,' say all the echoes in such a tone, so plaintive, I wish I had my flute.

Lloyd's four brothers are grown choice Lads—they swagger about Birmingham streets, and get drunk at Coffee houses, and beat the Watch—almost as great a metamorphosis to some of them, as the transformation of Roderick Random, the carrotty waggon-passenger and co-mate of Barber Strap[3] into a fine gent and [. . .] about town—**all** the world. [. . .]

Do you trouble your head about Peace?[4] or the Northern Confederacy? I want to know where you bestow your Interest—for every man has an interest, such as it is, in his breast—as Lord Hamlet says—

'every man has business and affairs.'— I feel as if I were going to leave off business—

Don't mistake me, I only feel so just now. Sometimes I am very busy about nothing.

But seriously what do you think of this Life of ours? Can you make head or tail on't? How we came here (that I have some tolerable bawdy[5] hint of) what we came here for (that I know no more than [an] Ideot.)

You dropt a word whether in jest or earnest, as if you would join me in some work, such as a review or series of papers, essays, or any-thing.— Were you serious? I want some occupation, and I more want money. Had you any scheme, or was it, as G. Dyer says, en passant? If I don't have a Legacy left me shortly, I must get into pay with some newspaper for small gains. Mutton is twelve-pence a pound.

There, there is a full three sides for you.—

C. L.

MS: unrecovered. Text: Lucas (1935), I, 270–271. Address, from Bertram Dobell, "Some Unpublished Letters of Charles Lamb," *The Athenaeum*, No. 4097 (May 5, 1906), 546: Mr. Manning/Mr. Crisp's/near St. Mary's/Cambridge. Neither text indicates the extent of the cancellations or missing portions.

1. *Post-chaise Companion; or, Travellers' Directory through England and Wales* (2d ed.; 1782), by Carington Bowles (1724–1793), in his time a well-known print seller in St. Paul's Churchyard. It is James White of whom Lamb writes below.

2. "To slander an absent friend" (Horace, *Satires*, I, iv, 81). The Coleridges' home at Keswick was near Derwent Water. Ullswater, mentioned below, is to the east. The Lloyd mentioned in the next paragraph is probably Charles.

3. In Tobias Smollett's *Roderick Random*.

4. Between England and France. The Preliminaries of Peace were signed in London on October 1, 1801. The Treaty of Amiens was concluded on March 25, 1802. Napoleon's Northern Confederacy, referred to following, had been broken up when Lord Nelson destroyed the Danish fleet in the Battle of Copenhagen, the city herself having fallen on April 2, 1801. The conclusion of the next sentence is a variation of *Hamlet*, I, v, 130.

5. Dobell's text indicates an omission in place of this word and a sentence missing at the end of this paragraph.

114. *C. L. to Rickman*

Octor. 9th or thereabouts [1801]

I called lately upon our common friend G. Dyer of Clifford's Inn. I found him inconsolable and very dirty. It seems that Gilbert Wake-

field[1] is dead, and George had not got his tribute ready for Mr. Phillips's magazine this month, and Dr. Aikin had sent a little tribute, and Miss Aikin had also sent a *tribute,* and the world would expect a tribute from his pen. At first I imagined that George was touched with some sense of kindred mortality, such as Methusaleh himself must have felt, when he was qualmish; but no, all that disturbed George was, that he had not got a *tribute. George* the *second,* George Burnett, supt with me last night. He is not got quite well of the metaphyz, but I hope & trust that last night's paroxysm will be the last, and that his disorder has come to its crisis. He maintained that if a highwaymen, who is going to kill you, *spares* your *life* on your expressly promising to *spare his,* that is, not to prosecute, you are under no obligation to keep your word, because you were in a state of violence, when the promise was made, and the **Good of the Whole,** which may be partially endangered by suffering that man to live, is to be preferred to any such promise in such circumstances made. If I ever turn free-booter, and light upon George Burnett in my travels, I shall remember what I have to trust to. But saving his metaphyz (which goes off after the first heats of youth like the green Sickness) George the 2d has good parts. He only wants fortune. He as ill becomes adversity, as George the first[2] would do prosperity, if any one should leave him a rich legacy. Another of fortune's *humble servants* is a visitor of mine, who in the language of antiquity would have been nominated Simonds-with-the-slit-lip. I cannot say his linen was of Tarsus, nor quite so robust as Russian, but it certainly craved bleaching, but saving his dirty shirt, and his physiognomy and his 'bacco box, together with a certain kiddy air in his walk, a man could have gone near to have mistaken him for a Gentleman. He has a sort of ambition to be so misunderstood. It seems the Treasury does not pay with that weekly promptitude, and accommodating periodicalness, it was wont; & some constitutions *cannot wait.*— He craved the Loan of a half guinea; could I refuse a **Gentleman**[3] who seemed in distress? He dropt some words, as if he were desirous of trying what effect the Irish Air would have upon a *poor* constitution. Could'nt you make him a door keeper, or a game-keeper, or find some post for him, not altogether so brilliant as useful? Some situation under the *mint-master?*— I leave him to your mercy and ability. There is no hurry, for what you have given him will keep him in *work* some time, & for *pay,* why tis just as his Majesty's Min-

isters shall please.— — **So, Cottle's** Psalms[4] are come out hot press'd
for six shillings. Of course I shall send you a copy. "Poetry is never
more delightfully employed than when in the service of its Creator."
Vide Preface to the Translation (if he had writ one, but he has not).

Quid majus!—[5] the Professor is not married, the Plough is yet in
posse—peace is all the cry here—fireworks, lights &c. abound—.
White stationed himself at Temple Bar among the boys, and threw
squibs; burned one man's cravat.— This is the cream of London
intelligence—you shall have the earliest tidings of all new movements—

C L

MS: Huntington Library. Pub.: Ainger (1904), I, 206–208; Harper, III, 39–41;
Lucas (1935), I, 277–278. Address: Jno. Rickman Esqr/Dublin Castle.

1. Gilbert Wakefield (b. 1756), the classical scholar and controversial religious
and political writer, had died on September 9. In Richard Phillips' *Monthly
Magazine,* 12 (October 1801), 220–221, 225–230, and 190, are the tributes of
Dyer, who had known Wakefield since about 1780; of the physician and author
John Aikin (1747–1822), the editor of the magazine from 1796 to 1807, the son
of Wakefield's fellow tutor and scholar at Warrington Academy Dr. John Aikin
(1713–1780), and the brother of the miscellaneous writer Mrs. Anna Letitia
Barbauld (1743–1825); and of the younger Dr. Aikin's daughter the biographer
and historical writer Lucy Aikin (1781–1864).

2. George Dyer. Simonds, or Simmonds (below), nicknamed the Goul, or
Goule, and Slit-lips, is somewhat identified in Rickman's letter to Southey of
November 7, 1801 (*Rickman,* p. 58), as one to whom Rickman had given lowly
employment, of the kind Rickman had given Burnett, working on the population
returns in the cockpit, or privy council offices, Whitehall. The expression "linen
. . . of Tarsus" presumably alludes to linen finely made. The originator of the
expression, if not Lamb, has not been identified.

3. Underscored twice.

4. Joseph Cottle's *A Version of the Psalms of David, Attempted in Meter,*
which Longman's had just issued.

5. "Something more." The "Professor," following, is Godwin. The phrase *in
posse* translates, "in control."

115. *C. L. to Rickman*

[Late October or early November 1801]

A letter from G. Dyer will probably accompany this. I wish I could
convey to you any notion of the whimsical scenes I have been witness
to in this fortnight past. Twas on Tuesday week the poor heathen
scrambled up to my door about breakfast time. He came thro' a violent
rain with no neckcloth on & a *beard* that made him a spectacle to
men & angels and tap'd at the door. Mary open'd it & he stood stark

still & held a paper in his hand importing that he had been ill with a fever. He either wouldn't or couldn't speak except by signs. When you went to comfort him he put his hand upon his heart & shook his head & told us his complaint lay where no medicines could reach it. I was dispatch'd for Dr. Dale,[1] Mr. Phillips of St. Paul's Church yard & Mr. Frend who is to be his executor. George solemnly delivered into Mr. Frend's hands & mine an old burnt preface that had been in the fire with injunctions which we solemnly vow'd to obey that it should be printed after his death with his last corrections & that some account should be given to the world why he had not fulfill'd his engagement with subscribers. Having done this & borrow'd two guineas of his bookseller[2] (to whom he imparted in confidence that he should leave a great many loose papers behind him which would only want methodizing & arranging to prove very lucrative to any bookseller after his death) he laid himself down on my bed in a mood of complacent resignation. By the aid of meat & drink put into him (for I all along suspected a vacuum) he was enabled to sit up in the evening, but he had not got the better of his intolerable fear of dying; he expressed such philosophic indifference in his speech & such frightened apprehensions in his physiognomy that if he had truly been dying and I had known it I could not have kept my countenance. In particular when the doctor came & ordered him to take little white powders, (I suppose of chalk or alum to humour him) he ey'd him with a *suspicion* which I could not account for; he has since explain'd that he took it for granted Dr. Dale knew his situation & had ordered him these powders to hasten his departure that he might suffer as little pain as possible. Think what an aspect the heathen put on with these fears upon a dirty face. To recount—all his freaks for two or three days while he thought he was going & how the fit operated & sometimes the man got uppermost & sometimes the author & he had this excellent person to serve & he must correct some proof sheets for Phillips & he could not bear to leave his subscribers unsatisfy'd but he must not think of these things now, he was going to a place where he should satisfy all his debts—& when he got a little better he began to discourse what a happy thing it would be if there was a place where all the good men & women in the world might meet meaning heav'n & I really believe for a time he had doubts about his soul for he was very near, if not quite light-headed. The fact was he had not had a good meal for some

days & his little dirty Neice (whom he sent for with a still dirtier Nephew[3] & hugg'd him; & bid them farewell) told us that unless he dines out he subsists on tea & gruels. And he corroborated this tale by ever & anon complaining of sensations of gnawing which he felt about his *heart* which he mistook his stomach to be & sure enough these gnawings were dissipated after a meal or two & he surely thinks that he has been rescued from the jaws of death by Dr. Dale's white powders. He is got quite well again by nursing & chirps of odes & lyric poetry the day long—he is to go out of town on Monday & with him goes the dirty train of his papers & books which follow'd him to our house. I shall not be sorry when he takes his nipt carcase out of my bed which it has occupied & vanishes with all his Lyric lumber. but I will endeavour to bring him in future into a method of dining at least once a day. I have proposed to him to dine with me & he has nearly come into it whenever he does not go out & pay me. I will take his money beforehand & he shall eat it out.[4] If I don't it will go all over the world. Some worthless relations of which the dirty little devil that looks after him & a still more dirty nephew are component particles, I have reason to think divide all his gains with some lazy worthless authors that are his constant satellites. The literary Fund has voted him seasonably £20 & if I can help it he shall spend it on his own carcase. I have assisted him in arranging the remainder of wh[at] he calls Poems & he will get rid of 'em I hope in another mo[nth . . .] be about a history of [. . .] *a Life!* My [. . .]

I promised Burnet to write when his parcel went. He wants me to certify that he is more awake than you think him. I believe he may be by this time but he is so full of self-opinion that I fear whether he & Phillips will ever do together.[5] What he is to do for Phillips he whimsically seems to consider more as a favor done *to* P. than a job *from* P.— He still persists to call employment *dependence* & prates about the insolence of booksellers & the tax upon geniuses. poor devil! he is not launched upon the ocean & is sea-sick with afore thought. I write plainly about him & he would stare & yawn finely if he read this treacherous epistle but I really am anxious about him & that nettles me to see him so proud & so helpless. If he is not serv'd he will never serve himself. I read his long letter to Southey[6] which I suppose you have seen. He had better have been furnishing copy for Phillips than luxuriating in tracing the causes of his imbecillity. I be-

lieve he is a little wrong in not ascribing more to the structure of his own mind. He had his yawns from nature, his pride from education.

I hope to see Southey soon, so I need only send my remembrance to him now. Doubtless I need not tell him that Burnett is not to be foster'd in self-opinion. His eyes want opening to see himself a man of middling stature. I am not oculist enough to do this. The booksellers may one day remove the film. I am all this time on the most cordial supping terms of amity with G. Burnett & really love him at times: but I must speak freely of people behind their backs & not think it back biting. It is better than Godwin's way of telling a man he is a fool to his face.

I think if you could do *any* thing for George[7] in the way of an office (God knows whether you can in any haste but you did talk of it) it is my firm belief that it would be his *only chance* of settlement; he will never live by his *literary exertions* as he calls them—he is too proud to go the usual way to work & he has no talents to make that way un- necessary. I know he talks big in his letter to Southey that his mind is undergoing an alteration & that the die is now casting that shall con- sign him to honor or dishonor. but these expressions are the convulsions of a fever not the sober workings of health. Translated into plain English he now & then perceives he must work or starve & then he thinks he'll work: but when he goes about it there's a lion in the way. He came dawdling to me for an Encyclopædia yesterday. I recom- mended him to Norris' library[8] & he said if he could not get it there Phillips was bound to furnish him with one. It was Phillips' interest to do so & all that. This was true with some restrictions—but as to Phillips' interest to oblige G. B! Lord help his simple head! P. could, by a *whistle* call together a host of such authors as G. B. like Robin Hood's merry men in green. P. has regular regiments in pay. Poor writers are his crab-lice & suck at him for nutriment. His round pud- ding chops are their *idea* of plenty when *in their idle fancies they aspire* to be rich.[9]

What do you think of a life of G. Dyer? I can scarcely conceive a more amusing novel. He has been connected with all sects in the world & he will faithfully tell all he knows. Every body will read it; & if it is not done according to my fancy I promise to put him in a novel when he dies. Nothing shall escape *me*. If you think it feasible, whenever you write you may encourage him. Since he has been so close with me I

have perceiv'd the workings of his inordinate vanity, His gigantic attention to particles & to prevent open vowels in his odes his solicitude that the public may not lose any tittle of his poems by his death & all the while his utter ignorance that the world do'nt care a pin about his odes & his criticisms, a fact which every [bo]dy knows but himself,— he *is a rum genius*

C L

MS: unrecovered; a copy: The University of Texas Library, Austin, Texas. Pub.: Harper, III, 44–50; Lucas (1905), VI, 230–233; Lucas (1912), V, 234–238; Lucas (1935), I, 279–282. Address: John Rickman Esqr/Dublin Castle. Rickman's letter to Southey of November 7 (*Rickman*, pp. 57–60) establishes the dates for this and the next letter by its mention of this letter, its transcription of Dyer's letter to Rickman that accompanied this letter, and its references to Burnett's packet to Rickman on which Lamb comments in this and the next letter.

1. Perhaps Dr. Thomas Dale (1729–1816), of Devonshire Square, Bishopsgate. The Phillips referred to following is Richard. See Vol. I, Letter 5, note 5, for William Frend. See Vol. I, Letter 77, note 2, about the burned preface, the Preface to Dyer's *Poems* (1800).

2. The firm of Longman and Rees.

3. The children of George Dyer's brother John, a lighterman who in November 1804 was living with his wife and children (who have not been identified) in St. Dunstan's Court, Fleet Street.

4. Lamb here and in his preceding sentence may mean this: "I have proposed to him to dine with me & pay me whenever he decides not to dine elsewhere, & he has nearly accepted my proposal. I will take his money before-hand, & he shall eat up its worth." The literary fund mentioned below was perhaps that of the Inner Temple, or perhaps (as is intimated in Letter 126) one with which Frend was associated. Dyer's poems are those that with other writings form *Poems and Critical Essays* (2 vols.; 1802). The greater portion of three lines concluding this paragraph has been torn from the bottom of the sheet.

5. Richard Phillips had employed Burnett to write for William Fordyce Mavor's *Universal History*. See Vol. I, Letter 29, note 2.

6. Who had sailed for Dublin on October 11 to accept an appointment that Rickman had obtained for him as private secretary to Isaac Corry (1755–1813), at this time chancellor of the Irish exchequer and surveyor of Irish Crown lands. But Southey remained for only about two weeks, returned to Keswick, and in the first week of November settled in London to serve Corry there.

7. Burnett.

8. That of the Inner Temple and under the care of Randal Norris. See Vol. I, Introduction, p. xxix.

9. The last three words may also be underscored, but the manuscript is so faded that I cannot be certain if they are.

116. *C. L. to Rickman*

[Early November 1801]

I was the moon-struck man, that was inspired to write on the pacquet "for John Rickman"; & must hasten to clear Burnett of that part of his *Indictment*. He brought to me his Letter and his Essay, or rather two Essays, and desired me to write myself, and put up altogether in a parcel. I had no leisure to write then, but I did up his things, and when I had done so, the enormous bulk staggered me, and I preferred that obnoxious indorsement to enlarging it with another cover. I was guided by the usages of the India House, where I have often received superscriptions similar, and escaped shot free. I will never practise upon your pocket in the like manner again, but Burnett stands acquitted. None but the Bishop[1] could have composed that illustrious specimen of ignorance, which you extract. And he alone, in all England, would not understand the absurdity of it, if it were to be pointed out. Still I wish something could be done for him, even if he waited six weeks, *or a day over,* for it. Methinks! (as the Poets say) I see Preferment waiting at the door, *afraid to come in,* 'till his worship has finished his Introduction, that She may not deprive the World of his matchless Labours.— I admire your Commitation[2] of Pork: it is quite authentic and Apostolic. .— A gift of Tongues: I should sin against the Holy Ghost to refuse it. How, like their clever Ancestors, will they descend in a red shower upon my parched and gaping Larder.

I have nothing to communicate, but my thanks, and to assure you that I retain a very lively memory of our old smoking evenings in Southampton Buildings. G. Dyer, our illustrious Co-Puffer, has emigrated to Enfield, where some rich man,[3] that has got two country Houses, allows him the use of a very large one, with a Library, where he is getting the final vol. of his Poems ready, & then I shall set him about his Life: by *use,* in a sentence back, I mean dirting & littering.—

Southey is not arrived—

<div align="right">Yours sinerely
C L</div>

I forgot to notice an anachronism in your 1st Letter, which I am glad to see you correct in a subsequent—you accost me my dear *Sir.*[4]

By what twist of association in your unlucky Pericranium have you connected that Honor with my Cognomen?——

Mary thanks you, but she prefers **Rum.**

I have literally *this moment* recd. your packet for Southey. I mean Burnett's History of his own times. And your Letter. For your kind mention of slit-lips take my warmest thanks. He will have no objection to wait 6 weeks or *a day over,* tho' it may be damnably more inconvenient for him to **Wait** than for the Bishop. The fact of the "strange flesh"[5] which he is reported to have eaten, astounds me, but I can believe & tremble.— Never mind the ceremony of franking to me. John Company pays.——

MS: Huntington Library. Pub.: Ainger (1904), I, 210–212; Harper, III, 50–52; Lucas (1935), I, 283–284. Address: John Rickman Esqr/Dublin Castle.

1. Burnett. Lamb gives him the title of Gilbert Burnet, bishop of Salisbury, author of *History of His Own Times.* See Vol. I, Letter 60, note 3, and the last postscript in this letter.
2. "Commutation" was presumably the word intended.
3. Unidentified.
4. Underscored twice.
5. *Antony and Cleopatra,* I, iv, 67.

117. *C. L. to Godwin*

[Early November 1801]

Your Letter[1] cannot be better. I have ventured to substitute in *my copy,* top of 4th page, "A spirit of humanity *in** the author" for *"the* humanity & *benevolence of* the Author" which was scarce modest.— I have left you to adopt it, or not, in your copy.— I would suggest another alteration—your own copy 2d page 9th line *"entire* persuasion"—. that is not true—. in your pamphlet your words are "I hope & trust" a colloquial phrase expressing usually a low degree of persuasion. What if, adverting to your own words, you say "I aver my *hope & trust,"*? marking the words emphatically, as if your readers did not advert to the force of them in their place

<div align="right">In haste—yours truly
C L</div>

I have not compared my copy. *Do you.*——

*or "sufficient evidences of humanity in" &c—if you please—

MS: Lord Abinger. Unpublished.

1. Dated November 10 and to the editor of the *Monthly Magazine,* 12 (December 1, 1801), 387–388, in response to a letter signed "W." in the magazine for November 1 (pp. 304–305) charging that Godwin revealed himself a defender of infanticide in his pamphlet *Thoughts. Occasioned by the Perusal of Dr. Parr's Spital Sermon, Preached at Christ's Church, April 15, 1800: Being a Reply to the Attacks of Dr. Parr, Mr. Mackintosh, the Author of an Essay on Population, and Others* (1801). Named or alluded to in that title are the pedagogue Samuel Parr (1747–1825), James Mackintosh (see Letter 108, note 2), and the political economist Thomas Robert Malthus (1766–1834). Of the quotations below (apparently from a manuscript copy of the letter that Godwin had sent to Lamb) only *"entire* persuasion," transformed into "I aver my persuasion," is somewhat in the published letter. "I hope, and trust" is in the pamphlet. See *Uncollected Writings (1785–1822): Articles in Periodicals and Six Pamphlets, One with Coleridge's Marginalia, by William Godwin. Facsimile Reproductions with Introductions,* ed. Jack W. Marken and Burton R. Pollin (Gainesville, Fla.: Scholars' Facsimiles and Reprints, 1968), pp. 376 and 356.

118. *C. L. to Robert Lloyd*

[November 18, 1801]

I am not dead nor asleep. But Manning is in town, & Coleridge is in town, and I am making a thorough alteration in the structure of my play for Publication. My brain is overwrought with variety of worldly-intercourse. I have neither time nor mind for scribbling. Who shall deliver me from the body of this Death?—

Only continue to write & to believe that when the **Hour** comes, I shall strike like Jack of the Clock, id est, I shall once more become a regular correspondent of Robt. & Plumstead. How is the benevolent, loud-talking, Shakspere-loving, Brewer?—[1]

To your enquiry respecting a selection from B'p Taylor I answer— it cannot be done, & if it could it would not *take* with John Bull.— It cannot be done, for who can disentangle and unthread the rich texture of Nature & Poetry sewn so thick into a stout coat of theology, without spoiling both *lace* & *coat?* how beggarly and how bald do even Shakespeares Princely Pieces look, when thus violently divorced from *connexion* & *circumstance*! when we meet with To be or not to be[2]— or Jacques's moralizings upon the Deer—or Brutus and Cassius' quarrel & reconciliation—in an Enfield speaker or in Elegant Extracts—how we stare & will scarcely acknowledge to ourselves (what we are conscious we feel) that they are flat & have no power. Something exactly like this have I experienced when I have picked out similes & stars

from Holy Dying and shewn them per se, as you'd shew specimens of minerals or pieces of rock—. Compare the grand effect of the Star-paved firmament—& imagine a boy capable of picking out those pretty twinklers **one by one** & playing at chuck farthing with them.— Every thing in heaven & earth, in man and in story, in books & in fancy, acts by **Confederacy,** by juxaposition, by circumstance & **place**—. Consider a fine family—(if I were not writing to you I might instance your own) of sons & daughters with a respectable father & a handsome mother at their head, all met in one house, & happy round one table—. Earth cannot shew a more lovely & venerable sight,[3] such as the Angels in heaven might lament that in their country there is no marrying or giving in marriage—. Take & split this Body into individuals—shew the separate caprices, vagaries, &c. of Charles, Rob. or Plum. one a quaker, another a churchman.— The eldest daughter seeking a husband out of the pale of parental faith—another warping perhaps—the father a prudent, circumspective, do-me-good sort of a man *blest* with children whom no ordinary rules can circumscribe—. I have not room for all particulars—but just as this happy & venerable Body of a family loses by splitting & considering individuals too nicely, so it is when we pick out **Best Bits** out of a great writer.[4] Tis the *Sum* total of his mind which *affects* us

C [L]

MS: Henry W. and Albert A. Berg Collection, The New York Public Library, Astor, Lenox and Tilden Foundations. Pub.: Ainger (1900), II, 40–42; Macdonald, I, 216–217; Ainger (1904), I, 190–191; Harper, III, 56–58; Lucas (1935), I, 284–286. Address: Mr. Robert Lloyd/Ch Lloyd Esqr/Birmingham. Postmark: November 18, 1801.

1. Plumstead Lloyd, conjecturally.

2. *Hamlet,* III, i, 55–89. See *As You Like It,* II, i, 47–57, and *Julius Caesar,* IV, ii, 37–52, and iii, 1–162, for the speeches referred to next. See Vol. I, Letter 5, note 3, for *Elegant Extracts.*

3. One wonders if Wordsworth did not see this letter within the next few months, remember this passage, and turn it into the opening line of "Composed upon Westminster Bridge, September 3, 1802"—"Earth has not anything to show more fair."

4. As Lamb did in *Specimens of English Dramatic Poets* and "Extracts from the Garrick Plays" (*Works,* IV, 397–505). But in the Preface to the former work he pointed out that wherever he could he gives "entire scenes, and in some instances successive scenes, rather than to string together single passages and detached beauties, which I have always found wearisome in the reading in selections of this nature" (*Works,* IV, xi).

119. *C. L. to Rickman*

Tuesday 24th Novr. 1801

Dr. Rickman—

I have just put my finishing hand to my play to alter it for publishing. I have made a thorough change[1] in the structure of the latter part, omitting all those scenes which shew'd John under the first impression of his father's death. I have done this, because I had made him too weak, and to expose himself before his servants, which was an indecorum; & from a theory, that poetry has nothing to do to give *pain,* the imbecillities, and deformities, the dotages of human nature, are not fit objects to be shewn. Instead of these rejected scenes I have told his feelings in a *narrative* of the old Servant to Margaret, which is a relief to the oppression of John so often *talking* in his own person.—— I have cut out all the interview of John & Simon, and they do not meet at all, & I have expunged Simon's bloody resolution, which offended you so much from him. I have sent him to *improve himself* by travel, and it is explained that his presence (who is the *good son* in my *parable*) would have been too much a reproach & a pain to *my prodigal* in the first hour of his grief.— The whole ends with Margaret's Consolation, where it *should* end, without any pert incident of surprise & trick to make a catastrophe.— Moreover, I have excluded the two tales of the Witch & the Gentleman who died for Love, having since discovered by searching the parish register of St. Mary Ottery, that his disorder was a stranguary, tho' some rimes upon his grave-stone did a little lean to my hypothesis.— Moreover, I have gone thro' & cut out all the Ahs! & Ohs! and sundry weak parts, which I thought so fine three or four years ago. When it comes out, you must let me know, in what manner I can transmit you a copy or two.— — I have been so particular, because you have shewn more liking to my Margaret, than most people, and my alterations were *in part* the offspring of your suggestions; not wholly, for I have long smelt a jumble. I hope you will find it now nearly all of a piece. I am to Christen it "John Woodvil" simply—not Pride's cure.— As Dyer says, "I am no enemy to candid & ingenious criticism, I only deprecate the arrows of calumny": vide most of the prefaces of G. Dyer.— Dyer regularly

dines with me when he does not go a visitg. and brings his shilling. He has pick'd up amazingly. I never saw him happier. He has had his Doors listed, & his casements puttied, and bought a handsome *screen* of the last century. Only his poems do not get finished. One volume is printing, but the second wants a good deal doing to it. I do not expect that he will make much progress with his Life and Opinions, till his detestable Lyric Poetry is delivered to Subscribers. I shall make him not deliver one vol. till both are ready, else he would infalli[b]ly have made two troubles & two expences of it. He talks of marrying,[2] but this en passant (as he says) & entre nous, for God's sake dont mention it to him, for he has not forgiven me for betraying to you his purpose of writing his own Life. He says, that if it once spreads, so many people will expect and wish to have a place in it, that he is sure he shall disoblige all his friends. .————

G. Burnet shewed me your rouzing Letter. If I had not have known your theory and design, I must have called it a very cruel Letter, and sure as I was that your general idea of the treatment, which is best for Burnetts & George the Seconds,[3] was right, I could not help thinking you had gone too far, even so far that he could not put up with it or you ever after, without doing a moral injury to himself. But you must pursue your own course, which 9 times out of ten will be more judicious than mine. The less of interference in these cases, the better. I was principally (if not only) sorry, that you assured him of Southey's opinion of the mediocrity of his understanding perfectly agreeing with your own. Southey was the last plank of the scaffold which propt up George in his opinion of himself. But I dare not affirm you did wrong. I am not a teacher in Israel.[4]

<div style="text-align:right">Yours truly
C Lamb</div>

MS: Huntington Library. Pub.: Ainger (1904), I, 208–210; Harper, III, 41–44; Lucas (1935), I, 286–288. Address: John Rickman Esqr/Dublin Castle.

1. For this and other changes made in "Pride's Cure," which G. and J. Robinson had published with other writings by February 4, 1802, as *John Woodvil: A Tragedy. To Which Are Added, Fragments of Burton, the Author of the Anatomy of Melancholy,* see *Works,* V, 350–367. See also Letter 125 and Vol. I, Letter 38, note 3.

2. Southey wrote Rickman on February 17, 1802, that the Lambs had talked Dyer into falling in love with Elizabeth Ogilvy Benger (see Vol. I, Letter 66, note 2) and had gotten him into a "quagmire and cannot get him out again, for

they have failed in the attempt to talk Miss Bungay or Bungey or Benjey into love with him. This is a cruel business," Southey added, "for he has taken the injection, and it may probably soon break out in sonnets and elegies" (*Rickman,* p. 76).

3. Still Burnett, presumably. See Letter 114, first paragraph.

4. John 3:10.

120. *C. L. to Rickman*

[Early December 1801]

I sincerely thank you for your repeated offer, but I have just received as much as £50 an old debt which I told you of, and that will a good deal more than cover the expences of printing. I expect to be able to send you some copies in a few weeks. I have not had a proof sheet yet.— I have nothing to claim upon Dyer's account. He paid me from the beginning as near as I can calculate, and I solemnly protest it, to a penny for all the expences he put me to, & whenever he dines with us he regularly brings his shilling, which is a fair average for what his gluttony devours. To be sure he has occasionally an eleemosynary whiff of tobacco, for which I cannot sconse the Poet.[1] I am afraid he sometimes does not come, when he has not got a shilling, and I cannot force him, for now his health is come back, he is the most unmanageable of God's creatures. He goes about fetching & carrying for Ladies, and always thinking he *must* call upon this Lady & tother Gentleman. His 1st vol. is nearly printed, but he is projecting new odes and impertinences for the 2d. & I cannot foresee a period. Still he seems by fits bent upon writing his Life, and will do it, if the Prototype is not overtaken with death. I quite give up any hope of reducing him to common sense & human conduct. All that can be done is to bolster up his carcase by a daily habit of **Dining,** until he finishes his mortal pilgrimage. Poor G. Burnett is very ill and reduced. You would deposit your fierce anger, if you saw the metaphysician. He has brought his Introduction[2] to a finish at last, but he is not in a capacity to go on. Coleridge has recommended him to the Editor of the Morning Post, who has promised to employ him. But a Lion is in his footpath, and he cannot *begin yet.* I suppose he will write to you, and it will be needless to say more of him here.— The Goul has a Gouless & two, if not three, young Gouls. The Goul has not paid me the pittance, for twas not

much, he borrowd of me, but I have reason to believe his circum-
stances are so squalid, that it would be more to expect of him, than
can be expected from man or goul, to divert his Comings in from the
service of genuine Hunger and thirst. Fenwick's Plough (how one idea
of Poverty introduces another!) is degenerated already from a daily
to a weekly paper. I wish it may not vanish into thin air, or come
out the same day as Burnett's Historia Romana issues from the press.
I meantime have made some overtures to the Editor of the Morning
Post thro' Coleridge, who writes for that paper, & hope I am on the
point of being engaged.—. I have seen Southey several times. His Wife
is considerably improved, & will talk if she is talked to, but she bitterly
complains that when literary men get together, they never speak to the
women. Mrs. Lovel is also in town & Southey's mother,[3] who is
dying:—"so am not I said the foolish fat scullion." Do you remember
our unfeeling behaviour at the funeral of that dear young Lady, who
was withered in her bloom by the untimely stroke of Death, & lies in
what-d'ye-call-em Church yard? The tear is falling, while I remember—
dont you perceive the Ink rather *brackish?* as G. Burnett asked in a
company at my brothers the other day, Whether the Thames Water at
Blackfriars Bridge was not a little **Brackish.**— The Professor has not
yet thrown himself away. I am sorry to find, he is about to commit a
folly, for I hear that **She** has no fortune & has one child, & they
propose that she shall ease the burden of the family expences by
translating from the French.— **Fell,**[4] the inevitable shadow of every
thing which Godwin does, is absolutely writing a **Play.** It is a **Comedy.**
It is just finished, and I go this evening in the hope to see it. It will
have one trait in it. There can be no mirth in it. An Owl making a
Pun would be no bad emblem of the unnatural attempt.—— —

To your enquiry whether Mary swallows certain mixed Liquors,
she answers that I unfortunately misunde[r]stood that advice, as if it
had been addrest to me, and ha[ve] almost killed myself by the
Blunder. But she will profit by the correction. She desires her love &
remembrance—. White often enquires after you, and as often desires
to be mentioned to you, which I as regularly forget.— Stoddart[5] is
going to begin the study of Civil Law at the Commons. I still keep my
attachment to Brandy & Tobacco, which "grow with my decay &
strengthen with my weakness," but better is a crazy house with good

cellars in it than a magnificent mansion with small beer. I certainly get more of a Christian than ever, for no man *repents* more than I do.

farewell, old Comrade & new Secretary—

thine

C L

You must send up your St. Helena[6] Letter *immediately,* and I will drop it in our Box. I ca'nt frank it. John Company never franks *outwards.* A ship, the Marquis of Ely, goes at **Xmas**——. The Armston goes next **We'nsday**——

Since I wrote last Leaf, I have read Fell's Comedy, and am surprized to find it contain, if not sterling wit or character, a liveliness & knowledge of the present popular taste, which has astonish'd me. The serious parts are dann'd flat. But I should not at all wonder, he having a pretty good introduction, even if it should please highly. He has been a minute observer of what *takes* in Reynolds's plays,[7] and has had real Actors continually in his view.— Who knows, but Owls *do* make Puns, when they hoot by moonshine? I shall hear from the Morning Post this day, and shall endeavor to get the Theatrical reports, not *all,* but Kemble's chief characters & **Cooke's** &c—— ——

MS: Huntington Library. Pub.: Ainger (1904), I, 212–214; Harper, III, 52–56; Lucas (1935), I, 288–290. Address: John Rickman Esqr/Dublin Castle. See especially note 3 for the dating.

1. Five canceled lines follow.

2. To Mavor's *Universal History* (see below and Vol. I, Letter 29, note 2), whose first seven volumes treat the Roman epoch and are announced as completed in the *Monthly Magazine,* 13 (June 1802), 465. To "a Lion is in his footpath," below, cf. Proverbs 26:13. See Letter 114, note 2, about the Goul.

3. Margaret Hill Southey (b. 1752), who had arrived with Mary, the widow of Robert Lovell, in the evening of November 30, 1801, and would die of consumption on January 5, 1802. (See Vol. I, Letter 1, note 2, and *New Southey Letters,* I, 259 and 266.) The word *"dying,"* in the following clause, is underscored twice. The quotation is from *Tristram Shandy,* Vol. V, ch. vii. The deceased young lady is probably the one identified in Letter 124, note 1.

4. Ralph Fell (d. 1814), who had known Godwin since 1790, had introduced him to John Fenwick, and had been introduced to Lamb by Godwin or Fenwick. In addition to the (unidentified) comedy mentioned below, Fell was the author of *A Tour through the Batavian Republic* (1801) and a *Life of Charles James Fox* (1808). By September 1802, according to Lamb's subsequent letters, which seem to be the only sources of further information on him, he had become the editor of some naval chronicle, by January 1804 had been reduced to extreme want and seeking through Lamb employment from Rickman, and in January 1806 was on his way into Newgate, leaving his wife and four children to make their way into some poor-law parish. His death is recorded in the *Gentleman's Magazine,* 84 (April 1814), 412.

5. Dr. John Stoddart. (See Vol. I, Letter 3, note 28.) By "the Commons,"

following, Lamb refers to Doctors' Commons, or the College of Advocates, or (formally) The College of Doctors of Law Exercent in the Ecclesiastical and Admiralty Courts, which was located, until its dissolution in 1857, on Knightrider Street at Godliman Street. The quotation is an adaptation of Pope's *An Essay on Man*, II, 136. A canceled line and one-half follow the close of this paragraph.

6. Where the mail carried by outward- and inward-bound East Indiamen was usually exchanged.

7. *Werter* (1785), *Eloisa* (1786), and *The Dramatist* (1789), for instance, by Frederic Reynolds (1764–1841), of Westminster School and the Middle Temple. The last sentence in this letter seems to contain allusions to theatrical reports written, or about to be written, by Lamb. If so, one report could be "G. F. Cooke in 'Richard the Third,'" which is Lamb's and is in the *Morning Post* of January 4, 1802. Another could be, by its mention of John Philip Kemble (see Vol. I, Letter 56, note 1), "Theatre: Covent Garden," which is thought to be Lamb's and is in the *Morning Post* of January 9, 1802. See *Works*, I, 36–38 and 399–400, and the next two letters.

121. *C. L. to Rickman*

[Saturday,] 9th January [1802]

I am to be sure much gratified with your use of Margaret[1] as a kind of rack to extort confession from women. But dont give me out as your Rack-maker, lest the women retort upon me the fate of Perillus, which you may read in your Ainsworth under the article Phalaris: or you may find the story more at large by perusing the Controversy between Bentley & Boyle. . I have delayed to write (I believe I am telling a Lye) until I should get a book ready to send (but I believe this has been all along a pretext recurred to, a kind of after-motive, when the resolution was taken a priori, rather than the true cause, which was mixed up of busy days & riotous nights,[2] doing the Company's business in a morning, straining for Jokes in the afternoon, and retailing them (not being yet published) over punch at night). The Lungs of Stentor could not long sustain the Life I have led. I get into parties, or treat them with Pope Joan four times in a week—. You have dropt in eer now when Norris was courting at such a Party, and you know the game. I stick to it like any *Papist*. Tis better than Poetry, Mechanics, Politics, or Metaphysics—. That's a stop—there's pope— you did not take your ace—what a magic charm in sounds— —. I begin not to wonder at the blood shed which dyed Christian Europe concerning **Omousia & Omoiousia**[3]—a party of people's *faces* about a fire grinning over cards and forgetting that they have got to go home is the supreme felicity **the Maximum Bonum**. White has or is

about to write you at my suggestion. We desire nothing so vigorously as to see Master Secretary in these parts—. There are Liquors and **fumes** extant, which have power to detain a Bachelor from his cold **Bed** till cock crow.——

Fenwick gives routs & balls & suppers (not balls) but splendid entertainments out of the first fruits of the Plow—he had some hundreds of pounds **from** unthinking Nobility—. It is no breach of Charity to suppose that part is expended—his wife & daughter have got magnificent Hats, which Mary waggishly has christen'd Northumberland Hats, from his great Patron at Charing Cross.——[4]

Dyer has at last met with a madman more mad than himself—the Earl of Buchan brother to the Erskines & eccentric biographer of Fletcher of Saltoun—this old man of near eighty is come to London in his way to France, & George & he go about every where—. George brought the mad Lord up to see me—I wa'nt at home but Mary was washing—a pretty pickle to receve an Earl in! Lord have mercy upon us a **Lord** in my Garratt! my utmost ambition was some time or other to receve a Secretary! well, I am to breakfast with this mad Lord on Sunday. I am studying manners. George & my Lord of Buchan went on thursday last to Richmond[5] in the **Long Coach** to pay their devotions to the shrine of Thompson! the coldest day in the year. Enough to Cool a Jerusalem-Padder. George is as proud as a Turkey Cock & can talk of nothing else; always taking care to hedge in at the end, that he don't value Lords, & that the Earl has nothing of the Lord about him. O human nature! human Nature! for my part I have told every Body, how I had an **Earl** come to **see me**— —. George describes the Earl as a very worthy man, who has his hobby horses, for instance, George says, he will stop you in the street, when you are walking with him, & hold you by the button, and talk so Loud, that all the Passers by look at you. So you may guess *why* he cleaves to **George the first**—. If you have read the Post,[6] you may have seen a dissertation **on Cookes Richard the 3d.** which is the best thing I have done. It was in Last Monday; Stray **Jokes** I will not *mark,* hoping you will always take the Good ones to be mine, and the bad ones to be done by John a Nokes &c.

<div style="text-align: right;">

in haste

happy year to Master Secretary— —

C L

</div>

I had, before your injunction came, given a hint to the Goul, that you were disposed to serve him: this to rear him from the dreary state of despair he was in. But, now, *mum.* I wish to God you may do any thing: for all the Elements have fought against him—

My Play will most likely accompany my *next.* Fell's goes on slow & sure, like his own Long stories—. It is *much much* better than I could believe. Some of it is very *good farce,* which is all a modern play need be.—

Please to send me *one* Letter with the *Broad Seal,*[7] for a friend who is curious in impressions.

MS: Huntington Library. Pub.: Ainger (1904), I, 215–217; Harper, III, 58–61; Lucas (1935), I, 290–292. Address: Jno. Rickman Esqr/Dublin Castle.

1. In *John Woodvil.* Perillus of Athens, below, was the inventor and first victim of the brazen bull in which Phalaris (ca. 570–554 B.C.), tyrant of Acragas, Sicily, was also burned. For the story Lamb directs Rickman first to the *Thesaurus linguae Latinae compendiarius* (1736), by Robert Ainsworth (1660–1743), and then to the controversy that arose between the scholar and critic Richard Bentley (1662–1742) and Charles Boyle, fourth Earl of Orrery and first Baron Marston (1676–1731). Bentley, in an essay in the second edition of *Reflections upon Ancient and Modern Learning* (1697), by William Wotton (1666–1727), had sought to show that the epistles of Phalaris, edited by Boyle in 1695 and with a Preface containing insolent references to Bentley, were forgeries. Boyle and his supporters answered Bentley in *Dr. Bentley's Dissertation on the Epistles of Phalaris* (1698). Bentley silenced them with his *Dissertation on the Letters of Phalaris* (1699). Jonathan Swift made the controversy famous in *The Battle of the Books* (1704).

2. Cf. Luke 15:13; *John Woodvil,* II, ii (*Works,* V, 147); and (with a pun in mind) *King Lear,* I, iii, 6, and II, i, 94. The Greek herald Stentor, below and in the *Iliad,* V, 785, had a voice equal to that of fifty men and died supposedly in a shouting contest with Hermes, the crier of the gods. Pope Joan is a card game. Norris is Randal Norris. A "stop" is a situation in Pope Joan. The pope is the seven or nine of diamonds.

3. A reference to the dispute between the orthodox and the followers of the heretical Arius (d. 336) over the substance of the Father and the Son. In its center were the Homoii, who spoke of a general likeness of the Son to the Father. At the left were the Anomoii, who held with Arius that the Son was not like the Father. At the right were both the Homoousians, who adopted the Nicene, or orthodox, belief that the Son was "of the same substance" as the Father, and the Homoiousians, who thought to preserve the content of the Nicene doctrine without having to adopt it, by proposing that the Son had "a likeness of nature" with the Father.

4. The location of Northumberland House, since razed, the ancient London residence of the Percys. (See Letter 108, note 1.) The "madman," below, is David Steuart Erskine, eleventh Earl of Buchan (1742–1829), the author, among other works, of *Essay on the Lives of [Andrew (1655–1716)] Fletcher of Saltoun and the Poet Thomson* (1792). His brothers were Henry (1746–1817), lord advocate, and Thomas, later first Baron Erskine (1750–1823) and lord chancellor of England.

5. Where James Thomson lived and in whose churchyard he is buried. Mr. R.

W. Burchfield, editor of the *Oxford English Dictionary Supplement,* believes "Jerusalem-Padder" as it is used below means "pilgrim."
6. The *Morning Post* of January 4. Mentioned at the end of the paragraph is the comic actor James Noke, or Nokes (d. 1692?).
7. The Great Seal of England. Rickman was deputy keeper of the privy seal.

122. *C. L. to Rickman*

[Mid-January 1802]

You may suspect as much as you please (suspicion ever haunts the guilty mind) that I did not do that thing about Richard, but I tell you I did, and I also made the Lord Mayor's Bed,[1] which you are welcome to rumple as much as you please. I plead guilty to certain "felicities of phrase"—*noviciate* used as an adjective I myself suspected, but did not know that *novice* was any other than a substantive. But what the devil's all this coil for about delightful artifices and elastic minds? and how should a man at Bantry Bay know any thing about good English?— the fact is, that it was but an unfinished affair at first, and by the *intelligent artifice* of the Editor it was made more chaotic still. As it stands, it is more than half *introduction*: half of which was to be *note*. But it is most probably the last theatrical morceau I shall do: for they want 'em done the same night, and I tried it once, & found myself non compos. I ca'nt *do* a thing against time. If I use do & did to excess, tis because I know 'em to be good English, that you ca'nt deny. My Editor uniformly rejects all that I do considerable in length. I shall only do paragraphs, with now & then a slight poem such as Dick Strype,[2] if you read it, which was but a long Epigram. So I beg you not to read with much expectation, for my poor paragraphs do only get in, when there are none of any body's else. Most of them are rejected; all, almost, that are *personal,* where my forte lies. And I cannot get at once out of the delightful regions of scurrility, the "Delectable Mountains" of *Albion* where whilom I fed my sheep,[3] into the Rickshaws of fashionable tittle tattle, which I *must learn.* I cannot have the conscience to order a Paper for Xt Church, on the Hypothesis that it is on my account (which is modest) for no paragraphs can be worth 8 guineas a year. However I will try & see, if I can get it at an under price as you proposed.— I sent 'em mottoes for 12th day at their own

desire—how did they serve me? the first day they put in mottoes by another (most stupid) hand, and the next day mottoes by ditto with some of mine tacked to 'em. They rejected a pretty good one on Dr. Solomon[4]

My namesake, sprung from Jewish Breeder,
Knew *from* the Hyssop *to* the Cedar,
But I, unlike the Jewish Leader,
Scarce know the Hyssop *from* the Cedar.

Another of the rejected ones, on Count Rumford

I deal in Aliments fictitious,
And teaze the Poor with soups nutritious:
Of bones & flint I make dilution,
And belong to the National Institution.

Maybe you did'nt see what were *in* of mine.—— — the **Best** was

Addington
I put my night cap on my head,
And went as usual to my bed,
And most surprizing to relate!
I woke a Minister of State!——

Another
Frere & Canning
At Eton School brought up with dull boys,
We shone like *men* among the *school boys;*
But since we in the world have been,
We are but *schoolboys* among men.—

Your advice about getting a share of the Post *as fast as I can*! ! I shall certainly follow. I wish I may hold my two guinea matter

My scrawl costs you nothing; & me only so much Ink. Mary's Love. We are just setting out on a night expedition freezing (the glass at 23 as I *hear,* for I dont know a thummometer from a Bareumter) to Pentonville to see Mister Comedy Fell and his pretty Spousa.—

Yours &c
C L.

MS: Huntington Library. Pub.: Ainger (1904), I, 217–219; Harper, III, 62–64; Lucas (1935), I, 293–295. Address: John Rickman Esqr/Dublin.

1. "Grand State Bed," in "The Fashionable World" column of the *Morning Post* of January 4, 1802, and Lucas (1935), I, 295. The locutions "felicities of phrase" and *"noviciate,"* below, are in "G. F. Cooke in 'Richard the Third'" (*Works*, I, 36, 37, and 38). Although Lamb below expresses annoyance with his editor, Daniel Stuart, Lamb in "Newspapers Thirty-five Years Ago" called him "one of the finest tempered of Editors . . . [and] frank, plain, and English all over" (*Works*, II, 220).

2. "Dick Strype; or, the Force of Habit. A Tale—by Timothy Bramble," in the *Morning Post* of January 6, 1802, and Lucas (1935), I, 295–297.

3. They are the Delectable Moutains and sheep of Immanuel's Land in John Bunyan's *The Pilgrim's Progress*. (See esp. Part 1.) The next two sentences and portions of the next four letters concern a request of Rickman that a subscription to the *Morning Post* be entered in the name of his father at Christchurch. Having failed to obtain a discount, Lamb offers to share the expense of the newspaper with the understanding that the Reverend Mr. Rickman share the newspaper with Mary.

4. Samuel Solomon (d. 1819), a notorious quack and the author of health manuals. The second epigram is on Sir Benjamin Thompson, Count von Rumford (1753–1814), a scientific investigator, social reformer, and founder of the Royal Institution. The third, in the *Morning Post* of January 7, 1802, and *Works*, V, 102, is on Henry Addington, later first Viscount Sidmouth (1757–1844), who in 1801 had been suddenly requested by George III to become prime minister. The fourth, in the *Morning Post* of January 8, 1802, and *Works*, V, 102, is on the Etonians, anti-Jacobins, and government ministers John Hookham Frere and George Canning. (See Vol. I, Letter 44, note 9.) Lamb's other epigrams are indistinguishable from those by others in the paper during this period.

123. *C. L. to Rickman*

18th January [1802]

Dr Rickman

I have not been able to find a chapman, who will pay half thy father's Newspapers. I already read the post upon nearly a similar Plan, 7 or 8 of us subscribe. One keeps it & pays $\frac{1}{2}$. But to avert thy wrath and indignation, which I know will burn most furiously if I omit thy Commission, I have ordered one at full cost, and there will go the first with the same Post which carries this. As Mary seldom sees a Paper, she will thank your father for the liberty of reading it first and take care duly to send it by the same day's Post. She will pay such proportion as a Jury before Lord Kenyon[1] shall award.

Dinner is smoking.—

Yours truly
C. Lamb

Geoe. the 2*nd* has just arrived

has stayed over his time!! & written to Ld. Stanhope[2] without telling his L'ship where to find him, accordingly must write again

MS: unrecovered; a copy: Huntington Library. Pub.: Ainger (1904), I, 219; Harper, III, 64–65; Lucas (1935), I, 297–298. Address, from Lucas (1935): To John Rickman, Esq.,/Dublin Castle.

1. Lord Chief Justice Lloyd Kenyon, first Baron Kenyon (1732–1802), reputedly one of the strictest judges ever to sit in chancery.

2. Charles Stanhope, third Earl Stanhope, who was the son of Philip Stanhope, second Earl Stanhope (1717–1786), and of his wife, Grizel (d. 1811). She, a daughter of the poet Charles Hamilton, by courtesy Lord Binning (1697–1733), is referred to in the next letter. In addition to the next letter and its note 4 see Vol. I, Letter 5, note 5, and Letter 29, note 2.

124. *C. L. to Rickman*

[February ?1, 1802]

Dear Rickman,

Not having known the sweet girl[1] deceased, your humble Servant cannot endite with true passion a suitable Epitaph. Here is a kind of Substitute for feeling—but your own Prose, or nakedly the Letter which you sent me, which was in some sort an Epitaph, & the best one, would do better on her grave stone, than the cold Lines of a Stranger——

A Heart which felt Unkindness, yet complain'd not,
A Tongue which spake the simple Truth, and feign'd not,
A Soul as White as the pure marble Skin
(The beauteous Mansion it was lodged in)
Which, unrespected, could itself respect:
 On Earth was all the Portion of a Maid,
 Who in this common Sanctuary laid
Sleeps unoffended by the World's Neglect.——

I have not seen Southey to talk with him about it, but I conclude you addrest a Letter to that import to him, as *his* came along with mine.— If you stay a little, perhaps he or I may hit upon a Better, for I suspect [it] is sadly of common place.—

I had hoped e'er this to send you a Book, but the Boarders[2] are shockingly dilatory, & seem never to have heard of the faboulous stories of the Anxiety of Authors & Parents——

You will see almost as soon as the Receipt of this a first Number of a Paper in the Morning Post, which I have undertaken Solus, to be called the **Londoner;**[3] I think you will like the First Number, as it jumps with your Notions about a Country Life &ca— — —. I have done no more, so I have all the World before me where to chuse. I think you could give me hints. I have seen light Papers in the Agricult. Mag. which would suit the Londoner to a tittle.— G Burnett surprized us with a visit yesterday. His Two young Lords have run away—George deposes, that he was Teaching them their Lesson, when he was called down by Ld. Stanhope to be introduced to his Ldships Mother; when he returned his Pupils were flown. They had gone out of Window with their best Coats & Linen.— The Eldest Son of Ld. S. served him exactly the same Trick, and his Lordship sets it down, that these Striplings as well as the former (who never came back) were spirited away by the Pitt & Grenville Party, to whom he is allied by Marriage.[4] He says, that Pitt will make them Villains. Ministers have already bought off his Son & his Son in Law: & he meant to bring up these young ones (the eldest 16) to mechanics or manufactures. It is very probable what he says—for the P's & G's (writing to a Secretary I dare not be more explicit) would go some steps to stop the growth of Democratic **Peers.**— George declares, that he is only sorry on Lord Stanhope's account, who is much agitated, but on his own he dont care at all: nay I have no doubt he is ready to leap at his heart, for Lord S. desires he will stay in his house, & he will try to get him something. So George has got his old desirable prospect of food & clothing with no Duty to perform for it. I could fill vols. with a History of his absurdities since the date of my Last— —. Take one or 2. Imprimis he overstay'd his 3 weeks—then he wrote to Lord S from town to write to him, but forgot to mention his own address—then he was forced to write again to say he forgot, & begg'd his Lordship to tell him the Exact situation where his Lordships House stood, that he might have no trouble in finding it! ! ! to write to a **Peer** of the Realm to tell the Number of his house! Then he determines to set off for Chevening[5] next morng. & writes that he will come down by the 8 oClock stage—then he comes to us the Night before at 11 & complains bitterly of the difficulty of getting up so early—then he goes away & White & I lay wagers that he wont go at all. Next Morning 11 oClock —Enter Geo. the 2d. in a dirty neckloth—he could not go, because he

had no Linen, & he had not time to go to Southey to borrow it, & inadvertently slips out that to be sure there was a Coach went at $\frac{1}{2}$ pas 10—then my Tutor gapes & stares, & borrows a neckloth & sets off with all proper humility to My Lord's in a **Post Chaise**—drives up to the Door in Style—& there I leave him bowing and gaping to see the fine Pictures—

<div align="right">

Yours Truly

C Lamb
</div>

Mary's grateful thanks for your indulgence, by which she reads My Works————[6]

MS: Huntington Library. Pub.: Ainger (1904), I, 220–222; Harper, III, 65–68; Lucas (1935), I, 298–300. Address: Jno. Rickman Esqr/Dublin Castle. See note 3 for the dating.

1. Mary Druit, or Druitt (1782?–1801), who died of consumption and is buried at Wimborne, Dorsetshire. Neither the epitaph here, which is also in *Works,* V, 323, nor that given in Letters 129 and 142 is on her tombstone. In his letter to Rickman of February 6, 1802 (*New Southey Letters,* I, 268), Southey also agreed to write an epitaph for her, but it appears he never did.

2. The bookbinders.

3. "The Londoner," which is in the *Morning Post* of February 1, 1802; in Letter 127; and in *Works,* I, 39–40. Lamb never went on with the series. The next sentence concludes with *Paradise Lost,* XII, 646. The agricultural magazine would be the one Rickman had conducted. See Vol. I, Letter 86, note 4.

4. Lord Stanhope's first wife, to whom he was married in 1774, was Lady Hester Pitt Stanhope (1755–1780), the sister of the statesman William Pitt (1759–1806) and the daughter of William Pitt, first Earl of Chatham (1708–1778), and his wife, Lady Hester Grenville Pitt, Baroness Chatham. By his first wife Lord Stanhope had three daughters—Lady Hester Lucy Stanhope (1776–1839), who became her uncle William Pitt's confidante, an Eastern traveler, and an eccentric; Lady Griselda Stanhope (1778–1851), who in 1800 became the wife of John Tickell, or Teckell, of Hambleton, Hampshire; and Lady Lucy Rachael Stanhope (1780–1814), who in 1796 became the wife of Thomas Taylor of Sevenoaks, Kent, the family apothecary and afterward (through the influence of William Pitt) controller general of the customs. Lord Stanhope's second wife, to whom he was married in 1781, was Louisa Grenville Stanhope (d. 1829), the daughter and sole heiress of the Honorable Henry Grenville (1717–1784), who was the brother of the statesmen Richard Temple Grenville-Temple (1711–1779) and George Grenville (1712–1770) and was the governor of Barbados from 1746 to 1756, ambassador to the Porte in 1762, M.P., and commissioner of the customs. By his second wife Lord Stanhope had three sons—Philip Henry Stanhope, to become fourth Earl Stanhope (1781–1855), keeper of the records in Birmingham Tower, Dublin, and M.P.; Charles Banks Stanhope (1785–1809), to become a major and die in the Battle of Corunna; and James Hamilton Stanhope (1788–1825), to become a lieutenant-colonel. It was probably Philip Henry Stanhope and clearly Thomas Taylor whom William Pitt's ministers had "bought off" (below). Lord Stanhope later disinherited all his children.

5. The Stanhope family seat, in Kent.

6. In the *Morning Post.*

125. *C. L. to Rickman*

4th Febry [1802]

Dear Rickman

I send you three Copies.[1] Keep one yourself, and distribute the others. Perhaps you will send one to her, "whom you in sport do call your Margaret," but this is mere conjecture.—

G Dyer is sitting by me, he begs to be kindly remembered. He has brought news, that a Mr. Wainewright, with a Mr. Frend the Pamphletteer, and Mr. Perry the Chronicleer, have set up as a Committee to procure him an Annuity by subscription. Ld. Stanhope has sent £50——

Talking of money, you owe me £2.2—which I paid in advance for your father's Papers.

Yours Truly
C L

MS: Huntington Library. Pub.: Ainger (1904), I, 222; Harper, III, 68–69; Lucas (1935), I, 300.
1. Of *John Woodvil*. The quotation below, an adaptation of *As You Like It*, IV, iii, 156, is explained by a remark in Rickman's note to Southey of December 5, 1801: "I wrote to Lamb the other day, and am quite pleased to think I have been accessory to the regeneration and *first* edition of my noble Margaret (the heroine of *John Woodvil*). I shall be desperately in love when I meet her counterpart" (*Rickman,* p. 68). Wainewright has not been identified. Perry is James Perry of the *Morning Chronicle.*

126. *C. L. to Rickman*

[?Sunday, February ?14, 1802]

"I take thy Groat in earnest of Revenge."[1] One and twenty Margarets fall to the disposal of your dainty Cousin. I hope he wo'nt debauch them. I sup with him at Southey's on Tuesday, God willing. — Your Guineas (which let me tell you are too much, but you shall have your way) are not absolutely mal-a-pros, for by a cruel reverse of Fortune, that Dame who is painted with a Wheel to signify to you, that she is changes, and rowlings, & mutabilities, I am no longer Paragraph spinner. The fact is, that Stuart was wonderfully polite and civil at first, I suppose because Coleridge recommend me, from

whose assistance in the Paper he expected great things, but Coleridge from ill health & unsettlement having hung an Arse, as the saying is, I gradually got out of favor, and Stuart has at last twice told me, that I must take more pains about my paragraphs, for he has not been able to draw above one in five from what I have sent him.[2] This in connection with his altered behavior was hint quite enough for me, who do not require hints as big as St. Paul's Church to make me understand a coldness, excited my magnanimous Spirit to endite a Valorous Letter of Resignation, which I did with some qualms, when I remembered what I gave up: but to tell truth, the Little I have done has been very irksome, and rendered ten times more so from a sense of my employer not being fully satisfied: and that little has subtracted from my pleasures of walking, reading, idling, &c. which are as necessary to me as the "golden vapour"[3] of Life itself. My health (silly as it seems to relate) has suffered bitterly. The Routine has been drinking one night in noisy Company, & writing the next upon a head ach. My Spirits absolutely require freedom & leisure, & I think I shall never engage to do task work any more, for I am **sick.**— I must cut closer, but better is something (I forget what but it is scriptural) than a stalled ox, &c—[4]

I am almost ashamed at my capriciousness, as must seem to you, but upon a serious review I do approve of what I've done. I've foolishly involved you (I fear) in an expence of 8 guineas a Year, which I *think* was on my accot. but as it is for *whom* it is, I must not call it foolish. A Paper in a Country Town is a kind of London. But I would gladly purchase your acquiescence by paying half, which I know you wont accept—

I have given this up only two days, & I feel myself at elbow room, free & happy. I can scribble now at my heart's Leisure, if I have an impulse, & tho' I know I speak as a fool, I am sure I can write better gratis.— Give me one Curse and then for God's sake say no more about it. I have weighed my loss & my gain, & I write *Profit*—

I may yet do the Londoners at my Leisure.—[5]

This Letter is short, for I have got a bad Head Ach.— Mr. Abbots Elevation, you may be sure, surprized me. I take it for granted you will not be a **Loser.** I am sure I shall be a gainer, if an Easterly Wind wafts you to England.

Frend was here yesterday. He desires me to set down every day Dyer dines with me, & the Committee will pay me, as George is to have no money of his own. George contrives constantly to dine here, when he says he shant over night which is very *convenient* & vice versa. It is the damned Vanity of being supposed to be always engaged. Now he is got well, he is as freakish as King David at Gath.[6] Nothing can be done with him; save that the Committee will preserve him from felo de se, that he shant starve himself.

George the 2d discharges his important Trust, of doing *nothing* for Ld. S.—with fidelity & diligence. His Lordship sends him to town upon any fiddle faddle errand, & George fancies himself essential to his L'ships Comfort. He looks more important than Mr. **Dressin,**[7] King's Messenger.—

Mary always desires to be most kindly remembered by you. She bids me *not* tell you, that an Epigram called **Helen** in my little Book, is of her writing. But it is, every tittle of it. I hope you do not dislike it. We remain

<div align="right">

Yours truly

C and M L[8]

</div>

MS: Huntington Library. Pub.: Ainger (1904), I, 223–225; Harper, III, 69–71; Lucas (1935), I, 300–302. Address: Jno Rickman Esqr/Dublin Castle. The date, which except for "Sunday" previous editors show as part of the letter, is properly an estimate from especially the remark near the reference to note 5.

1. *Henry V*, V, i, 63. Rickman's cousin who had ordered the copies of *John Woodvil* (the "Margarets," following) was a maternal cousin, a Beaumont whose first name has not been determined. He was killed in 1807 at Montevideo, Uruguay, while serving under Sir Samuel Auchmuty (1756–1822) in the British expeditionary force responsible for its capture. See *Rickman,* pp. 67 and 69, and Letter 222, near the reference to note 9.

2. As "for good Charles Lamb," Stuart later recalled, "I never could make any thing of his writings. Coleridge often and repeatedly pressed me to settle him on a salary, and often and repeatedly did I try; but it would not do. Of politics he knew nothing; they were out of his line of reading and thought; and his drollery was vapid, when given in short paragraphs fit for a newspaper: yet he has produced some agreeable books, possessing a tone of humour and kind feeling, in a quaint style, which is amusing to read, and cheering to remember" (*Gentleman's Magazine,* N.S. 9 [June 1838], 577).

3. Cf. Edmund Spenser, *The Faerie Queene,* III, ix, 179.

4. "Better *is* a dinner of herbs where love is, than a stalled ox and hatred therewith" (Proverbs 15:17).

5. See Letter 124, note 3. Charles Abbot (see below and Vol. I, Letter 86, note 4) had on February 10 been made speaker of the House of Commons.

6. See 1 Samuel 27.

7. Whose first name has not been determined. But then his last name sounds

like Lamb's invention. For "Helen," mentioned below and published with *John Woodvil,* see Vol. I, Letter 82.

8. Although this letter is signed "C and M L," the author, as indicated by the numbered heading, is Lamb. The author of letters similarly signed will be similarly indicated.

127. *C. L. to Manning*

Monday 15th February 1802

Not a sentence, not a syllable, of **Trismegistus** shall be lost through my neglect. I am his word-banker, his store-keeper of puns & syllogisms.[1] You cannot conceive (and if Trismegistus cannot, no man can) the strange joy, which I felt at the Receipt of a Letter from Paris. It seemed to give me a learned importance, which placed me above all, who had not Parisian Correspondents. Believe, that I shall carefully husband every Scrap, which will save you the trouble of memory, when you come back. You cannot write things so trifling, let them only be about Paris, which I shall not treasure. In particular, I must have parallels of Actors & Actresses. I must be told if any Building in Paris is at all comparable to St. Paul's, which contrary to the usual mode of that part of our Nature, called Admiration, I have looked up to with unfading Wonder, every morning at ten oClock, ever since it has lain in my way to business. At noon I casually glance upon it, being hungry; and Hunger has not much taste for the fine arts. Is any night-walk comparable to a Walk from St. Pauls to Charing Cross, for Lighting, & Paving, Crowds going & coming without respite, the rattle of coaches, & the chearfulness of shops? Have you seen a man Guillotined yet? is it as good as Hanging? are the Women *all* painted, & the men *all* monkeys? or are there not a few that look like *rational* of *both sexes?* Are you & the first Consul[2] *thick?* All this expence of ink I may fairly put you to, as your Letters will not be solely for my proper pleasure, but are to serve as memoranda & notices, helps for short memory, a kind of Rumfordizing recollection, for yourself on your return. Your Letter was just what a letter should be, crammed, and very funny. Every part of it pleased me, till you came to Paris, & your damned philosophical indolence or indifference stung me. You cannot stir from your rooms till you know the Language! what the Devil! are men nothing but word-trumpets?,

are men all tongue & ear? have these creatures, that you & I profess to know *something about*, no faces, gestures, gabble, no folly, no absurdity, no induction of French education upon the Abstract Idea of Men & Women, no similitude nor dissimilitude to English! Why, thou *damned* **Smelfungus!**[3] Your account of your Landing and reception & Bullen (I forget how you spelt it) it was spelt *my* way in Harry the 8ths ti[me,] was exactly in that *minute* styl[e] which strong impressions *inspire* (writing to a Frenchman I write as a Frenchman would)—. It appears to me, as if I should die with joy at the first Landing in a foreign Country. It is the nearest Pleasure, which a grown man can substitute for that unknown one, which he can never know, the pleasure of the first entrance into Life from the Womb.— I dare say, in a short time my Habits would come back lik[e] a "stronger man" armed,[4] and drive out that new pleasure; & I should soon sicken for known objects. Nothing has transpired h[ere] that seems to me of sufficient importance to send dry-shod over the Water: but I suppose you will want to be told some news. The Best & the Worst to me is, that I have given up Two Guineas a week at the Post, & regained my health & spirits, whic[h] were upon the wane. I grew **sick,** & Stuart unsatisfied. Ludisti satis, tempus abire est.[5] I must cut closer thats' all. In all this time I have done but one thing, which I reckon tolerable: & that I will transcribe, because it may give you pleasure, being a Picture of *my* hungers. You will find it in my last Page. It absurdly is a first Number of a Series, thu[s] strangled in Embryo. **More News.** The Professor's Rib has come out to be a damn'd disagreeable woman, so much as to drive me & some more old **Cronies** from his House. If a man will keep **Snakes** in his House, he must not wonder if People are shy of coming to see him **because of the Snakes. Mister Fell** or as you with your usual **faceteness**[6] and drollery call him Mr. F+ll has stopt short in the middle of his Play, like what is called **being taken short.** Some *friend* has told him that it has not the least merit in it. O! that I had the rectifying of the Litany! I would put in a Libera *Nos* (*Scriptores* videlicet) ab *amicis!* That's all the **News.** *A pro pos* (is it *Pedantry*, writing to a Frenchman, to express myself sometimes by a French Word, when an English one would not do as well? methinks, my thoughts fall naturally into it)

A pro pos, I think you wrong about *my* Play.[7] *All* the **omissions** are *right.* And the supplementary Scene in which Sandford *narrates* the

manner in which his master is affected, is the **Best** in the Book. It
stands, where a Hodge podge of German puerilities used to stand. I
insist upon it, that you like that Scene. Love me, love that scene. I will
now transcribe the Londoner (No. 1) & wind up all with Affection &
Humble Servant at the end. *The Londoner* (I write *small,* in regard to
your good eyesight): "In compliance with my own particular humour,
no less than with thy laudable curiosity, Reader, I proceed to give thee
some accot. of my history & habits. I was born under the Nose of St.
Dunstan's Steeple, just where the conflux of the eastern & western in-
habitants of this two-fold City meet & justle in friendly opposition at
Temple Bar. The same day, which gave me to the world, saw London
happy in the celebration of her great Annual Feast.[8] This I cannot help
looking upon as a lively type or omen of the great good will, which I
was destined to bear toward the City, resembling in kind that Solici-
tude, which every Chief Magistrate is supposed to feel for whatever
concerns her interest & well being. Indeed I consider myself in some
sort a *speculative Lord Mayor of London:* for tho' circumstances
*un*happily preclude me from ever arriving at the dignity of a gold
chain & spital sermon,[9] yet thus much will I say of myself in truth,
that Whittington himself with his **Cat** (just emblem of *vigilance* &
a *furred gown*) never went beyond me in affection, which I bear to
the Citizens. Shut out from serving them in the most honorable mode, I
aspire to do them benefit in another scarcely less honorable: & if I
cannot by virtue of office commit vice & irregularity to the *material
Counter,* I will at least erect a *spiritual one,* where they shall be laid
fast by the heels. In plain words, I will do my best endeavors to write
them down. To return to Myself (from whence my zeal for the public
good is perpetually causing me to digress) I will let thee, Reader, into
certain more of my peculiarities. I was born (as you have heard) bred,
& have past most part of my time in a *crowd.* This has begot in me
an entire affection for that way of life, amounting to an almost in-
surmountable aversion from solitude & rural scenes. This aversion was
never in[terrup]ted or suspended, except for a few years in the younger
part of my Life, during a period, in whi[ch I ha]d fixed my affections
upon a charming young woman.[10] Every man, while the **Passion** is
upon him, [is for a] ti[m]e at least addicted to groves & meadows &
purling streams. During this short period of my existence, I contracted

just enough familiarity with rural objects, to understand tolerably well ever after the **Poets,** when they declaim in such passionate terms in favor of a country Life. For my own part, now the fit is long past, I have no hesitation in declaring, that a mob of happy faces, crowding up at the **Pit Door** of Drury Lane Theatre just at the hour of 5, give me ten thou'san[d] finer pleasures, than I ever received from all the flocks of silly sheep,[11] that have whitened the plains of Arcadia or **Epsom Downs.** This passion for Crowds is no where feasted so full as in London. The man must have a rare recipe for melancholy, who can be dull in Fleet Street. I am naturally inclined to Hypochondria; but in London it vanishes, like all other ills—. Often, when I have felt a weariness or distaste at home, have I rushed out into her crowded *Strand,* and fed my humour till tears have wetted my cheek for inutterable sympathies with the multitudinous moving picture, which she never fails to present at all hours, like the shifting scenes of a skilful Pantomime. The very deformities of London, which give distaste to others, from habit do not displease me. The endless succession of Shops, where Fancy (miscalled Folly) is supplied with perpetual new gauds & toys, excite in me no puritanical aversion. I gladly behold every appetite supplied with its proper food. The obliging Customer, & the obliged Tradesman—things which live by bowing, & things which exist but for homage, do not affect me with disgust; from habit, I perceive nothing but urbanity, where other men, more refined, discover meanness. I love the very Smoke of London, because it has been the medium most familiar to my vision. I see grand principles of honor at work in the dirty ring, which encompasses two Combatants with fists, & principles of no less eternal justice in the tumultuous detectors of a pickpocket. The salutary astonishment, with which an Execution is surveyed, convinces me more forcibly than an 100 vols. of abstract Polity, that the universal instinct of man in all ages has leaned to Order & good government. Thus, an **Art** of extracting morality from the commonest incidents of a Town **Life** is attained by the same well-natured Alchemy, with which the **Forresters** of **Arden,** in a beautiful country, "Found tongues in trees, books in the running brooks, Sermons in stones, & Good in ev'ry thing."[12] Where has **Spleen** her food but in London?—humour, interest, curiosity, suck at her measureless breasts without a possi-

bility of being satiated. Nursed amid her noise, her crowds, her be-
loved smoke, what have I been doing all my life, if I have not lent out
my heart with *usury* to such scenes?[13] Reader, in the course of my peri-
grinations about this Great City; it is hard, if I have not picked up
Matters which may serve to amuse thee, as it has done me, a summer
evening long. **Farewell.**"———

What is all this about?, said Mrs. Shandy——. A story of a Cock &
a Bull, said Yorick;[14] & so it is—but Manning will take good-naturedly
what *God will send him* across the water: only I hope he wont *shut*
his *eyes* & *open* his *mouth*, as the Children say, for that is a way to
gape & not to *read*. Manning, continue your Laudable Purpose of
making me your **Register.** I will render back all your **Remarks,** &
I, not you, shall have received **Usury** by having read them.—

In the mean time, may the **Great Spirit,** have you in his keeping; &
preserve our English-man from the inoculation of frivolity & sin upon
French Earth.—

Allons (or what is it you say instead of *good bye?*)—

Mary sends her kind Remembrance, & covets the Remarks equally
with me.

<div align="right">C Lamb</div>

MS: Huntington Library. Pub.: Talfourd (1837), I, 215–216 and 248–251;
Sala, I, 372–373 and 380–382; Purnell, I, 372–373 and 380–382; Fitzgerald, II,
205–206 and 213–215; Hazlitt, I, 310 and 330–332; Ainger (1888), I, 179–180
and 196–198; Ainger (1900), II, 58–63; Macdonald, I, 218 and 236–238; Ainger
(1904), I, 225–228; Harper, III, 72–76; Lucas (1905), VI, 233–237; Lucas
(1912), V, 240–244; Lucas (1935), I, 303–307. Address: Mr. Thos. Manning/
Maeson Magnan/No. 342 Boulevard Italien/Paris. Postmark: 1802.

1. For in his letter of January 28–February 2 Manning requested Lamb to keep
his letters from abroad should Manning make "some observations, that I shall
wish to recall to my memory when I return to England" (*Manning-Lamb Let-
ters*, p. 59).

2. Napoleon. "Rumfordizing," below, alludes to Sir Benjamin Thompson, Count
von Rumford, as the inventor of the Rumford stove, to which Manning alluded
in his letter.

3. Laurence Sterne's name for Tobias Smollett in *A Sentimental Journey
through France and Italy.* In the third of the three chapters called "In the Street,
Calais," Sterne wrote that Smollett traveled from Boulogne to Paris, and "from
Paris to Rome—and so on—but he set out with the spleen and jaundice, and
every object he pass'd by was discoloured or distorted—He wrote an account of
them, but 'twas nothing but the account of his miserable feelings." So for his own
reasons Manning wrote that "Paris to a stranger is a desert full of Knaves &
Whores—like London. I have not yet seen much of the interior of private houses

—very very little,—but I have the means in my power, when I please; in fact I speak the language so ill, that I have been desirous of standing aloof for a short time, & this solitariness with respect to the gay world has kept me from publick places, for what pleasure could I take in a masquerade, when I don't know a soul. So as I am not yet *au fait* with respect to Paris, I shall say nothing about it" (*Manning-Lamb Letters,* p. 62). "Bullen," in the following sentence, is the archaic variant for "Boulogne" that Lamb would adopt in *The King and Queen of Hearts* (*Works,* III, 343). The adjective *"minute"* derives from the French. The verb *"inspire,"* which is underscored twice, derives from the Old French.

4. Luke 11:21.

5. "You have played enough; it is time to go away" (Horace, *Epistles,* II, ii, 214–215).

6. *Perhaps* "facetiousness" was intended. The Latin below translates, "Deliver Us (namely *Writers*) from *friends!*" Lamb may have in mind the aphorism Maréchal Claude Louis Hector de Villars (1653–1734) supposedly made when taking leave of Louis XIV: "Defend me from my friends; I can defend myself from my enemies."

7. Manning thought *John Woodvil* had been too much retrenched: "I miss the Beautiful Branches you have lopped off and regret them. In some of the Pages the sprinkling of words is so thin as to be quite outré. There you were wrong again" (*Manning-Lamb Letters,* p. 63). The supplementary scene, about which Manning said nothing, is that between Sandford and Margaret at the end of the fourth act. See *Works,* V, 168–169.

8. Lord Mayor's Day, November 9. Lamb was in fact born on February 10.

9. One preached on Easter Monday and Tuesday originally from a special pulpit in St. Mary Spital. The expression "furred gown," below, is from *Measure for Measure,* III, ii, 7, and *King Lear,* IV, vi, 165.

10. Ann Simmons. See Vol. I, Introduction, p. xxxiv.

11. See Vol. I, Letter 100, note 3.

12. *As You Like It,* II, i, 16–17.

13. See Vol. I, Letter 98, at the reference to note 9.

14. In Sterne's *Tristram Shandy,* Vol. IX, ch. xxxiii. Said Manning: "I like your Londoner very much, there is a deal of happy fancy in it, but it is not strong enough to be seen by the generality of readers. Yet if you would write a volume of Essays in the same stile you might be sure of its succeeding" (*Manning-Lamb Letters,* p. 74).

128. *C. L. to Rickman*

16 Mitre Court Buildings, Inner Temple

[April 10, 1802]

Dear Rickman,

The enclosed Letter explains itself. It will save me the danger of a Corporal interview with the Man-eater, who, if very sharp set, may take a fancy to me, if you will give me a short note, declaratory of probabilities. These from Him, who hopes to see you once or twice

more, before he goes hence, to be no more seen: for there is no tipple
nor tobacco in the grave, whereunto he hastneth.

<div align="right">C Lamb</div>

how cleanly the Goul writes, and like a Gentleman!

MS: Huntington Library. Pub.: Purnell, II, 87–88; Fitzgerald, III, 8–9;
Hazlitt, I, 311; Ainger (1888), I, 180; Ainger (1900), II, 63; Macdonald, I,
219; Ainger (1904), I, 228; Harper, III, 76; Lucas (1905), VI, 239; Lucas
(1912), V, 246; Lucas (1935), I, 309. Address: Mr. Jno. Rickman/Old Palace
Yard/Westminster. Postmark: April 10, 1802. The enclosure, a letter apparently
from Simonds (become, I gather, the Man-eater as well as the Goul), has not
been recovered.

129. *C. L. to Manning*

<div align="right">[April 23, 1802]</div>

My dear Manning,

Although something of the latest, and after two month's waiting,
your Letter was highly gratifying. Some parts want a little explication,
for example, "the Godlike face of the First Consul."[1] *What God* does
he most resemble, Mars, Bacchus, or Apollo? or the God Serapis, who
flying (as Egyptian Chronicles deliver) from the fury of the Dog
Anubis (the Hieoroglyph of an English Mastiff) lighted upon Mono-
motapa (or the Land of Apes) by some thought to be old France, and
there set up a Tyranny &c.— Our London Prints of him represent him
gloomy & sulky, like an angry Jupiter.— I hear, that he is very small,
even less than me, who am "less than the least of the Apostles,"[2] at
least less than they are painted in the Vatican. I envy you your access
to this Great Man, much more than your seances & conversationis,
which I have a shrewd suspicion must be something dull.— What you
assert concerning the Actors of Paris, that they exceed our Comedians,
bad as ours are, is *impossible*. In one sence it may be true, that their
fine Gentlemen, in what is called Genteel Comedy, may possibly be
more brisk & degagee than Mister Caulfield[3] or Mr. Whitfield, but
have any of 'em the power to move *laughter in excess?* or can a
Frenchman *laugh?* Can they batter at your judicious Ribs, till they
shake, nothing loth to be so shaken? This is John Bull's Criterion, and
it shall be mine. You are Frenchified. Both your taste and morals are
corrupt and Perverted. Bye and bye you will come to assert, than[4]

Bonaparte is as great a General as the Old Duke of Cumberland, & deny that one Englishman can beat three Frenchman. Read Henry the Fifth, to restore your Orthodoxy.—— ——

All things continuee at a stay-still in London. I cannot repay your new Novelties with my stale Reminiscences. Like the Prodigal, I have spent my Patrimony, and feed upon the superannuated chaff & dry husks of repentance:[5] yet sometimes I remember with Pleasure the Hounds and Horses, which I kept in the days of my Prodigality. I find nothing new, nor any thing that has so much of the Gloss and Dazzle of Novelty, as may rebound in narrative, and cast a reflective glimmer across the channel: Something I will say about People, that you & I know. Fenwick is still in Debt, & the Professor has not done making Love to his new Spouse. I think he never looks in an Almanac, or he would have found by the Calendar, that the Honeymoon was extinct a moon ago. Lloyd[6] has written to me, & names you. I think a Letter from Maison Magnan (is *that* a Person or a Thing?) would gratify him. G. Dyer is in love with an Ideot, who loves a Doctor, who is incapable of loving any thing but himself. A puzzling circle of perverse providences! a Maze as un-get-out-again-able as the **House** which Jack built. Southey is Sec. to the Chanc. of the Irish Exchecq. £400 a year. Stoddart is turn'd Dr. of Civil Law, & dwells in Drs. Commons: I fear *his* Commons are short, as they say. Did I send you an Epitaph[7] I scribbled upon a poor girl who died at 19—a good girl, and a pretty girl, and a clever girl, but strangely neglected by all her friends & kin—?

> Under this cold marble stone
> Sleep the sad remains of **One,**
> Who, when alive, by few or none
> Was lov'd, as lov'd she might have been,
> If she prosp'rous days had seen,
> Or had thriving been, I ween.
> Only this cold funeral stone
> Tells, she was belov'd by One,
> Who on the marble graves his moan.——*

I send you this, being the only piece of Poetry I have *done*, since the Muses all went with T. M. to Paris.— I have neither stuff in my brain, nor Paper in my Draw, to write you a longer letter. Liquor and

Company and wicked Tobacco a' nights, have quite dis-pericraniated me, as one may say: but you, who spiritualize upon Champagne, may continue to write long long Letters, and stuff 'em with amusement to the end— —. Too long they cannot be, any more than a Codicil to a Will, which leaves me sundry Parks & Manors, not specify'd in the deed. But dont be *two months* before you write again.

These from merry old England, on the day of her valiant Patron St. **George.**—

<div align="right">C Lamb</div>

*Brief and Pretty and tender. Is't not?

MS: Huntington Library. Pub.: Talfourd (1837), I, 251–254; Sala, I, 383–385; Purnell, I, 383–385; Fitzgerald, II, 216–218; Hazlitt, I, 337–339; Ainger (1888), I, 202–204; Ainger (1900), II, 92–95; Macdonald, I, 245–247; Ainger (1904), I, 248–250 and 394; Harper, I, facsimile, and III, 120–123; Lucas (1905), VI, 240–241, and VII, 968; Lucas (1912), V, 246–248; Lucas (1935), I, 310–312. Address: Mr. T. Manning/Maison Magnan/No. 342 Boulevard Italien/Paris. Lamb gives the day he wrote in his last paragraph. A postal endorsement shows the letter was forwarded to Montmartre on *11 floreal an 10*—May 1, 1802.

1. Manning had seen Napoleon at the Tuileries and so described him to Lamb on April 6. (See the *Manning-Lamb Letters*, p. 69.) Serapis, or Hermes, in the following sentence, was the state god of Egypt during the reign of the Ptolemies (ca. 367–247 B.C.). Anubis, usually represented as a jackal, was the ancient Egyptian god associated with the mortuary and the afterworld. Monomotapa appears on old maps of southeast Africa designating an extensive region on the Zambezi.

2. 1 Corinthians 15:9. Napoleon was about five and one-half feet tall, and Lamb, according to *Mary and Charles Lamb*, p. 222, short enough for Charles Tween of Widford, the husband of Randal Norris' younger daughter, Elizabeth, to place his hands under Lamb's arms and lift him easily over a stile. Major S. Butterworth in "Charles Lamb: Some New Biographical and Other Details," *The Bookman*, 60 (July 1921), 165, announced a record showing that on June 14, 1814, Lamb weighed 129 1/2 pounds in boots.

3. Thomas Caulfield (d. 1815), who performed as a comedian and mimic at Drury Lane and made his debut in America in 1806. John Whitfield, mentioned next, was acting at Drury Lane by 1776 and later moved to Covent Garden.

4. For "that." William Augustus, Duke of Cumberland (1721–1765), mentioned below, commanded the force that defeated the rebels at Culloden in 1746.

5. See Luke 15:13–17.

6. Probably Charles Lloyd. The "Ideot," below, is conjecturally Elizabeth Ogilvy Benger. The doctor has not been identified.

7. Titled "Epitaph on a Young Lady Who Lived Neglected and Died Obscure" in the *Morning Post* of February 7, 1804, and *Works*, V, 80. See Letter 124, note 1.

130. *Mary Anne Lamb to Sarah Stoddart*

Temple
21st July 1802

My dear Miss Stoddart

I am ashamed of having your kind letter so long by me unanswerd:
it lies upon the table and reproaches me all day long—when I beged
you would write to me, I forgot to inform you—I am much fonder of
receiving letters, than writing them: but I believe this is no very un-
common case. Charles received a letter from your brother the same day
I did yours, and like me neglected to answer it 'till yesterday, when
after writing and burning a dozen sheets of paper (which perhaps you
do not know is his usual habit) he sent your brother a little short
nothing-at-all-about letter[1] of six lines: as I shall do you. I am always
a miserable letter writer, and I feel the want, in writing to a new
friend of being able to talk of the days "O lang syne": but this is a
defect I trust time will remedy.

I am very glad the waistcoats puzzled you, you were so proud you
would not let me do them: I intend when your brother returns to
town to offer my services to him for anything he wants in the *mending*
way, and that will be a very noble offer for *me* to make, who am you
know naturally very lazy. I rejoice exceedingly to hear you have hopes
of being in town again next winter——the evenings we spent together,
were the pleasantest I have known for a *very* long time: yet I fear you
have somehow procured a false character to obtain permission to
return to us, I will with pleasure sign any paper of that kind you may
have occasion for—I will protest you are the most amusing, good-
humoured, good sister, and altogether excellent girl I know, or any
other fibs you will please to dictate to me.

My brother has got a bad inflamation in his eyes, and is unwell, and
out of spirits, he desires his kindest remembrance to you: I believe a
little game at romps would do him good——

We have heard nothing of Allan;[2] I long very much to see him; I
have the recollection of much kind shewn to us by Allen, and kindness
unacknowledged, and seemingly forgotten; for soon after Allan had
been uncommonly attentive and good to us, when we were in distress

from severe illness, he married, and it so happened I do not know why, we never saw him afterwards.

Will you present my compliments to the Lady[3] I drank tea with at your brothers, I forget her name, but I mean the Lady you promised to read your choice Extracts to———if balloons were a common and a cheap conveyance, I would like to come over and make a list'ner of your party, now and then of an evening when I had a few hours to spare.

I am happy to hear you father and mother are well, a stranger's compliments seem mere compliments or I would send mine to them.

<div style="text-align: right">

I will ever be

Your affectionate friend
</div>

write soon—I should like to contrive to get you into the way of writing two or three letters for one. remember I pay no postage, and you do, and you can always scribble a few lines to me, when you are disposed to enclose a letter to any other friend, and you know it is not any inconvenience to my brother to receive them.

MS: University of Bristol Library. Pub.: John R. Barker, "Some Early Correspondence of Sarah Stoddart and the Lambs," *Huntington Library Quarterly,* 24 (1960), 65–66. Address: Miss Stoddart/Salisbury. Postmark: July 21, 1802. Sarah Stoddart (1774–1840), the sister of Dr. John Stoddart and to become after a succession of suitors the first wife of William Hazlitt, had apparently met the Lambs while visiting London shortly before July 16, 1802. For at the library and transcribed on page 65 in the article cited above is a note to her of that date from her brother instructing her to answer him and to forward her letter through Lamb at the East India House to save postage. "In the cover," Stoddart concluded, "you may give your remembrances to Miss Lamb." Mary's letters to her come to be engagingly revelatory of the natures of both women.

1. Unrecovered.

2. Robert Allen (see Vol. I, Introduction, p. xxxi), who was about to tour Scotland with Stoddart.

3. Perhaps Isabella Moncreiff (see Vol. I, Letter 3, note 28) or Anna Fullarton, the daughter of General William Fullarton (1754–1808), commissioner of Trinidad. Stoddart was seeing both women at this time. She to whom Mary refers might also have been the (unidentified) Miss Keir mentioned in the next letter.

131. *C. L. to Sarah Stoddart*

<div style="text-align: right">

Monday 9th (I believe) [August 1802]
</div>

My dear Miss Stoddart,

Mary finding it utterly impossible to write (what with the warm

weather, which relaxes the thumbs, & what with a Journey into Cumberland,[1] which we are about to undertake tomorrow, which causes much speculation) I am obliged (O sweet necessity!) to take up the pen. You will continue to address your Letters, as usual. I have given directions, they shall be sent.—

I certainly put in **Miss Keir's.** I suppose the young Lady was too idle or too busy to answer it immediately.

We are to be a month out. Mr. Fenwick, that drunken Swain (who was never drunker than last night) is to occupy our apartments while we are gone.—

Mary promises to write a Letter of respectable Longitude, the first thing she does on her return.—Accept this "Posy for a Ring"[2] from

Yours truly

C Lamb

MS: University of Bristol Library. Pub.: John R. Barker, "Some Early Correspondence of Sarah Stoddart and the Lambs," *Huntington Library Quarterly*, 24 (1960), 67. Address: Miss Stoddart/Salisbury. Postmark: August 10, 1802.

1. To the Coleridges at Keswick, to the younger Charles Lloyds at Ambleside, and to Dove Cottage. There in the absence of the Wordsworths, who were in Calais visiting Anne Marie, or "Annette," Vallon (1766–1841) and her daughter by Wordsworth, Caroline (bapt. 1792), the Lambs were received by the philanthropist and abolitionist Thomas Clarkson (1760–1846) of Eusemere, Pooley Bridge, at the upper end of Ullswater, and his wife, Catherine (1772–1856), the eldest daughter of William Buck (1747–1819) of Bury St. Edmunds and the former Sarah Corsbie.

2. *Hamlet,* III, ii, 152.

132. *C. L. to Samuel Taylor Coleridge*

[East India House]
Wensday [September 8, 1802]

Dear Coleridge,

I thought of not writing till we had performed some of our Commissions, but we have been hindered from setting about them, which yet shall be done to a tittle.— We got home very pleasantly on Sunday. We had Miss Buck's Company[1] nearly all the way. Mary is a good deal fatigued, and finds the difference of going *to* a place & coming *from* it.— I feel that I shall remember your mountains to the last day I live. They haunt me perpetually. I am like a man who has been

falling in Love unknown to himself, which he finds out when he leaves the Lady. I do not remember any very strong impression while they were present, but being gone their Mementoes are shelved in my brain—.[2] We past a very pleasant little time with the Clarksons. Lloyd's hospitality is not extinct; it only was past into *them*.— The Wordsworths are at Montague's rooms, near neighbors to us. They dined with us yesterday, & I was their guide to Bartlemy fair!—

I shall put your Letter in the penny post, and shall always do so, if you have no objection, for I dont want to see Stuart: our Dissolution was rather ambiguous, & I am not sure he is not displeased.—

I was pleased to recognize your Blank verse Poem (the Picture)[3] in the Morng Post of Monday. It reads very well & I feel some dignity in the notion of being able to understand it better than most **Southern Readers.**—

I hope you got over the fatigue of Helvellin. I shall expect little **Notes** now & then to accompany yours to Stuart, which will pay me for the pang I must feel! in defrauding the Company.— Mind, if you think the Penny Post not safe or had otherwise rather I dropt 'em in myself, I will, but I hate to encounter that impudent **Clerk** . .

I yesterday hunted about at Lackingtons[4] &c. for Miltons Prose Works, which if I could have got reasonably I should have beg'd your acceptance. The only one I met with, the best Quarto, was 6 guineas.— But I dont despair—

Observe the **Lamb***e* (but dont mark it) on those Letters I am not to open— —

My next Letter I hope will contain some account of our Commissions.—

I am hurryi[n]g this off at my Office where I am got for the first time to day, & very awkward I feel and strange at Business. I forget the names of Books, and feel myself not half so great a man as when I [was] a scrambler among mountains. I feel debased. But I shall soon break in my mountain Spirit—

Particularly tell me about little *Pi-pos*[5] (or flying Opossum) the only child (but one) I had ever an inclination to **steal** from its parents. That one was a Beggar's brat, that I might have had cheap. I hope his little Rash is gone.

But dont be jealous. I have a very affectionate memory of you all, besides Pi-pos: but *Pipos* I especially love.—

Remember me kindly to Hartly & Hartley's old friends at Greta Hall & very kindly to Sara. I may venture to add Mary's Love, I am sure, tho' she does not sit beside me. Public Offices scare away familiar faces & make ugly faces too familiar. Have you seen Stoddart & Allen. We past S. on the road

<div align="right">God bless you all
C L</div>

MS: Huntington Library. Pub.: Talfourd (1837), I, 220; Sala, I, 132; Purnell, I, 132; Fitzgerald, I, 414; Hazlitt, I, 313; Ainger (1888), I, 180–181; Ainger (1900), II, 63–64; Macdonald, I, 219–221; Ainger (1904), I, 228–229; Harper, III, 77–79; Lucas (1905), VI, 242–243; Lucas (1912), V, 248–249; Lucas (1935), I, 312–313. Address: Mr Coleridge/Greta Hall/Keswick/Cumberland. Postmark: September 1802. See note 2 for the dating.

1. That of Ann Buck, the sister of Mrs. Clarkson and after the autumn of 1812 the wife of John Corsbie.

2. Bryan Waller Procter (1787–1874), the barrister and poet who wrote under the pseudonym Barry Cornwall, recorded in his *Charles Lamb: A Memoir* (Boston: Roberts, 1866), pp. 237–238, that when someone asked Lamb "how he felt when amongst the lakes and mountains of Cumberland, he replied that he was obliged to think of the Ham and Beef shop near Saint Martin's Lane; this was in order to bring down his thoughts from their almost too painful elevation to the sober regions of every-day life." The Wordsworths, referred to below, had returned from Calais to London on August 30 and were staying in Paper Buildings, Inner Temple, in the rooms of Basil Montagu (1770–1851), who ultimately gained eminence in chancery and the bankruptcy courts and as a legal writer and an editor of *The Works of Francis Bacon* (16 vols.; 1825–1836). He was the acknowledged natural son of John Montagu, fourth Earl of Sandwich (1718–1792), and his mistress, the singer Martha Ray (d. 1779). In 1786 Basil Montagu entered Christ's College, Cambridge, where he met Coleridge and earned the B.A. in 1790 and the M.A. in 1793. In 1790 or 1791 he was married to Caroline Matilda Want (d. 1793) of Brampton, Huntingdonshire, and by her had Basil Caroline (1792–1830), who became the original of Edward in Wordsworth's "Anecdote for Fathers" and "To My Sister." In 1795 Montagu settled in Lincoln's Inn and met Wordsworth. After some months fearing for Basil Caroline's well-being in the midst of Montagu's poverty and depression, Wordsworth (in Montagu's words) "proposed to take my child from my Chambers in London in[to] Dorsetshire, where he was about to settle with his Sister" (autobiographical MS, *Wordsworths' Letters,* I, 147). In 1801 Montagu was married to Laura (1782–1806), the eldest daughter of Sir William Beaumaris Rush, a landholder of Roydon, in Suffolk, and of Wimbledon, in Surrey. In 1808 Montagu was married to the former Anna Dorothea Benson, the daughter of a wine merchant of York, the widow of Thomas Skepper (a lawyer of York) and the mother of Anne Benson Skepper (1799–1888). Anne Benson Skepper in 1824 became the wife of Procter. She, her mother, and Montagu are noticed in "Oxford in the Vacation" (*Works,* II, 11). Bartlemy, or Bartholomew, Fair was a four-day affair beginning on the eve of St. Bartholomew's Day, September 3, and held in West Smithfield.

3. "The Picture: Or the Lover's Resolution," in the *Morning Post* of September 6, whose setting Lamb found familiar from his visits in Cumberland.

4. Lackington, Allen and Company, a book shop in Finsbury Square known as The Temple of the Muses. Its principals were James (1746–1815) and George (1768–1844) Lackington and Robert Allen (not the Robert Allen the friend of the Lambs). About "Lamb*e*," in the next paragraph, see Vol. I, Letter 76, note 6.

5. Derwent Coleridge. The nickname arose from his "inability to pronounce the words 'flying opossum' under a picture in one of his books" (Lucas [1905], VI, 250).

133. C. L. to Manning

London
24th Sep. 1802

My dear Manning,

Since the date of my last letter I have been a traveller. A strong desire seized me of visiting remote regions. My first impulse was to go and see Paris.[1] It was a trivial objection to my aspiring mind, that I did not understand a word of the language: since, I certainly intend some time in my life to see **Paris** and equally certainly intend never to learn the language: therefore that could be no objection. However I am very glad I did not go, because you had left Paris (I see) before I could have set out.— I believe, Stoddart promising to go with me another year prevented that plan. My next scheme (for to my restless ambitious mind London was become a bed of thorns)[2] was to visit the far famed Peak in Derbyshire, where the Devil sits, they say, without breeches. *This* my purer mind rejected, as indelicate. And my final resolve was a Tour to the Lakes. I set out with Mary to Keswick, without giving Coleridge any notice, for my time being precious did not admit of it; he received us with all the hospitality in the world, and gave up his time to shew us all the wonders of the country. He dwells upon a small hill by the side of Keswick, in a comfortable house, quite enveloped on all sides by a net of mountains: great floundering bears & monsters they seem'd, all couchant & asleep. We got in in the evening, travelling in a Post Chaise from Pe[n]rith, in the midst of a gorgeous sun shine, which transmuted all the mountains into colours, purple &c. &c. We thought we had got into Fairy Land. But that went off (as it never came again, while we stayed, we had no more fine sun sets) and we entered Coleridge's comfortable study just in the dusk, when the moun-

tains were all dark with clouds upon their heads. Such an impression I never received from objects of sight before, nor do I suppose that I can ever again. Glorious creatures, fine old fellows, Skiddaw &c.[3] I never shall forget ye, how ye lay about that night, like an intrenchment, gone to bed as it seemed for the night, but promising that ye were to be seen in the morning. Coleridge had got a blazing fire in his study, which is a large antique ill-shaped room, with an old fashioned organ, never play'd upon, big enough for a church, Shelves of scattered folios, an Eolian Harp, & an old sofa, half bed &c. And all looking out upon the last fading view of Skiddaw & his broad-breasted brethren: What a night!— Here we staid three full weeks, in which time I visited Wordsworth's cottage, where we stayed a day or two with the Clarksons (good people & most hospitable, at whose house we tarried one day & night) & saw Lloyd. Wordsworths were gone to Calais. They have since been in London, & past much time with us: he is now gone into Yorkshire to be married,[4] to a girl of small fortune, but he is in expectation of augmenting his own, in consequence of the death of Lord Londsdale, who kept him out of his own, in conformity with a plan my Lord had taken up in early life of making every body unhappy. So we have seen Keswick, Grasmere, Ambleside, Ulswater (where the Clarksons live) and a place[5] at the other end of Ulswater, I forget the name, to which we travelled on a very sultry day over the middle of Helvellyn.— We h[a]ve clambered up to the top of Skiddaw, & I have waded up the bed of Lodore. In fine I have satisfied myself, that there is such a thing as that, which tourists call *romantic,* which I very much suspected before: they make such a spluttering about it, and toss their splendid epithets around them, till they give as dim a light, as four oClock next morning the Lamps do after an illumination. Mary was excessively tired, when she got about half way up Skiddaw, but we came to a cold rill (than which nothing can be imagined more cold, running over cold stones) & with the reinforcemt. of a draught of cold water, she surmounted it most manfully.— O its fine black head & the bleak air a top of it, with a prospect of mountains all about & about, making you giddy, & then Scotland afar off & the border countries so famous in song & ballad—. It was a day that will stand out, like a mountain, I am sure, in my life.— But I am returned (I have now been come home near 3 weeks (I was a month out)) & you cannot conceive the degradation I felt at first, from being accustommed

to wander free as air among mountains, & bathe in rivers without being controuled by any one, to come home & *work:* I felt very *little*. I had been dreaming I was a very great man. But that is going off, & I find I shall conform in time to that state of Life, to which it has pleased God to call me. Besides, after all, Fleet Street & the Strand are better places to live in for good & all than among Skiddaw: Still, I turn back to those great places, where I wandered about, participating in their greatness. After all I could not *live* in Skiddaw: I could spend a year, two, three years, among them, but I must have a prospect of seeing Fleet Street at the End of that time: or I should mope & pine away, I know. Still Skiddaw is a fine Creature. My habits are changing, I think; i.e. from drunk to sober: whether I shall be happier or no, remains to be proved. I shall certainly be more happy in a morning, but whether I shall not sacrifice the fat & the marrow & the kidneys, i.e. the Night, the glor[iou]s, care-drowning, night, that heals all our wrongs, pours wine into our mortifications, changes the scene from indifferent & flat to bright & brilliant—. O Manning, if I should have formed a diabolical resolution, by the time you come to England, of not admitting any spirituous liquors into my house, will you be my guest on such shame worthy terms? Is life, with such limitations, worth trying.— The truth is that my liquors bring a nest of friendly harpies about my house, who consume me.—

This is a pitiful tale to be read at St. Gothard:[6] but it is just now nearest my heart.— Fenwick is a ruined man. He is hiding himself from his Creditors, and has sent his wife & children into the Country. Fell, my other drunken companion (that has been: nam hic cæstus artemque repono) is turned Editor of a Naval Chronicle. Godwin (with a pitiful artificial Wife) continues a steady friend: tho' the same facility does not remain of visiting him often. That Bitch[7] has detached Marshall from his house: Marshall, the man who went to sleep when the Ancient Mariner was reading, the old steady, unalterable, friend of the Professor— —. Holcroft is not yet come to town. I expect to see him & will deliver your messag[e.] Ho[w I hat]e *this part* of a letter. [T]hings come crowding in to say, & no room for 'em. Some things are too little to be told, i.e. to have a preference: some are too big & circumstantial.— Thanks for yours, which was most delicious.

Would I had been with you, benighted &c— I fear, my head is turned with wandering. I shall never be the same acquiesct. being.— farewell.———

Write again **quickly,** for I shall not like to hazard a letter, not knowing where the fates have carried you. farewell, my dear fellow.

<div align="right">C Lamb</div>

MS: Huntington Library. Pub.: Talfourd (1837), I, 221–226; Sala, I, 373–377; Purnell, I, 373–377; Fitzgerald, II, 206–210; Hazlitt, I, 314–317; Ainger (1888), I, 181–184; Ainger (1900), II, 65–69; Macdonald, I, 221–225; Ainger (1904), I, 229–232; Harper, I, facsimile, and III, 80–84; Lucas (1905), VI, 243–245, and VII, 968; Lucas (1912), I, 250–253; Lucas (1935), I, 314–317. Address: A Monsieur Manning/Poste Restante/à Touluse.

1. Which he and Mary did see in 1822 and which Manning had left on July 14, 1802, for Switzerland, Milan, Savoy, Valence, Avignon, Marseilles, and ultimately Toulouse. He stayed there until about early November.

2. Cf. "beds of roses," in Christopher Marlowe's "The Passionate Shepherd to His Love," line 9. The "far famed Peak in Derbyshire," referred to next, possibly Camden, is described almost the way Lamb describes it here in Michael Drayton's *Poly-Olbion,* Song 26, line 406.

3. One and one-quarter lines are canceled following.

4. Wordsworth would be married at Brompton Church on October 4 to Mary Hutchinson, who brought perhaps £400 to the marriage. Wordsworth had about £70 annually and what he occasionally earned from his writings. Dorothy, who would live with them, had arranged to be financially independent by obtaining promises of the continuance of annual allowances of £20 from each of her brothers Christopher (see Vol. I, Letter 41, source note) and John (1772–1805), the latter the commander of the East Indiaman *Earl of Abergavenny,* and of an additional annual £20 from her brother Richard (1768–1816), an attorney of Staple Inn, London. But those arrangements became unnecessary when it appeared that money long due them all would be paid. John Wordsworth (1741–1783), their father, who from 1764 had been the law agent and land steward in Cumberland and Westmorland for James Lowther, first Earl of Lonsdale (1736–1802), had died without receiving the nearly £5,000 Lord Lonsdale owed him for his services. When the administrators of the estate of John Wordsworth—his brother Richard (1733–1794) and his brother-in-law Christopher Cookson Crackanthorpe, later Christopher Cookson (1745–1799)—could not collect, they took the matter to court. Litigation followed until 1791, when the parties agreed to settle out of court. But no settlement was made during the years left to Lord Lonsdale. When he died he left his estate to his third cousin William Lowther, later first Earl of Lonsdale of the second creation (1757–1844), and stipulated that his just debts be paid. William Lowther accordingly cleared the account, though not until 1804, with a payment to the Wordsworths jointly of £8,500, which represented the original indebtedness and most of the interest it would have earned.

5. Probably Patterdale, just south of Ullswater.

6. The pass in the Alps on the main route from Switzerland to Italy through which Manning had walked. The Latin, below, is from the *Aeneid,* V, 484, and translates, "for here I give up the gloves and the profession [of boxing]."

7. Mrs. Godwin. Manning's message, mentioned below and given in Manning's

letter of September 10, 1802 (*Manning-Lamb Letters,* p. 81), consists only of remembrances to the dramatist and miscellaneous writer Thomas Holcroft (1745– 1809); to Louisa (d. 1853), Holcroft's fourth wife, the daughter of the French playwright and critic Louis Sebastien Mercier (1740–1814), the sister of the T., or B., Mercier with whom Holcroft attempted to establish a printing business in London in 1802–1803, and to become, in 1812, the wife of the dramatist James Kenney (1780–1849); and to Fanny, Holcroft's daughter by an earlier marriage. Fanny Holcroft became the translator of plays of Vittorio Alfieri, Pedro Calderón de la Barca, Leandro Fernandez de Moratín ("Inarco Celenio") Gotthold Lessing, and Christian Felix Weisse for her father's *Theatrical Recorder* (1805), the translator as well of Louis Joseph de Bourbon's *Memoirs of the Life of the Great Condé* (1807), and the author of *Fortitude and Frailty: A Novel* (1817). Manning had met the Holcrofts earlier in the year in Paris, where since January 1801 Holcroft had been working on his *Travels from Hamburg, through Westphalia, Holland, and the Netherlands, to Paris* (1804).

134. *C. L. to Coleridge*

[October 5, 1802]

Carolus Agnus Coleridgio suo S.

Carissime,

Scribis, ut nummos scilicet epistolarios solvam et postremo in **Tartara** ubeam: immo tu potius **Tartaricum** (ut aiunt) deprehendisti, qui me vernaculâ meâ linguâ pro scribâ conductitio per tot annos satis eleganter usum ad Latinè impure et canino fere ore latrandum per tuasmet epistolas benè compositas et concinnatas percellire studueris. Conabor tamen: Attamen vereor, ut Ædes istas nostri Christi, inter quas tantâ diligentiâ magistri improbâ bonis literulis quasi per clysterem quendam injectis, infrà suprà que olim penitùs imbutus fui, Barnesii et Marklandii doctissimorum virorum nominibus adhuc gaudentes, barbarismis meis peregrinis et aliunde quæsitis valde dehonestavero. Sed pergere quocunque placet. Adeste igitur, quotquot estis, conjugationum declinationumve turmæ, terribilia spectra, et tu imprimis ades, **Umbra et Imago** maxima obsoletæ (Diis gratiæ) **Virgæ,** quâ novissime in mentem receptâ, horrescunt subito natales, et parum deest quo minùs braccas meas ultro usque ad crura demittam, et ipse puer pueriliter ejulem.

Ista tua Carmina Chamouiana satis grandia esse mihi constat; sed hoc mihi nonnihil displicet, quòd in iis illæ montium Grisosonum inter se responsiones totidem reboant anglicè, **God, God,** haud aliter atque temet audivi tuas montes Cumbrianas resonare docentes, **Tod, Tod,**

nempe Doctorem infelicem: vocem certe haud **Deum Sonantem.** Pro cæteris plaudo.

Itidem Comparationes istas tuas satis callidas et lepidas certè novi: sed quid hoc ad verum? cum illi Consulari viro et *mentem irritabilem* istum Julianum, et etiam *astutias frigidulas* quasdem Augusto propriores, nequaquam congruenter uno afflatu comparationis causâ insedisse affirmave*ris*: necnon nescio quid similitudinis etiam cum Tiberio tertio in loco solicite produxeris. Quid tibi equidem cum uno vel altero Cæsare, cum universi Duodecim ad comparationes tuas se ultro tulerint?— Præterea, vetustati adnutans, comparationes iniquas odi.

Istas Wordsworthianas nuptias (vel potius cujusdam *Edmundii* tui) te retulisse mirificum gaudeo. Valeas, Mariae, fortunata nimium, et antiquæ illæ **Mariæ** Virgini (comparatione plusquam Cæsareanâ) forsitan comparanda, quoniam **Beata inter Mulieres:** et etiam fortasse Wordsworthium ipsum tuum maritum Angelo Salutatori æquare fas erit, quoniam e **Cælo** (ut ille) descendunt et Musæ et ipsæ Musicolæ: at Wordsworthium Musarum observantissimum semper novi. Necnon te quoque affinitate haĉ nova, **Dorothea,** gratulor: et tu certe alterum *donum Dei.*

Istum Ludum, quem tu, Coleridgi, Americanum garris, a Ludo (ut Ludi sunt) maximè abhorrentem prætereo: nempe quid ad Ludum attinet, totius illæ gentis Columbianæ, a nostrâ gente, eadem stirpe ortâ, ludi singuli causa voluntatem perperam alienare? Quæso ego materiam ludi: tu Bella ingeris.

Denique valeas, et quid de Latinitate meâ putes, dicas: facias ut **opossum** illum nostrum volantem vel (ut tu malis) quendam Piscem erratundum, a me salvum et pulcherrimum esse jubeas. Valeant uxor tua cum Hartleiio nostro. Soror mea salva est et ego: **Vos** et ipsa salvere jubet. Ulterius progrediri non liquet: homo sum æratus.

P. S. Pene mihi exciderat, apud me esse Librorum a Johanno Miltono Latinè scriptorum volumina duo, quæ (Deo Volente) cum cæteris tuis libr[is] ocyùs is [?] per maria ad te missura curabo: sed me in hoc tali genere rerum nullo modo *festinantem* novisti: habes confitentem reum. Hoc solum dici restat, prædicta volumina pulchra esse et omnia opera Latina J. M. in se continere. Circa Defensionem istam Pro Popo. Ango. acerrimæm in præsens ipse præclaro gaudio moror.

Jussa tua Stuartina faciam ut diligenter colam.—

Iterum Iterumque valeas.——

et facias memor sis nostri

MS: Berg Collection, New York Public Library. Pub.: Talfourd (1837), I, 227–230; Sala, I, 133–135; Purnell, I, 133–135; Fitzgerald, I, 415–417; Hazlitt, I, 317–319; Ainger (1888), I, 185–187; Ainger (1900), II, 70–72; Macdonald, I, 225–227; Ainger (1904), I, 233–235; Harper, III, 85–87; Lucas (1905), VI, 246–247; Lucas (1912), V, 253–255; Lucas (1935), I, 318–319. Address: Mr Coleridge/Keswick/Cumberland. Postmark: October 5, 1802.

[Translation]

Charles Lamb to His Friend Coleridge, Greeting

Dear Friend,

You write that I am to pay my debt, to wit in coin of correspondence, and finally that I am to go to **Tartarus:** no but it is you have caught a **Tartar** (as the saying is), since after all these years employing my own vernacular tongue, and prettily enough for a hired penman, you have set about to drive me by means of your well composed and neatly turned epistles to gross and almost doggish barking in the Latin. Still, I will try: And yet I fear that the Hostel of our Christ,—wherein by the exceeding diligence of a relentless master I was in days gone by deeply imbued from bottom to top with polite learning, instilled as it were by a clyster—which still glories in the names of the erudite Barnes and Markland,[1] will be vilely dishonored by my outlandish and adscititious barbarisms. But I am determined to proceed, no matter whither. Be with me therefore all ye troops of conjugations and declensions, dread spectres, and approach thou chief, greatest **Shade and Phantom** of the disused (thank Heaven) **Birch,** at whose entry to my imagination a sudden shiver takes my rump, and a trifle then more would make me begin to let down my breeches to my calves, and turning boy, howl boyishly.

That your Ode at Chamounix[2] is a fine thing I am clear; but here is a thing offends me somewhat, that in the ode your answers of the Grison mountains to each other should so often echo in English, **God, God,** in the very tone that I have heard your own lips teaching your Cumbrian mountains to resound, **Tod, Tod,** meaning the un-

lucky doctor: a syllable assuredly of no **Godlike Sound.** For the rest, I approve.

Moreover, I certainly recognize that your comparisons[3] are acute and witty: but what has this to do with truth? since you have given to the great Consul at once that *irritable mind* of Julius, and also a kind of *cold cunning,* more proper to Augustus, attributing incongruous characteristics in one breath for the sake of your comparison: nay, you have even in the third instance laboriously drawn out some likeness to Tiberius. What had you to do with one Caesar, or a second, when the whole Twelve offered themselves to your comparison?— Moreover, I agree with antiquity, and think comparisons odious.

Your Wordsworth nuptials[4] (or rather the nuptials of a certain *Edmund* of yours) fill me with joy in your report. May you prosper, Mary, fortunate beyond compare, and perchance comparable to that ancient Virgin **Mary** (a comparison more than Caesarean) since **blessed art thou among women:** perhaps also it will be no impiety to compare Wordsworth himself your husband to the Angel of Salutation, since (like the angel) from **Heaven** descend both Muses and the servants of the Muses: whose devoutest votary I always know Wordsworth to be. Congratulations to thee, ***Dorothea,*** in this new alliance: you also assuredly are another *gift of God.*[5]

As for that game with America you talk of, Coleridge, I pass it by as quite unfit for a game (as games go) : for, tell me, what fun is there in wickedly estranging the whole Columbian people from our people, who are of the same stock, for the sake of a single jest? I seek the material for fun: you press War upon me.[6]

Finally, fare you well, and pray tell me what you think of my Latinity: kindly wish health and beauty from me to our flying **opossum** or (as you prefer to call it) roving Fish. Good health to your wife and our Hartley. My sister and I are well: **She** also sends you greeting. I do not see how to get on farther: I am a bankrupt.

P. S. I had almost forgot, I have by me two volumes of the Latin writings of John Milton,[7] which (Deo Volente) I will have sent you sooner or later by sea: but you know me no way *precipitate* in this kind: the accused pleads guilty. This only remains to be said, that the aforesaid volumes are handsome and contain all the Latin works of

J. M. At present I dwell with much delight on his vigorous defence of the English people.

I will be sure to observe diligently your Stuartial orders.—

Again and Again farewell.——

and pray be mindful of me

[Adapted from the translation in Lucas (1935), I, 319–321]

1. Joshua Barnes (1654–1712) and Jeremiah Markland (1693–1776), Christ Hospitalers, classicists, and Cantabrigians. Barnes was regius professor of Greek at Emmanuel College from 1695 and an editor of Euripides, Anacreon, and Homer. Markland was a fellow and tutor at Peterhouse, or St. Peter's College, from 1717; later a resident of Milton Court, Dorking; and a scholar of Horace, Statius, and Cicero.

2. "Hymn before Sun-rise, in the Vale of Chamouni," which is in the *Morning Post* of September 11, 1802, as "Chamouny, the Hour before Sunrise: A Hymn." The passage there that Lamb complains about below and that Coleridge later replaced with the present lines 58–63 reads so:

God! God! the torrents like a shout of nations
Utter! the ice-plain bursts and answers God!
God, sing the meadow-streams with gladsome voice,
And pine-groves with their soft and soul-like sound,
The silent snow-mass, loos'ning thunders God!

By "the unluckly doctor" Lamb means the divine and author Dr. William Dodd (1729–1777), who was hanged at Tyburn for forging a bond worth £4,200 in the name of his former pupil Philip Stanhope, fifth Earl of Chesterfield (1755–1815). Dodd was hanged in spite of the pleadings of Dr. Johnson and others for his pardon. In one of Coleridge's notebooks, according to Mrs. Gertrude Alison Anderson, the editor of the *Manning-Lamb Letters* (see my Vol. I, Introduction, p. lxxxviii, and Lucas [1935], I, 321), Coleridge stated that he made the mountains echo Dodd's name.

3. Coleridge's essay "Comparison of the Present State of France with That of Rome under Julius and Augustus Caesar," which is serialized in the *Morning Post* of September 21, 25, and October 2, 1802.

4. "Dejection, an Ode, Written April 4, 1802," which is in the *Morning Post* of October 4, 1802, Wordsworth's wedding day. There the name "Edmund" is used instead of the present "Lady." The expression "blessed art thou among women," below, is from Luke 1:28.

5. The meaning of "Dorothy," or "Dorothea."

6. A Mr. Rendall wrote to Lucas regarding this paragraph: "Coleridge was evidently meditating an attack on America, but the game he proposed cannot now be identified. Bonaparte in this year demanded restraints on the English press, and the dismissal from England of French persons obnoxious to him. Coleridge, perhaps, wished to retaliate, by making fun of Lafayette, notorious as Washington's man in America, and as putting the American Declaration of Independence as a model before the National Assembly. Lafayette was hated by the Jacobins for his moderation, but Coleridge, with his 'Once a Jacobin, always a Jacobin' in the *Morning Post* [of October 21, 1802] at this time, would not choose to see that" (Lucas [1935], I, 321).

7. In his next letter Lamb corrects this statement. He had, rather, the edition by Thomas Birch (1705–1766), *A Complete Collection of the Historical, Political, and*

Miscellaneous Works of John Milton . . . With an Historical and Critical Account of the Life and Writings of the Author (1738). See Letter 137 for Lamb's lengthier comments on Milton's defenses of the English, mentioned below, and the next letter for the "orders" of Daniel Stuart.

135. *C. L. to Coleridge*

[October 11, 1802]

Dear Coleridge,

Your offer about the German Poems is exceedingly kind; but I do not think it a wise speculation, because the time it would take you to put them into prose would be nearly as great as if you versified them.[1] Indeed I am sure you could do the one nearly as soon as the other: so that instead of a division of labour, it would be only a multiplication. But I will think of your offer in another light. I dare say I could find many things (of a light nature) to suit that paper, which you could not object to pass upon Stuart as your own; and I should come in for some light profits, and Stuart think the more highly of your assiduity. Bishop Hall's characters[2] I know nothing about, having never seen them. But I will reconsider your offer, which is very plausible. For as to the drudgery of going every day to an Editor with my scraps, like a Pedlar, for him to pick out & tumble about my ribbands & posies, and to wait in his lobby &c. no money could make up for the degradation: You are in too high request with him to have any thing unpleasant of that sort to submit to—

It was quite a slip of my pen, in my Latin Letter, when I told you I had Milton's Latin Works: I ought to have said his **Prose** Works in 2 volumes Birch's edition, containing all both Latin & English, a fuller & better edition than Lloyd's of Toland.[3] It is completely at your service, & you must accept it from me: at the same time I shall be much obliged to you for your Latin Milton, which you think you have at Howell's; it will leave me nothing to wish for, but the Hist. Engl. which I shall soon pick up for a trifle: I will send you the Milton with any choice Books you may want from Howel's ⅌ Waggon; or if you prefer it, all your Books by sea: but I suppose in the latter case there is a hazard of their not coming to hand. Wordsworth has got the Oil Silk you bespoke, Mary did not make it up for fear of not doing it

right, and you must have **soles** of **Cork** or something to your feet, or
you will rub the silk to pieces the first time of using: these she did not
know how to put on: or I promise you she would not have spared any
trouble. . Wordsworth has also some Snuff for you secundum recipe.—
And he forgot to take, what we have still for you, a black Cap: but
you must write me word whether the Cap & Miltons are worth paying
Carriage for. You have a Milton: but it is pleasanter to eat ones own
peas out of ones own garden, than to buy them by the Peck at Covent
Garden: And a Book reads the Better, which is our own, & has been
so long known to us, that we know the topography of its blots &
dogears, and can trace the dirt in it to having read it at Tea with
[bu]tterd muffins, or over a **Pipe,** which I think is the maximum.—
But Coleridge you must accept these little things & not think of return-
ing money for them: for I do not set up for a factor or general
Agent.— As for fantastic debts of £15, I'll think you were dreaming, &
not trouble myself seriously to attend to you.—

My bad Latin you properly correct: but natales for natis was an
inadvertency: I knew better. Progrediri or Progredi I thought in-
different; my Authority being Ainsworth.—[4] However as I have got a
fit of latin, you will now & then indulge me with an **Epistola**. I pay
the postage of this, & propose doing it by turns. In that case I can
now & then write to you without remorse: not that you would mind
the money, but you have not always ready cash to answer small
demands, the *Epistolarii* nummi:[5]—I had one reason for writing
now.— What you will be extremely glad to hear: I have just received
intelligence, that **Billy Winch** is doing extremely well. He went out
to **India** on the Bengal Estabm. as **Cadet,** & is come to be a Lieuten-
ant; he is extremely respected, has learnd the language, & is thought
a clever man. The **Rogue** was courting his **Colonel's** Daughter, when
my informer heard last of him. He had not any encour[a]gement from
the family; but the esteem he was in secured him from any mortifying
repulse.— My authority is a goodnatured young man, who was a
little time at **Xts,** is now in the India House, Robinson:[6] he says he &
his father travelld into Devonshire with you, & you were very kind
to him.—

Your Epigram on the Sun & Moon in Germany is admirable. Take
'em all together, they are as good as Harrington's.— I will muster up

all the conceits I can, & you shall have a packet some day. You & I together can answer all demands surely: you mounted on a terrible charger (like Homer in the Battle of the Books) at the head of the Cavalry. I will lead the light horse.[7]

I have just heard from Stoddart. Allen & he intend taking Keswick in their way home.— Allen wished particularly to have it a secret, that he is in Scotland, & wrote to me accordingly very urgently: as luck was, I had told not above 3 or 4; but Mary had told Mrs. **Green** of **Xts** Hospital!——[8]

Lloyd has written me a fine Letter of friendship all about himself & Sophia & love & cant: which I have not answered. I have not given up the idea of writing to him; but it will be done very plainly & sincerely without acrimony.—

For the **present,** farewell: never forgetting **Love** to **Pi=Pos** & his friends

C Lamb

MS: British Museum, London. Pub.: Talfourd (1837), I, 238–241; Sala, I, 135–137; Purnell, I, 135–137; Fitzgerald, I, 417–419; Hazlitt, I, 319–321; Ainger (1888), I, 187–188; Ainger (1900), II, 73–75; Macdonald, I, 227–229; Ainger (1904), I, 235–236; Harper, III, 90–92; Lucas (1905), VI, 250–251; Lucas (1912), V, 257–258; Lucas (1935), I, 321–324. Address: Mr. Coleridge/Greta Hall/Keswick/Cumberland. Postmark: October 11, 1802.

1. Evidently Stuart had asked Coleridge for translations of certain German poems for publication in the *Morning Post*. Coleridge had in turn offered to supply Lamb with their prose paraphrases and give him credit if Lamb would versify them as he had done in 1800 with Thekla's song, or "Ballad from the German," for Coleridge's translation of Schiller's *The Piccolomini; or, the First Part of Wallenstein*. (See Vol. I, Letter 65, second paragraph.) Nothing came of the proposal, in spite of Lamb's acceptance of it in the next letter.

2. *Characters of Virtues and Vices* (1608), by Bishop Joseph Hall (1574–1656), which the poetaster (though poet laureate) and dramatist Nahum Tate (1652–1715) versified in 1691 and from which Lamb in 1820 took a couplet for the epigraph to "Barron Field's Poems" (*Works,* I, 197 and 469).

3. The deist John Toland (1670–1722), whose edition of Milton's prose works appeared in 1698. Howell's, mentioned in the following sentence, was the home of Stuart's tailor at 10 King Street, Covent Garden, where Coleridge lodged from time to time from November 1801. The "Hist. Engl." has not been identified. Coleridge wanted it for use in preparing a contemplated history of English prose. (See *Coleridge's Letters,* II, 776 and esp. 877.) The symbol is for "per."

4. Robert Ainsworth. See Letter 121, note 1.

5. The "coin of *Letters.*" William Winch (1780–1806), discussed below, was a Christ's Hospitaler and the son of William and Elizabeth Winch of London. He was appointed a cadet in 1795, was promoted to ensign in 1796, and went out to India and was raised to lieutenant in the First Native Infantry in 1797 and to captain in 1804. He died, unmarried, at Supa, Bundelkhand. He is listed in V. C.

P. Hodgson's *Officers of the Bengal Army, 1758–1834* (London: n.p., 1834),
IV, 501.

6. William Robinson, who was in receipt of salary from the transfer accountant's
department since 1798. In 1805, according to Samuel McKechnie's "Charles Lamb
of the India House," in the *CLSB* of May 1949, he was sent as an assistant ac-
countant to the company's station at Penang, where he later became the accountant
general and a member of the court of judicature of the island. His father has not
been identified. Coleridge's "On the Curious Circumstance, That in the German
Language the Sun Is Feminine, and the Moon Is Masculine," mentioned below,
is in the *Morning Post* of October 11, 1802. Lamb found it and Coleridge's other
epigrams equal to those by the wit Sir John Harington (1561–1612) that are
published, among other places, with his translation (1591) of Ariosto's *Orlando
Furioso.*

7. Which Swift in *The Battle of the Books* assigned to Abraham Cowley and to
the poet and critic Nicolas Boileau-Despréaux (1636–1711).

8. Mrs. Katherine Green, who worked at Christ's Hospital from about 1790 to
1841. Its records additionally show only that she was a matron in the London
school in 1828 and 1833 and the infirmary nurse in the Hertford branch in 1841.
She was remembered by the (anonymous) author of "Recollections of a New Boy,"
in *Gleanings from "The Blue." Being a Selection of Poetry and Prose from the
Magazine of Christ's Hospital in the Years 1870–71 and 1874–81* (Hertford:
Austin, 1881), pp. 63–64. Lloyd and Sophia, mentioned below, are the younger
Charles Lloyd and his wife.

136. *C. L. to Coleridge*

[East India House
October 23, 1802]

Your kind offer I will not a second time refuse. You shall send me
a packet, and I will do them into English with great care. Is not there
one about Wm. Tell, and would not that in the present state of dis-
cussions be likely to *tell?*— The Epigrams I meant are to be found at
the end of Harrington's Translation of Orlando Furioso: if you could
get the book, they would some of them answer your purpose to modern-
ize. If you ca'nt, I fancy I can. Baxter's Holy Co̅mo̅nwealth[1] I have
luckily met with, and when I have sent it, you shall if you please con-
sider yourself indebted to me 3/6 the cost of it: especially as I
purchased it after your solemn injunctions. The plain case with regard
to my presents (which you seem so to shrink from) is that I have not
at all affected the character of a Donor, or thought of violating your
sacred Law of **Give & Take:** but I have been *taking* & partaking the
good things of your House (when I know you were not over-abound-
ing) and I now *give* unto you of mine: and by the grace of God I

happen to be myself a little super-abundant at present. I expect I shall be able to send you my final parcel in about a week: by that time I shall have gone thro' all Milton's Latin works. There will come with it the Holy Comonwealth, and the identical North American Bible[2] which you helped to dogs ear at Xt's.— I call'd at Howell's for your little Milton, and also to fetch away the White Cross Street Library Books, which I have not forgot: but your Books were not in a state to be got at then, & Mrs. H. is to let me know when she packs up. They will be sent by sea; & my little præcursor will come to you by the Whitehaven waggon, accompanied with pens penknife &c.— — Mrs. Howell was as usual very civil; & asked with great earnestness, if it were likely you would come to Town in the winter. She has a friendly eye upon you.—[3] I read daily your political Essays. I was particularly pleased with Once a Jacobin: tho' the argument is obvious enough, the style was less swelling than your things sometimes are, and it was plausible ad populum.

A vessel has just arrived from Jamaica with the news of poor Sam Le Grice's death. He died at Jamaica of the yellow fever. His course was rapid and he had been very foolish, but I believe there was more of kindness and warmth in him than almost any other of our school-fellows. I have had no account a long time of Favell.[4] The annual meeting of the Blues is tomorrow at the London Tavern, where poor Sammy dined with them two years ago, and attracted the notice of all by the singular foppishness of his dress. When men go off the stage so early, it scarce seems a noticeable thing in their epitaphs, whether they have been wise or silly in their lifetime.—

I am glad the snuff & Pi-pos's Books please.— Goody Two Shoes[5] is almost out of print. Mrs. Barbauld['s] stuff has banished all the old classics of the nursery; & the Shopman at Newbery's hardly deign'd to reach them off an old exploded corner of a shelf, when Mary ask'd for them. Mrs. B's & Mrs. Trimmer's nonsense lay in piles about. Knowledge insignificant & vapid as Mrs. B's books convey, it seems, must come to a child in the *shape* of *knowledge,* & his empty noddle must be turned with conceit of his own powers, when he has learnt, that a Horse is an Animal, & Billy is better than a Horse, & such like: instead of that beautiful Interest in wild tales, which made the child a man, while all the time he suspected himself to be no bigger than a child. Science has succeeded to Poetry no less in the little walks of

Children than with Men.—: Is there no possibility of averting this sore evil? Think what you would have been now, if instead of being fed with Tales and old wives fables in childhood, you had been crammed with Geography & Natural History.? **Damn them.** I mean the cursed Barbauld Crew, those **Blights & Blasts** of all that is **Human** in man & child.—

As to the Translations, let me do two or three hundred Lines, & then do you try the Nostrums upon Stuart in any way you please. If they go down, I will bray more. In fact, If I got or could but get £50 a year only in addition to what I have, I should live in affluence.

Have you anticipated it, or could not you give a Parallel of Bonaparte with Cromwell, particularly as the contrast in their deeds affecting *foreign* states: Cromwell's interference for the Albigenses, B's against the Swiss. Then Religion would come in; &. Milton & you could rant about **our Countrymen** of that Period.—6 This is a hasty suggestion, the more hasty because I want my Supper.— I have just finished Chapman's Homer. Did you ever read it? it has *most* the continuous power of interesting you all along, like a rapid original, of any: & in the uncommon excellence of the more finish'd parts goes beyond Fairfax or any of 'em.— The Metre is 14 Syllables & capable of all sweetness & grandeur. Cowper's damn'd blank verse detains you every step with some heavy Miltonism.— Chapman gallops off with you his own free pace.— Take a simile for an example—The Council breaks up.—

> —Being abroad, the Earth was overlaid
> With flockers to them, that came forth: as when of frequent **Bees**
> Swarms rise out of a hollow rock, repairing the degrees
> *Of their egression endlessly, with ever rising new*
> From forth their sweet nest: as their store, still as it faded, gr[ew,]
> *And never would cease sending forth her clusters to the Spring,*
> They still crowd out so; this flock here, that there, belabouring
> The loaded flowers. So &c. &c. —
> (what *Endless egression of phrases* the Dog commands)!

Take another, Agamemnon wounded, bearing his wound heroically for the sake of the Army (look below) to a Woman in Labor.—

> He with his lance, sword, mighty stones, pour'd his Heroic wreak
> On other squadrons of the foe, whiles yet warm blood did break

Thro' his cleft veins: but when the wound was quite exhaust &
 crude,
The eager anguish did approve his princely fortitude.
As when most sharp & bitter pangs distract a labouring Dame,
Which the divine Ilithiæ, that rule the painful frame
Of human childbirth pour on her: th' Ilithiæ that are
The daughters of Saturnia: with whose extreme repair
The woman in her travail strives, to take the worst it gives;
With Thought, **it *must be,* tis *Love's Fruit,*** the end for which
 she liv[es;]
The mean to make herself new born, what comforts will redound.
So &c.—

I will tell you more about Chapman & his peculiarities in my next.[7]
I am much interes[ted] in him.—

<div align="right">Yours ever affect. & Pi-pos's &c—</div>
<div align="right">C L</div>

MS: Huntington Library. Pub.: Talfourd (1837), I, 234–238; Sala, I, 137–
140; Purnell, I, 137–140; Fitzgerald, I, 419–422; Hazlitt, I, 322–324; Ainger
(1888), I, 189–191; Ainger (1900), II, 75–78; Macdonald, I, 229–232; Ainger
(1904), I, 237–239; Harper, I, facsimile, and III, 92–97; Lucas (1905), VI, 252–
254, and VII, 968–969; Lucas (1912), V, 259–262; Lucas (1935), I, 324–327.
Address: Mr Coleridge/Keswick/Cumberland. Postmark: October 23, 1802.
 1. *A Holy Commonwealth, Opening the True Principles of Government: For
the Healing of the Mistakes, and Resolving the Doubts, That Most Endanger and
Trouble England at This Time* (1659), by the Presbyterian divine Richard Baxter
(1615–1691).
 2. *Mamussee Wunneetupanatamwe Up-Biblum God naneeswe Nukkone Testa-
ment kah wonk Wusku Testament-Ne quoshkinnumuk nashpe Wuttinneumoh
Christ noh assoowesit John Eliot* (1653; "The Whole Holy His-Bible God both
Old Testament and also New Testament This Turned by the-Servant-of-Christ
Who Is Called John Eliot")—the translation of the Bible into the Massachusetts
dialect of the Algonquian language by John Eliot (1604–1690), a colonial clergy-
man originally of Widford, Hertfordshire, England, who became known as the
Indian Apostle. Whitecross Street, whose library is mentioned below, is in Cripple-
gate.
 3. Mrs. Howell, Stuart recorded in the *Gentleman's Magazine*, N.S. 9 (May
1838), 487, "was a cheerful good housewife, of middle age, who I knew would
nurse Coleridge as kindly as if he were her son; and he owned he was comfortably
taken care of." Coleridge's "Once a Jacobin Always a Jacobin," mentioned below,
is in the *Morning Post* of October 21, 1802.
 4. Samuel Favell (1775–1812), who was the son of John, a house painter at
Cambridge, attended Christ's Hospital with Lamb and Coleridge and in 1795 was
matriculated at Pembroke College, Cambridge, where he became a pantisocrat. He
was not graduated, but with Samuel Le Grice (see Vol. I, Introduction, pp. xxxi–

xxxii) accepted a commission in the army from the Duke of York, rose to captain, and died on the plains of Salamanca. He is described in "Christ's Hospital Five and Thirty Years Ago," as W—— in "Poor Relations" (*Works*, II, 22 and 160), and in *Hunt's Autobiography*, I, 81. (In *Works*, II, 323 and 409–410, his first name is given as Joseph; in *Hunt's Autobiography* as Robert; but in *Alumni Cantabrigienses* as Samuel.) The "Blues," below, designates the Christ's Hospitalers.

5. *Goody Two-shoes*, sometimes ascribed to Oliver Goldsmith. It was published by John Newbery (1713–1767), the originator of children's books and the founder, in 1745 in St. Paul's Churchyard, of the bookselling establishment mentioned below and to which his son Francis (1743–1818) succeeded in 1767. Mrs. Anna Letitia Barbauld's books for the young are *Early Lessons for Children* (1778), *Lessons for Children, of Three Years Old* (1779), *Hymns in Prose for Children* (1781), and one Mrs. Barbauld wrote with her brother Dr. John Aikin, *Evenings at Home; or, the Juvenile Budget Opened. Consisting of a Variety of Miscellaneous Pieces for the Instruction and Amusement of Young Persons* (1792–1796). Mrs. Sarah Trimmer, née Kirby (1741–1810), was the author of books for elementary and church schools and *Easy Introduction to the Knowledge of Nature* (1782), *Sacred History, Selected from the Scriptures, with Annotations and Reflections Adapted to the Comprehension of Young Persons* (1782–1784), and *Story of the Robins*, which was first published as *Fabulous Histories* (1786). Lamb's attack on children's books at the end of the paragraph is interesting in light of the fact that he and Mary were shortly to write six of their own.

6. Coleridge never acted on the suggestion. Lamb next commends the translations (1611 and 1614) of the *Iliad* and the *Odyssey* by George Chapman (1559?–1634); considers them as superior to Edward Fairfax's translation (1600) of Tasso's *Gerusalemme Liberata* and to William Cowper's translations (1791) of Homer; and quotes from Chapman's translation of the *Iliad*, II, 70–77, and XI, 228–239. Lamb later paraphrased Chapman's translation of the *Odyssey* in *The Adventures of Ulysses* (1808).

7. Which has either not been recovered or is the next letter. But in the next letter is nothing about Chapman.

137. *C. L. to Coleridge*

Nov. 4th, 1802

 Observe, there comes to you, by the Kendal waggon to-morrow, the illustrious 5th of November, a box, containing the Miltons, the strange American Bible, with White's brief note, to which you will attend; Baxter's 'Holy Commonwealth,' for which you stand indebted to me 3s. 6d.; an odd volume of Montaigne, being of no use to me, I having the whole; certain books belonging to Wordsworth, as do also the strange thick-hoofed shoes, which are very much admired at in London. All these sundries I commend to your most strenuous looking after. If you find the Miltons in certain parts dirtied and soiled with a crumb of right Gloucester[1] blacked in the candle (my usual supper), or peradventure a stray ash of tobacco wafted into the crevices, look to that

passage more especially: depend upon it, it contains good matter. I have got your little Milton which, as it contains Salmasius—and I make a rule of never hearing but one side of the question (why should I distract myself?)—I shall return to you when I pick up the *Latina opera*. The first Defence is the greatest work among them, because it is uniformly great, and such as is befitting the very mouth of a great nation speaking for itself. But the second Defence, which is but a succession of splendid episodes slightly tied together, has one passage which if you have not read, I conjure you to lose no time, but read it; it is his consolations in his blindness, which had been made a reproach to him. It begins whimsically, with poetical flourishes about Tiresias[2] and other blind worthies (which still are mainly interesting as displaying his singular mind, and in what degree poetry entered into his daily soul, not by fits and impulses, but engrained and innate); but the concluding page, *i.e.* of *this passage* (not of the *Defensio*) which you will easily find, divested of all brags and flourishes, gives so rational, so true an enumeration of his comforts, so human, that it cannot be read without the deepest interest. Take one touch of the religious part:— Et sane haud ultima Dei cura cæci—(*we blind folks,* I understand it, not *nos* for *ego*)—sumus; qui nos, quominus quicquam aliud præter ipsum cernere valemus, eo clementius atque benignius respicere dignatur. Væ qui illudit nos, væ qui lædit, execratione publica devovendo; nos ab injuriis hominum non modo incolumes, sed pene sacros divina lex reddidit, divinus favor: nec tam *oculorum hebetudine* quam *Cœlestium alarum umbrâ* has nobis fecisse tenebras videtur, factas illustrare rursus interiore ac longe præstabiliore lumine haud raro solet. Huc refero, quod et amici officiosius nunc etiam quam solebant, colunt, observant, adsunt; quod et nonnulli sunt, quibuscum Pyladeas atque Theseas alternare voces verorum amicorum liceat.

> Vade gubernaculum mei pedis.
> Da manum ministro amico.
> Da collo manum tuam, ductor autem viæ ero tibi ego.[3]

All this, and much more, is highly pleasing to know. But you may easily find it;—and I don't know why I put down so many words about it, but for the pleasure of writing to you and the want of another topic.

Yours ever,

C. Lamb

To-morrow I expect with anxiety S. T. C.'s letter to Mr. Fox.[4]

MS: unrecovered. Text: Lucas (1935), I, 328–329. Also pub.: Talfourd (1837), I, 241–243; Sala, I, 141–142; Purnell, I, 141–142; Fitzgerald, I, 423–424; Hazlitt, I, 324–326; Ainger (1888), I, 191–192; Ainger (1900), II, 79–81; Macdonald, I, 233–234; Ainger (1904), I, 239–240; Harper, III, 97–100; Lucas (1905), VI, 255–256; Lucas (1912), V, 262–264.

1. A cheese. The work referred to below of Claudius Salmasius, or Claude Saumaise (1588–1653), the French classical scholar, is his vindication of Charles I and its accompanying attack on the British Commonwealth, titled *Defensio regia pro Carolo I* (1649). It had provoked Milton to write *Pro populo Anglicano defensio* (1651), his first defense of the English people. Lamb also refers to, and quotes from, Milton's second defense—*Joannis Miltoni Angli pro populo Anglicano defensio secunda* (1654)—which was in response to (the anonymous) *Regii sanguinis clamor ad coelum adversus parricidas Anglicanos* (1652; "The Cry of the Royal Blood to Heaven against the English Parricides"). Milton believed its author was the Protestant divine Alexander More (1616–1670). Its author was the Anglican Peter du Moulin (1601–1684).

2. The celebrated legendary blind prophet of Thebes.

3. "And, in truth, we who are blind, are not the last regarded by the providence of God; who, as we are the less able to discern any thing but himself, beholds us with the greater clemency and benignity. Woe be to him who makes a mock of us; woe be to him who injures us; he deserves to be devoted to the public curse. The divine law, the divine favour, has made us not merely secure, but, as it were, sacred, from the injuries of men; nor would seem to have brought this darkness upon us so much by inducing a dimness of the eyes, as by the overshadowing of heavenly wings; and not unfrequently is wont to illumine it again, when produced, by an inward and far surpassing light. To this I attribute the more than ordinary civilities, attentions, and visits of friends; of whom there are some, with whom, as with true friends, I may hold the dialogue of Pylades and Orestes:

[*Orestes*] Go slowly on, and be the rudder of my feet.
[*Pylades* Precious is my charge.]

[Euripides, *Orestes*, line 795]

Give your hand to your friend and helper.
Throw your arm about my neck, and I will be your guide."

[Euripides, *Hercules Furens*, lines 1398 and 1402]

[*Joannis Miltoni Angli pro populo Anglicano defensio secunda*, tr. George Burnett, in *The Works of John Milton*, ed. Frank Allen Patterson *et al.* (New York: Columbia University Press, 1933), VIII, 73 and 75]

4. The first letter to the statesman Charles James Fox (1749–1806) is in the *Morning Post* of November 4, 1802. The second is in its issue of November 9. In them Coleridge denounced Fox for his hypocrisy and ambitions; for his support of the Treaty of Amiens, whose terms many Englishmen had come to regard as an indignity to them; for the pleasure he took in the thought, which he had made public at a tavern dinner on October 10, that the treaty was glorious to France; and for his trip to Paris that included his acceptance of the hospitality and other favors of Napoleon and Talleyrand.

138. *C. L. to Joseph Cottle*

Monday aftn [November 8, 1802?]

My dear Sir,

Will you oblige me by putting off our meeting tomorrow to some other day which you shall name yourself, this week?— A friend[1] of mine has unknowing of my prior engagement, engaged a party to meet me, and it will be difficult for him to disarrange his guests. Will you oblige me by sending back by the messenger, what other day this week your kindness is willing to substitute?

Yours truly

C Lamb

MS: The Historical Society of Pennsylvania, Philadelphia. Pub.: Thomas Ollive Mabbott and John Howard Birss, "Some Uncollected Letters of Charles Lamb," *Notes and Queries,* 165 (1933), 298. Address: Mr Cottle/Crane Court. Notation: "Autograph of Charles Lamb/J. C." The date is suggested by the address—Cottle and Nathaniel Biggs (see Vol. I, Letter 4, note 5) printed the 1802 edition of *Lyrical Ballads* at Crane Court, Fleet Street—and by Lamb's discussion of Cottle in the next letter, first paragraph.

 1. Unidentified.

139. *C. L. to Manning*

[Mid-November 1802]

My dear Manning,

I must positively write, or I shall miss you at Toulouse. I sit here like a decayed minute hand (I lye, that does not *sit*) and being myself the exponent of no time, take no heed how the Clocks about me are going. You possibly by this time may have explored all Italy, and toppled unawares into Ætna, while you went too near those rotten jaw'd gap-tooth'd[1] old worn out chaps of hell;—while I am meditating a quiescent letter to the honest Post Master of Toulouse. But in case you should not have been felo de se, this is to tell you, that your Letter was quite to my palat—in Particular your just remarks upon Industry, *damned* Industry (tho' indeed you left me to explore the reason) were highly relishing—. Iv'e often wish'd I liv'd in the Golden age when

Shepherds lay, stretch'd upon flowers, and loused themselves at their leisure—the genius there is in a man's natural idle face, that has not learn'd his multiplication table! before doubt, and propositions, & corollaries got into the world. *Now,* as **Joseph Cottle,** a Bard of Nature Sings, going up **Malvern Hills**—

> How steep! how painful the ascent?
> It needs the evidence of *close deduction,*
> To know that ever I shall gain the Top.[2]

You must know that **Joe is Lame,** so that he had some reason for so singing. These two Lines I assure you are taken totidem Literis from a very *popular* Poem. Joe is also an Epic Poet as well as a descriptive, and has written a Tragedy, tho' both his Drama & **Epopoiea** are strictly *descriptive;* & chiefly of the *Beauties* of *Nature,* for Joe thinks *man* with all his passions and frailties not a proper subject of the *drama.* Joe's Tragedy hath the following surpassing speech in it. Some King is told, that his Enemy has engaged Twelve Archers to come over in a Boat from an Enemy's country & waylay him, he thereupon pathetically exclaims

> *Twelve* dost thou say? **Curse** on those dozen villains.

Cottle read 2 or 3 acts out to us, very gravely on both sides, till he came to this heroic touch, and then he ask'd what we laughd at. I had no more muscles that day—. A poet that chuses to read out his own verses, has but a limited power over you; there is a bound, where his authority ceases.

A propose, if you should go to Florence or to Rome, inquire what works are extant in Gold Silver Bronze or Marble of **Benevenuto Cellini,** a Florentine Artist, whose Life[3] doubtless you have read, or if not, without controversy you must read, so hark 'ye, send for it immediately from Lane's circulating Library. It is always put among the romances, very properly—but you have read it, I suppose. In particular enquire at Florence for his Colossal Bronze Statue (in the Grand Square, or some where) of **Perseus.** You may read the story in Tooke's Pantheon.—

Nothing material has *transpired* in these parts. Coleridge has endited a violent Philippic against Mr. Fox in the Morning Post, which is a compound of expressions of humility Gentleman-ushering-in most

arrogant charges. It will do Mr. Fox no real Injury among those that know him.[4] [. . .]

MS: Huntington Library. Pub.: Talfourd (1837), I, 217–218; Talfourd (1848), I, 128–129; Sala, I, 367–369; Purnell, I, 367–369; Fitzgerald, II, 200–202; Hazlitt, I, 326–327; Ainger (1888), I, 193–194; Ainger (1900), II, 81–83; Macdonald, I, 234–236; Ainger (1904), I, 241–242; Harper, III, 100–102; Lucas (1905), VI, 256–258; Lucas (1912), V, 265–266; Lucas (1935), I, 330–332. Address: [A Monsieur Mannin]g/[Poste Restan]te/[à Toulou]se/[Fran]ce. The date of the letter is estimated from its last paragraph.

1. Cf. Chaucer's Prologue to "The Wife of Bath's Tale," line 609. This sentence and the Latin in the next allude together to Manning as the Greek philosopher and statesman Empedocles (ca. 490–430 B.C.), who according to one legend threw himself into the volcano Etna. The comments on industry refer to the notice Manning took in his letter of October 6–14, 1802 (*Manning-Lamb Letters,* esp. p. 87), of its promotion—"damned industry" he too called it—and the consequent decline of mirth among the French peasantry since the revolution. Lamb's wish for the retired life of another, a golden, age foreshadows "The Superannuated Man" (*Works,* II, 193–199).

2. "Malvern Hills," lines 33–35, in Joseph Cottle, *Malvern Hills, with Minor Poems, and Essays* (4th ed.; 2 vols; London: Cadell, 1829), I, 2. The Latin, below, translates, "in just so many words." Cottle's epic is *Alfred.* (See Vol. I, Letter 82, note 6.) Cottle's tragedy has not been identified and was not published. "Epopoiea," properly "epopœia," is the archaic form of "epopee"—an epic or epic poetry.

3. *The Life of Benvenuto Cellini: A Florentine Artist . . . Written by Himself* (1771), a translation by the miscellaneous writer Thomas Nugent (1700?–1772) of *La vita di Benvenuto Cellini scritta da lui medesimo* (1728). Lamb would have Manning obtain it from the circulating library in Leadenhall Street founded by William Lane (1745?–1814). There is a short account of Lane in the *Gentleman's Magazine,* 84 (March 1814), 301. Cellini's bronze group, mentioned below, called "Perseus Holding the Head of Medusa," is located in the Loggia dei Lanzi in Florence. The legend it portrays, of Perseus' being sent from Seriphos by Polydectes to behead Medusa so that Polydectes would be free to love Perseus' mother, is told in Andrea Tooke (1673–1732), *The Pantheon, Representing the Fabulous Histories of the Heathen Gods and Most Illustrious Heroes* (1698; rev. 1717).

4. See Letter 137, note 4. The remainder of the leaf, about two-thirds of the whole, has been torn away. On the verso of the remaining fragment are nine canceled lines above what is left of the address.

140. *M. A. L. to Sarah Stoddart*

Decr 1 [1802]

My dear Miss Stoddart

I am truly and heartily ashamed of myself, I have been so very long without writing to you. I have nothing to offer in excuse. I have been very ill but that has been only these few weeks past: and it is many months that I have been several kind letters in your debt: pray now

forgive me, and believe, what is *indeed* the truth, that some teazing thing has always happened to prevent me, when I have intended writing to you.

I have been to the Lakes,—in a long jouney of three hundred miles, and a month passed in scenes so new and strange to me, I ought to have picked up something worth telling you about, but my dull head, cannot just now recollect a single circumstance I think will entertain you. My poor head is just now full of the memory of our walks together —driving along the Strand so fast (lest the scotch broth should be spoiled in our absence) we were ashamed of shewing of red faces at your friend's in westminster,[1] or bustling down Fleet-Market-in-all-its-glory of a saturday night, admiring the stale peas and co'lly flowers and cheap'ning small bits of mutton and veal for our sunday's dinner's, returning home in all haste, to be scolded for not laying the cloth in time for supper (albeit it being nine o'clock) and then chidden for laughing in an unseemly manner. I have never half liked being at your brothers rooms since you left them:—they[2] sit and preach about learned matters, while I turn over an old book, and when I am weary look in the window in the corner where you and your work-bag used to be, and wish for you to rout them up and make us all alive.

Your brother promises you shall be in town again after christmas, I look forward to the time with very great pleasure, I hope to God nothing will happen to disappoint us—upon the whole you had but a dull time of it when you was here—your brother must be well and we will all endeavour to make you more comfortable when you come again—yet I think in general you did not look *so very melancholy then* considering—. I have seen the famous Dr Stoddart in his fine scarlet robes, unfortunately the wig was at the barbers, so that I saw but half the show: we will have another grand exhibition when you come, if you will promise not to laugh.

It is merely my own private fancy, but I think your brother is very much more disposed to relish his profession than he used to be—it used to strike me he never *talked about* it, but since he has been *admitted* he is often talking of trials and affairs belonging to trials, and law business to my thinking is got more into his head.

I hope your Mother is better, I am very sorry a[lso (?)] to hear such an indifferent account of her health

If you will forgive my ill usage and be a good natured girl and write

to me directly I will promise always to answer your letters immediately, and I will try to be less-dull another time, but I am not yet half well, my head ach's, and my spirits are very indifferent.

God bless you, Charles sends his love

<div align="right">I am your most affectionate friend

M Lamb</div>

remember me to your kind neighbour[3]

you not only do not write to me but you never enc[l]ose a letter, have you too neglected all your correspondents

MS: University of Bristol Library. Pub.: John R. Barker, "Some Early Correspondence of Sarah Stoddart and the Lambs," *Huntington Library Quarterly,* 24 (1960), 68–69. Address: Miss Stoddart/Salisbury. Postmark: December 1, 1802.

1. Barker (see p. 69 of his article, cited above) determined the friends to be Mr. and Mrs. William Osborne of 3 Barton Street and Broom Hall, with whom Miss Stoddart again stayed, when she came to London early in 1803.

2. Lamb and Stoddart.

3. Unidentified.

PART V

Letters 141–187
16 Mitre Court Buildings, Inner Temple
February 19, 1803 — December 25, 1805

141. *C. L. to Manning*

London
19th February 1803

My dear Manning,

The general scope of your letter[1] afforded no indications of insanity, but some particular points raised a scruple. For God's sake don't think any more of 'Independent Tartary.' What have you to do among such Ethiopians? Is there no *lineal descendant* of Prester John?

Is the chair empty? Is the sword unswayed?[2]—depend upon't they'll never make you their king, as long as any branch of that great stock is remaining. I tremble for your Christianity. They'll certainly circumcise you. Read Sir John Mandevil's travels to cure you, or come over to England. There is a Tartarman now exhibiting at Exeter Change. Come and talk with him, and hear what he says first. Indeed, he is no very favorable specimen of his Countrymen! But perhaps the best thing you can do, is to *try* to get the idea out of your head. For this purpose repeat to yourself every night, after you have said your prayers, the words Independent Tartary, Independent Tartary, two or three times, and associate with them the *idea of oblivion* ('tis Hartley's method[3] with obstinate memories), or say, Independent, Independent, have I not already got an *Independence?* That was a clever way of the old puritans—pun-divinity. My dear friend, think what a sad pity it would be to bury such *parts* in heathen countries, among nasty, unconversable, horse-belching, Tartar people! Some say, they are Cannibals; and then conceive a Tartar-fellow *eating* my friend, and adding the *cool malignity* of mustard and vinegar! I am afraid 'tis the reading of Chaucer has misled you; his foolish stories about Cambuscan and the ring, and the horse of brass.[4] Believe me, there's no such things, 'tis all the poet's *invention;* but if there were such *darling* things as old Chaucer sings, I would *up* behind you on the Horse of Brass, and frisk off for Prester John's Country. But these are all tales; a Horse of Brass never flew, and a King's daughter never talked with Birds! The Tartars, really, are a cold, insipid, smouchey set. You'll be sadly moped (if you are not eaten) among them. Pray *try* and cure yourself. Take Hellebore[5] (the counsel is Horace's, 'twas none of my thought

originally). Shave yourself oftener. Eat no saffron, for saffron-eaters contract a terrible Tartar-like yellow. Pray, to avoid the fiend. Eat nothing that gives the heart-burn. *Shave the upper lip.* Go about like an European. Read no books of voyages (they're nothing but lies) : only now and then a Romance, to keep the fancy *under.* Above all, don't go to any sights of *wild beasts. That has been your ruin.* Accustom yourself to write familiar letters on common subjects to your friends in England, such as are of a moderate understanding. And think about common things more. There's your friend Holcroft now, has written a play.[6] You used to be fond of the drama. Nobody went to see it. Notwithstanding this, with an audacity perfectly original, he faces the town down in a preface, that they *did like* it very much. I have heard a waspish punster say, 'Sir, why did you not laugh at my jest?' But for a man boldly to face me out with, 'Sir, I maintain it, you did laugh at my jest,' is a little too much. I have seen H. but once. He spoke of you to me in honorable terms. H. seems to me to be drearily dull. Godwin is dull, but then he has a dash of affectation, which smacks of the coxcomb, and your coxcombs are always agreeable. I supped last night with Rickman, and met a merry *natural* captain,[7] who pleases himself vastly with once having made a Pun at Otaheite in the O. language. 'Tis the same man who said Shakspeare he liked, because he was so *much of the Gentleman.* Rickman is a man 'absolute in all numbers.'[8] I think I may one day bring you acquainted, if you do not go to Tartary first; for you'll never come back. Have a care, my dear friend, of Anthropophagi! their stomachs are always craving. But if you do go among [them] pray contrive to *stink* as soon as you can that you may [not (?)] hang a [on (?)] hand at the Butcher's. 'Tis terrible to be weighed out for 5d. a-pound. To sit at table (the reverse of fishes in Holland), not as a guest, but as a meat.[9]

God bless you: do come to England. Air and exercise may do great things. Talk with some Minister. Why not your father?

God dispose all for the best. I have discharged my duty.

<div style="text-align: right">

Your sincere frd,

C. Lamb

</div>

MS: unrecovered. Text: Lucas (1935), I, 333–335. Also pub.: Talfourd (1837), I, 245–248; Sala, I, 377–380; Purnell, I, 377–380; Fitzgerald, II, 210–213; Hazlitt, I, 328–330; Ainger (1888), I, 194–196; Ainger (1900), II, 83–86; Macdonald, I, 238–240; Ainger (1904), I, 242–244; Harper, III, 102–105; Lucas

(1905), VI, 258–259; Lucas (1912), V, 266–268. Address, from Macdonald (as is "London" in the heading): Mr Manning,/Hotel de Paris,/Rue de la Loi, à Paris.

1. Of February 10, 1803, the last extant letter before the one postmarked May 12, 1806, when Manning sailed from Portsmouth for China. (See the *Manning-Lamb Letters*, pp. 90–92 and 94–95.) Prester John, or Presbyter Johannes, mentioned below, was a fabulous Christian potentate who according to Asiatic legend and various travel narratives—John Mandeville's among thèm (see Vol. I, Letter 48, note 5)—ruled remote regions in Asia and Africa from the twelfth to perhaps the beginning of the fourteenth century.

2. *Richard III*, IV, iv, 469.

3. An allusion to the doctrine of association as expounded by David Hartley, in his *Observations on Man* (1749).

4. In "The Squire's Tale," as is Canace (of whom Lamb writes below), the daughter of King Cambuscan. The tale is set in Tartary.

5. Used by the ancients as a remedy for mental disease. Horace, as Lamb points out following, counseled such a use for it, in *Satires*, II, iii, 82–87.

6. *A Tale of Mystery*, which was performed at Covent Garden on November 13, 1802, and published in the same year.

7. James Burney (1750–1821), the son of the musician and author Dr. Charles (1726–1814) and his first wife, the former Esther Sleepe (d. 1761); the brother of the novelist Frances, or Fanny, Burney, who became Madame d'Arblay (1752–1840), and of the classical scholar Dr. Charles (1757–1817); and the friend since 1802 of Rickman and Southey. James Burney entered the navy in 1764, sailed in 1772 with Captain James Cook on his second voyage, and in 1773 was promoted to lieutenant. In 1776 he joined Cook on his third voyage, and consequent to Cook's death in 1779 commanded the *Discovery* on its voyage back to England. He was confirmed as commander in 1780, elevated to captain in 1782, took part in the action off Cuddalore in 1783, and returned home in failing health and did not serve again. He thereafter gave his time to literature and the composition of such works as *A Chronological History of the Discoveries in the South Sea or Pacific Ocean* (1817), *A Chronological History of North-eastern Voyages of Discovery and of the Early Eastern Navigations of the Russians* (1819), and *An Essay on the Game of Whist* (1821). At the time of his death he was a rear admiral on the retired list. He is noticed in Lamb's "Barron Field's Poems" (*Works*, I, 197), as he is in this letter, as having punned in Tahiti. His sister the novelist Sarah Harriet Burney (1770?–1844) is celebrated in "Sonnet: To Miss Burney, on Her Character of Blanch in 'Country Neighbours,' a Tale" (V, 82–83). His wife, Sarah (d. 1832), was possibly the model for Mrs. Battle in "Mrs. Battle's Opinions on Whist" (II, 32–37). The marriage of their daughter, Sarah, or Sally, to her cousin John Thomas Payne of Pall Mall in 1821 is the subject of "The Wedding" (II, 239–243). Their son, Martin Charles (1788–1852), who became an attorney and a lifelong friend of the Lambs, and to whom Lamb dedicated the second volume of *Works* (1818), in the sonnet "To Martin Charles Burney, Esq." (V, 42), is recalled in "Detached Thoughts on Books and Reading" (II, 176). Articles on the Burneys by Winifred Woodham and Phyllis G. Mann are in the *CLSB* of May 1951, July 1952, November 1957, and March 1963.

8. *Paradise Lost*, VIII, 421.

9. As in Andrew Marvell's "The Character of Holland," lines 29–30: "The fish ofttimes the burgher dispossessed / And sat not as a meat but as a guest."

142. *C. L. to William Wordsworth, with a postscript from John Stoddart*

5th March 1803

Dear Wordsworth,

having a Guinea of your sister's left in hand,[1] after all your commissions, and as it does not seem likely that you will trouble us, as the phrase is, for some time to come, I send you a pound note, and with it the best things in the verse way, I have lit upon for many a day. I believe, they will be new to you. You know Cotton,[2] who wrote a 2d part to Walton's Angler. A volume of his miscellaneous poems is scarce. Take what follows from a poem call'd Winter. I omit 20 verses, in which a storm is described, to hasten to the best.—

21

Louder, and louder, still they* come,
Nile's Cataracts to these are dumb,
The Cyclops to these Blades are still,
Whose anvils shake the burning hill.

22

Were all the stars-enlighten'd skies
As full of ears, as sparkling eyes,
This rattle in the crystal hall
Would be enough to deaf them all.

23

What monstrous Race is hither tost,
Thus to alarm our British Coast,
With outcries such as never yet
War, or confusion, could beget?

24

Oh! now I know, them, let us home,
Our mortal Enemy is come,
Winter, and all his blustring train,
Have made a voyage o'er the main

27

With bleak, and with congealing winds,
The earth in shining chain he binds;
And still as he doth further pass,
Quarries his way with liquid glass.

28

Hark! how the Blusterers of the Bear
Their gibbous Cheeks in triumph tear,
And with continued shouts do ring
The entry of their palsied king!

29

The squadron, nearest to your eye,
Is his forlorn of Infantry;
Bow men of unrelenting minds,
Whose shafts are feather'd with the winds.

30

Now you may see his vanguard rise
Above the earthy precipice,
Bold Horse, on bleakest mountains bred,
With hail, instead of provend, fed.

31

Their lances are the pointed locks,
Torn from the brows of frozen rocks,
Their shields are chrystal as their swords,
The steel the rusted rock affords.—

32

See, the Main Body now appears!
And hark th' Æolian Trumpeters
By their hoarse levets do declare,
That the bold General rides there.

33

And look where mantled up in white
He sleds it, like the Muscovite.
I know him by the port he bears,
And his lifeguard of mountaineers.

34

Their caps are furr'd with hoary frosts,
The bravery their cold kingdom boasts;
Their spungy plads are milk white frieze,
Spun from the snowy mountain's fleece.

35

Their partizans are fine carv'd glass,
Fring'd with the morning's spangled grass;
And pendant by their brawny thighs
Hang cimetars of burnish'd ice.

38

Fly, fly, the foe advances fast.
Into our fortress let us haste,
Where all the roarers of the north
Can neither storm, nor starve, us forth.

39

There under ground a magazine
Of sovran juice is collar'd in,
Liquor that will the siege maintain,
Should Phoebus ne'er return again.

40

Tis that, that gives the poet rage,
And thaws the gelly'd blood of age,
Matures the young, restores the old,
And makes the fainting coward bold,

41

It lays the careful head to rest,
Calms palpitations in the breast,
Renders our live's misfortunes sweet,
And Venus frolic in the sheet.

42

Then let the chill Sciorocco blow,
And gird us round with hills of snow,
Or else go whistle to the shore,
And make the hollow mountains roar.

43

Whilst we together jovial sit
Careless, & crown'd with mirth & wit,
Where tho' bleak winds confine us home,
Our fancies thro' the world shall roam.

44

We'll think of all the friends we know,
And drink to all, worth drinking to;
When, having **drunk all thine & mine,**
We rather shall want health than wine!

45

But, where friends fail us, we'll supply
Our friendships with our Charity.
Men that remote in sorrows live,
Shall by our lusty bumpers thrive.

46

We'll drink the wanting into wealth,
And those that languish into health,
Th' afflicted into joy, th' opprest
Into security & rest.

47

The worthy in disgrace shall find
Favor return again more kind,
And in restraint who stifled lye,
Shall taste the air of liberty.—

48

The brave shall triumph in success,
The lovers shall have mistresses,
Poor unregarded virtue praise,
And the **neglected Poet** bays.—

49

Thus shall our healths do others good,
While we ourselves do all we wou'd,
For freed from envy, and from care,
What would we be, **but what we are?**

50

Tis the plump Grape's immortal juice,
That does this happiness produce,
And will preserve us free together,
Maugre mishance, or wind, & weather.

51

Then let old Winter take his course,
And roar abroad till he be hoarse,
And his lungs crack with ruthless ire,
It shall but serve to blow our fire.

52

Let him our little castle ply
With all his loud artillery,
Whilst sack & claret man the fort,
His fury shall become our sport.

53

Or let him **Scotland** take, & there
Confine the plotting Presbyter;
His zeal may freeze, whilst we kept warm
With love & wine can know no harm.—

How could Burns miss the series of lines from 42 to 49?—

There is also a long poem from the Latin[3] on the inconveniences of
old age. I c'ant set down the whole, tho' right worthy, having dedi-
cated the remainder of my sheet to something else. I just excerp here
& there, to convince you, if after this you need it, that Cotton was a
first rate. Tis old Gallus speaks of himself, once the delight of the
Ladies and Gallants of **Rome.**—

The beauty of my shape & face are fled,
And my revolted form bespeaks me dead,
For fair, and shining age, has now put on
A bloodles, funeral complexion.
My skin's dry'd up, my nerves unpliant are,
And my poor limbs my nails plow up & tear.
My chearful eyes now with a constant spring
Of tears bewail their own sad suffering;

And those soft lids, that once secured my eye
Now rude, & bristled grown, do drooping lie,
Bolting mine eyes, as in a gloomy cave,
Which there on furies, & grim objects, rave.
Two'uld fright the full-blown Gallant to behold
The dying object of a man so old.
And can you think, that once a man he was,
Of human reason who no portion has.
The letters split, when I consult my book,
And every leaf I turn does broader look.
In darkness do I dream I see the light,
When light is darkness to my perishd sight.

 * * * *

Is it not hard we may not from men's eyes
Cloak, & conceal Age's indecencies.
Unseeming spruceness th' old man discommends,
And in old men, only to live, offends.

 * * * *

How can I him a living man believe,
Whom light, & air, by whom he panteth, grieve;
The gentle sleeps, which other mortals ease,
Scarce in a winter's night my eye-lids seize.

 * * *

The boys, & girls, deride me now forlorn,
And but to call me, Sir, now think it scorn.
They jeer my countnance, & my feeble pace,
And **scoff that nodding head,** that awful was.

 * * * * *

A Song written by Cowper which in stile is much above his usual,
and emulates in noble plainness any old balad I have seen. Hayley has
just published it &c. with a Life.—[4] I di[d] not think Cowper *up*
to it.—

Song
On the Loss of the Royal George—

Toll for the Brave!
The Brave, that are no more!

All sunk beneath the wave,
Fast by their native shore.—

2

Eight hundred of the Brave,
 Whose courage well was tried,
Had made the vessel heel,
 And laid her on her side.

3

A Land breeze shook the shrouds,
 And she was over set;
Down went the Royal George,
 With all her sails complete.

4

Toll for the Brave!
 Brave Kempenfelt is gone:
His last sea-fight is fought;
 His work of glory done.—

5

It was not in the battle,
 No tempest gave the shock;
She sprang no fatal leak;
 She ran upon no rock. .

6

His sword was in its sheath;
 His fingers held the pen,
When Kempenfelt went down,
 With twice four hundred men.

7

Weigh the vessel up!
 Once dreaded by our foes!
And mingle with the cup
 The tear that England owes.

8

Her timbers yet are sound,
 And she may float again,

Full charg'd with England's thunder,
And plow the distant main

9

But Kempenfelt is gone,
His victories are oer;
And he, and his eight hundred,
Shall plow the wave no more.

In your obscure part of the world, which I take to be ultima Thule, I thought these verses out of Books which cannot be accessible, would not be unwelcome. Having room, I will put in an Epitaph[5] I writ for a *real occasion,* a year or two back.

On Mary Druit who died
aged 19.

Under this cold marble stone
Sleep the sad remains of **One,**
Who, when alive, by few or none

2

Was lov'd, as lov'd she might have been,
If she prospr'ous days had seen,
Or had thriving been, I ween.

3

Only this cold funeral stone
Tells, she was belov'd by One,
Who on the marble graves his moan.[6]

I conclude with Love to your Sister & Mrs. W.—

Yours affecty.
C Lamb

Mary sends Love &c.

On consulting Mary, I find it will be foolish inserting the Note, as I intended, being so small, and as it is possible, you *may*[7] have to *trouble* us again e'er long; so it shall remain to be settled hereafter. However, the verses sha'nt be lost.

N. B. all **orders** executed with fidelity & punctuality by C & M Lamb

I beg to open this for a minute to add my remembrances to you all, and to assure you I shall ever be happy to hear from or see, much more to be useful to any of my old friends, at Grasmere

J Stoddart

A *lean* paragraph of the Docto[r]'s.

C Lamb

*the winds

MS: University of Texas Library. Pub.: Harper, III, 107–115; Lucas (1905), VI, 262–268; Lucas (1912), V, 270–277; Lucas (1935), I, 337–344. Address: Mr. Wordsworth/Grasmere/near Ambleside/Westmoreland. Postmark: March 5, [180]3.

1. Apparently from the money Dorothy Wordsworth had left with Mary for purchases while Miss Wordsworth was in London between February 23 and the date of this letter. See *Wordsworths' Letters*, I, 385.

2. Charles Cotton (1630–1687), from whose "Winter," published in Cotton's *Poems on Several Occasions* (1689), Lamb quotes below. Wordsworth subsequently quoted from the same poem, in his Preface to the 1815 edition of *Lyrical Ballads*, and Coleridge commended Cotton's pure style in the *Biographia Literaria* (1817). Cotton's addition to Izaak Walton's *The Compleat Angler* (1653), an addition called "The Second Part of the Compleat Angler, Being Instructions How to Angle for a Trout or Grayling In a Clear Stream," first appeared in the edition of 1676.

3. One of Cotton's "Translations out of Several Poets," here a translation from the Roman poet Gallus Cornelius (ca. 70–26 B.C.), titled "Ch. Cornelii Galli; vel potius Maximiani Elegia I" in the first (1689) edition of Cotton's *Poems on Several Occasions*, pp. 600–607. Lamb, below, quotes lines 135–154, 185–188, 259–262, and 304–307.

4. William Hayley's *The Life and Posthumous Writings of W. Cowper* (2 vols., 1803; Vol. III, 1804; Vol. IV, 1806). Cowper's song laments the loss of Rear Admiral Richard Kempenfelt (1718–1782) and the at least eight hundred crewmen and passengers who perished with him when the *Royal George* went down under his command while being refitted at Spithead on August 29, 1782, before she was to have proceeded to Gibraltar. The precise cause of her sinking remains uncertain, but it is known that she developed a leak a few inches beneath her water line, was slightly heeled over by running her guns on the opposite side so that the leak could be repaired, and was either overturned by a sudden breeze or broke up with the shifting of her weight. Whatever the reason, a large section of her bottom came loose and she sank almost instantly.

5. See Letter 124, note 1.

6. Twelve canceled lines follow.

7. Underscored twice.

143. *C. L. to Manning*

dear Manning,

I send you some verses I made on the death of a young Quaker[1] (you may have heard me speak of as being in love with for some years, while I lived at Pentonville, tho' I had never spoken to her in my life). She died about a month since. If you have interest with the Abbe de Lisle! you may get 'em translated. He has done as much for the Georgics.—

What think you of destroying Xtianity by some such familiar couplets as these; easy to be remember'd from their briefness, and affecting from their particularity, Videlicet————

> Among those whom by the Prophet's command the Bears eat up
> Was pretty little Master Jacky Jupp.—

Such things come home to a parent's bosom.—

Yours &c.—
C Lamb

Hester Savory.—
When maidens such as Hester die,
Their place ye may not well supply,
Though ye among a thousand try
 With vain endeavor.

A month or more hath she been dead,
Yet cannot I by force be led
To think upon the wormy bed,
 And her together.

A springy motion in her gait,
A rising step, did indicate
Of pride and joy no common rate,
 That **flush'd** her spirit.

I know not by what name beside
I shall it call; if twas not pride,

It was a joy to *that* allied,
 She did inherit.

Her parents held the Quaker rule,
Which doth the human feeling cool;
But she was train'd in Nature's school;
 Nature had blest her.—

A waking eye, a prying mind,
A heart that stirs, is hard to bind;
A hawk's keen sight ye cannot blind;
 Ye could not Hester's!

My sprightly neighbour! gone before
To that unknown and silent shore,
Shall we not meet? as heretofore,
 Some summer morning,

When from thy chearful eyes a ray
Hath struck a bliss upon the day,
A bliss that would not go away;
 A sweet forewarning!

MS: Huntington Library. Pub.: Sala, I, 382–383; Purnell, I, 382–383; Fitz-gerald, II, 215–216; Hazlitt, I, 333; Ainger (1888), I, 198; Ainger (1900), II, 87; Macdonald, I, 241; Ainger (1904), I, 244; Harper, III, 106–107; Lucas (1905), VI, 261; Lucas (1912), V, 269–270; Lucas (1935), I, 335–337. Address: Mr. Manning/Hotel de Paris/Rue de la loi/Paris. Postmark: [March] 23 [1803].

1. See Vol. I, Letter 87, note 5. The Abbé de Lisle, mentioned below, is Jacques Delille (1738–1813), poet, professor of Latin poetry at the Collège de France, abbot of Saint-Sévérin. He is best known for his *Les Géorgiques de Virgile, traduites en vers français* (1769), which in 1774, on the recommendation of Voltaire, gained him membership in the Académie française.

144. *C. L. to Coleridge*

[April 13, 1803]

My dear Coleridge,

Things have gone on better with me since you left me.—[1] I expect to have my old house-keeper home again in a week or two. She has mended most rapidly.— *My* health too has been better, since you took

away that Montero cap. I have left off cayenned eggs, and such bolsters to discomfort.— There was death in that cap. I mischievously wished that by some inauspicious jolt the whole contents might be shaken, and the coach set on fire. For you said they had that property. How the old Gentleman,[2] who joined you at Grantham, would have clapt his hands to his knees, and not knowing but it was an immediate visitation of God that burnt him, how pious it would have made him;—him I mean, that brought the Influenza with him, & only took places for one.— A damned old sinner, he must have known what he had got with him!— However I wish the cap no harm for the sake of the *head it fits,* & could be content to see it disfigure my healthy side-board again.—[3]

What do you think of smoking? I want your sober, *average, noon opinion* of it.— I generally am eating my dinner about the time I should determine it. Morning is a Girl, & c'ant smoke—she's no evidence one way or other.— & Night is so evidently *bought over,* that *he* ca'nt be a very upright Judge—. May be the truth is that *one* pipe is wholesome, *two* pipes toothsome, *three* pipes noisom, four *pipes* fulsom, *five* pipes quarrelsome, and thats the *sum* on't.— But that is deciding rather upon rhime than reason. . After all our instincts *may* be best.— Wine, I am sure, good mellow, generous, Port, can hurt no body, unless they take it to excess, which they may easily avoid, if they observe the **rules** of temperance——[4]

Bless you, old **Sophist,** who next to **Human Nature** taught me all the corruption I was capable of knowing.— And bless your Montero Cap, and your trail (which shall come after you whenever you appoint) & your wife & children, **Pi pos** especially.—

When shall we two smoke again?—.[5] Last night I had been in a sad quandary of spirits in what they call the evening, but a pipe, & some generous Port, and King Lear (being alone) had its effects as a remonstrance. I went to bed pot-valiant. By the way may not the **Ogles** of Somersetshire be remotely descended from King **Lear?**—[6]

Love to Sara ʃ and ask her what Gown she means by saying that Mary has got of hers. I know of none but what went with Miss Wordsworths things to Wordsth. & was paid for out of their money. I allude to a part which I may have read imperfectly in a Letter[7] of hers to you.—

<div align="right">C L</div>

MS: Huntington Library. Pub.: Talfourd (1848), I, 134–136; Sala, I, 145–147; Purnell, I, 145–147; Fitzgerald, I, 427–429; Hazlitt, I, 336–337; Ainger (1888), I, 201–202; Ainger (1900), II, 90–92; Macdonald, I, 243–245; Ainger (1904), I, 247–248; Harper, III, 118–120; Lucas (1905), VI, 268–269; Lucas (1912), V, 277–279; Lucas (1935), I, 344–345. Address: Mr Coleridge/Greta Hall/Keswick/Cumberland. Postmark: April 13, 1803.

1. Coleridge, who had been staying since February 20 at the home of the younger Josiah Wedgwood (see Vol. I, Letter 32, source note) at Gunville, Blandford, Dorsetshire, had left for London on March 14. There he had resided at least part of the time with the Lambs until the night of April 6 and returned to Keswick on the evening of April 8. On April 4 he had written to his wife of Lamb's "old house-keeper," Lamb's sister, Mary: "I had purposed not to speak of Mary Lamb—but I had better write it than tell it. The Thursday before last she met at Rickman's a Mr Babb [or Babbs—see Letter 207, at the reference to note 1], an old old Friend & Admirer of her Mother / the next day she *smiled* in an ominous way—on Sunday she told her Brother that she was getting bad, with great agony—on Tuesday morning [March 29] she layed hold of me with violent agitation, & talked wildly about George Dyer / I told Charles, there was not a moment to lose / and I did not lose a moment—but went for a Hackney Coach, & took her to the private Madhouse at Hogsden [Hoxton] / She was quite calm, & said—it was the best to do so—but she wept bitterly two or three times, yet all in a calm way. Charles is cut to the Heart" (*Coleridge's Letters,* II, 941; see also 934, 938, and 942). On March 30 Rickman wrote Southey that on the previous afternoon Lamb "came in somewhat abruptly, and at sitting down, shed some tears. . . . Poor Lamb recovered himself pretty well towards night, and slept at my house: he dines with me to-day, and then hopes that he will be steadied" (*Rickman,* p. 87). Mary was home again by May 20. A montero, a huntsman's, cap (see below) figures in Laurence Sterne's *Tristram Shandy,* Vol. VI, ch. xxiv.

2. From whom Coleridge had caught influenza on the coach ride from London to Keswick. See *Coleridge's Letters,* II, 942–943.

3. Four canceled lines follow. Two and one-half more are canceled following the third sentence below.

4. For Lamb's public expressions on smoking and drinking see "Confessions of a Drunkard" (*Works,* I, 133–139).

5. *Macbeth,* I, i, 1.

6. The pun is obvious, but in fact a Captain Nathaniel Ogle of Coleridge's army regiment had befriended Coleridge in March 1794, and in May of the same year signed the regiment's muster roll attesting that Coleridge had been discharged on April 10 by reason of insanity. See *Coleridge's Letters,* I, 71 and 76.

7. Unrecovered.

145. *C. L. to Coleridge*

[May 20, 1803]

Dr C.—

I do confess that I have not sent your books as I ought to be done. But you know how the human freewill is tethered, and that we perform promises to ourselves no better than to our friends. A watch is come for you. Do you want it soon, or shall I wait till some one travels

your way. You like me I suppose reckon the lapse of time from the waste thereof, as boys let a cock run to waste, too idle to stop it, and rather amused with seeing it dribble. Your poems[1] have begun printing. Longman sent to me to arrange them the old and the new together. It seems you have left it to him. So I classed them as nearly as I could, according to dates. First after the dedication (which must march first) and which I have transplanted from before the preface (which stood like a dead wall of prose between) to be the first Poem—then comes the **Pixies,** and the things most juvenile.— then on to Chatterton &c. on lastly to the Ode on Departn. Year & Musings which finish. Longman wanted the Ode first, but the arrangemt. I have made is precisely that mark'd out in the Dedication, following the order of time.— I told L. I was sure that you would omit a good portion of the first edition—I instanced in several sonnets &c.—but that was not his plan, and as you have done nothing in it, all I could do was to arrange 'em on the supposition that **all** were to be retained. A few I positively rejected, such as that of the *thimble,* & that of **flicker & flickers wife,** and that *not* in the manner of Spencer,[2] which you yourself had stigmatized.— &, the Man of Ross. I doubt whether I should this last. It is not too late to save it.— The first proof is only just come.— I have been forced to call that Cupid's Elixir **"Kisses."** It stands in your 1st V. as an Effusion.— So that instead of prefixing "the Kiss" to that of "one kiss dear maid &c." I have ventur'd to entitle it "to Sara." I am aware of the nicety of changing even so mere a trifle as a title to so short a piece, & subverting old associations, but **Two** called **"Kisses"** would have been absolutely ludicrous, & "effusion" is no name, & these poems come close together.— I promise you not to alter **one** word in any poem whatever, but to take your last text, where two are. Can you send any **wishes** about the book? Longman I think should have settled with you, but it seems you have left it to him. Write as soon as you possibly can, for without making myself responsible, I feel myself in some sort accessary to the selection, which I am to proof-correct. But I decidedly said to Biggs that I was sure you would omit more. Those I have positively rubbed off, I can swear to *individually* (except the M. of Ross, which is too familiar in Pope)[3] but no others.— You have your cue.— For my part I had rather all the juvenilia were kept memoriæ causa.—

Rob. Lloyd has written me a masterly Letter containing a character

of his father, see how different from Charles he views the old man
"literatim—my father smokes, repeats Homer in Greek & Virgil, & is
learning when from business with all the vigor of a young man Statian.[4]
He is really a wonderful man. He mixes Public & Private business, the
intricacies of discording life with his religion & devotion. No one more
rationally enjoys the romantic scenes of nature, & the chitchat & little
vagaries of his children; & tho' surrounded with an ocean of affairs, the
very neatness of his most obscure cupboard in the house passes not un-
noticed. I never knew any one view with such clearness, nor so well
satisfied with things as they are; & make such allowance for things
which must appear perfect Syriac to him."— by the last he means, the
Lloydisms of the younger branches.— His portrait of Charles (exact as
far as he has had opportunities of noting him) is most exquisite.—
"Charles is become steady as a Church, & as straitforward as a roman
road. It would distract him to mention any thing that was not as plain
as sense. He seems to have run the whole scenery of life, & **now rests
as the formal precision of non existence.**"— Here is genius, I think.—
and tis seldom a young man, a Lloyd, looks at a father (so differing)
with such good-nature, while he is alive.

<div align="center">write.—</div>

<div align="right">I am in post-haste
C L</div>

Love &c. to Sara P. & H.[5]
Mary sends love from home

MS: Huntington Library. Pub.: Talfourd (1848), I, 137–140; Sala, I, 143–
145; Purnell, I, 143–145; Fitzgerald, I, 425–427; Hazlitt, I, 333–335; Ainger
(1888), I, 199–201; Ainger (1900), II, 87–90; Macdonald, I, 241–243; Ainger
(1904), I, 245–247; Harper, III, 115–118; Lucas (1905), VI, 270–271; Lucas
(1912), V, 279–281; Lucas (1935), I, 346–348. Address: Mr Coleridge/Greta
Hall/Keswick/Cumberland. Postmark: M[ay] 20, 1803.
 1. *Poems* (1803), which Nathaniel Biggs was now printing for publication by
Longman and Rees and which Lamb, following to some extent the arrangement
of Coleridge's *Poems on Various Subjects* (1796) and to a greater extent Cole-
ridge's *Poems* (1797), was seeing through the press. The dedication, mentioned be-
low, is "To the Rev. George Coleridge of Ottery St. Mary, Devon. *With Some
Poems,"* which is also the dedicatory poem to *Poems* (1797).
 2. Those three poems are "The Silver Thimble. The Production of a Young
Lady [Coleridge's wife], Addressed to the Author [Joseph Cottle] of the Poems
Alluded to in the Preceding Epistle," "Written after a Walk before Supper," and
"Lines in the Manner of Spenser." The first two are not in *Poems* (1803). The
last and the "Man of Ross" are. The poem that Lamb retitled "Kisses" was in

My dear Wordsworth,

 If Gilpin's statement has afforded you any satisfaction, I can assure you that he was most explicit in giving it, and even seemed anxious (interrupting me) to do away any misconception. His statement is not contradicted by the last & fullest of the two Narratives, which have been published (the former being a mere transcript of the newspapers) which I would send you if I did not suppose that you would receive more pain from the unfeeling canting way in which it is drawn up, than satisfaction from its contents; and what relates to your brother in particular is very short. It states that your brother was seen talking to the First Mate but a few minutes before the ship sunk with apparent cheerfulness, & it contradicts the newspaper account about his depression of spirits procrastinating his taking leave of the Court of Directors; which the drawer up of the Narrative (a man high in the India House) is likely to be well informed of. It confirms Gilpin's account of his seeing your brother striving to save himself, & adds that "Webber, a Joiner, was near the Captain, who was standing on the hencoop when the ship went down, whom he saw washed off by a sea, which also carried him (Webber) overboard;—This is all which concerns your brother personally. But I will just transcribe from it, a Copy of Gilpin's account delivered in to the Court of Directors.—

"Memorandum respecting the Loss of the E. of A.—"

"At 10 A.M. being about 10 leagues to the Westward

IX. Facsimile of the first page of a letter from Charles Lamb to William Wordsworth, March 4, 1805 (Letter 172). Courtesy of the Humanities Research Center, The University of Texas at Austin.

the hope of sending you something from some of the
actual spectators, but I have been disappointed, & can
add nothing yet. Whatever I pick up, I will store for
you. . It is perfectly understood at the E. I. House,
that no blame whatever belongs to the Capt.ⁿ or Officers.
I can add no more but Mary's warmest love to
all. Write when you can write without trouble, do it,
for you are among the very chief of our interests
4 March –
Chamb.

Mr Wordsworth
Grasmere
near Ambleside
Westmorland

X. Facsimile of the fourth page of the letter of March 4, 1805.

1796 called Effusion XXVI and in 1797 "The Composition of a Kiss." That which he retitled "To Sara" was in 1796 called Effusion XXVIII and in 1797 "The Kiss."

3. In Pope's *Moral Essays*, "Epistle III. To Allen Lord Bathurst," lines 250–290. There Pope praised the charitable John Kyrle (1637–1724), the Man of Ross. The Latin below translates, "for the sake of memory."

4. Derived from the Latin poet Publius Papinius Statius (ca. 45–96).

5. "Pi-pos," or Derwent, and David Hartley.

146. *C. L. to Coleridge*

Saturday 27 [28] May 1803

My dear Coleridge,

the date of my last was one day prior to the receipt of your letter, full of foul omens. I explain this lest you should have thought mine too light a reply to such sad matter.— I seriously hope by this time you have given up all thoughts of journeying to the green islands of the blest, Voyages in time of war are very precarious, or at least that you will take them in your way to the Azores![1] Pray be careful of this letter till it has done its duty, for it is to inform you that I have booked off your watch (laid in cotton like an untimely fruit) and with it Condillac and all other books of yours which were left here. These set out on Monday next the 29th May by Kendal waggon from White horse Cripplegate. You will make seasonable enquiries, for a watch may'nt come your way again in a hurry.—

I have been repeatedly after Tobin,[2] and now hear that he is in the country; not to return till middle of June. I will take care & see him with the earliest. But cannot you write pathetically to *him*, enforcing a speedy mission of your books for literary purposes. He is too good a retainer to Literature to let her interests suffer thro' his default. And why in the name of Beelzebub are your books to travel from Barnard's Inn to the Temple, & thence circuitously to Cripplegate, when their business is to take a short cut down Holborn hill, up Snow do., on to Wood St. &c.—? the former mode seems a sad superstitious subdivision of labor.—

Well! the "Man of Ross" is to stand, Longman begs for it, the Printer stands with a wet sheet in one hand, and a useless Pica in the other, in tears pleading for it; I relent. Besides it was a Salutation poem, and has the mark of the beast "Tobacco" upon it. Thus much I have

done. I have swept off the lines about *widows* & *orphans* in 2d edition[3]
which (if you remember) you most awkwardly & illogically caused to
be inserted between two *If's* to the great breach & disunion of said *if's,*
which now meet again (as in 1st edition) like two clever Lawyers
arguing a case. Another reason for subtracting the pathos was, that— —
the Man of Ross is too familiar to need telling what he did, & especially
in worse lines than Pope told it: and it now stands simply as Reflec-
tions at an Inn about a known character, & sucking an old story into
an accommodation with present feelings.— Here is no breaking spears
with Pope! but a new, independent, & really a very pretty poem. In
fact tis as I us'd to admire it in the 1st vol. & I have even dared to
restore

 If neath this roof thy wine-chear'd moments pass
For Beneath this roof if thy cheard moments pass—[4]

"cheard" is a sad general word, "wine cheard" I'm sure you'd give me,
if I had a speaking trumpet to sound to you 300 miles. But I am your
fac totum, and that save in this instance which is a single case, & I
ca'nt get at you, shall be next to a **fac** nihil; at most a fac simile.—[5]
I have ordered "Imitation of Spencer" to be restored on Wordsworth's
authority. And now all that yo[u] will miss will be "Flicker & Flicker's
Wife" **the** "thimble" *"breathe dear harmonist"* and *I believe* "the
child that was fed with manna."— Another vol. will clear off all your
anthologic, morning-post-ian and epistolary miscellanies—but pray
dont put **Xtobel** therein.— dont **let** that **sweet** maid come forth at-
tended with Lady Holland's mob at her heels. Let there be a separate
vol of Tales, choice tales, ancient Mariners &c

 C L

 A Word of your health will be richly accept'ble

MS: Huntington Library. Pub.: Talfourd (1848), I, 141–144; Sala, I, 147–
149; Purnell, I, 147–149; Fitzgerald, II, 1–3; Hazlitt, I, 339–340; Ainger (1888),
I, 204–206; Ainger (1900), II, 95–98; Macdonald, I, 247–249; Ainger (1904), I,
250–252; Harper, III, 124–126; Lucas (1905), VI, 272–273; Lucas (1912), V,
282–283; Lucas (1935), I, 348–350. Address: Mr. Coleridge/Greta Hall/Keswick/
Cumberland. Postmark: May 28, 1803.

 1. From February to March Coleridge had expressed in his letters a desire to
accompany Thomas Wedgwood (see Vol. I, Letter 32, source note) to France,
Spain, and Italy. But poor health kept Coleridge in England, and Wedgwood left
on March 25 with another companion. It was probably the return of Wedgwood

on May 16—just as the war with France again broke out—and the account he would have given Coleridge of his travels that renewed Coleridge's desire for southern climates. "Condillac," below, refers to the *Logique* (1781) of Etienne Bonnot de Condillac (1715–1780), which Coleridge wished to examine in preparation for his proposed but never written "Organum verè Organum, or an *Instrument* of Practical Reasoning in the Business of Real Life." (See *Coleridge's Letters*, II, esp. 947.) "Monday next" was the thirtieth.

2. James Webbe Tobin (1767–1814). He was the eldest son of James Tobin (d. 1817), who was once of Bristol but had latterly become a planter on the island of Nevis, the West Indies. James Webbe Tobin was the brother of George (1768–1838), a naval officer advanced to rear admiral in 1837, and of the dramatist John (see Vol. I, Letter 90, note 3), and the friend of Coleridge and Wordsworth since 1797 named in a line Coleridge had written for the original version of Wordsworth's "We Are Seven." Failing eyesight prevented Tobin from entering the church after he was graduated from Wadham College, Oxford, in 1791. From 1795 to 1804 he resided with his brother John in London, assisting him with his dramas and contributing eight poems of his own to the second volume of Southey's *Annual Anthology*. In 1809 he left England for Nevis. He spent his remaining years there, in total blindness, superintending his father's plantation and working for the abolition of slavery. See *Wordsworths' Letters*, I, esp. 210.

3. Lines 9–14 in *Poems* (1797):
Friend to the friendless, to the sick man health,
With generous joy he view'd his modest wealth;
He hears the widow's heaven-breath'd prayer of praise,
He marks the shelter'd orphan's tearful gaze,
Or where the sorrow-shrivel'd captive lay,
Pours the bright blaze of Freedom's noon-tide ray.
The two *if*'s next referred to are in lines 5 and 15 in *Poems* (1797) and in lines 11 and 15 in the final version of the "Man of Ross."

4. The first line, line 11 in the final version of the poem, is in the texts of 1794 and 1803. The second line is in the texts of 1796, 1797, and 1828 and after.

5. The three Latin expressions translate, "do all," "do nothing," and "do like." The last two poems in the series following are "To the Rev. W. J. Hort while Teaching a Young Lady Some Song-tunes on His Flute" and "On the Christening of a Friend's Child." Coleridge took Lamb's advice and withheld "Christabel" and "The Rime of the Ancient Mariner." Lady Holland's Mob was formed of toughs, sometimes five thousand of them, who had assembled annually since the period of the Commonwealth at Smithfield on the eve of Bartholomew Fair to engage in rioting and outrageous lawlessness. William Hone, who characterized the mob in his *Every Day Book*, Vol. I, for September 5, 1825, stated that its size and activities had begun to decrease in about 1822.

147. *C. L. to Coleridge*

[June 1803]

By some fatality, unusual with me, I have mislaid the list of books which you want. Can you, from memory, easily supply me with another?

I confess to Statius,[1] and I detained him wilfully, out of a reverent regard to your style. Statius, they tell me, is turgid. As to that other

Latin book, since you know neither its name nor subject, your wants (I crave leave to apprehend) cannot be very urgent. Meanwhile, dream that it is one of the lost Decades of Livy.

Your partiality to me has led you to form an erroneous opinion as to the measure of delight you suppose me to take in obliging. Pray, be careful that it spread no further. 'Tis one of those heresies that is very pregnant. Pray, rest more satisfied with the portion of learning which you have got, and disturb my peaceful ignorance as little as possible with such sort of commissions.

Did you never observe an appearance well known by the name of the man in the moon? Some scandalous old maids have set on foot a report that it is Endymion.[2] Dr. Stoddart talks of going out King's Advocate to Malta. He has studied the Civil and Canon Law just three canon months, to my knowledge. *Fiat justitia, ruat cœlum.*

Your theory about the first awkward step a man makes being the consequence of learning to dance, is not universal. We have known many youths bred up at Christ's, who never learned to dance, yet the world imputes to them no very graceful motions. I remember there was little Hudson,[3] the immortal precentor of St. Paul's, to teach us our quavers: but, to the best of my recollection, there was no master of motions when we were at Christ's.

Farewell, in haste.

C. L.

MS: unrecovered. Text: Lucas (1935), I, 351–352. Also pub.: Talfourd (1837), I, 169–170; Sala, I, 113–114; Purnell, I, 113–114; Fitzgerald, I, 395–396; Hazlitt, I, 239–240; Ainger (1888), I, 119–120; Ainger (1900), I, 181–182; Macdonald, I, 146–147; Ainger (1904), I, 129–130; Harper, II, 233–234; Lucas (1905), VI, 165–166; Lucas (1912), V, 166–167. The month in which Lamb wrote this letter is indicated by its second paragraph, which is apparently in response to an acknowledgment by Coleridge that he had received the books Lamb had sent him on May 30.

1. Probably his *Silvae*. Coleridge quoted from it in his letter to Thomas Poole of December 26, 1796 (in *Coleridge's Letters*, I, 289, and *Coleridge's Poetical Works* [1912], II, 1113), dedicatory to the quarto (1796) edition of *Ode on the Departing Year*. The work referred to at the end of the paragraph is Livy's history of Rome, *Ab urbe condita libri*. It is divided into decades, many of which have been lost.

2. The lovely shepherd boy of Asia Minor beloved of Selene (or Artemis, Cynthia, Diana, and others associated with Selene), the goddess of the moon. The legend as it is usually told has Selene put Endymion into a profound sleep so that she might embrace him undisturbed. About Stoddart, mentioned following, his appointment and residence in Malta, see Vol. I, Letter 3, note 28. The Latin at the end of the paragraph translates, "Let justice be done though the heavens fall."

3. Robert Hudson (1731–1815), who in 1755 was appointed assistant organist

at St. Mildred's, London, and in 1756 made vicar-choral and in 1773 almoner and master of the children at St. Paul's. In 1784 he earned the Mus. Bac. degree at St. John's College, Cambridge. During a period that included the attendance of Lamb and Coleridge, Hudson served as music master of Christ's Hospital in addition to serving St. Paul's. He published a collection of songs called *The Myrtle* (1762) and church music.

148. *M. A. L. to Dorothy Wordsworth*

July 9th [1803]

My dear Miss Wordsworth

We rejoice with exceeding great joy to hear the delightful tidings[1] you were so *very* kind to remember to send us—I hope your dear sister is perfectly well, and makes an excellent nurse—are you not now the happiest family in the world.

I have been in better health and spirits this week past than since my last illness—I continued so long so very weak & dejected I began to fear I should never be at all comfortable again, I strive against low spirits all I can, but it is a very hard thing to get the better of.

I am very uneasy about poor Coleridge, his last letters are very melancholy ones, remember me affectionately to him & Sara, I hope you often see him—

Southey is in town, he seems as proud of his little girl[2] as I suppose your brother is of his boy, he says his home is now quite a different place to what it used to be—I was glad to hear him say this—it used to look rather chearless.

We went last week with Southey & Rickman & his sister[3] to Sadlers Wells, the lowest and most London-like of all our London amusements —the entertainments were Goody Two Shoes, Jack the Giant-Killer, and *Mary of Buttermere!* poor Mary was very happily married at the end of the piece, to a sailor her former sweetheart—we had a prodigious fine veiw of her fathers house in the vale of Buttermere—mountains very like large haycocks, and a lake like nothing at all: if you had been with us, would you have laughed the whole time like Charles & Miss Rickman or gone to sleep as Southey and Rickman did.

Stoddart is in expectation of going soon to Malta as Judges Advocate, it is likely to be a profitable situation, fifteen hundred a year or more— if he goes he takes with him his sister and as I hear from her as a very great secret a *wife;*[4] you must not mention this because if he stays in

England he may not be rich enough to marry for some years, I do not know why I trouble you with a secret which it seems I am unable to keep myself and which is of no importance to you to hear; if he succeeds in this appointment he will be in a great bustle for he must set out to Malta in a month, in the mean time he must go to Scotland to marry & fetch his wife and it is a match against her parents consent and they as yet know nothing of the Malta expedition; so that he expects many difficulties, but the young lady and he are determined to conquer them, he then must go to Salisbury to take leave of his father & mother who I pity very much, for they are old people and therefore are not very likely ever to see their children again.

Charles is very well and very *good* I mean very sober but he is very good in every sense of the word for he has been very kind and patient with me and I have been a sad trouble to him lately, he had shut out all his friends because he thought company hurt me, and done every thing in his power to comfort & amuse me, we are to go out of town soon[5] for a few weeks when I hope I shall get quite stout and lively.

You saw Fenwick when you was with us, perhaps you remember his wife and children were with his brother a tradesman at Penzance, he (the brother) who was supposed to be in a great way of business has become a bankrupt, they are now at Penzance without a home & without money; and poor Fenwick who has been Editor of a country newspaper lately is likely soon to be quite out of employ; I am distresed for them for I have a great affection for Mrs Fenwick.

how pleasant your little house and orchard must be now, I almost wish I had never seen it, I am always wishing to be with you, I could sit upon that little bench in idleness [all] day long. When you have a leisure hour, a letter from y[ou,] kind friend will give me the greatest pleasure—

We have money of yours and I want you to send me so[me] commission to lay it out are you not in want of anything.

I believe when we go out of town it will be to Margate—I love the seaside and expect much benefit from it, but your mountain scenery has spoiled us we shall find the flat country of the Isle of Thanet very dull.—

Charles joins me in love to your brother & sister and the little John, I hope you are building more rooms, Charles said I was so long answering your letter Mrs Wordsworth would have another little one before

you received it. our love and compliments to our kind Molly,[6] I hope she grows younger & happier every day—when, and where, shall I ever see you again, not I fear a very long time, you are too happy ever to wish to come to London—when you write tell me how poor Mrs Clarkson does.

God bless you & yours

<div align="right">I am your affectionate friend

M Lamb</div>

MS: University of Texas Library. Pub.: Harper, III, 126–130; Lucas (1905), VI, 274–276; Lucas (1912), V, 284–286; Lucas (1935), I, 352–354. Address: Miss Wordsworth/Grasmere/Westmorland. Postmark: July 11, 1803.

1. Of the birth on June 18 of the Wordsworths' son John (d. 1875), who would become a parish clergyman.

2. Margaret, who had been born on August 31, 1802, and would die at the end of August 1803.

3. Mary Rickman, according to *Rickman,* pp. 89, 162, and 327. All three of the entertainments mentioned below—the full title of the last is *Edward and Susan; or, the Beauty of Buttermere*—had been published by 1803. Their author, Charles Isaac Mungo Pitt Dibdin, known as Charles Dibdin, the younger (1768–1833), became a proprietor and the acting manager of Sadler's Wells. He was the elder son of the dramatist and song writer Charles Dibdin (1745–1814) and his mistress, Harriet Pitt, a dancer at Covent Garden who adopted the stage name Mrs. Davenet when Dibdin deserted her in 1774. The younger Dibdin was the brother of the actor and dramatist Thomas John (1771–1841) and the father of the musician Henry Edward (1813–1866) and of Lamb's later correspondent John Bates Dibdin. Mary of Buttermere was Mary Robinson, a beautiful Cumberland girl whom the cheat John Hatfield (1758?–1803) duped into marrying him on October 2, 1802, by assuming a fictitious name and a number of titles. He was convicted of forgery and deceit at Carlisle on August 15 and hanged on September 3, 1803. Funds were raised for her. She became the subject of many writings, including three by Coleridge, in the *Morning Post* of October 11, 22, and November 5, 1802. She ultimately settled into obscurity as the wife of a farmer.

4. Isabella Moncreiff (see Vol. I, Letter 3, note 28), who became Stoddart's wife within the next few weeks.

5. From July 18 to August 3, it would appear from the next two letters, and not to Margate, as Mary supposes below, but to Cowes, Isle of Wight, with the Burneys. It is first John and then Thomas Fenwick of whom Mary writes in her next paragraph.

6. Molly, or Mary, Fisher (1741?–1808), who lived with her brother John Fisher (1746?–1820) and his wife, the former Agnes Mackereth (d. 1804), across the road from Dove Cottage and had served the Wordsworths since December 1799. (See *Wordsworths' Letters,* I, 275.) Catherine (Mrs. Thomas) Clarkson, mentioned below, had gone or in a few days would go to her parents' home in Bury St. Edmunds to recover her health.

149. *C. L. to Rickman*

Saturday morning 16. July [1803]

Dear Rickman,

I enclose you a wonder, a letter from the shades.[1] A dead body wants to return, and be inrolled inter vivos. Tis a gentle ghost, and in this Galvanic age it may have a chance.

Mary and I are setting out for the Isle of Wight. We make but a short stay, and shall pass the time betwixt that place and Portsmouth, where Fenwick is. I sadly wanted to explore the **Peak**[2] this summer, but Mary is against steering without card or compass, and we should be at large in Darbyshire.—

We shall be at home this night and tomorrow, if you can come and take a farewell pipe.

I regularly transmitted your notices to the Morning Post, but they have not been duly honoured. The fault lay not in me.

Yours truly

C Lamb

MS: Huntington Library. Pub.: Purnell, II, 88; Fitzgerald, III, 9; Hazlitt, I, 341; Ainger (1888), I, 206; Ainger (1900), II, 98; Macdonald, I, 249; Ainger (1904), I, 252; Harper, III, 130; Lucas (1905), VI, 277; Lucas (1912), V, 287; Lucas (1935), I, 355. Address: John Rickman Esqr/New Palace Yard/Westminster. Postmark: July 16, 1803.

1. Probably from Burnett, who, having quarreled with Rickman and Southey earlier in the year, had at about this time sent a circular letter to his friends "announcing his recovery from 'mental distortion,' and asking Rickman for a place under the Government" (*Rickman*, p. 90). Although Rickman wrote Southey that he wanted nothing further to do with Burnett, Rickman arranged for Burnett's free tuition at Westminster Hospital when on July 28 Southey requested him (*New Southey Letters*, I, 321–322) to do what he could to satisfy Burnett's ambition to become a naval surgeon. The Latin in the next sentence translates, "among the living."

2. Camden, presumably. See Letter 133, note 2.

150. *C. L. to Rickman, written on the following letter from James Burney to Rickman*

[Cowes, Isle of Wight]
27 July 1803[1]

Dear Rickman

We are at Cowes, the whole flock, Sheep and Lambs—and in good pasturage—for notwithstanding that I joined or rather acquiesced in your dispraise of Cowes, in a dry summer like this it is a very pleasant place. We were much harassed by hot travelling and uncertainties till we fixed at this haven, and now I could feel myself thoroughly well disposed to indulge in a week of compleat idleness, if my senses were not invaded by the din of preparation, and the account which every day's paper brings of the universal bustle that prevails every where. We purpose however to stay here one week longer reckoning from this date, and then to return to the defence of the Capital after so well having guarded the Sea Coast. We have visited Newport and Carisbrook Castle where we saw a deep well and a cross old woman. We went by water and friend Lamb (to give a specimen of his Seamanship) very ingeniously and unconsciously cast loose the fastenings of the mast, so that Mast, sprit, sails, and all the rest tumbled overboard with a crash, and not less to his surprise than to the surprise of every other person in the boat. I doubt whether any of us will muster up sufficient activity to go to the South part of the Island. We do every thing that is idle, such as reading books from a circulating library, sauntering, hunting little crabs among the rocks, reading Church Yard poetry whh. is as bad at Cowes as any Church Yard in the Kingdom can produce. Miss Lamb is the only person among us who is not idle. All the cares she takes into her keeping. At Night however we do a little business in the smoking line, and Martin endeavours to make Conundrums, but alas! he is not equal to the atchievement. Such is the edifying life we lead at the Isle of Wight. Let us know how you take care of the Capital. An old sea saying is, 'Give a sprat to catch a Mackarel,' So pray send us your Mackarel and accept this sprat.

From the White Isle[2]

(date unknown) [July ?27]

I testify that this is a pretty good outline of our doings, but the filling it up requires the hand of a master. A volume might be made of Martins Blunders which parental tenderness omits. Such as his letting the packet boat's boat go without him from the quay at Southampton, while he stood hiatusing, smit with the love of a Naiad; his tumbling back over a stone twice the height of himself, and daubing himself; his getting up to bathe at six o Clock, and forgetting it, and in consequence staying in his room in a process of annihilation &c. &c. Then the time expended in *Martin being scolded* would serve as great a sinner as Judas to repent in. In short nothing in this house goes right till after supper, then a gentle circumambience of the weed serves to shut out Isle of Wight impertinent scenery and brings us back in fancy to Mutton Lane and the romantic alleys ever green of nether Holborn, green that owes nothing to grass, but the simple effect of cabbage water, tripe-cauls, children's st——s &c. .

The fact of my setting the mast upside down is partly true. Indeed it was never properly nailed down, or the accident could not have happened.— Capt Burney does nothing but teach his children bad habits. He surfeits them with cherries and black currents till they can eat no supper & then claps down the fruit expended to the common stock, and deducts what the surfeit saves from his part. There's a little girl[3] he's brought with him that has cost I dont know what in codlings.— No ordinary orchard would be a jointure for her. [Had all her sex been proportionate devourers of] apples, God would [have] saved by keeping them in Paradise.— To add to our difficulties Martin has brought down a Terence, which he renders out loud into canine Latin at Breakfast & other meals, till the eyes of the infatuated Parent let slip water for joy, and the ears of every body beside shed their wax for being tired. More I could add but it is unsafe.

C Lamb

MS: Huntington Library. Pub.: Ainger (1904), I, 253–255; Harper, III, 131–133; Lucas (1935), I, 356–357. Address: John Rickman Esqr.
1. From Burney.
2. From Lamb.

3. Unidentified. Codlings, mentioned below, are apples, a codling being a variety. The bracketed locutions, supplied from Lucas (1935), I, 357, are obscured by mending tape on the manuscript.

151. *M. A. L. to Sarah Stoddart*

Wednesday [September 21, 1803]

My dear Sarah

I returned home from my visit[1] yesterday, and was much pleased to find your letter, for I have been very anxious to hear how you were going on.— I could hardly help expecting to see you when I came in: yet though I should have rejoiced to have seen your merry face again, I believe it was better as it was—upon the whole, and all things considered, it is certainly better you should go to Malta.[2]

The terms you are upon with your Lover does (as you say it will) appear wondrous strange to me, however, as I cannot enter into your feelings, I certainly can have nothing to say to it, only th[a]t I sincerely wish you happy in your own way, however odd that way may appear to me to be. I would begin now to advise you to drop all correspondence with William but, as I said before, as I cannot enter into your feelings, and views of things, *your ways not being my ways,*[3] why should I tell you what I would do in your situation. So child take thy own ways and God prosper thee in them.

One thing my advising spirit must say—use as little *Secresy* as possible, and as much as possible make a friend of your sister-in-law——you know I was not struck with her at first sight, but upon your account, I have watched and marked her very attentively: and while she was eating a bit of cold mutton in our kitchen, we had a serious conversation, from the frankness of her manner I am convinced she is a person I could make a friend of, why should not you? We talked freely about you: she seems to have a just notion of your character, and will be fond of you, if you will let her.

My father had a sister lived with us, of course lived with my Mother her sister-in-law, they were in their different ways the best creatures in the world—but they set out wrong at first. They made each other miserable for full twenty years of their lives—my Mother was a perfect gentlewoman, my Aunty as unlike a gentlewoman as you can possibly

imagine a good old woman to be, so that my dear Mother (who though
you do not know it, is always in my poor head and heart) used to dis-
tress and weary her with incessant & unceasing attentions, and polite-
ness to gain her affection, The **Old woman** could not return this in
kind, and did not know what to make of it—thought it all deceit, and
used to hate my Mother with a bitter hatred, which of which of course
was soon returned with interest, a little frankness and looking into each
others characters at first would have spared all this, and they would
have lived as they died fond of each other, for the last few years of their
life when we grew up & harmonised them a little they sincerely loved
each other. My Aunt & my Mother were wholly unlike you and your
sister,[4] yet in some degree theirs is the secret history I believe of all
sisters-in-law—and you will smile when I tell you I think myself the
only woman in the world, who could live with a brothers wife, and
make a real friend of her. partly from [e]arly observation of the un-
happy example I have just given you, and partly from a knack I know
I have of looking into peoples real characters, and never expecting
them to act out of it—never expecting another to do as I would do in
the same case. When you leave your Mother and say if you never shall
see her again you shall feel no remorse, and when you make a *jewish*
bargain with your *Lover*, all this gives me no offence, because it is your
nature, and your temper, and I do not expect or want you to be
otherwise than you are, I love you for the good that is in you, and look
for no change.

But, certainly you ought to struggle with the evil that does most
easily beset you—a total want of politeness in behaviour, I would say
modesty of behaviour, but that I should not convey to you my idea of
the word modesty, for I certainly do not mean you want *real modesty,*
and what is usually called false, [o]r mock modesty, is [a qua]llity I
certainly do not wish you to possess; yet I trust you know what I mean
well enough.

Secresy, though you appear all frankness, is certainly a grand failing
of yours, it is likewise your *brothers* and therefore a family failing——
by secrecy I mean you both want the habit of telling each other at the
moment everything that happens,—where you go—and what you
do——that free communication of letters and opinions, just as they
arise, as Charles and I do, and which is after all the only groundwork
of [any (?)][5] friendship—your brother I will answer fo[r . . .] will

never tell his wife or his sister all tha[t is in (?)] his mind—he will receive letters and not s[. . .] this is a fault Mrs Stoddart can never te[ll him (?)] of, but she can, and will feel it, thoug[h on] the whole and in [ever]y other respect she i[s. . .] happy with him.— Begin for Gods sake a[t the] first and tell her every thing that passes—at first she may hear you with indifference, but in time this will gain her affection and confidence.— Show her all you[r] letters (no matter if she does not show hers). It is a pleasant thing for a friend to put into ones hand a letter just fresh from the post. I would even say begin with shewing her this, but that it is written freely and loosely, and some apology ought to be made for it, which I know not how to make, for I must write freely or not at all.

If you do this, she will tell your brother you will say, and what then quotha'?—it will beget a freer communication amongst you, which is a thing devoutly to be wished.——⁶

God bless you, and grant you may preserve your integrity, and return unmarried and penniless, and make William a good and a happy wife

your affectionate friend

M Lamb

Charles is very unwell, & my head aches, he sends his love, mine with my best wishes to your brother & sister.

I hope I shall get another letter from you.

MS: The Pierpont Morgan Library, New York. Pub.: Harper, III, 134–138; Lucas (1905), VI, 278–280; Lucas (1912), V, 288–291; Lucas (1935), I, 358–360. Address: Miss Stoddart/Dr Stoddart's/Ryde/Isle of Wight/To be left at the post office. Postmark: September 21, 1803.

1. Where is not known, but it becomes evident that the Stoddarts had recently visited the Lambs.

2. She did go, to join there her brother and his bride. The lover of Miss Stoddart referred to below was a Mr. Turner, who had succeeded (the unidentified) William. For an account of her attempts to find a husband before she found Hazlitt and of her cynical and financial approach to the institution of marriage generally, see John R. Barker, "Some Early Correspondence of Sarah Stoddart and the Lambs," *Huntington Library Quarterly*, 24 (1960), esp. 62–65. The expression "wondrous strange" is borrowed from *Hamlet*, I, v, 164.

3. Isaiah 55:8.

4. Properly sister-in-law, here and elsewhere. Sarah Stoddart had no sister.

5. The edge of the paper has been torn away. With it went one or two words at the ends of this line and each of the next seven lines.

6. *Hamlet*, III, i, 63.

152. *C. L. to Godwin*

[Monday, November 7, 1803]

Dr Sir

On wednesday we cannot possibly come, and we shall certainly be engaged for one day between that & sunday, what day is uncertain.—

So if you please, we will let the matter stand over till *Sunday,* on which day-evening you may expect us, if we hear nothing from you to the contrary.—

I have been strangely hindered in the review.[1] I set to it in earnest yesterday morning, & rap rap came a knock, & one of the Lloyds (whom you know I love!) from Birmingham, & no more business could be done that day.— But you shall certainly see the review before you see the reviewr.

Yours

C Lamb

MS: Lord Abinger. Pub.: Lucas (1935), I, 363. Address: Mr. Godwin/Polygon/ Somers-town. Postmark: November 7, 1803.

1. Which Lamb did not succeed in writing of Godwin's *The Life of Geoffrey Chaucer, the Early English Poet; Including Memoirs of His Near Friend and Kinsman, John of Gaunt, Duke of Lancaster: With Sketches of the Manners, Opinions, Arts and Literature of England in the Fourteenth Century.* Its first two volumes had come out in October 1803. Its final two volumes would come out in 1804. Lamb reveals in the next three letters the irritation the aborted review caused him, but never the name of the Lloyd, referred to below, who first hindered his formation of it.

153. *C. L. to Godwin*

Tuesday 8th Novr 1803

My dear Sir,

I have been sitting down for three or four days successively to the review which I so much wished to do well & to your satisfaction. But I can produce nothing but absolute flatness and nonsense. My health and spirits are so bad, and my nerves so irritable, that I am sure, if I persist, I shall teaze myself into a fever.— You do not know how sore and weak a brain I have, or you would allow for many things in me, which

you set down for whims. I solemnly assure you that I never more wished to prove to you the value which I have for you, than at this moment; but although in so seemingly trifling a service, I cannot get through with it. I pray you to impute it to this one sole cause, ill health. I hope I am above a subterfuge, and that you will do me this justice to think so.—

You will give me great satisfaction by sealing my pardon & oblivion in a line or two, before I come to see you, or I shall be too ashamed to come.—

<div align="right">Yours with great truth
C Lamb</div>

MS: Lord Abinger. Pub.: Hazlitt, I, 342; Ainger (1888), I, 207; Ainger (1900), II, 99; Macdonald, I, 250; Ainger (1904), I, 255; Harper, III, 138–139; Lucas (1905), VI, 281; Lucas (1912), V, 291; Lucas (1935), I, 360–361.

154. *C. L. to Godwin*

[November 10, 1803]

Dr. *Godwin*

You never made a more unlucky and perverse mistake than to suppose that the reason of my not writing that cursed thing was to be found in your book.— I assure you most sincerely that I have been even greatly delighted with Chaucer. I may be wrong but I think there is one considerable error runs through it which is a conjecturing spirit, a fondness for filling out the picture by supposing what Chaucer did and how he felt, where the materials are scanty.— So far from meaning to withhold from you (out of mistaken tenderness) this opinion of mine, I plainly told Mrs. Godwin that I did find *a fault*, which I would reserve naming until I should *see you* and *talk it over*. This she may very well remember, and also that I declined naming this fault, until she drew it from me by asking me, if there was not too much fancy in the work. I then confessed generally what I felt, but refused to go into particulars, till I had seen you.— I am never very fond of saying things before third persons, because in the relation (such is human nature) something is sure to be dropt. If Mrs. G. has been the cause of your misconstruction, I am very angry, tell her: yet it is not an **anger unto** death—

I remember also telling Mrs. G. (which she may have *dropt*) that I

was by turns considerably more delighted than I expected. But I wished
to reserve all this till I saw you. I even had conceived an expression to
meet you with, which was *thanking* you for some of the most exquisite
pieces of criticism I had ever read in my life.— In particular I should
have brought forward *that* on Troilus and Cressida, and Shakespear,[1]
which it is little to say delighted me and instructed me (if not absolutely
instructed me, yet put into *full-grown sense* many conceptions which
had arisen in me before in my most discriminating moods)— —all
these things I was preparing to say, and bottling them up till I came,
thinking to please my friend & host the author!—when lo! this deadly
blight intervened——

I certainly ought to make great allowances for your misunderstanding
me. You by long habits of composition, & a greater command gained
over your own powers, cannot conceive of the desultory & uncertain
way in which I (an author by fits) sometimes cannot put the thoughts
of a common letter into sane prose. Any work which I take upon myself
as an engagement, will act upon me to torment—e.g. when I have
undertaken, as 3 or 4 times I have, a school boy copy of verses[2] for
Merch. Taylor's boys at a guinea a copy, I have fretted over them, in
perfect inability to do them, & have made my sister wretched with my
wretchedness for a week together. The same, till by habit I have ac-
quired a mechanical command, I have felt in making paragraphs.—
As to reviewing in particular, my **head** is so whimsical a head, that I
cannot after reading another man's book, let it have been never so
pleasing, give any account of it, in any methodical way. I cannot follow
his train.— Something like this you must have perceiv'd of me in con-
versation. Ten thousand times I have confessed to you, talking of my
talents, my utter inability to remember in any comprehensive way what
I read.— I can vehemently applaud, or perversely stickle at *parts:* but
I cannot grasp at a whole. This infirmity (which is nothing to brag of)
may be seen in my two little compositions, the tale & my play.[3] In both
which no reader, however partial, can find *any story.*— I wrote such
stuff about Chaucer & got into such digressions, quite irreducible into
1 1/5 column of a paper, that I was perfectly *ashamed to shew it you.*
However it is become a serious matter that I should convince you, I
neither slunk from the task through a wilfull deserting neglect,— or
through any (most *imaginary* on your part) distaste of **Chaucer;** & I
will try my hand again, I hope with better luck. My health is bad &

my time taken up, but all I can spare between this & Sunday shall be employed for you, since you desire it.— & if I bring you a crude wretched paper on Sunday, you must burn it & forgive me; if it proves any thing better, than I predict, may it be a peace offering of sweet incense[4] between us.

<div align="right">C Lamb</div>

MS: Lord Abinger. Pub.: Hazlitt, I, 343–344; Ainger (1888), I, 207–209; Ainger (1900), II, 99–102; Macdonald, I, 250–252; Ainger (1904), I, 255–257; Harper, III, 139–142; Lucas (1905), VI, 281–283; Lucas (1912), V, 292–293; Lucas (1935), I, 361–363. Address: Mr. Godwin/Polygon/Somers-town. Postmark: November 10, 1803.

1. A canceled line and one-fifth follow.

2. Verses, which have not been recovered, that Lamb prepared for the students at the Merchant Taylors' School, London. Those students, according to Ainger (1904), I, 395, were permitted to seek outside assistance in constructing their weekly epigrams.

3. *Rosamund Gray* and *John Woodvil.*

4. The expression "sweet incense" is frequent in Exodus, in 25:6, for example. Other instances are in Leviticus 4:7 and 16:12, Numbers 4:16, and 2 Chronicles 2:4 and 13:11.

155. *C. L. to Godwin*

<div align="right">Monday night [November ?14, 1803]</div>

My dear Sir,

[I a]ssure you positively that what I had [begun] to write about Chaucer was so inconsider[able] that you could make no possible use of [i]t. I have it not, and if I could recover it, I should be extremely hurt to be obliged to shew it you.— I beg you to let the subject now rest, and unless you wish to teaze and vex me, that you will not mention it again. I hoped that I had said enough before.

<div align="right">Yours truly
C Lamb</div>

MS: Lord Abinger. Pub.: Lucas (1935), I, 363. The date is conjectured from the preceding letters. The bracketed locutions, supplied from Lucas (1935), I, 363, are obscured by a stain on the manuscript.

156. *C. L. to Rickman*

[January 13, 1804]

Dear Rickman,

You do not happen to have any place at your disposal which would suit a decayed literatus. I do not much expect that you have, or that you will go much out of your way to serve the object, when you hear it is *Fell.* But the case is, by a *mistaking* of his *turn,* as they call it, he is reduced I am afraid to extremities, and would be extremely glad of a place in an office. Now it does sometimes happen, that just as a man wants a place, a place wants him, and though this is a lottery to which none But G. Burnett would chuse to trust his all, there is no harm just to call in at Despair's office for a friend, and see if *his* number is **come up.** (Burnet's further case I inclose[1] by way of episode.)— Now if you should happen or anybody you know, to want a *hand,* here is a young man of solid but not brilliant genius, who would turn his hand to the making out dockets, penning a manifesto, or scoring a tally, not the worse (I hope) for knowing Latin & Greek and having in youth conv'rsed with the Philosophers. But of these follies I believe he thoroughly awakened, and would bind himself by a terrible oath never to imagine himself an extraordinary genius again.

Yours &

C Lamb

MS: Huntington Library. Pub.: Talfourd (1837), I, 282–283; Purnell, II, 89; Fitzgerald, III, 10; Hazlitt, I, 364–365; Ainger (1888), I, 223–224; Ainger (1900), II, 125–126; Macdonald, I, 272; Ainger (1904), I, 273–274; Harper, III, 200–201; Lucas (1905), VI, 332; Lucas (1912), V, 345–346; Lucas (1935), I, 332. Address: Jno Rickman Esqr/New Palace Yard/Westminstr. Postmark: January 13, 1804.

1. The enclosure has not been recovered.

157. *C. L. to Thomas Poole*

Temple
14 feb, 1804

Dear Sir

I am sorry we have not been able to hear of lodgings to suit young F.[1] but we will not desist in the enquiry. In a day or two something may turn up. Boarding houses are common enough, but to find a family where he would be safe from impositions within & impositions without is not so easy.—

I take this opportunity of thanking you for your kind attentions to the Lad I took the libery. of recommending. *His* mother was disposed to have taken in young F. but could not possibly make room

Your obliged &c
C Lamb

MS: British Museum. Pub.: Harper, III, 142–143; Lucas (1905), VI, 283–284; Lucas (1912), V, 294; Lucas (1935), I, 364. Address: T. Poole Esqr.
1. George Fricker (d. 1813), the brother of Mmes. Lovell, Southey, and Coleridge. Poole, Lamb, Southey, Coleridge, and Rickman were seeking lodgings and employment in London for him. Savary's Bank had employed him for several months in 1799–1800, Rickman now gave him temporary work on one of his statistical projects, and Coleridge seems to have obtained a clerk's position for him in April in the Sick and Wounded Office. (See Letter 167, note 7; *Coleridge's Letters,* I, 548, and II, 1064, 1067, and 1124; and *New Southey Letters,* II, 60.) The lad mentioned below has not been identified.

158. *C. L. to Coleridge*

[March 10, 1804]

Dr C.

I blunderd open this letter, its weight making me conjecture it held an inclosure; but finding it poetry (which is no man's ground, but waste & common) I perused it.— Do you remember that you are to come to us tonight?

C L

MS: University of Texas Library. Pub.: Harper, III, 143; Lucas (1905), VI, 284; Lucas (1912), V, 294; Lucas (1935), I, 364. Addresses, by Mrs. Coleridge:

⟨To/Mr. Lambe/India house/London⟩; by Lamb: Coleridge/Mr. Tobins/Barnards Inn/Holborn. Postmark: March 10, 1804. The note is written on the cover of an extract from Southey's *Madoc* that Coleridge had requested of Mrs. Coleridge in his letter to her of February 19, 1804. The date of his dinner with the Lambs Coleridge noted on one of the flyleaves of the 1659 selections in folio from Sir Thomas Browne's writings that Lamb, as Lamb also noted there, had purchased for Coleridge for the occasion. The book, whose title page is missing, is now in the New York Public Library. (See *Coleridge's Letters*, II, 1071 and 1080–1081.) Coleridge stayed with James Webbe Tobin until March 27, arrived in Portsmouth on March 28, and, seeking escape from the northern climate and home, sailed on the evening of April 8 from Spithead on board the *Speedwell* for Malta, to find work there and live with the Stoddarts. He lived with them until July 6. Then, not getting along with Stoddart, he moved into a suite of rooms in the governor's palace offered to him by Sir Alexander John Ball (1757–1809), a distinguished naval officer and the first governor of Malta. Coleridge became his private secretary from July 1804 to January 1805, his acting public secretary from January 18 to September 6, 1805, and wrote of him in *The Friend* (1809–1810).

159. *C. L. to Robert Lloyd*

Tuesday 13th March 1804

Dear Robert

I received your notes safe, and thank you for them. It seems you are about to be married.[1] Joy to you and uninterrupted satisfaction in that state. But who is the Lady? it is the character of your letters, that you omit facts, dates, names & matter, and describe nothing but feelings, in which as I cannot always partake, as being more intense in degree or different in kind from my own tranquil ones, I cannot always well tell how to reply. Your dishes are too much sauced and spiced and flavored, for me to suppose that you can relish my plain meats and vulgar aliment. Still, Robert, if I cannot always send you of the same, they have a smack & a novelty a Robert-ism about them, that make them a dainty stimulus to my palate at times.— I have little to tell you of. You are mistaken, I am disengaged from all newspaper connexions,[2] & breathe a freeer air in consequence. I was bound like Gulliver in a multitude of little chains, which by quotidian teazing swelled to a rack and a gibbet in the year's account. I am poorer but happier. Your three pounds came seasonably, but I doubt whether I am fairly intitled to them as a debt.—

I am obliged to break off here, and would not send this unfinished, but that you might otherwise be uneasy about the monies.—

Am I ever to see you? for it is like letters to the dead, or for a friend to write to his friend in the Fortunate Isles or the moon, or at the Antipodes, to address a line to one in Warwickshire that I am never to see in London. I shall lose the very face of Robt. by disuse, & I question if I were a painter, if I could now paint it from memory.

I could tell you many things, but you are so spiritual & abstracted, that I fear to insult you with tidings of this world. But may your approaching husband-hood humanize you. I think I see a dawn. I am sure joy is rising upon you, & I stand a tiptoe to see the **sun** ascending till it gets up & up, & "while a man tells the story"[3] shews at last a fair face & a full light.—

God bless you, Rob*t*

C L

MS: Huntington Library. Pub.: Ainger (1900), II, 103–104; Macdonald, I, 253–254; Ainger (1904), I, 258–259; Harper, III, 146–148; Lucas (1935), I, 365–366. Address: Mr R. Lloyd/Ch Lloyd Esqe/Birmingham. Postmark: [March] 13, 1804.

1. To Hannah Hart (see Vol. I, Letter 34, note 7), on August 2, 1804.

2. Most recently from those with the *Morning Post*. What Lloyd's three pounds, mentioned below, were for is not known, but the remark intimates a letter that has not been recovered from Lamb to Robert Lloyd.

3. Unidentified. The substance of this paragraph and the previous one reappears in "Distant Correspondents" (*Works*, II, 104–108).

160. *M. A. L. to Sarah Stoddart, with a postscript from C. L.*

[March ?27, 1804]

My dearest Sarah

I will just write a few hasty lines to say Coleridge is setting off sooner than we expected, and I every moment expect him to call in one of his great hurry's for this, Charles intended to write by him, but has not: most likely he will send a letter after him to Portsmouth if he does not you will certainly hear from him soon: We rejoiced with exceeding great joy to hear of your safe arrival: I hope your brother will return home in a few years a very rich man. Seventy pounds in one fortnight is a pretty beginning.—

I envy your brother the pleasure of seeing Coleridge drop in unexpectedly upon him—. We talk; but it is but wild and idle talk of

following him: he is to get my brother some little snug place of a thousand a year, and we are to leave all, and come and live among ye—*what a pretty dream.* — —

Coleridge is very ill: I dread the thoughts of his long voyage—write assoon as he arrives whether he does or not—and tell me how he is.

"Jamaica bodies use him weel"———[1]

he has got letters of recommendation to Governor Ball and God knows who, and he will talk, & talk, and be wondrously admired—. But I wish to write for him *a letter of recommendation* to Mrs Stoddart, and to yourself to take upon ye on his first arrival, to be to him kind affectionate nurses. and mind now that you perform this duty faithfully, and write me a good account of yourself. behave to him as you would to me, or to Charles if we came sick and unhappy to you.

I have no news to send you, Coleridge will tell you how we are going on—. Charles has lost the newspaper but what we dreaded as an evil has proved a great blessing, for we have both strangely recovered our health and spirits since this has happened. And I hope when I write next I shall be able to tell you Charles has begun something which will produce a little money, for it is not well to be *very poor* which we certainly are at this present writing.———

I sit writing here and thinking almost you will see it tomorrow, and what a long, long, time it will be before you receive this—.[2] When I saw your letter I fancy'd you were even just then in the first bustle of a new reception, every moment seeing new faces, & staring at new objects, when at that time every thing had become familiar to you, and the strangers, your new dancing partners had perhaps become gossipping fire-side friends—you tell me of your gay, splendid gdoings,[3] tell me likewise what manner of home-life you lead—is a quiet evening in a Maltese drawing room as pleasant as those we have passed in Mitre Court, & Bell yard, tell me all about it, every thing pleasant, & every thing unpleasant that befalls you

I want you to say a great deal about yourself. *are you happy, and do you not repent going out?* I wish I could see you for one hour only.—

remember me affectionately to your sister, and brother and tell me when when you write if Mrs Stoddart[4] likes Malta and how the climate agrees with her and with thee.—

We heard you were taken prisoners, and for several days believed the tale! .—

how did the pearls, and the fine court finery bear the fatigues of the voyage, & how often have they been worne, and admired?—

Rickman wants to know if you are going to be married yet—satisfy him in that little particul[ar] when you write——

The Fenwicks send their love, and Mrs Reynolds[5] her love—and the little old lady her best respects. Mrs Jeffries who I see now & then talks of you with tears in her eyes, and when she heard you was taken prisoner Lord! how frightened she was. she has heard (she tells me) that Dr Stoddart is to have a pension of two thousand a year whenever he chuses to return to England— —

God bless you, and send you all manner of comforts, & happinesses.

<div style="text-align:right">Your most affectionate friend
Mary Lamb</div>

how do? how do? no time to write, S T. C. going off in a great hurry
<div style="text-align:right">Ch. Lamb</div>

MS: Pierpont Morgan Library. Pub.: Harper, III, 143–146; Lucas (1905), VI, 285–286; Lucas (1912), V, 295–296; Lucas (1935), I, 366–368. Address: Miss Stoddart. The date is reasonably well established by the announcements here of the imminent departure of Coleridge and by these statements in his letter to Rickman of Monday, March 26 (*Coleridge's Letters,* II, 1105): "I have received *orders* from the Captain [of the *Speedwell*] . . . to be at Portsmouth by Wednesday early-morning. Accordingly, I have taken my place by the Tuesday Evening's Mail.—"

1. Burns, "On a Scotch Bard Gone to the West Indies," line 49.

2. The substance of this sentence reappears in "Distant Correspondents" (*Works,* II, 104–108).

3. Probably the resultant of having thought of both "goings" and "doings."

4. Still Miss Stoddart's "sister," properly sister-in-law. The Stoddarts' imaginary captors (see below) would have been the French.

5. Elizabeth Reynolds, Lamb's early teacher. (See Vol. I, Introduction, pp. xxviii–xxix.) The elderly lady next mentioned may be Mrs. Grant, Mary's elderly nurse. (See Letter 165, note 7.) Mrs. Jeffries has not been identified.

161. *C. L. to Coleridge*

[East India House]
Thursday [April 5, 1804]

My dear C.—

I but just received your commission-abounding letter. All shall be done, make your European heart easy in **Malta,** all shall be performed.— You say I am to transcribe off part of your letters & send to Somebody* (but the name is lost under the wafer, so you must give it me.)— I suppose Wordswth.—

I have been out of town since Saturday, the reason I had not your letter before. **N. B.** knowing I had 2 or 3 Easter holydays it was in my intention to have ask'd you, if my accompanying you to Portsmo. would have been pleasant. But you were not visible, except just at the critical moment of going off from the Inn, at which time I could not get at you.— So **Deus aliter disposuit,**[1] & I went down into hertfordshire—

I write in great bustle indeed.— God bl[e]ss you again—. Attend to what I have written mark'd * above, and dont merge any part of your **orders** under seal again.

C Lamb

Mary would send her best love; but I write at office—
the £1 came safe

MS: Huntington Library. Pub.: Harper, III, 148–149; Lucas (1905), VI, 287; Lucas (1912), V, 297; Lucas (1935), I, 368. Address: S. T. Coleridge Esqr/J. C. Mottley's Esqr/Portsmouth/Hants. Postmark: April 5, 1804. Mottley, to whom Daniel Stuart had given Coleridge a letter of introduction, was a Portsmouth bookseller and the Portsmouth correspondent for *The Courier.* He may still have been the Portsmouth correspondent for the *Morning Post* also, though Stuart had sold the *Morning Post* in August 1803. See *Coleridge's Letters,* II, esp. 1107 and 1111.
 1. "God arranged otherwise."

162. *C. L. to Poole*

Temple
4th May 1804

Dear Sir,

I have no sorts of connexion with the Morning Post at present, nor acquaintance with its late Editor (the present Editor of the Courier) to ask a favour of him with propriety; but if it will be of any use, I believe I could get the insertions[1] into the British Press (a Morning Paper) through a friend.—

Yours truly
C Lamb

MS: British Museum. Pub.: Harper, III, 149; Lucas (1905), VI, 287–288; Lucas (1912), V, 298; Lucas (1935), I, 369. Lucas and Harper presumably determined the addressee of this and the next letter from address leaves now missing.
1. Unidentified, as is Lamb's friend, mentioned below, associated with the *British Press*, or *Morning Literary Advertiser*.

163. *C. L. to Poole*

Temple
[Saturday,] 5th May 1804

Dear Sir,

I can get the insertions into the British Press without any difficulty at all. I am only sorry that I have no interest in the M. Post, having so much greater circulation.

If your friend chuses it, you will be so good as to return me the Critique, of which I forgot to take a copy, and I suppose on Monday or Tuesday it will be in. The sooner I have it, the better—

Yours &c
C Lamb

I did formerly assist in the Post, but have no longer any engagement.—

MS: British Museum. Pub.: Harper, III, 149–150; Lucas (1905), VI, 288; Lucas (1912), V, 298; Lucas (1935), I, 369.

164. *C. L. to Dorothy Wordsworth*

June 2. 1804

Dear Miss Wordsworth,

the task of letter-writing in my family falls to me; you are the organ of correspondence in yours, so I address you rather than your brother. We are all sensibly obliged to you for the little scraps (Arthur' o Bower[1] and his brethren) which you sent up; the bookseller has got them, and paid Mrs. Fenwick for them. So while some are authors for fame, some for money, you have commenced author for charity.— The least we can do, is to see your commissions fulfilled; accordingly I have **booked this 2d June 1804** from the Waggon Inn in Cripplegate the **watch** & books which I got from your brother Richard, together with Purchas's Pilgrimage[2] and Brown's Religio Medici which I desire your brother's acceptance of, with some *pens,* of which I observed no great frequency when I tarried at Grasmere. (I suppose you have got Coleridge's letter)—. These things I have put up in a deal box directed to Mr Wordsworth Grasmere near Ambleside, **Kendal,** by the **Kendal** waggon. At the same time I have sent off a parcel by C's desire to Mr. T. Hutchinson to the care of Mr. *"T Monkhouse[3] or T Markhouse"* (for C's writing is not very plain) Penrith by the Penrith waggon this day; which I beg you to apprize them of, lest my direction fail—. In your box, you will find a little parcel for Mrs. Coleridge, which she wants as soon as possible; also for yourselves, **the Cotton, Magnesia, bark & Oil, which come to** £2.3.4 thus

	sh—
Thread & needles	17
Magnesia_____	8
⟨Oil⟩ **bark**_____	9.8
⟨Ear⟩ **Oil** _____	8.8
	2.3.4
packing case_____	2.6
	2.5.10

$$
\left.\begin{array}{l}
\text{deduct a guinea I owe} \\
\text{you, which C. was to} \\
\text{pay, but did not—}
\end{array}\right\} \underline{\hspace{3cm}} \quad 1.1
$$

leaves you indebted_____ 1.4.10

whereby[4] you may see, how punctual I am—

I conclude with our kindest remembran[c]es to your brother & Mrs. W——. We hear, the young John is a Giant.—

And should you see Charles Lloyd, pray *forget* to give my love to him

<div align="right">

Yours truly

Dr. Miss W——

C Lamb
</div>

I send you two little copies of verses[5] by Mary L——b.—

Dialogue between a Mother and Child

Child. "O Lady, lay your costly robes aside,
(sings) No longer may you glory in your pride."

Mother Wherefore to day art singing in mine ear
Sad songs were made so long ago, my dear?
This day I am to be a bride, you know.
Why sing sad songs were made so long ago?

Child "O Mother lay your costly robes aside,"
For you may never be another's bride:
That line I learnt not in the old sad song.

Mother I pray thee, pretty one, now hold thy tongue;
Play with the bride maids, and be glad, my boy,
For thou shalt be a second father's joy.

Child One father fondled me upon his knee:
One father is enough alone for me—

Suggested by a print of 2 females after Leon[ardo da] Vinci, called Prudence & Beauty, which hangs up in our ro[om.]
O! that you could see the **print! !**—

The Lady Blanch, regardless of all her lovers' fears,
To the Urseline Convent hastens, & long the Abbess hears:

"O Blanch my child repent thee of the courtly life ye lead!"
Blanch looked on a rose bud, and little seem'd to heed;—
She looked on the rose bud, she looked round, and thought
On all her heart had whisper'd, & all the **Nun** had taught.
"I am worshipped by lovers, & brightly shines my fame,
"All Christendom resoundeth the noble **Blanch's** name;
"Nor shall I quickly wither like the rose bud from the tree,
"My **Queen-like** graces shining when my beauty's gone from me.
"But when the sculptur'd marble is raised o'er my head,
"And the matchless Blanch lies lifeless among the noble dead,
"This saintly Lady Abbess has made me justly fear,
"It nothing will avail me that I were worship **here**"—

I wish they may please you; we in these parts are not a little proud
of them

 C L

MS: University of Texas Library. Pub.: Harper, III, 150–153; Lucas (1905), VI, 288–290; Lucas (1912), V, 299–300; Lucas (1935), I, 369–371.

1. Which in *The Cherry Tree*, ed. Geoffrey Grigson (New York: Vanguard Press, 1959), p. 389, is titled "The High Wind" and reads thus:
 Arthur o' Bower has broken his band
 And he comes roaring up the land;
 The King of Scots with all his power
 Cannot stop Arthur of the Bower.
Lucas, who was informed by the Wordsworth scholar the late William Knight that this and the other scraps were copied, not written, by Miss Wordsworth, provided a slightly different version of the piece. (See Lucas [1935], I, 372.) The bookseller mentioned following has not been identified.

2. Samuel Purchas (1575?–1626), *Purchas, His Pilgrimage; or, Relations of the World and the Religions Observed in All Ages* (1613), the work that in the summer of 1797 had prompted the reverie that Coleridge fashioned into "Kubla Khan."

3. Thomas Monkhouse (1785–1825), at this time of Penrith but later of Budge Row, London, where he became successful in business, famous for his hospitality, and interested in literature. He was the son of George Monkhouse (1756–1802) of Penrith and the former Mary Hall (1760–1790) and a first cousin of Thomas Hutchinson (see Vol. I, Letter 44, note 6) and Mrs. Wordsworth. He became the esteemed friend of Lamb, Coleridge, Henry Crabb Robinson, and other literati.

4. A canceled line and two-thirds precede.

5. In *Works*, V, 31–32 and 38. The Leonardo, also called "Modesty and Vanity," that suggested the second poem is reproduced in *Works*, V, facing p. 300.

165. *M. A. L. to Sarah Stoddart, with a postscript from C. L.*
[Mid-June 1804]

My dearest Sarah

Your letter which contained the news of Coleridge's arrival was a most welcome one, for we had began to entertain very unpleasant apprehensions for his safety. And your kind reception of the forlorn wanderer gave me the greatest pleasure, & I thank you for it in my own, & my brothers name. I shall depend upon you for hearing of his welfare, for he does not write himself: but as long as we know he is safe, and in such kind friends hands, we do not mind.[1] Your letters my dear Sarah are to me very, very precious ones, they are the kindest, best, most natural ones I ever received. The one containing the account of the arrival of Coleridge, perhaps the best I ever saw, & your old friend Charles is of my opinion. We sent it off to Mrs Coleridge, & the Wordsworths, as well because we thought it our duty to give them the first notice we had of our dear friends safety, as that we were proud of shewing our Sarahs pretty letter. The letters we received a few days after from you, & your brother were far less welcome ones, I rejoiced to hear your sister is well, but I grieved for her loss of the dear baby.[2] And I am sorry to find your brother is not so successful as he at first expected to be, and yet I am almost tempted to wish his illfortune may send him over to us again, he has a friend I understand who is now at the head of the Admiralty. Why may he not return & make a fortune here?

I cannot condole with you very sincerely upon your little failure in the fortune-making-way. If you regret it. So do I. But I hope to see you a comfortable English Wife, & the forsaken, forgotten William of English-Partridge memory, I have still a hankering after. However I thank you for your frank communication, & I beg you will continue it in future, & if I do not agree with a good grace to your having a Maltese husband, I will wish you happy, provided you make it a part of your marriage articles, that your husband shall allow you to come over-sea & make me one visit, else may neglect, & overlookedness be your portion while [y]ou stay there.

I would condole with you upon the misfortune has befallen your

poor leg, but such is the blessed distance we are at from each other, that I hope before you receiv[e] this you have forgot it ever happened.[3]

Are compliments the high ton at the Maltese Court, your brother is so profuse of them to me, that being as you know so unused to them, they perplex me sadly, [i]n future I beg they may be discontinued. They always remind me of the free, & I believe very improper letter[4] I wrote to you while you were at the Isle of Wight, the more kindly you & your brother & sister took the impertinent advice contain[e]d in it, the more certain I feel that it was unnecessary, & therefore highly improper. Do not let your brother compliment me into the memory of it again.

My brother has had a letter from your Mother which has distressed him sadly——about the postage of some letters being paid by my brother——your silly brother it [s]eems has informed your Mother (I did not think your brother could have been so silly) that Charles had grumbled at paying the said postage. The fact was, just at that time we were very poor, having lost the Morning Post, & we were be- gining to practice a strict economy. My brother who never makes up his mind whether he will be a Miser, or a Spendthrift, is at all times a strange mixture of both, of this failing the even economy of your correct brother's temper makes him an ill judge. The miserly part of Charles, at that time smarting [u]nder his recent loss, then happened to reign triumphant, and he would not write, or let me write, so often as he wished, because the postage cost two and four pence, then came two or three of your poor Mother's letters nearly together, & the two & four pences he wished, but grudged to pay for his own, [h]e was forced to pay for hers. In this dismal distress he applied to Fenwick [t]o get his friend Motley to send them free from Portsmouth, this Mr Fenwick could have done for half a words speaking, but this he did not do! Then Charles foolishly, & unthinkingly complained to your brother in a half serious, half joking way, & your brother has wickedly, & with malice aforethought told your Mother, O fye upon him, what will your Mother think of us. I too feel my share of blame in this vexatious busi- ness, for I saw the unlucky paragraph in my brothers' letter,[5] & I had a kind of foreboding that it would come to your Mothers' ears although I had a higher notion of your brothers good sense than I find he de- served. By entreaties & prayers I might have prevailed on my brother

to say nothing about it. But I make a point of conscience never to interfere, or cross my brother in the humour he happens to be in. It always seems to me to be a vexatious kind of Tyranny that women have no business to exercise over men, which merely because *they having a better judgement* they have the power to do. Let *men* alone, and at last we find they come round to the right way, which *we* by a kind of intuition perceive at once. But better, far better, that *we* should let them often do wrong, than that they should have the torment of [a] Monitor always at their elbows. Charles is sadly fretted now, & knows not what to say to your Mother—. I have made this long preamble about it, to induce you if possible to reinstate us in your Mothers good graces, say to her it was a jest misunderstood, tell her Charles Lamb is not the shabby fellow she & her son took him for, but that he is now & then a little whimsical, or so. I do not ask your brother to do this, for I am offended with him for the mischief he has made.——

I feel that I have too lightly passed over the interresting account you sent me of your late disappointment. It was not because I did not feel & comple[te]ly enter into the affair with you. You surprize & please me with the frank & generous way in which you deal with your Lovers, taking a refusal from their cold prudential hearts, with a better grace, & more good humour than other women accept a suitors service.—— Continue this open artless conduct & I trust you will at last find some man who has sense enough to know you are well worth risking a probable life of poverty for.

I shall yet live to see you, a poor, but happy English Wife. Remember me most affectionately to Coleridge—, & I thank you again, & again for all your kindness to him. To dear Mrs Stoddart & your brother I beg my bes[t] love, and to you all I wish health & happiness, & a *soon* return to Old England

I have sent to Mr Burrels[6] for your kind present, but unfortunately he is not in town. I am impatient to see my fine silk handkerchiefs, & I thank [y]ou for them, not as a present, for I do not love presents, but [as a . . . remembrance of your old] friend. Farewell

I am my best Sarah,
your most affectionate friend
Mary Lamb

Good wishes & all proper remembrances from old nurse,[7] Mrs Jeffries, Mrs Reynolds, Mrs Rickman &c &c &c.

Long Live Queen Hoop-oop-oop-ooo
and all the old merry phantoms

My dear Miss Stoddart,

Mary has written so fully to you that I have nothing to add but that in all the kindness she has exprest, & loving-desire to see you again, I bear my full part. You will perhaps like to tear this half from the sheet, and give your brother only his strict due, the remainder. So I will just repay your late kind letter with this short post-script to hers. Come over here, & let us all be merry again.

C Lamb

MS: Lockwood Library, State University of New York at Buffalo. Pub.: Sala, I, 429; Purnell, I, 429; Fitzgerald, II, 262; Hazlitt, I, 346–347; Macdonald, I, 254; Harper, III, 153–158; Lucas (1905), VI, 291–294; Lucas (1912), V, 301–304; Lucas (1935), I, 372–375. The date is estimated from the fact that Coleridge landed at Malta on May 18; from the completion date of June 11 of his first letter back to his wife, which she seems not yet to have received; and from Wordsworth's letter of June 14 to Walter Scott, where it is apparent that Wordsworth had not received the letter from Miss Stoddart to Mary that was forwarded to him announcing Coleridge's arrival. See *Coleridge's Letters,* II, 1135, and *Wordsworths' Letters,* I, 481.

1. Three and one-half canceled lines follow.
2. A girl, who had died on the night of her birth, June 5, 1804. (See *Coleridge's Letters,* II, 1139.) Stoddart's friend referred to below, apparently of the admiralty in London, has not been identified.
3. This thought too Lamb developed in "Distant Correspondents" (*Works,* II, esp. 104–105).
4. Presumably Letter 151.
5. Unrecovered.
6. Unidentified. The bracketed passage, below, now illegible in the manuscript and containing one word illegible to Lucas, is supplied from Lucas (1935), I, 375.
7. Mrs. Mary Grant (b. 1740?) of Maidenhead, Ram Court, Fleet Street, and after October 1809 a patient in the incurable ward of Westminster Hospital. (See Vol. III, Letter 233, notes.) Lamb's postscript begins with "Long Live . . ."

166. *C. L. to Robert Lloyd*

[September 13, 1804]

Dear Robert,

I was startled in a very pleasant manner by the contents of your letter. It was like your good self, to take so handsome an opportunity of renewing an old friendship. I thank you kindly for your offers to

My dear Mrs Clarkson

Your kind letter would have given me great pleasure but for the concern I feel at the uneasiness you express at the unjust reports you have heard of John Wordsworth. It is upon your own account alone that I am distressed at it: for my own part I totally disbelieve it, and so does my brother and he desires me to tell you in the strongest terms I can think of, his full conviction that the injurious falsehood you have heard is entirely void of foundation. The report coming from an underwriter Charles says makes it easy to be accounted for, because it is a well known fact that they always impute blame to the Captain whenever a Ship is lost.

My brother says that he never heard a whisper at the India House, (or any where else) of poor John Wordsworth being drunk, which had that been the case would certainly he says have been known and talked of there. He is quite certain the India Directors were perfectly satisfied with his conduct, and that no blame has ever been imputed to him.

+ We are very glad you have not told Wordsworth, and earnestly beg you never will tell him, because it may not be easy to get at evidence strong enough to make him perfectly satisfied. It was with great difficulty that my brother got at the intelligence he sent to Wordsworth, the survivors almost all being gone out to India in other ships. We think we can trace the story of his being drunk to this slight foundation: A gentleman of the name of Burgoyne, a cornet in the army, who was a passenger in the Ship told at the India House that a few minutes

XI. Facsimile of the first page of a letter from Mary Anne Lamb to Mrs. Thomas Clarkson, March 13, 1806 (Letter 197). Courtesy of Brown University Library.

been very much with us lately, and we love him dearly. —
You say nothing about yourself, & you give a very cross reason
because I set you the example. You do not even say how you
are in health, but it must have been your anxiety about poor
John Wordsworth made you forget what you must know we were
so very anxious to hear. Will you be so kind as to write soon
for I shall be uneasy till I hear your mind is if you are more
satisfied about this injurious report. I wish you would feel as I
do that it is most certainly a wicked & malicious falsehood

XII. Facsimile of the fourth page of the letter of March 13, 1806.

bring me acquainted with Mrs. Ll. I cannot come now, but assuredly I will some time or other, to see how this new relation sits upon you. I am naturally shy of new faces;[1] but the Lady who has chosen my [o]ld friend Robert, cannot have a repelling one. Assure her of my sincere congratulations & friendly feelings. Mary joins in both with me, and considers herself as only left out of your kind invitation by some **lapsus styli**.— We have already had all the holydays we can have this year. We have been spending our usual summer month at Richmond, from which place we traced the banks of the old Thames for ten & tw[en]ty miles, in daily walks or rides, & found beauties which may compare with Ulswater & Windermere. We visited Windsor, Hampton &c. &c.—but this is a deviation from the subject with which I began my letter.—

Some day I certainly shall come and see you, in your new light; no longer the restless (but good) Robert; but now the staid, sober (& not less good) married Robert. And how does Plumstead the impetuous take your getting the start of him? When will he subside into matrimony?[2] **Priscilla** has taken a long time indeed to think about it. I will suppose that her first choice is Now her final; though you do not expressly say that she is to be a Wordsworth. I wish her, and dare promise her, all happiness.—

All these new nuptials do not make me unquiet in the perpetual prospect of celibacy.[3] There is a quiet dignity in old-bachelorhood, a leisure from cares, noise &c. an enthronization upon the armed-chair of a man's feeling that he may sit, walk, read, unmolested, to none accountable—but hush! or I shall be torn in pieces like a churlish Orpheus by young married women & bride-maids of Birmingham.— The close is this, to every man that way of life, which is his election, is best. Be as happy in yours, as I am determined to be in mine, and we shall strive lovingly who shall sing best the p[ra]ises of matrimony, & the praises of singleness. Adieu my old friend in a new character, and believe me that no "wounds" have pierced our friendship: only a long want of **seeing** each other has disfurnished us of topics on which to talk. Is not your new fortunes a topic, which may hold us for some months (the honey months at least)?

MS: Huntington Library. Pub.: Ainger (1900), II, 104–106; Macdonald, I, 254–256; Ainger (1904), I, 259–260; Harper, I, facsimile, and III, 159–160;

Lucas (1935), I, 376–377. Address: Mr Robert Lloyd/Nott and Lloyd's/Birmingham. Postmark: September 13, 1804. "Nott" Lamb should have spelled "Knott." See Vol. I, Letter 34, note 7.

1. A confession made public in "New Year's Eve" (*Works*, II, 27). The Latin, below, translates, "slip of a pen."

2. Also this year, as would Priscilla Lloyd, mentioned following, and Christopher Wordsworth. See Letter 104, note 4, and Vol. I, Letter 41, source note.

3. In "Mackery End, in Hertfordshire" (*Works*, II, 75) Elia claimed, "I, for one, find in myself no sort of disposition to go out upon the mountains, with the rash king's offspring, to bewail my celibacy."

167. *C. L. to William Wordsworth, with letters from M. A. L. to Dorothy Wordsworth and Mrs. Samuel Taylor Coleridge and a postscript from C. L. to Mrs. Coleridge*

[October 13, 1804]

Dear Wordsworth,

I have not forgot your commissions.— But the truth is, and why should I not confess it? I am not plethorically abounding in Cash at this present. Merit, God knows, is very little rewarded; but it does not become me to speak of myself. My motto is **"Contented** with little **yet** wishing for more."— Now the books you wish for would require some pounds, which I am sorry to say I have not by me: so I will say at once, if you will give me a draft upon your town-banker for any sum you propose to lay out, I will dispose of [it] to the very best of my skill in choice old books, such as my own soul loveth.—[1] In fact, I have been waiting for the liquidation of a debt to enable myself to set about your commission handsomely, for it is a scurvy thing to cry **Give me** the money first, & I am the first of the family of the Lambs that have done it for many centuries: but the debt remains as it was, and my old friend that I accommodated has generously forgot it!—

The books which you want I calculate at about **£8.**— Ben Jonson is a Guinea Book. Beaumont & Fletcher in folio, the right folio, not now to be met with; the octavos are about £3.— As to any other old dramatists, I do not know where to find them except what are in Dodsly's old plays, which are about £3 also: Massinger I never saw but at one shop, but it is now gone, but one of the editions of Dodsley contains about a fourth (the best) of his plays.— Congreve and the rest of King Charles's moralists are cheap & accessible.— The works

on Ireland I will enquire after, but I fear, Spenser's[2] is not to be had apart from his poems; I never saw it. But you may depend upon my sparing no pains to furnish you as complete a library of old Poets & Dramatists as will be prudent to buy; for I suppose you do not include the £20 edition of Hamlet, single play, which Kemble has.— Marlow's plays & poems are totally vanished; only one edition of Dodsley retains one, & the other two, of his plays: but John Ford is the man after Shakespear.[3] Let me know your will & pleasure soon: for I have observed, next to the pleasure of buying a bargain for one's self is the pleasure of persuading a friend to buy it. It tickles one with the image of an imprudency without the penalty usually annex'd.

<div align="right">C Lamb</div>

(turn over leaf for more letters)

My dear Miss Wordsworth[4]

I writ a letter immediately upon the receipt of yours, to thank you for sending me the welcome tidings of your little neice's birth, and Mrs Wordsworths safety, and waited till I could get a frank to send it in, not being able to procure one, I will defer my thanks no longer for fear Mrs Wordsworth should add another little baby to your family before my congratulations in the birth of the little Dorothy arrives.

I hope Mrs Wordsworth, & the pretty baby, & the young philosopher are well, they are three strangers to me whom I have a longing desire to be acquainted with.

My brother desires me not to send such a long gossiping letter as that I had intended for you, because he wishes to fill a large share of the paper with his acknowledgments to Mr Wordsworth for his [le]tters, which he considers as a very uncommon favor, your brother seldom writing letters. I must beg my brother will tell Mr Wordsworth how very proud he has made me also by praising my poor verses. Will you be so kind as to forward the opposite page to Mrs Coleridge; this sheet of paper is quite a partnership affair, when the Parliament meets, you shall have a letter for your sole use.— —

My brother and I have been this summer to Richmond; we had a lodging there for a month, we passed the whole time there in wandering about, & comparing the views from the banks of the Thames with your mountain scenery, and tried, & wished to persuade ourselves that

it was almost as beautiful. Charles was quite a Mr Clarkson in his admiration, and his frequent exclamations, for though we had often been at Richmond for a few hours we had no idea it was so beautiful a place as we found it on a months intimate acquaintance.

We rejoice to hear of the good fortune of your brave sailor-brother,[5] I should have liked to have been with you when the news first arrived

Your very friendly invitations have made us long to be with you, & we promise ourselves to spend the first money my brother earns by writing certain books (Charles often plans but never begins) in a journey to Grasmere.—

When your eyes (which I am sorry to find continue unwell) will permit you to make use of your pen again I shall be very happy to see a letter in your own hand writing.

I beg to be affectionately remembered to your brother & sister

& remain ever your affectionate friend

M Lamb

Compliments to old Molly.

My dear Mrs Coleridge

I have had a letter written ready to send to you which I kept hoping to get a frank, and now I find I must write one entirely anew, for that consisted of matters not now in season, such as condolence on the illness of your children[6] who I hope are now quite well, & comfortings on your uncertainty of the safety of Coleridge with wise reasons for the delay of the letters from Malta, which must now be changed for pleasant congratulations. Coleridge has not written to us, but we have had two letters from the Stoddarts since the one I sent to you, containing good accounts of him, but as I find you have had letters from himself I need not tell you the particulars.

My brother sent your letters to Mr Motley according to Coleridge's direction & I have no doubt but he forwarded them.

One thing only in my poor letter the time makes no alteration i[n, which is] that I have half a bed ready for you, & I shall rejoice with exceeding great joy to have you with me,[7] pray do not change your mind for I shall be sadly disappointed if you do. Will Hartly be with you? I hope he will, for you say he goes with you to Liverpool, and I conclude you come from thence to London.

I have seen your brother lately, and I find he entertains good hopes from Mr Salte, & his present employment I hear is likely to continue a considerable time longer, so that I hope you may consider him as good as provided for. He seems very steady, and is very well spoken of at his office.

I have lately been often talking of you with Mrs Hazlitt.[8] William Hazlitt is painting my brothers picture which has brought us acquainted with the whole family. I like William Hazlitt & his sister very much indeed, & I think Mrs Haslitt a pretty goodhumoured woman. She has a nice little girl of the Pypos kind, who is so fond of my brother that she stops strangers in the street to tell them when *Mr Lamb is coming to see her.*

I hope Mr Southey and your sister & the little Edith[9] are well. I beg my love to them.

God bless you, and your three little darlings, & their wandering father, who I hope will soon return to you in high health & spirits

I remain ever your affectionate friend

Mary Lamb

Compliments to Mr Jackson[10] & darling friend. I hope they are well.

C Lamb particularly desires to be remembered to Southey & all the Southeys, as well as to Mrs C. and her little Coleridges—Mrs. C's letters have all been sent as Coleridge left word, to Motley's Portsmouth—

MS: University of Texas Library. Pub.: Talfourd (1837), I, 170–172; Sala, I, 233–234; Purnell, I, 233–234; Fitzgerald, II, 68–69; Hazlitt, I, 265–266; Ainger (1888), I, 142–143; Ainger (1900), I, 217–218; Macdonald, I, 173–174; Ainger (1904), I, 154–155; Harper, II, 267–269; Lucas (1905), VI, 294–298; Lucas (1912), V, 305–309; Lucas (1935), I, 377–381. Address: Mr Wordsworth/ Grasmere/near Ambleside/Westmoreland. Postmark: October 13, 1804.

1. In a letter dated December 27 [1804] (*Wordsworths' Letters,* I, 523) Wordsworth asked his brother John to have ten pounds ready for Lamb at Richard Wordsworth's chambers to pay for the books. (See below, Letter 211, note 1.) Lamb's debtor, alluded to below, has not been identified.

2. *View of the Present State of Ireland* (1633).

3. Ford, Lamb maintained in *Specimens of English Dramatic Poets* (*Works,* IV, 218), "was of the first order of Poets. He sought for sublimity, not by parcels in metaphors or visible images, but directly where she has her full residence in the heart of man; in the actions and sufferings of the greatest minds. There is a grandeur of the soul above mountains, seas, and the elements."

4. From Mary. Dorothy, or Dora (d. 1847), mentioned below, had been born

to the Wordsworths on August 16. She would become, in 1841, the wife of the poet Edward Quillinan (1791–1851). The "young philosopher" is the Wordsworths' son John.

5. John Wordsworth, who had brought the *Earl of Abergavenny* back to England from China on August 14 and been scheduled for a "better voyage" (*Wordsworths' Letters*, I, 511), to Bengal and China, for the season 1804–1805.

6. Now including Sara (d. 1852), who had been born on December 23, 1802, would in 1829 be married to her cousin and her father's literary executor, Henry Nelson Coleridge (1798–1843), and would edit her father's writings.

7. Whether Mrs. Coleridge came soon to visit the Lambs is not known. George Fricker, the brother referred to below, was possibly seeking employment in the wholesale linen drapery firm variously listed in the London directories for 1799 and 1808 as William Salte, W. and G. Salte, or William and W. G. Salte, of 20 Poultry Street.

8. The former Mary Pierce, or Pearce, of Portsea, Hampshire. She had been the wife since about 1793 of William Hazlitt's brother, John (1767–1837), a professional miniature painter at whose home at 109 Great Russell Street William, who was now painting Lamb in the dress of a Venetian senator (frontispiece), frequently resided from about 1799 to 1807. She was thus the sister-in-law of the amateur painter Margaret Hazlitt (1770–1841) and was ultimately the mother of Harriet, Mary, William (1805?–1885), and the son (b. 1807) mentioned in Letter 216, near the reference to note 2. The meeting of the Lambs and William Hazlitt had occurred at a dinner party at the Godwins' on March 22, 1803. In 1823 in "My First Acquaintance with Poets" (*Hazlitt's Works*, XVII, 122) Hazlitt recalled the moment there when Lamb, Holcroft, and Coleridge "were disputing fiercely which was the best man—*Man as he was, or man as he is to be.* 'Give me,' says Lamb, 'man as he is *not* to be.' This saying was the beginning of a friendship between us, which I believe still continues." See *Hazlitt*, p. 153, for the date of the dinner; *The Journals of Margaret Hazlitt:Recollections of England, Ireland, and America,* ed. Ernest J. Moyne (Lawrence: University of Kansas Press, 1967), pp. 124–125, for a reliable genealogy of the Hazlitt family; and *The Hazlitts,* p. xiii, for a fairly complete list of William Hazlitt's paintings done mainly between 1802 and 1804, and pp. 334–337 for a list of John Hazlitt's paintings exhibited at the Royal Academy.

9. Edith May (d. 1871), who had been born to the Southeys on May 1, 1804. In 1834 she would become the wife of John Wood Warter (1806–1878), a divine, an antiquary, and an editor of Southey's works and letters.

10. William Jackson (1748–1809), the owner of Greta Hall. His friend, mentioned next, was probably a Mrs. Wilson, his housekeeper and the Coleridge children's "Wilsy." (See *Coleridge's Letters*, I, 644, and *Wordsworths' Letters*, I, 447.) The final paragraph is Lamb's.

168. C. L. to Robert Southey

7 Nov 1804

Dr. Southey,

 You were the last person from whom we heard of Dyer, and if you know where to forward the news I now send, to him, I shall be obliged to you to lose no time. D's sister in Law, who lives in St.

Dunstans' court wrote to him about three weeks ago to the Hope Inn Cambridge, to inform him that **Squire Houlbert** or some such name of Denmark Hill has died, & left her husband a thousand pounds, and two or three hundred to Dyer.[1] Her letter got no answer, and she does not know where to direct to him, so she came to me, who am equally in the dark. Her story is, that Dyer's immediately coming to town now, & signing some papers, will save him a considerable sum of money: how, I dont understand; but it is very right he should hear of this— —. She has left me barely time for the post; so I conclude with all Love &c— —to all at Keswick.—

Dyer's brother, who by his wife's account has got £1000 left him, is father of the little dirty girl, Dyer's neice & fac-totum—

<div align="right">In haste—
Yours truly
C Lamb</div>

If you send George this, Cut off the last paragraph—
D's laundress had a letter a few days since; but George **never dates.**

MS: Berg Collection, New York Public Library. Pub.: Sala, I, 201–202; Purnell, I, 201–202; Fitzgerald, II, 53–54; Hazlitt, I, 345–346; Ainger (1888), I, 209–210; Ainger (1900), II, 106–107; Macdonald, I, 256; Ainger (1904), I, 260–261; Harper, III, 163–164; Lucas (1905), VI, 298–299; Lucas (1912), V, 309–310; Lucas (1935), I, 381–382.

1. Mrs. Gertrude Alison Anderson determined that the will of a Richard Holburt was proved on October 10, 1804, stipulating that £1,000 in 3 percent stock go to John Dyer (see Letter 115, note 3) and £250 to George Dyer, both to be paid "before the dividend day occurring next after his decease" (Lucas [1935], I, 382).

169. *C. L. to William Wordsworth*

<div align="right">[18th Feby 1805]</div>

My dear Wordsworth,

the subject of your letter[1] has never been out of our thoughts since the day we first heard of it, and many have been our impulses towards you, to write to you, or to write to enquire about you; but it never seemed the time. We felt all your situation, and how much you would want Coleridge at such a time, and we wanted somehow to make up to you his absence, for we loved & honoured your Brother, & his death always occurs to my mind with something like a feeling of reproach,

as if we ought to have been nearer acquainted, & as if there had been
some incivility shewn him by us, or something short of that respect
which we now feel: but this is always a feeling, when people die, and
I should not foolishly offer a piece of refinement, instead of sympathy;
if I knew any other way of making you feel how little like indifferent
his loss has been to us. I have been for some time wretchedly ill &
low, and your letter this morning has affected me so with a pain in my
inside & a confusion, that I hardly know what to write or how. I have
this morning seen Stewart[2] the 2d mate who was saved: but he can
give me no satisfactory account, having been in quite another part of
the ship when your brother went down. But I shall see Gilpin tomor-
row, and will communicate your thanks, & learn from him all I can.
All accounts agree that just before the vessel going down, your brother
seemed like one overwhelmed with the situation, & careless of his own
safety. Perhaps he might have saved himself; but a Captain who in
such circumstances does all he can for his ship & nothing for himself,
is the noblest idea. I can hardly express myself, I am so really ill. But
the universal sentiment is, that your brother did all that duty required:
and if he had been more alive to the feelings of those distant ones
whom he loved, he would have been at that time a less admirable
object; less to be exulted in by them: for his character is high with all
that I have heard speak of him, & no reproach can fix upon him.
Tomorrow I shall see Gilpin, I hope, if I can get at him, for there is
expected a complete investigation of the causes of the loss of the ship
at the East India House, & all the Officers are to attend: but I could
not put off writing to you a moment. It is most likely I shall have some-
thing to add tomorrow, in a second letter. If I do not write, you may
suppose I have not seen G. but you shall hear from me in a day or two.
We have done nothing but think of you, particularly of Dorothy.
Mary is crying by me while I with difficulty write this: but as long as
we remember any thing, we shall remember your Brother's noble
person, & his sensible manly modest voice, & how safe & comfortable
we all were together in our apartment, where I am now writing. When
he returned, having been one of the triumphant China fleet, we
thought of his pleasant exultation (which he exprest here one night)
in the wish that he might meet a Frenchman in the seas; & it seem'd
to be accomplished, all to his heart's desire.— I will conclude from

utter inability to write any more, for I am seriously unwell: & because I mean to gather something like intelligence to send to you tomorrow: for as yet, I have but heard second hand, & seen one narrative, which is but a transcript of what was common to all the Papers. God bless you all, & reckon upon us as entering into all your griefs.

[C. Lamb]

MS: University of Texas Library. Pub.: Harper, III, 164–166; Lucas (1905), VI, 299–300; Lucas (1912), V, 310–311; Lucas (1935), I, 382–383. Address: Mr. Wm. Wordsworth/Grasmere/near Ambleside/Westmoreland. Postmark: February 18, 1805. The date and signature, which have been cut from the end of the letter, I have transcribed from their substitutions written above the missing piece presumably by the person who took it.

1. Unrecovered, but apparently requesting details concerning the loss of John Wordsworth and the *Earl of Abergavenny*. She had sailed from Portsmouth under his command on February 1 with between 386 and 402 passengers, troopers, and crew. In the late afternoon of the fifth she had been drawn onto the Shambles, a reef two miles off Portland Bill. She had been freed in the evening, but had gone down in eleven or twelve fathoms two miles off Weymouth Beach between 11:00 p.m. and 2:00 a.m. as a result of the rent in her hull. Her 100 to 155 survivors had reached the East India House on the morning of the seventh, and news of the disaster had been made public that afternoon. Captain Wordsworth's body was recovered on March 20 and the next day interred with the other victims in a common grave in Wyke Regis churchyard, Weymouth, Dorsetshire.

2. W. E. G. Stewart, according to Frank Prentice Rand's *Wordsworth's Mariner Brother* (Amherst, Mass.: The Jones Library, 1966), p. 104. Thomas Gilpin, referred to below, was the fourth mate.

170. *C. L. to William Wordsworth*

Tuesday [February 19, 1805]

My dear Wordsworth,

I yesterday wrote you a very unsatisfactory letter. To day I have not much to add, but it may be some satisfaction to you that I have seen **Gilpin,** & thanked him in all your names for the assistance he tried to give: and that he has assured me that your Brother did try to save himself, and was doing so when Gilpin called to him, but he was then struggling with the waves & almost dead.— G heard him give orders a very little before the vessel went down with all possible calmness, & it does not at all appear that your Brother in any absence of mind neglected his own safety. But in such circumstances the memory of those who escaped cannot be supposed to be very accurate; and there

appears to be about the Persons that I have seen a good deal of re-
servedness & unwillingness to enter into detail, which is natural, they
being Officers of the Ship, and liable to be examined at home about its
loss. The examination is expected today or tomorrow, and if anything
should come out, that can interest you, I shall take an early opportunity
of sending it to you; ⟨and procure a⟩—

Mary wrote some few days since to Miss Stoddart, containing an
account of your Brother's death, which most likely Coleridge will have
heard, before the letter comes:[1] we both wish it may hasten him back.
We do not know any thing of him, whether he is settled in any post
(as there was some talk) or not. We had another sad account to send
him, of the death of his schoolfellow **Allen**; tho' this, I am sure, will
much less affect him. I dont know whether you knew Allen; he died
lately very suddenly in an apoplexy. When you do & can write, par-
ticularly inform us of the healths of you all. God bless you all. Mary
will write to Dorothy as soon as she thinks **she** will be able to bear it.
It has been a sad tidings to us, & has affected us more than we could
have believed. I think it has contributed to make me worse, who have
been very unwell, & have got leave for some few days to stay at home:
but I am ashamed to speak of myself, only in excuse for the unfeeling
sort of huddle which I now send. I could not delay it, having seen
Gilpin, & I thought his assurance might be some little ease to you.

We will talk about the Books, when you can better bear it. I have
bought none yet. But do not spare me any office you can put me on
now or when you are at leisure for such things. Adopt me as one of
your family in this affliction; & use me without ceremony as such.

<div style="text-align: right;">Mary's kindest Love to all—</div>

<div style="text-align: right;">C L[2]</div>

MS: University of Texas Library. Pub.: Harper, III, 167–168; Lucas (1905),
VI, 301–302; Lucas (1912), V, 312–313; Lucas (1935), I, 384–385. Address:
Mr. Wordsworth/Grasmere/near Ambleside/Westmoreland. Postmark: February
19, 180[5].

1. This letter and that mentioned below containing the account of Robert
Allen's death have not been recovered. The latter letter is mentioned in the third
paragraph of Letter 178 as having been (with other letters) taken by the French.
The Wordsworths had hoped Coleridge would not learn of their brother's
death until he returned to England. But Mary, Lady Ball, the former Mary
Wilson, abruptly told him of it at an embassy gathering on March 31. "I at-
tempted to stagger out of the room (the great Saloon of the Palace with 50
people present)," he wrote Mrs. Coleridge on July 21, "and before I could reach

the door fell down on the ground in a convulsive hysteric Fit / —I was confined to my room for a fortnight after / —and now I am afraid to open a Letter / & I never dare ask a question of any newcomer" (*Coleridge's Letters,* II, 1170).

 2. A postscript about a line long is canceled.

171. *C. L. to Manning*

<div align="right">

16 Mitre Court Buildings Inner Temple
Saturday 24 [23] feb. 1805
</div>

Dear Manning,

 We have executed your commissions. There was nothing for you at the White Horse. I have been very unwell since I saw you. A sad depression of spirits, a most unaccountable nervousness: from which I have been partially relieved by an odd accident. You knew **Dick Hopkins**[1] the swearing Scullion of Caius'? This fellow by industry and agility has thrust himself into the important situations (no sinecures believe me) of Cook to Trinity Hall & Cauis College: and the generous creature has contrived with the greatest delicacy imaginable to send me a present of Cambridge Brawn. What makes it the more extraordinary is that the man never saw me in his life that I know of. I suppose he has *heard* of me. I did not immediately recognize the donor: but one of Richard's cards, which had accidentally fallen into the straw, detected him in a moment. **Dick** you know was always remarkable for flourishing. His card imports that "Orders (to-wit for Brawn) from any part of England, Scotland, or Ireland will be duly executed" &c. . At first I thought of declining the present: but Richard knew my blind side when he pitched upon **Brawn.** Tis of all my hobbies the supreme in the eating way. He might have sent, sops from the pan, skimmings, crumplets, chips, hog's lard, the tender brown judiciously scalped from a fillet of veal (dextrously replaced by a salamander) the tops of asparagus, fugitive livers, runaway gizzards of fowls, the eyes of martyr'd Pigs, tender effusions of laxative woodcocks, the red spawn of lobsters, leveret's ears, and such pretty filchings common to cooks: but these had been ordinary presents, the every-day courtesies of Dish-washers to their sweethearts. Brawn was a noble thought. It is not every common Gullet-fancier than[2] can properly esteem of it. It is like a picture of one of the choice old Italian masters. It's gusto is of that hidden sort. As Wordsworth sings of a modest poet: you

must love him ere to you he will seem worthy of your love: so Brawn, you must taste it ere to you it will seem to have any taste at all. But tis nuts to the adept: those that will send out their tongue and feelers to find it out. It will be wooed & not unsought be won. Now **Ham**-essence, lobsters, turtle, such popular minions absolute *court you*, lay themselves out to strike you at first smack, like one of **David's** Pictures[3] (they call him *Darveed)* compared with the plain russet-coated wealth of a Titian or a Corregio, as I illustrated above. Such are the obvious glaring **heathen** virtues of a Corporation dinner compared with the reserved collegiate worth of Brawn.

Do me the favor to leave off the business which you may be at present upon, and go immediately to the Kitchens of Trinity & Caius', and make my most respectful compli[ments] to Mr. Richard Hopkins, and assure him that his Brawn is most excellent, and that I am moreover obliged to him for his **inuendo** about Salt water & Bran: which I shall not fail to improve. I leave it to you whether you shall chuse to pay him the civility of asking him to dinner while you stay in Cambridge, or in whatever other way you may best like to shew your gratitude to *my friend*. Richard Hopkins considered in many points of view is a very extraordinary character. .— **Adieu.** I hope to see you to supper in London soon, where we will taste Richard's brawn, and drink his health in a chearful but moderate cup. We have not many such men in any rank of life as Mr. R. Hopkins. **Crisp**[4] the Barber of St. Mary's was just such another. I wonder *he* never sent me any little token, some chestnuts, or a puff, or two pound of hair: just to remember him by. **Gifts** are like nails. **Præsens ut absens:** that is, your *Present* makes amends for your absence.—

<div align="right">Yours.
C Lamb</div>

MS: Huntington Library. Pub.: Talfourd (1837), I, 256–259; Sala, I, 385–387; Purnell, I, 385–387; Fitzgerald, II, 218–220; Hazlitt, I, 348–349; Ainger (1888), I, 210–212; Ainger (1900), II, 107–110; Macdonald, I, 258–260; Ainger (1904), I, 261–263; Harper, III, 169–171; Lucas (1905), VI, 302–303; Lucas (1912), V, 313–315; Lucas (1935), I, 385–386. Address: Thos. Manning Esqr./ Caius' College/Cambridge. Postmark: February 23, 1805.

1. Who called himself "Cook of Trinity Hall and Caius College" in an advertisement in the *Cambridge Chronicle* of February 8, 1806. The advertisement goes on to say that Richard Hopkins "begs leave to inform the Nobility, Gentry, &c. that he has now ready for sale, BRAWN, BRAWN HEADS & CHEEKS. All orders will be thankfully received, and forwarded to any part of the kingdom" (quoted

from Lucas [1935], I, 387). It was of course Manning who had ordered the brawn sent to Lamb, whose letter is one of the many precursors of "A Dissertation upon Roast Pig" (*Works*, II, 120–126).

2. For "that." Wordsworth's words, below, occur in "A Poet's Epitaph," lines 43–44.

3. Those by Jacques Louis David (1748–1825).

4. See Vol. I, Letter 53, source note. The Latin below translates, "Present as absent" (Terence, *Eunuchus*, I, i, 112). Lamb considered gifts and givers further in "Thoughts on Presents of Game, &c." and "That We Must Not Look a Gift-horse in the Mouth" (*Works*, I, 343–344; and II, 261–263).

172. *C. L. to William Wordsworth*

4 March [1805]

My dear Wordsworth,

If Gilpin's statement has afforded you any satisfaction, I can assure you that he was most explicit in giving it, and even seemed anxious (interrupting me) to do away any misconception. His statement is not contradicted by the last & fullest of the two Narratives,[1] which have been published (the former being a mere transcript of the newspapers) which I would send you if I did not suppose that you would receive more pain from the unfeeling canting way in which it is drawn up, than satisfaction from its contents; and what relates to your brother in particular is very short. It states that your brother was seen talking to the First Mate[2] but a few minutes before the ship sunk with apparent cheerfulness, & it contradicts the newspaper account about his depression of spirits procrastinating his taking leave of the Court of Directors; which the drawer up of the Narrative (a man high in the India House) is likely to be well informed of. It confirms Gilpin's account of his seeing your brother striving to save himself, & **adds** that **"Webber,** a Joiner, was near the Captain, who was standing on the hencoop when the ship went down, whom he saw washed off by a sea, which also carried him (Webber) overboard";—this is all which concerns your brother personally. But I will just transcribe from it, a Copy of Gilpin's account delivered in to the Court of Directors.—

"Memorandum respecting the Loss of the E. of A"—— "At 10 A.M. being about 10 leagues to the Westward of Portland, the Commodore made the signal to bear up—did so accordingly. At this time having main top gallant mast struck, fore & mizen do. on deck & the jib boom

in the wind about W.S.W. at 3 P.M. got on board a Pilot, being about
2 leagues to the westward of Portland; ranged & bitted both cables at
about ½ past 3, called all hands & got out the jib boom at about
4. While crossing the east End of the shambles, the wind suddenly died
away, & a strong tide setting the ship to the westward, drifted her into
the breakers, & a sea striking her on the larboard quarter, brought her
to, with her head to the northward, when she instantly struck, it being
about 5 P.M: Let out all the reefs, & hoisted the top sails up, in hopes
to shoot the ship across the Shambles. About this time the wind shifted
to the N.W. The surf driving us off, & the tide setting us on alternately,
sometimes having 4½ at others 9 fathoms, sand of the sea about 8 feet,
continued in this situation till about ½ past 7, when she got off. During
the time she was on the Shambles, had from 3 to 4 feet water; kept the
water at this height about 15 minutes, during the whole time the
pumps constantly going. Finding she gained on us, it was determined
to run her on the nearest shore. About 8 the wind shifted to the east-
ward: the leak continuing to gain upon the pumps, having 10 or 11
feet water, found it expedient to bale at the forescuttle & hatch way.
The ship would not bear up—kept the helm hard a starboard, she
being water-logg'd: but still had a hope she could be kept up till we
got her on Weymouth Sands. Cut the lashings of the boats—could not
get the Long Boat out, without laying the main-top-sail aback, by
which our progress would have been so delayed, that no hope would
have been left us of running her aground. & there being several sloops
in sight, one having sent a small skiff on board, took away 2 Ladies &
3 other passengers, & put them on board the sloop, at the same time
promising to return & take away a hundred or more of the people:
she finding much difficulty in getting back to the Sloop, did not return.
About this time the Third Mate[3] & Purser were sent in the cutter to
get assistance from the other ships. Continued pumping & baling till
11 P.M. when she sunk. Last cast of the lead 11 fathoms; having fired
guns from the time she struck till she went down, about 2 A.M. boats
came & took the people from the wreck about 70 in number. The
troops, in particular the Dragoons, pumped very well.

(Signed) Thos. Gilpin"

And now, my dear W.— I must apologize for having named my
health. But indeed it was because what with the ill news, your letter

coming upon me in a most wretched state of ill spirits, I was scarce able to give it an answer, & I felt what it required. But we will say no more about it. I am getting better. And when I have persisted **time enough** in a course of **regular living** I shall be well. But I am now well enough; & have got to business afresh—. Many thanks for your invitation. I have wished myself with you daily since the news. I have wished that I were Coleridge, to give you any consolation. You have not mourned without one to have a feeling of it. And we have not undervalued the intimation of your friendship. We shall one day prove it by intruding on your privacy, when these griefs shall be a little calmed. This year, I am afraid, it is impossible: but I shall store it up as among the good things to come, which keep us up when life & spirits are sinking.

If you have not seen or wish to see the wretched narrative I have mentioned, I will send it. But there is nothing more in it affecting you. I have hesitated to send it, because it is unfeelingly done; & in the hope of sending you something from some of the actual spectators, but I have been disappointed, & can add nothing yet. Whatever I pick up, I will store for you. . It is perfectly understood at the E. I. House, that no blame whatever belongs to the Captn. or Officers.

I can add no more but Mary's warmest Love to all. When you can write without trouble, do it, for you are among the very chief of our interests—

C Lamb

MS: University of Texas Library. Pub.: Harper, III, 172–176; Lucas (1905), VI, 304–306; Lucas (1912), V, 315–318; Lucas (1935), I, 387–389. Address: Mr Wordsworth/Grasmere/near Ambleside/Westmoreland. Postmark: March 5, 1805.
1. *An Authentic Narrative of the Loss of the Earl of Abergavenny, East Indiaman, off Portland . . . Corrected from the Official Returns at the East-India House* (London: Stockdale, February 13, 1805) and *An Authentic Narrative of the Loss of the Earl of Abergavenny, East Indiaman, Captain John Wordsworth . . . By a Gentleman in the East-India House* (London: Minerva Press, February 21, 1805). The Preface to the second is dated February 19 and signed with the initials of William Dalmeida (d. 1830), who had been appointed a clerk in the secretary's office of the East India House in 1777 and was retired in 1817.
2. Samuel Baggot, who, according to the first of the two pamphlets and therefore also the newspapers, observed that at the end, when he told Captain Wordsworth that all efforts to save the ship were in vain, Captain Wordsworth "stedfastly looked him in the face, and, at last, with every appearance of a heart-broken man, faintly answered 'Let her go! God's will be done.' These," Baggot concluded, "were the last words he uttered." The pamphlet remarks as well about the "extraordinary fact, that Captain Wordsworth felt such an unaccountable depression

of spirits, that he could not be persuaded to go through the usual ceremony of taking leave of the Court of Directors [of the East India Company] on the day appointed; and it was not till the Wednesday following, which was specially fixed for that purpose, that he yielded to the wishes of his friends, and reluctantly attended the Court" (quoted from *Wordsworths' Letters,* I, 550 and 565). William Webber, referred to below, is correctly termed a seaman in the next letter.

3. Joseph Wordsworth (bapt. 1782), a son of William's cousin Richard Wordsworth (1752–1816). That Richard Wordsworth was an attorney of Branthwaite, near Cockermouth, Cumberland. Cosmas Henry Stewart was the purser, referred to next.

173. *C. L. to William Wordsworth*

21st March 1805

Dear Wordsworth,

Upon the receipt of your last letter before that which I have just received, I wrote myself to Gilpin putting your questions to him; but have yet had no answer.[1] I at the same time got a person in the India House to write a much fuller enquiry to a relative of his who was saved, one Yates a midshipman. Both these officers (& indeed pretty nearly all that are left) have got appointed to other ships & have joined them. Gilpin is in the **Comet** India-man, now lying at Gravesend. Neither Yates nor Gilpin have yet answered, but I am in daily expectation. I have sent your letter of this morning also to Gilpin. The waiting for these answers has been my reason for not writing you. I have made very particular enquiries about Webber, but in vain. He was a common seaman (not the ship's carpenter) and no traces of him are at the I. House: it is most probable that he has entered in some Privateer, as most of the crew have done. I will keep the £1 note till you find out something I can do with it.— I now write idly, having nothing to send: but I cannot bear that you should think I have quite neglected your commission. My letter to G. was such as I thought he could not but answer: but he may be busy. The letter to Yates I hope I can promise, will be answered. One thing, namely why the other ships sent no assistance, I have learn'd from a person on board one of them: the firing was never once heard, owing to the very stormy night, & no tidings came to them till next morning. The **sea** was quite high enough to have thrown out the most expert swimmer, & might not your brother have received some blow in the shock, which disabled him?— We are glad to hear poor Dorothy is a little better. None of you are

able to bear such a stroke. To people oppressed with feeling, the loss of a good-humoured happy man that has been friendly with them, if he were no brother, is bad enough. But you must cultivate his spirits, as a legacy: & believe that such as he cannot be lost. He was a chearful soul! God bless you. Mary's love always.

<div align="right">C Lamb</div>

MS: University of Texas Library. Pub.: Harper, III, 176–177; Lucas (1905), VI, 306–307; Lucas (1912), V, 318–319; Lucas (1935), I, 390. Address: Mr. Wordsworth/Grasmere/near Kendal/Westmoreland. Postmark: March 21, 1805.

1. Thomas Gilpin's answer to Lamb's letter is included below as part of Letter 175. Neither Lamb's letter to Gilpin nor the Wordsworth letters to which Lamb refers have been recovered. The answer of Midshipman Benjamin Yates to the enquiry mentioned, from his cousin Benjamin Yates (d. 1814)—he had been in the accountant general's department of the East India House since 1793—is included as part of the next letter.

174. *C. L. to William Wordsworth, written on a letter from Midshipman Benjamin Yates to Benjamin Yates of the East India House, with two interpolations by C. L.*

<div align="right">[East India House?
April 2, 1805]</div>

My dear Wordsworth,

this is Yates the [midshipman] to his Cousin of the India Ho. to some of m[y questions] as he wrote it. You will make allowance [. . .] your own knowledge of your Brother will tell you to [. . .] can belong to this young seaman's surmises. So thing[s . . .] did not know, as you did, the inner man. I though[t his words would] please better than my garbling them. **One** word in the midst of [his account of] your brother's behavior, I take to be *"composed"*: but it is horrib[ly written] and perhaps will be no information to you after Capt. Wordsworth's acct. .[1] [. . .] say's C. talks of coming home directly. I am in hope of more informat[ion soon.]

<div align="right">Yours ever sincerely
C L</div>

Gravesend

Mar[ch ?31—April 2, 1805]

Answer to the first Question. The way we made after the Ship got clear of the shambles was about 3 Miles per Hour the water increased in the Hold and forward withall retar'd our progress very much about nine o clock P M she was quite Water loggd the Jebb, in addition to the foresail where Ropt up in hopes she would pay her head but to no effect it was ebb tide that threw us on the flood rose in our favour after half an hour had the ship been managable it would have run us in quite shallow water.

Answer to the second the reason why the the Boats where not hoisted out was it would have deterd the Men paying that attention to the sails pumping and bailing in the second place the anxiety of saving life would have caused an exertion in every one the Boats from the sea most likely would have swampt along side in last or else the ship would have gon down in deep water when the distruction of every body though ever so good a swimmer would have been inevetable.

Answer to the third Capt W at the time the ship sunk was on the fore part of the Poop between the Mizzen and th[e] and the ladder close into the starbord side which leads down on the quarter deck.

Answer to the forth Mr Y² saw Capt W. that Instant the ship sunk.

Answer to the fifth see Question the third

Answer to Question the sixth Mr. Y. requested Capt W. to ascend the mizzen rigging having no reply made me I concluded from the screams of every on[e] in this distressed scen rendered me deaf to any answer he could make.

Answer to the seventh Question Mr. Y perfectly well recolects the last words of Capt W. was to haul on board the main tack which I have every reason to suppose hurred her down as it was a pressing sail

Answer to the 8th Capt W appeard quite composd the whole time he repeatedly called out to haul the main tack on board Mr. Baggot and the Pilot³ mentioned their was no occasion for any after sails as the ships head would not Pay off. Answer to the 10 they kept pumping and bailing untill the ship sunk Answer to the 11th *the reason why Capt. W.* was not saved *I cannot* define I have no reason to suppose he was thrown into the eddy the ship was quite full from the Main Mast forward the first scend⁴ the second entirely covered her and from

certain belief in my own mind he never had a wish to survive the loss of his property—

Answer to the 12th the reason why the ship (*went down* seems to be her[e] wanting) by the head was the water as it increased float'd all the loose things from the stern.

Answer to the 13th the only reason I can urge the other Ships where shut in round the point when the accident happened the Wind NE. did away the intention of our signal guns blew away the sound entirely from the harbour

Dear Cousin

I have answered your [questions] as near as come, [wi]thin my own observa[tion. Had] I been more acquainted with the s[hip I] probab[l]y would have been more s[ure. You will] I hope excuse my not answer[ing sooner, but] the bustle on board preven[ted . . .] it a perticular favour i[f you were] to give your oppinion of the answers &c. Give my best respects to Mr. Yates and Mr. C Yates and your sister[5]

<div style="text-align:right">and I am your sincere Cousin
B Yates</div>

MS: Wordsworth Library, Grasmere. Pub.: Carl H. Ketcham, "The Death of Wordsworth's Brother John: Manuscript Materials in the Cornell-Dove Cottage Collection," *Cornell Library Journal,* No. 11 (Spring 1970), 31–33. Addresses, by Midshipman Yates: ⟨Mr. B. Yates/[. . .]/Near Islington⟩; by Lamb: Mr. Wordsworth, Grasmere near Kendal/Westmoreland. Postmarks: April 1 and 2, 1805. The considerable though indeterminable number of missing locutions is due to a portion of the last leaf of the manuscript having been torn away. It is on the last leaf that Lamb wrote. Some of the conjectured readings are supplied from Ketcham's text.

1. That by John Wordsworth (1754–1819), William's cousin. That John Wordsworth had preceded William's brother John as the commander of the *Earl of Abergavenny* before his retirement from the service of the East India Company in January 1801. Coleridge, referred to next, did not leave Malta until about September 23, 1805. Then he traveled to Syracuse, Naples, Rome, Florence, and Leghorn. He sailed from Leghorn on June 23, 1806, and arrived at Lower Halstow, Kent, on August 17, 1806.

2. Midshipman Yates himself.

3. Unidentified.

4. A heaving upward by the force of a swell; a pitching downward, at either the bow or the stern, deep into the trough of a wave. The property of Captain Wordsworth referred to at the end of this paragraph was an investment in the voyage of perhaps £20,000 in money and cargo, which he had hoped to turn into a profit by private trade. It was rumored that Captain Wordsworth had chosen

to perish rather than suffer bankruptcy. (See *Wordsworths' Letters*, I, 535 and 548.) The parenthesis in the next paragraph and "urge" in the one following that are Lamb's.

5. Those members of the Yates family have not been identified.

175. *C. L. to William Wordsworth, written on a letter from Thomas Gilpin to C. L., with two glosses by C. L.*

[East India House
April 5, 1805]

Dear Wordsworth.

I have this moment received this letter from **Gilpin** in reply to 3 or 4 short questions I put to him in my letter before yours for him came. He does not notice having recd. yours, which I sent immediately. Perhaps he has already answered it to you. You see that his hand is sprain'd, & your questions being more in number, may delay his answer to you. My first question was, when it was he called to your brother: the rest you will understand from the answers. I was beginning to have hard thoughts of G. from his delay, but now I am confirm'd in my first opinion that he is a rare goodhearted fellow. How is Dorothy? & all of you.

Yours sincerely
C Lamb

I think I did not mention in my last, that I sent yours to T. Evans,[1] *Richmond*. I hope you have got an answer.— —

Comet, Northfleet
March 31st[—April 5], 1805

Sir

I did not receive yours of 16th Inst till this day, or shd have answerd it sooner——to your first Question, I answer after the Ship had sunk—to your second, my answer is, I was in the Starboard Mizen Rigging—I thought I see the Captn hanging by a Rope—that was fast to the Mizen Mast—I came down & haild him as loud as I could, he was about 10 feet distant from me I threw a rope which, fell close to him, he seem'd quite Motionless, & insensible (it was excessive cold) and was, soon after, sweep'd away, & I see him no more it was near

about five minutes after the Ship went down——With respect to the Captn & Webber, being on the same Hencoop I can give no answer, all I can say, I did not see them—your fourth* Question, I cannot answer, as I did not see Captn Wordsworth at the moment the Ship was going down, tho I was then, on the Poop less than one minute before I see the Captn their—the Statement in the printed Pamphlet, is by no means correct— I have sprained my Wrist, most violently, and am now in great pain which will I hope, be an apology, for the shortness of this Letter

<div align="right">

believe me truly yours[†]
Thos Gilpin
</div>

This Letter as been detained till April 5th—

*4th question was, was Capt. W. standing near the shrouds or any place of safety at the moment of sinking?

[†]this is merely a kind way of expressing himself, for I have no acquaintance with him, nor ever saw him but that once I got introduced to him.—

MS: University of Texas Library. Pub.: Harper, III, 177–179; Lucas (1905), VI, 307–308; Lucas (1912), V, 319–320; Lucas (1935), I, 391–392. Addresses, by Gilpin: (Mr Lamb/Accountants Office/Indiahouse); by Lamb: Mr. Wordsworth/Grasmere/near Kendal/Westmoreland. Postmark: April 5, 1805.

1. Thomas Evans (d. 1810), who had been with the East India Company since 1778, for some time as one of its senior merchants in Bengal. In 1804–1805 he was on leave and living in Richmond, Surrey. With his daughter Emilia, her companion Mrs. Margaret Blair (one of the victims of the disaster), and his niece Rebecca Jackson he had sailed on the *Earl of Abergavenny* in an attempt to return to his duties. For his letter to Wordsworth and Wordsworth's reply see *Wordsworths' Letters*, I, 581–582 and 578–580. (This Thomas Evans is not the Thomas Evans identified in my Vol. I, Letter 3, note 29.) *"Richmond,"* following, is underscored twice.

176. *M. A. L. to Dorothy Wordsworth*

<div align="right">

[May 7, 1805]
</div>

My dear Miss Wordsworth

I thank you my kind friend for your most comfortable letter, till I saw your own hand-writing I could not persuade myself that I should do well to write to you, though I have often attempted it, but I always

left off dissatisfied with what I had written, & feeling that I was doing
an improper thing to intrude upon your sorrow, I wished to tell you,
that you would one day feel the kind of peaceful state of mind, and
sweet memory of the dead which you so happily describe as now almost
begun, but I felt that it was improper, and most grating to the feelings
of the afflicted, to say to them that the memory of their aff[l]iction
would in time become a constant part not only of their "dream, but of
their most wakeful sense of happiness."[1] That you would see every
object with, & through your lost brother, & that that would at last be-
come a real & everlasting source of comfort to you, I felt, & well knew
from my own experience in sorrow, but till you yourself began to feel
this I did not dare tell you so, but I send you some poor lines which I
wrote under this conviction of mind, and before I heard Coleridge was
returning home. I will transcribe them now before I finish my letter,
lest a false shame prevent me then, for I know they are much worse
than they ought to be, written as they were with strong feeling and on
such a subject, every line seems to me to be borrowed, but I had no
better way of expressing my thoughts, and I never have the power of
altering or amending anything I have once laid aside with dissatisfaction.

> Why is he wandering o'er the sea?
> Coleridge should now with Wordsworth be.
> By slow degrees he'd steal away
> Their woe, and gently bring a ray
> (So happily he'd time relief)
> Of comfort from their very grief.—
> He'd tell them that their brother dead
> When years have passed o'er their head,
> Will be remember'd with such holy,
> True, & perfect melancholy,
> That ever this lost brother John
> Will be their hearts companion.
> His voice they'll always hear, his face they'll always see,
> There's nought in life so sweet as such a memory.[2]

Mr and Mrs Clarkson came to see us last week, I find it was at your
request they sought us out, you cannot think how glad we were to see
them, so little as we have ever seen of them, yet they seem to us like
very old friends. poor Mrs. Clarkson looks very ill indeed, she walked

near a mile, and came up our high stairs which fatigued her very much, but when she had sat a while her-own natural countenance with which she cheared us in your little cottage seemed to return to her, & then I began to have hopes she would get the better of her complaint. Charles does not think she is so much altered as I do I wish he may be the better judge. We talked of nothing but you, she means to try to get leave of Dr Beddoes[3] to come & see you—her heart is with you, & I do not think it would hurt her so much to come to you, as it would distress you to see her so ill.

She read me a part of your letter wherein you so kindly express your wishes that we would come & see you this summer. I wish we could for I am sure it would be a blessed thing for you, & for us to be a few weeks together—I fear it must not be.— Mrs Clarkson is to be in town again in a fortnight and then they have promised we shall see more of them.

I am very sorry for the poor little Dorothy's illness—I hope soon to hear she is perfectly recovered. Remember me with affection to your brother, & your good sister, what a providence it is that your brother & you have this kind friend, & these dear little ones—I rejoice with her & with you that your brother is employed upon his poem[4] again—

pray remember us to old Molly, Mrs Clarkson says her house is a pattern of Neatness, to all her neighbours—such good ways she learnt of "Mistress." how well I remember the shining ornaments of her kitchen, & her old friendly face not t[he] least ornamental part of it.

Excuse the hast I write in, I am unexpectedly to go out to dinner, else I think I have much more to say, but I will not put it off till next post, because you so kindly say I must not write if I feel unwilling— you do not know what very great joy I have in being again writing to you,

Thank you for sending the letter of Mr Evans, it was a very kind one, have you received one from a Cornet Burgoine,[5] my brother wrote to him & desires he would direct his answer to your brother.—

God bless you & yours my dear friend

<div align="right">I am yours affectionately
M Lamb</div>

MS: University of Texas Library. Pub.: Talfourd (1848), II, 233–234; Sala, I, 322–324; Purnell, I, 322–324; Lucas (1905), VI, 308–310; Lucas (1912), V,

320–322; Lucas (1935), I, 392–394. Address: Miss Wordsworth/Grasmere/near Kendal/Westmoreland. Postmark: May 7, 1805.

1. Probably quoted from the letter of Miss Wordsworth, who expressed the same sentiment in her letter of May 4, 1805 (*Wordsworths' Letters,* I, 591–592), to Margaret, Lady Beaumont (1756–1829). She was the wife of Sir George Howland Beaumont, seventh baronet (1753–1827). He was a patron of the arts, of Wordsworth and Coleridge, and an amateur landscape painter.

2. In *Works,* V, 301–302.

3. Dr. Thomas Beddoes (1760–1808), who had known Coleridge since at least 1795 and possibly through Coleridge had come to know the Lambs, Wordsworths, and Clarksons. He was the author and editor of medical and other books and had in 1798 helped to establish the Pneumatic Institute at Clifton for the treatment of diseases by inhalation. He had been treating Mrs. Clarkson since about 1803. His wife was Anna Maria (1773–1824), a daughter of the author Richard Lovell Edgeworth (1744–1817) and the former Anna Maria Elers (d. 1773) and a sister of the novelist Maria Edgeworth (1767–1849). The Beddoeses' son was the poet and physiologist Thomas Lovell Beddoes (1803–1849). For the letter from Miss Wordsworth to Mrs. Clarkson mentioned in the next paragraph see *Wordsworths' Letters,* I, esp. 585.

4. *The Prelude.*

5. Cornet G. A. Burgoyne, the commander of the Eighth Regiment of Light Dragoons on board the *Earl of Abergavenny* and the author of *A Correct Narrative of the Loss of the Earl of Abergavenny East Indiaman, J. Wordsworth, Esq. Commander, Which Foundered in Weymouth Roads, on Tuesday Night, February the 5th, 1805* (Weymouth: n.p., n.d.). In Letter 197 Mary recounts his story of the two glasses of liquor and the gossip derived from it, that John Wordsworth was drunk when his ship went down. Lamb's letter to Burgoyne, to which Mary alludes following, has not been recovered, and Burgoyne seems never to have written to Wordsworth.

177. *C. L. to Godwin*

Thursday morng, 13 June 1805

Dear Godwin,

Your letter came while I was in the country,[1] where I have been spending some days, being left *alone* by the illness of poor Mary. She cannot come with me, but I purpose spending Monday evening with you, if I do not hear from you to the contrary. The intermediate evenings I am engaged.

With respects to Mrs. G.

Yours truly

C Lamb

P. S. I do not perfectly understand some parts of your letter, quià enigmatical. If you have met with any accident, I must postpone my sympathy till I come to understand it.—

, MS: Lord Abinger. Unpublished. Address: Mr. Godwin/Polygon/Somers-town. Postmark: June 13, 1805.
1. Where is not known. Mary had been placed in an asylum, as the next letter shows, on Monday, June 3. The Latin in the postscript translates, "because."

178. *C. L. to Dorothy Wordsworth*

friday 14th June 1805

My dear Miss Wordsworth,

Your long kind letter has not been thrown away (for it has given me great pleasure to find you are all resuming your old occupations, and are better) but poor Mary to whom it is addrest cannot yet relish it. She has been attacked by one of her severe illnesses, and is at present *from home*. Last Monday week was the day she left me; and I hope I may calculate upon having her again in a month, or little more. I am rather afraid late hours have in this case contributed to her indisposition. But when she begins to discover symptoms of approaching illness, it is not easy to say what is best to do. Being by ourselves is bad, & going out is bad. I get so irritable & wretched with **fear,** that I constantly hasten on the disorder. You cannot conceive the misery of such a foresight. I am sure that for the week before she left me, I was little better than light-headed. I now am calm, but sadly taken down, & flat. I have every reason to suppose that this illness, like all her former ones, will be but temporary. But I cannot aways feel [s]o.[1] Meantime she is **dead** to me,—and I miss a [prop]. All my strength is gone, and I am like a [fool, bere]ft of her co-operation. I dare not think, lest I [should think] wrong; so used am I to look up to her [in the least] & the biggest perplexity. To say *all that* [I know of her] would be more than I think any body could [believe or even under]stand; and when I hope to have her well [again with me] it would be sinning against her feelings to go about to praise her: for I can conceal nothing that I do from her. She is older, & wiser, & better than me, and all my wretched imperfections I cover to myself by resolutely thinking on her goodness. She would share life & death, heaven & hell with me. She lives but for me. And I know I have been wasting & teazing her life for five years past incessantly with my cursed drinking & ways of going on. But even in this up-braiding of myself I am offending against her;

for I know that she has cleaved to me **for better, for worse;** and if the balance has been against her hitherto, it was a **noble trade.**

I am stupid & lose myself in what I write. I write rather what answers to my feelings (which are sometimes sharp enough) than express my present ones, for I am only flat & stupid.———

Poor Miss Stoddart! she is coming to England under the notion of passing her time between her mother & Mary, between London & Salisbury.[2] Since she talk'd of coming, word has been sent to Malta that her Mother is gone out of her mind. This Lette[r] with mine to Stoddart with an account of Allen's death &c. has miscarried (taken by the French) [and] she is coming home, with no soul to receiv[e her.] She has not a woman-friend in London.

I am sure you will excuse my writing [no more, knowing I] am very poorly. I cannot resist tra[nscribing] three or four Lines which poor Mary made upon a Picture (a Holy Family) which we saw at an Auction **only one week before she left home.** She was then beginning to shew signs of ill boding. They are sweet Lines, and upon a sweet Picture. But I send them, only as the last memorial of her.

> Virgin & Child. L. da Vinci.——[3]
> **Maternal Lady** with the **Virgin-grace,**
> Heaven-born thy **Jesus** seemeth sure,
> And thou a virgin pure.
> **Lady** most perfect, when thy angel face
> **Men look** upon, they wish to be
> **A Catholic,** Madona fair, to worship thee.

You had her lines about the "Lady Blanch." You have not had some which she wrote upon a copy of a girl from Titian, which I had hung up where that print of Blanch & the Abbess (as she beautifully interpreted two female figures from L. da Vinci) had hung, in our room.— Tis light & pretty.

> Who are thou, fair one, who usurp'st the place
> Of Blanch, the Lady of the matchless grace?
> Come, fair & pretty, tell to me
> Who in thy life-time thou mightst be?
> Thou pretty art & fair,
> But with the Lady Blanch thou never must compare.

No need for Blanch her history to tell,
Whoever saw her face, they there did read it well.
But when I look on thee, I only know,
There liv'd a pretty maid some hundred years ago.

This is a little unfair, to tell so much about ourselves, & to advert so little to your letter, so full of comfortable tidings of you all. But my own cares press pretty close upon me, & you can make allowance. That you may go on gathering **strength & peace** is the next wish to Mary's recovery.—

I had almost forgot your repeated invitation. Supposing that Mary will be well & able, there is another *ability* which you may guess at, which I cannot promise myself. In prudence we ought not to come. This illness will make it still more prudential to wait. It is not a balance of this way of spending our money against another way, but an absolute question of whether we shall stop now, or go on wasting away the little we have got beforehand, which my **wise conduct** has already incroachd upon **one half.**— My best Love, however, to you all; & to that most friendly creature Mrs. Clarkson, & better health to her, when you see or write to her

C. Lamb

MS: University of Texas Library. Pub.: Talfourd (1837), I, 262–265; Talfourd (1848), II, 210–212; Sala, I, 239–242; Purnell, I, 239–242; Fitzgerald, II, 74–77; Hazlitt, I, 350–352; Ainger (1888), I, 212–214; Ainger (1900), II, 110–114; Macdonald, I, 260–262; Ainger (1904), I, 263–265; Harper, III, 180–183; Lucas (1905), VI, 311–313; Lucas (1912), V, 323–325; Lucas (1935), I, 394–397. Address: Miss Wordsworth/Grasmere/near Kendal/Westmorland. Postmark: June 14, 1805.

1. The lower left corner of the first leaf has been torn away. The bracketed readings in this paragraph are supplied from Lucas (1935), I, 395. Those in the third and fourth paragraphs are my conjectures.

2. Miss Stoddart was in Salisbury by September 18, 1805. See Letter 170, near the reference to note 1, for the first mention of Lamb's letter mentioned below.

3. Titled "On the Same" in *Works*, V, 39. The next poem is titled "Lines: *On the Same Picture Being Removed to Make Place for a Portrait of a Lady by Titian*" in *Works*, V, 38–39. The first poem is upon Leonardo's "The Virgin of the Rocks," which is reproduced in *Works*, V, facing p. 302. The second poem is in part upon a Titian that has not been identified. See Letter 164 for Mary's lines on Lady Blanch.

179. *C. L. to Manning*

Saturdy Hot Noon [July 27? 1805]

Dear Archimedes,

Things have gone on badly with thy ungeometrical friend, but they are on **the turn.** My old housekeeper has shewed signs of convalescence, and will shortly resume the power of the Keys. So I sha'nt be cheated of my tea and liquors. Wind in the west, which promotes tranquillity. Have leisure now to anticipate seeing thee again. Have been taking leave of Tobacco in a rhyming address.[1] Had thought *that vein* had been long since closed up. But the L——d opened Sara's bag after years of unproduction. Find I can rhime & reason too. Think of studying mathematics, to **restrain the fire** of my genius: which G. D. recommends. Have frequent bleedings at the nose: which shews plethoric. May'be shall try the **sea** myself, that great scene of wonders. Got incredibly sober & regular: shave oftener, & hum a tune, to signify chearfulness & gallantry.

Suddenly disposed to sleep, having taken a quart of peas with bacon, and stout. Will not refuse Nature; who had done such things for me!—

Nurse, dont call me, unless Mr. Manning comes. What, the Gentleman in spectacles? Yes.

Dormit[2]

C L

MS: Huntington Library. Pub.: Talfourd (1837), I, 188–189; Sala, I, 388; Purnell, I, 388; Fitzgerald, II, 221; Hazlitt, I, 353–354; Ainger (1888), I, 216; Ainger (1900), II, 114–115; Macdonald, I, 263; Ainger (1904), I, 266; Harper, III, 183–184; Lucas (1905), VI, 313; Lucas (1912), V, 325–326; Lucas (1935), I, 397–398. Address: Mr T. Manning/Caius' College/Cambridge. Postmark: [July?] 2[7?], 1805. The date is taken from the text of Hazlitt, who presumably could read in its entirety the (now partially illegible) postmark.

1. "A Farewell to Tobacco." (See Letter 182.) For the conception of Sarah, referred to below, see Genesis 21:1–3. See also Letter 219, note 1. "G. D." is a reference to George Dyer.

2. "He sleeps."

180. *C. L. to Manning*

Saturday [autumn 1805?]

Dear Manning,

I sent to Brown's immediately. Mr. Brown (or Pijou, as he is called by the moderns) denied the having received a letter from you. The **one** for you he remember'd receiving, and remitting to Leadenhall Street; whither I immediately posted (it being the middle of dinner) my teeth unpicked.— There I learned that if you want a letter set right, you must apply at the first door on the left hand **before one** oClock. I returned, and picked my teeth. And this morning I made my application in form, & have seen the vagabond letter, which most likely accompanies this. If it dos not, I will get Rickman to name it to the **Speaker,** who will not fail to lay the matter before Parliament the **next sessions;** when you may be sure to have all abuses in the **Post Department** rectified.—

N. B. There seems to be some informality epidemical. You direct yours to me in Mitre Court; my true address is Mitre Court Buildings. By the pleasantries of Fortune, who likes a joke or a double entendre as well as the best of us her children, there happens to be **another Mr Lamb**[1] (that there should be **two ! !**) in Mitre Court, His duns & *girls* frequently stumble up to me, and I am obliged to *satisfy* **both** in the best way I am able. Farewell and think upon it

C L

MS: Huntington Library. Pub.: Talfourd (1837), I, 259–260; Sala, I, 365–366; Purnell, I, 365–366; Fitzgerald, II, 198–199; Hazlitt, I, 355; Macdonald, I, 203–204; Harper, III, 19; Lucas (1905), VI, 329; Lucas (1912), V, 222; Lucas (1935), I, 255. Watermark: 1804. The business with Brown, who has not been identified, suggests that Lamb may have written the letter when Manning was planning to come to town to begin his medical studies at Westminster Hospital. See Vol. I, Letter 53, source note.

1. Unidentified.

181. *M. A. L. to Sarah Stoddart*

Wednesday Morning [September 18, 1805]

My dear Sarah

I have made many attempts at writing to you, but it has always

brought your troubles, and my own so strongly into my mind, that I have been obliged to leave off, & make Charles write for me—I am resolved now however few lines I write, this shall go, for I know my kind friend, you will like once more to see my own handwriting.

I have been for these few days past in rather better spirits, so that I begin almost to feel myself once more a living creature, and to hope for happier times, and in that hope I include the prospect of once more seeing my dear Sarah in peace and comfort in our old garret. how did I wish for your presence to chear my drooping heart when I returned home from banishment.

Is your being with, or near, your poor dear Mother necessary to her comfort? does she take any notice of you? and is there any prospect of her recovery? how I grieve for her & for you.— — — —

I went to the Admiralty about your Mothers pension,[1] from thence I was directed to an Office in Lincolns Inn where they are paid—they informed me at the Office that it could not be paid to any person except Mr Wray without a letter of Attorney from your Mother, and as the stamp for that will cost one pound, it will perhaps be better to leave it till Mr Wray comes to town, if he does come before Christmas, they tell me it can be received any thursday between this & Christmas, if you send up a letter of Attorney let it be in my name—if you think notwithstanding their positive assurance to the contrary that you can put me in any way of getting it without, let me know—. Are you acquainted with Mr Pearce[2] and will my taking another letter from you to him be of any service, or will a letter from Mr Wray be of any use though I fear not for they said at the Office they had orders to pay no pension without a letter of Attorney.— The attestation you sent up they said was sufficient & that the same must be sent every year.— Do not let us neglect this business, & make use of me, in any way you can.—

I have much to thank you and your kind brother for, I kept the dark silk as you may suppose—you have made me very fine, the broche is very beautiful. Mrs Jeffries wept for gratitude when she saw your present, she desires all manner of thanks & good wishes—your maids sister[3] was gone to live a few miles from town, Charles however found her out and gave her the handkerchiefs.——

I want to know if you have seen William & if there is any prospect in future there. All you said in your letter from Portsmouth that related

to him was burnt so in the fumigating, that we could only make out that it was unfavourable but not the particulars, tell us again how you go on, & if you have seen him, I conceit affairs will some how be made up between you at last.

I want to know how your brother goes on. Is he likely to make a very good fortune, & in how long a time? And how is he in the way of home comforts, I mean is he very happy with Mrs Stoddart? This was a question I could not ask while you were there, and perhaps is not a fair one now; but I want to know how you all went on, and in short twenty little foolish questions that one ought perhaps rather to ask when we meet than to write about. But do make me a little acquainted with the inside of the good Doctors house, and what passes therein

Was Coleridge often with you, or did your brother & Col argue long arguements, till between the two great argue-ers there grew a little coolness, or perchance the mighty friendship between Coleridge & your Sovereign Governor Sir Alexander Ball might create a kind of jealousy, for we fancy something of a coldness did exist from the little mention ever made of C—— in your brothers letters.—

Write us my good girl a long gossiping letter, answering all these my foolish questions—and tell me any silly thing you can recollect— any the least particular will be interesting to us, and we will never tell tales out of school; but we used to wonder & wonder how you all went on, and when you was coming home we said, "now we shall hear all from Sarah."

God bless you my dear friend

I am ever your affectionate
Mary Lamb

If you have sent Charles any commissions he has not executed write me word—he says he has lost or mislaid a letter desiring him to inquire about a wig——

Write two letters one of business and pensions and one all about Sarah Stoddart & Malta.——

Is Mr Moncrief[4] doing well there.—

We have got a picture of Charles, do you think your brother would like to have it? if you do can you put us in a way how to send it.—

MS: Pierpont Morgan Library. Pub.: Lucas (1905), VI, 314–315; Lucas (1912), V, 326–328; Lucas (1935), I, 398–400. Address: Miss Stoddart/Salisbury. Postmark: September 18, 1805.

1. Due to her as the widow of a naval officer. Mr. Wray, mentioned below, apparently the late John Stoddart's attorney, was possibly the William Wray of Malton, Yorkshire, who later subscribed to and solicited and prepared extracts for *The Friend.* See *The Friend,* ed. Barbara Rooke, II, 467.

2. Probably the William Pearce listed in the 1799 and 1808 London directories as a clerk in the admiralty office, Charing Cross.

3. Neither the maid nor her sister has been identified. The William of the next sentence is still Miss Stoddart's former lover.

4. William Wellwood Moncreiff (d. 1813), the younger Mrs. John Stoddart's eldest brother. He became a judge advocate for Malta. The picture of Lamb referred to below would probably have been a copy of either the Hancock drawing (Vol. I, frontispiece) or the Hazlitt painting (Vol. II, frontispiece).

182. *C. L. to William and Dorothy Wordsworth*
28th. Sep 1805

My dear Wordsworth (or Dorothy rather, for to you appertains the biggest part of this answer by right.)—

I will not again deserve reproach by so long a silence. I have kept deluding myself with the idea that Mary would write to you, but she is so lazy, or I believe the true state of the case, so diffident, that it must revert to me as usual. Though she writes a pretty good style, and has some notion of the force of words, she is not always so certain of the true orthography of them & that & a poor handwriting (in this **Age of female Callography**) often deter her where no other reason does.— We have neither of us been very well for some weeks past. I am very nervous and she most so at those times when I am: so that a merry friend, adverting to the noble consolation we were able to afford each other, denominated us not unaptly **Gum Boil** and **Tooth Ache:** for they use to say that a Gum Boil is a great relief to a Tooth Ache. We have been [on] two tiny excursions this summer, for three or four days each: to a place near Harrow, & to Egham where Cooper's Hill[1] is: and that is the total history of our Rustications this year, alas! how poor a Sound to **Skiddaw,** and **Helvellyn,** & **Borrodaile** and the magnificent **sesquipedalia** of the **year 1802.** Poor old Molly! to have lost her pride, that "last infirmity of **Noble Mind,**" and her Cow—. Providence need not have set her wits to such an old Molly. I am heartily sorry for her. Remember us lovingly to her. And in particular remember us to Mrs. Clarkson in the most kind manner.

I hope by southwards you mean that she will be at or near London, for she is a great favorite of both of us, and we feel for her health as much as is possible for any one to do. She is one of the friendliest, comfortablest women we know; & made our little stay at your cottage one of the pleasantest times we ever past. We were quite strangers to her.— Mr. C is with you too?— our kindest separate remembrances to him.— ——

As to our special affairs, I am looking about me. I have done nothing since the beginning of last year when I lost my newspaper job, and having had a long idleness, I must do something or we shall get very poor. Sometimes I think of a farce—but hitherto all schemes have gone off,—an idle brag or two of an evening vaporing out of a **pipe**, & going off in the Morning—but now I have bid farewell to my **"Sweet Enemy"**[2] Tobacco, as you will see in my next page. , I perhaps shall set soberly to work. Hang Work! I wish that all the year were holy day. I am sure that **Indolence indefeazible Indolence** is the true state of man, & business the invention of **the Old Teazer** who persuaded Adam's Master to give him an apron & set him a houghing—. **Pen & Ink & Clerks, & desks** were the refinements of this old torturer a thousand years after **under pretence of Commerce** allying distant shores, promoting & diffusing knowledge, good &c——

A Farewell to Tobacco——

May the Babylonish curse[3]
Strait confound my stammering verse,
If I can a passage see
In this word—perplexity,
Or a fit expression find,
Or a language to my mind,
(Still the phrase is wide an acre)
To take leave of thee, **Tobacco**;
Or in any terms relate
Half my Love or half my Hate,
For I hate yet love thee so,
That whichever Thing I shew,
The plain truth will seem to be
A constrain'd hyperbole,

And the passion to proceed
More from a Mistress than a Weed.

Sooty retainer to the vine,
Bacchus' black servant, negro fine,
Sorcerer that mak'st us doat upon
Thy begrim'd complexion,
And for thy pernicious sake
More and greater oaths to break
Than reclaimed Lovers take
'Gainst women: Thou thy siege dost lay
Much too in the female way,
While thou suck'st the labouring breath
Faster than Kisses; or than Death.—

Thou in such a cloud dost bind us,
That our worst foes cannot find us,
And Ill Fortune (that would thwart us)
Shoots at rovers, shooting at us;
While each man through thy height'ning steam
Does like a smoking Etna seem,
And all about us does express
(Fancy and Wit in richest dress)
A Sicilian Fruitfulness.
Thou through such a mist dost shew us,
That our best friends do not know us;
And, for those allowed features,
Due to reasonable creatures,
Liken'st us to fell Chimeras,
Monsters, that, who see us, fear us,
Worse than Cerberus,[4] or Geryon,
Or, who first loved a cloud, Ixion.
Bacchus we know, and we allow
His tipsy rites. But what art thou?
That but by reflex canst shew
What his deity can do,
As the old Egyptian spell
Aped the true Hebrew miracle.

Some few vapours thou may'st raise,
The weak brain may serve to amaze,
But to the reins and nobler heart
Canst nor life nor heat impart.

Brother of Bacchus, later born,
The old world was sure forlorn,
Wanting thee; that aidest more
The God's victories, than before
All his panthers, and the brawls
Of his piping bacchanals;
These, as stale, we disallow,

Or

Or judge of **thee** meant: only thou
His true Indian Conquest art;
And, for Ivy round his dart,
The reformed God now weaves
A finer Thyrsus[5] of thy leaves.
Scent to match thy rich perfume
Chymic Art did neer presume
Through her quaint alembic strain;
None so sovran to the brain.
Nature, that did in thee excell,
Framed again no second smell;
Roses, violets, but toys
For the smaller sort of boys,
Or for greener damsels meant;
Thou 'rt the only manly scent.—.
Stinking'st of the stinking kind,
Filth of the mouth and fog of the mind,
Africa that brags her foyson,[6]
Breeds no such prodigious poison,
Henbane, nightshade, both together,
Hemlock, aconite. **Nay** rather,
Plant divine of rarest virtue,
Blisters on the tongue would hurt you;
Twas but in a sort I blamed thee,
None eer prosper'd wh[o] defamed thee:

Irony all and feign'd abuse,
Such as perplext Lovers use
At a need, when in despair
To paint forth their fairest fair,
Or in part but to express
That exceeding comeliness
Which their fancies does so strike,
They borrow language of **Dislike,**
And instead of Dearest Miss,
Honey, Jewel, Sweetheart, Bliss,
And those forms of old admiring,
Call her Cockatrice and Syren,
Basilisk & all that's evil,
Witch, Hyena, Mermaid, Devil,
Ethiop wench & Blackamoor,
Monkey, **Ape,** and twenty more,
Friendly Trait'ress,[7] Loving Foe:
Not that she is truly so,
But no other way they know
A contentment to express,
Borders so upon excess,
That they do not rightly wot,
Whether it be pain or not.—
Or, as men constrain'd to part
With what's nearest to their heart,
While their sorrow's at the height,
Lose discrimination quite,
And their hasty wrath let fall,
To appease their frantic gall,
On the **darling thing** whatever,
Whence they feel it death to sever,
Though it be, as they, perforce,
Guiltless of the sad divorce.—
For I must, (nor let it grieve thee,
Friendliest of plants, that I must) leave thee.
For thy sake, **Tobacco, I**
Would do any thing but die;

And but seek to extend my days
Long enough to sing thy praise.
But as **she,** who once has been
A king's consort, is a **Queen**
Ever after; nor will bate
Any tittle of her state,
Though a widow, or divorced,
So I, from thy converse forced,
The old name and style retain,
(A right Katherine of Spain)[8]
And a seat too 'mongst the joys
Of the blest **Tobacco** Boys:
Where, though I by sour physician
Am debarr'd the full fruition
Of thy favors, I may catch
Some collateral sweets, and snatch
Sidelong odours, that give life
Like glances from a neighbour's wife;
And still dwell in the by places,
And the suburbs of thy graces,
And in thy borders take delight,
An Unconquer'd **Canaanite.**————— ———[9]

I wish you may think this a handsome farewell to my "Friendly Traitress." Tobacco has been my evening comfort & my morning curse for these five years: & you know how difficult it is from refraining to pick one's lips even, when it has become a habit. This Poem is the only one which I have finished since so long as when I wrote "Hester Savory"—.[10] I have had it in my head to do it these two years, but Tobacco stood in its own light when it gave me head aches that prevented my singing its praises. Now you have got it, you have got **all my store** for I have absolutely not another **Line.** No more has Mary.— We have nobody about us that cares for Poetry, and who will rear grapes when he shall be the sole eater? Perhaps if you encourage us to shew you what we may write, we may do something now & then before we absolutely forget the quantity of an English line for want of practice. The "Tobacco" being a little in the way of **Withers**

(whom Southey so much **likes**) perhaps you will somehow convey it to him **with** my kind remembrances. **Then,** everybody will have seen it that I wish to see it: I having sent it[11] to Malta.

I remain Dear W. & D—

Yours truly

C Lamb

MS: University of Texas Library. Pub.: Talfourd (1837), I, 265–266; Talfourd (1848), I, 148–150; Sala, I, 243–246; Purnell, I, 243–246; Fitzgerald, II, 78–81; Hazlitt, I, 356–358; Ainger (1888), I, 216–218; Ainger (1900), II, 115–118; Macdonald, I, 263–265; Ainger (1904), I, 266–268; Harper, III, 184–191; Lucas (1905), VI, 316–320; Lucas (1912), V, 329–333; Lucas (1935), I, 400–405. Address: Mr Wor[dsworth]/Grasmere/near Kendal/Westmoreland. Postmark: September 28, 1805.

1. Cooper's Hill, Surrey, was the home of Sir John Denham (1615–1669) after 1634 and is the principal setting of his "Cooper's Hill." See Letter 133 for the account of the Lambs' excursion into Cumberland in 1802. I cannot say what specifically had happened to Molly, or Mary, Fisher. The quotation is of Milton's "Lycidas," line 71.

2. Sir Philip Sidney, *Astrophel and Stella*, Sonnet 41, line 4. "A Farewell to Tobacco" is in *Works*, V, 32–35. The "Old Teazer," below, is renamed "Sabbathless Satan" in the eighth line of "Work" (*Works*, V, 55–56), a sonnet that Lamb formed from the substance of the remainder of this paragraph. The word "houghing" is a variation of "hoeing."

3. Of Genesis 11:1–9.

4. The three-headed dog that guarded the gates of the infernal regions. Geryon was the triple-bodied winged giant whose herd of red cattle was guarded by the two-headed dog Orthrus. The cloud that Ixion loved and on which he fathered the Centaurs was that which Hera substituted for herself when Ixion attempted to seduce her.

5. The staff tipped with a pine cone, at times twined with ivy, carried by Bacchus and his votaries.

6. An obsolete form of "foison": plenty, as of a crop or resources.

7. Cf. *All's Well That Ends Well*, I, i, 167–170. To "Loving Foe," following, cf. *Hamlet*, I, ii, 182.

8. Catherine of Aragon, the first queen of Henry VIII. She had refused to accept the Act of Succession after her husband was married to Anne Boleyn.

9. See Joshua 17:12–18 and Judges 1.

10. See Letter 143.

11. In a letter that has not been recovered.

183. *M. A. L. to Sarah Stoddart*

[Early November 1805]

My dear Sarah

Certainly you are the best letter writer (besides writing the best hand) in the world. I have just been reading over again your two long

letters, & I perceive they make me very envious, I have taken a bran new pen & put on my *spectacles*, & am peering with all my might to see the lines in the paper, which the sight of your even lines had well nigh tempted me to rule, & I have moreover taken two pinches of snuff extraordinary to clear my head which feels more cloudy than common this fine chearful morning.

All I can gather from your clear, & I have no doubt, faithful history of Maltese politics, is, that the good Doctor though a firm friend, an excellent fancier of Brooch's a good husband, an upright Advocate, and in short all that they say upon tomb stones, (for I do not recollect that they celebrate any fraternal virtues there) yet is he but a moody brother—. That your sister in law is pretty much like what all sister's in law have been since the first happy invention of the happy marriage state.— That friend Coleridge has undergone no alteration by crossing the Atlantic, for his friendliness to you as well as all the oddities you mention are just what one ought to look for from him. And that you my dear Sarah have proved yourself just as unfit to flourish in a little proud Garrison Town as I did shrewdly suspect you were before you went there.

If I possibly can I will prevail upon Charles to write to your brother by the conveyance you mention, but he is so unwell I almost fear the fortnight will slip away before I can get him in the right vein, indeed it has been sad & heavy times with us lately, when I am pretty well his low spirits, throws me back again & when he begins to get a little chearful then I do the same kind office for him—. I heartily wish for the arrival of Coleridge, a few such evenings as we have sometimes passed with him would wind us up and set us a going again

Do not say any thing when you write of our low spirits it will vex Charles. You would laugh, or you would cry, perhaps both, to see us sit together looking at each other with long and rueful faces, & saying how do you do? & how do you do? & then we fall a crying & say we will be better on the morrow—he says we are like tooth ach & his friend gum bile, which though a kind of ease, is but an uneasy kind of ease, a comfort of rather an uncomfortable sort.—

I rejoice to hear of your Mothers amendment, when you can leave her with any satisfaction to yourself which as her sister[1] I think I understand by your letters is with her I hope you may soon be able to do, let me know upon what plan you mean to come to Town, your

brother proposed your being six months in Town, & six with your Mother, but he did not then know of your poor Mothers illness, by his desire I enquired for a respectable family for you to board with, & from Capn Burney I heard of one I thought would suit you at that time, he particularly desired I would not think of your being with us, not thinking I conjecture the home of a single man *respectable* enough. Your brother gave me most unlimitted orders to domineer over you, to be the inspector of all your actions, & to direct, & govern you with a stern voice & a high hand, to be in short a very elder brother over you—does not the hearing of this my meek pupil make you long to come to London. I am making all the proper enquiries against the time of the newest & most approved modes (being myself mainly ignorant in these points) of etiquette & nicely correct maidenly manners—. But to speak seriously I mean when we mean[2] that we will lay our heads together & consult & contrive the best way of making the best girl in the world the fine Lady her brother wishes to see her, & believe me Sarah it is not so difficult a matter as one is sometimes apt to imagine—. I have observed many a demure Lady who passes muster admirably well who I think we could easily learn to imitate in a wee[k or two.][3] We will talk of these things when we meet[. In the] mean time I give you free licence to be happy [and] merry at Salisbury in any way you can, Has the partridge season opened any communication between you & William—as I allow you to be imprudent till I see you, I shall expect to hear you have invited him to taste his own birds. Have you scratched him out of your Will yet. Rickman is married, & that is all the news I have to send you.

Your Wigs were sent by Mr Varvell[4] above five months ago, therefore the[y] could have arrived when you came away.

I seem upon looking over my letter again to have written too lightly of your distresses at Malta, but however I may have written believe me I enter very feelingly into all your troubles. I love you, & I love your brother, & between you, both of whom I think have been to blame I know not what to say—only this I say try to think as little as possible of past miscarriages. it was perhaps so ordered by providence that you might return home to be a comfort to your poor Mother. And do not I conjure you let her unhappy malady afflict you too deeply—I speak from experience & from the opportunity I have had of much observation in such cases that insane people in the fancy's they take

into their heads do not feel as one in a sane state of mind does under the real evil of poverty the perception of having done wrong or any such thing that runs in their heads.

Think as little as you can, & let your whole care be to be certain that she is treated with *tenderness*. I lay a stress upon this, because it is a thing of which people in her state are uncommonly susceptible, & which hardly any one is at all aware of, a hired nurse *never*, even though in all other respects they are good kind of people. I do not think your own presence necessary unless she *takes to you very much* except for the purpose of seeing with your own eyes that she is very kindly treated. I do long to see you. God bless & comfort you

<div align="right">

yours affectionate[l]y.

M. Lam[b]

</div>

MS: Pierpont Morgan Library. Pub.: Lucas (1905), VI, 321–323; Lucas (1912), V, 334–337; Lucas (1935), I, 406–409. Address: Miss Stoddart/Salisbury. Watermark: 1804. The opening of the next letter and the mention below of John Rickman's marriage, on October 30 to Susannah Postlethwaite (see Vol. I, Letter 86, note 4), establish the date of this one.

1. Unidentified.
2. For "meet."
3. This locution and the bracketed locutions following went with the piece that has been cut from the edge of the second manuscript leaf. They are supplied from Lucas (1935), I, 408.
4. Probably the John Varvell listed in the London directories for 1805–1807 as a hair manufacturer and perfumer of 34 Southhampton Street and 25 Tavistock Street, Covent Garden.

184. *M. A. L. to Sarah Stoddart*

<div align="right">

⟨Novr 9⟩ [and 14, 1805]

</div>

My dear Sarah

After a very feverish night I writ a letter to you, and I have been distressed about it ever since—. In the first place I have thought I treated too lightly your differences with your brother—which I truly enter into & feel for, but which I rather wished to defer saying much about till we meet—but that which gives me most concern is the way in which I talked about your Mothers illness & which I have since feared you might construe into my having a doubt of your showing her proper attention without my impertinent interference. God knows nothing of this kind was ever in my thoughts, but I have entered very

deeply into your affliction with regard to your Mother, & while I was writing, the many poor souls in the kind of desponding way she is in whom I have seen, came afresh into my mind, & all the mismanagement with which I have seen them treated was strong in my mind, & I wrote under a forcible impulse which I could not at that time resist, but I have fretted so much about it since, that I think it is the last time I will ever let my pen run away with me.

Your kind heart will I know even if you have been a little displeased forgive me when I assure you my spirits have been so much hurt by my last illness that at times I hardly know what I do—I do not mean to alarm you about myself, or to plead in excuse that I am very much otherwise than you have always known me—I do not think any one perceives me altered, but I have lost all self confidence in my own actions, & one cause of my low spirits is that I never feel satisfied with any thing I do—a perception of not being in a sane state perpetually haunts me. I am ashamed to confess this weakness to you, which as I am so sensible of I ought to strive to conquer. But I tell you that you may excuse any part of my letter that has given offence, for your not answering it, when you are such a punctual correspondent has made me very uneasy.

Write immediately my dear Sarah, but do not notice this letter, nor do not mention anything I said relative to your poor Mother. Your hand writing will convince me you are friends with me—& if Charles who must see your letter was to know I had first written foolishly & then fretted about the event of my folly, he would both ways be angry with me.

I would desire you to direct to me at home but your hand is so well known to Charles that that would not do, therefore take no notice of my megrums till we meet, which I most ardently long to do, an hour spent in your company would be a cordial to my drooping heart.

Pray write directly and believe me ever

Your affectionate friend
M Lamb

Novr 14

I have kept this by me, till today hoping every day to hear from you, if you find the seal a clumsy one, it is because I opened the wafer

Write I beg by the return of the post, & as I am very desirous of

hearing if you are as I fear dissatisfied with me, you shall if you please direct my letter to Nurse, her direction is, Mrs Grant, at Mr Smiths, Maidenhead, Ram Court, Fleet Street.

I was not able you know to notice when I writ to Malta your letter concerning an insult you received from a vile wretch there, and as I mostly shew my letters to Charles I have never named it since. Did it ever come to your brother['s] knowledge?— Charles & I were very uneasy at your account of it.— I wish I could see you.—

<div style="text-align:right">yours ever
M Lamb</div>

I do not mean to continue a secret correspondence but you must oblige me with this one letter—in future I will always shew my letters, before the[y] go, which will be a proper check upon my wayward pen

MS: Lockwood Library, State University of New York at Buffalo. Pub.: Lucas (1905), VI, 327–328; Lucas (1912), V, 341–342; Lucas (1935), I, 412–414. Address: Miss Stoddart/Salisbury. Postmark: November 14, 1805.

185. *C. L. to William Hazlitt*

<div style="text-align:right">10 Nov. 1805</div>

Dear Hazlitt,

I was very glad to hear from you, and that your journey[1] was so *picturesque.* We miss you, as we foretold we should. One or two things have happened which are beneath the dignity of epistolary communication, but which seated about our fire at night (the winter hands of pork have begun) gesture and emphasis might have talked into some importance.— Something about Rickmans wife, for instance how tall she is & that she visits prank'd up like a **Queen of the May** with green streamers—a good natured woman tho', which is as much as you can expect from a friend's wife, whom you got acquainted with a bachelor.— Somethings too about **Monkey**[2] which ca'nt so well be written—how it set up for a fine Lady & thought it had got Lovers & was obliged to be convinced of its age from the parish register, where it was proved to be only twelve, and an edict issued that it should not give itself airs yet these four years: and how it got leave to be called **Miss** by grace: **these and such like Hows were**

in my head to tell you, but who can **write?** **Also** how Manning's come
to town in spectacles, and studies physic: is melancholy and seems to
have something in his head, which he do'nt impart:[3] Then how I am
going to leave off smoking.— **O la!** your Leonardos of Oxford made
my mouth water. I was hurried thro' the gallery, and they escaped
me. What do I say? I was a Goth then, and should not have noticed
them. I had not settled my notions of Beauty. I have now forever!—the
small head, the long Eye—that sort of peering curve,
the wicked Italian mischief, the stick-at-nothing Herodia's daughter-
kind of grace. You understand me. But you disappoint me in passing
over in absolute silence the Blenheim Leonardo. Did'nt you see it?
Excuse a Lover's curiosity.

 I have seen no pictures of note since, except Mr. **Dawe's** gallery.[4]
It is curious to see how differently two great men treat the same
subject, yet both excellent in their way: for instance **Milton** and Mr.
Dawe. Mr. **Dawe** has chosen to illustrate the story of Sampson exactly
in the point of view in which Milton has been most happy: the inter-
view between the Jewish Hero blind & captive, & Dalilah. Milton has
imagined his **Locks** grown again, strong as Horse hair or porcupine's
bristles, doubtless shaggy & black as being hairs "which of a nation
armed contain'd the strength."[5] I dont remember, he *says* black: but
could Milton imagine them to be **yellow?** do you?— Mr. Dawe with
striking originality of conception has crowned him with a thin yellow
wig,—in colour precisely like Dyson's, in curl and quantity resembling
Mrs. Professor's: his Limbs **rather stout** about such a man as my
Brother or Rickman: but no Atles nor Hercules, nor yet so bony as
Dubois the Clown of Sadler's wells.[6] This was judicious, taking the
spirit of the story rather than the fact: for doubtless God could com-
municate national salvation to the trust of flax & tow as well as hemp
& cordage, and could draw down a Temple with a golden tress as soon
as with all the **Cables** of the *British Navy.*— Miss Dawe *is* about a
portrait of sulky Fanny Imlay alias Godwin: but Miss Dawe is of
opinion that her subject is neither **reserved** nor sullen, and doubtless
she will **persuade** the picture to be of the same opinion. However the
features are tolerably like.— Too much of Dawes!— Was'nt you
sorry for Lord Nelson?[7] I have followed him in fancy ever since I saw
him walking in Pall Mall (I was prejudiced against him before)

looking just as a **Hero** should look: and I have been very much **cut** about it indeed. He was the only pretence of a Great Man we had. Nobody is left of **any name** at all. His Secretary died by his side. I imagined him, a Mr. Scott, to be the man you met at Hume's: but I learn from Mrs. Hume that it is not the same. I met Mrs. H one day & agreed to go on the Sunday to **Tea,** but the rain prevented us & the distance. I have been to apologize, & we are to dine there the first fine Sunday! ! Strange perverseness. I never went while you staid here, & now I go to *find you.* . ———

What other news is there, Mary?— What puns have I made in the last fortnight? You never remember them. You have no relish of the **Comic.** O! tell Hazlitt not to forget to send the American Farmer.[8] I dare say it is'nt so good as he fancies: but a Book's a Book. .— ———

I have not heard from Wordsworth or from Malta since. .— Charles Kemble, it seems, enters into possession tomorrow. We sup at 109 Russell St. this evening. I wish your brother would'nt drink. It's a blemish in the greatest characters. You send me a Modern quotation poetical. How do you like this in an old play?[9] Vittoria Corombona a spunky Italian Lady, a Leonardo one, nick-named the White Devil, being on her trial for murder &c.—and questioned about seducing a Duke from his wife & the State, makes answer:

> Condemn you me for that the Duke did love me?
> So may you blame some fair & chrystal River
> For that some melancholic distracted man
> Hath drown'd himself in it.—

N. B. I shall expect a Line from you, if but a bare Line, whenever you write to Russell St. & a Letter often when you do not. I pay no postage. But I will have consideration for you, until parliament time & franks. Luck to Ned Search[10] & the new art of colouring,—; Monkey sends her Love: & Mary 'specially.

<div align="right">

Your's truly.
C Lamb

</div>

our ticket was a £20. alas! !—are both yours blanks?
P. S. Godwin has ask'd after you several times.——

MS: By permission of the Harvard College Library, Cambridge, Mass. Pub.: Talfourd (1837), I, 266–271; Sala, I, 419–422; Purnell, I, 419–422; Fitzgerald, II, 252–255; Hazlitt, I, 359–362; Ainger (1888), I, 219–221; Ainger (1900), II, 118–122; Macdonald, I, 266–268; Ainger (1904), I, 269–271; Harper, III, 192–196; Lucas (1905), VI, 323–325; Lucas (1912), V, 337–339; Lucas (1935), I, 409–411. Address: Mr. Wm. Hazlitt/Revd. Mr. Hazlitt/Wem/Shropshire. Postmark: [November] 11, 1805.

1. From London to the home of his parents, William Hazlitt (1737–1820), the Unitarian minister at Wem, and the former Grace Loftus (1746–1837). Hazlitt did not return to London until mid-spring 1806. (See *Hazlitt*, p. 156.) By "pork," below, Lamb may refer to the two-handed card game piquet. His remarks on Mrs. Rickman he later expanded into "A Bachelor's Complaint of the Behaviour of Married People" (*Works*, II, 126–132).

2. Louisa Martin (1793?–1858), the subject of "To Louisa M——, Whom I Used to Call 'Monkey'" and "The Ape" (*Works*, V, 76–77 and 80–81). The Lambs had met her possibly through the John Hazlitts and remained exceptionally fond of her for the rest of their lives. Later letters show that by 1808 she was attending a Mrs. Howell's school in Watford, Hertfordshire; in 1830 was at Chelsea College; and in 1834 was, with the assistance of Lamb and Wordsworth, attempting to open a school of her own in Carlisle. She did open it, according to Roger Ingpen, who wrote of a conversation he had with Mrs. Fulton, a daughter-in-law of Miss Martin's sister Sarah ("A Friend of Charles Lamb," *The Bookman*, 60 [September 1921], 245–246), with a legacy she received upon the death of a Sir Thomas Acland, in whose Devonshire household she had served for years as a governess. (That could have been the household of either Sir Thomas Dyke Acland, ninth baronet [1752?–1794], or Sir Thomas Dyke Acland, tenth baronet [1787–1871], but in neither case, given those dates, could the money have been a death legacy from either of those principal Aclands.) Ingpen additionally records that she later established a school in Kensington High Street, London; moved to Maidenhead, Berkshire, in 1844; returned to London about 1850; and died at Maida Vale. The Lambs also knew Louisa's mother and sisters—Sarah, who became Mrs. Fulton, and Hannah, who tutored the daughters of Henry George Herbert, second Earl of Carnarvon (1772–1833), and by him was left a lifetime annuity.

3. Four canceled lines follow. The Oxford Leonardos that Lamb could have seen are those at Christ Church college: the drawings "A Grotesque Bust of a Man," "Allegories of Envy, Ingratitude, Pleasure, and Pain," a sheet of scientific studies, "Study for the Sleeve of the Angel in the Uffizi 'Annunciation,'" "Allegory on the Political State of Milan," and, on the verso of the last, "Allegory of Fame and Envy"; and four paintings, which in Lamb's time were thought to have been by Leonardo—two fragments of a reduced copy of Leonardo's "Virgin and Child with St. Anne" and, from the school of Leonardo, "The Virgin and Child with the Yarn-winder" and "Virgin and Child Seated on a Parapet." The picture at Blenheim is probably "The Virgin and Child" by Leonardo's pupil Giovanni Antonio Beltraffio, or Boltraffio (1467–1516), but once attributed to his master. Herodias' (not "Herodia's") daughter, by Herod Philip, was Salome. See Matthew 14:3–11 and Mark 6:17–28.

4. That of the portrait painter and mezzotint engraver George Dawe (1781–1829), of whom Lamb wrote in "Recollections of a Late Royal Academician" (*Works*, I, 331–336), and there again mentioned Dawe's "Sampson in the Lap of Dalilah." He was a son of the mezzotint engraver Philip (fl. 1780) and the brother of the painter and mezzotint engraver Henry Edward (1790–1848) and of the miniature painter Elizabeth Dawe (fl. 1800–1805). In 1803 he won the gold medal from the Royal Academy and in 1814 was elected to its membership. In

1816–1817 he was introduced at large to the English aristocracy through his portraits of Princess Charlotte Augusta and her husband, Prince Leopold of Saxe-Coburg, and worked largely under its patronage through 1818. In 1819 he accepted an invitation from Czar Alexander to live in St. Petersburg and paint what over the next nine years amounted to almost four hundred portraits of high-ranking Russian officers who had fought against Napoleon. He returned to England in 1828; left in 1828 for Berlin, St. Petersburg, and Warsaw; came back to London in August 1829. In October he died in Kentish Town at the home of his brother-in-law, the engraver and portrait painter Thomas Wright (1792–1849). Godwin and Coleridge sat for Dawe, and Lamb possibly also. For Eliza Rutherford, the former Eliza Fenwick, remarked in a letter to her mother of September 30, 1812 (*The Fate of the Fenwicks*, p. 132), that Rutherford and others had fancied from a picture of Lamb that Dawe had given to her that she and Lamb had been lovers. But neither that nor the portrait, commented on later in this letter, that Elizabeth Dawe was doing of Fanny Imlay (1794–1816), the daughter of Godwin's first wife (Mary Wollstonecraft) by the American soldier and author Gilbert Imlay (1754?–1828), is listed in the catalogues or biographies.

5. *Samson Agonistes*, line 1494. Milton did not describe the color of Samson's hair. Dyson, referred to below, the translator and painter George Dyson (d. 1822), was an acquaintance of the London radicals and an early friend and correspondent of Godwin, who included him with the dissenting minister and poet Joseph Fawcett (1758?–1804), Holcroft, and Coleridge as the "four principal oral instructors to whom I feel my mind indebted for improvement" (*Godwin*, I, 17). Mrs. Professor is Mrs. Godwin.

6. Dubois had come to London near the end of the eighteenth century, allegedly from Italian comedy, and first appeared as the main character in the harlequinades at Sadler's Wells. He performed at Drury Lane from 1789, at the Haymarket in 1792, and at Covent Garden from December 1803. Although his Christian name and his dates are not known, it is known that he was a contemporary of the pantomimist Giuseppe Grimaldi, who was the father of the famous clown Joseph Grimaldi (1799–1837), and that Dubois instructed Joseph Grimaldi in the skills basic to his profession. An engraved portrait of Dubois, published in the *Thespian Magazine* of 1794, is in the Theatre Section of the Victoria and Albert Museum. General references to him are in Maurice Willson Disher's *Clowns & Pantomimes* (1925; rpt. New York and London: Blom, 1968), pp. 88 and 94–96.

7. Who was killed by a musket shot from the *Redoubtable* while his *Victory* was engaged with her and the *Bucentaure* off Cape Trafalgar, Spain, on October 21, 1805. Alexander John Scott (1768–1840), the private secretary and interpreter of Nelson and the chaplain of the *Victory*, did not die at his side, as Lamb remarks below, but attended Nelson at his death. Scott was later presented with the Crown living of Catterick, Yorkshire. In 1816 he was appointed chaplain to George, Prince Regent, afterward George IV. The Scott that Hazlitt had met at Joseph Hume's has not been identified. Joseph Hume (1767–1843), of Montpelier House, Notting Hill, Kensington, was a clerk in the victualling office, Somerset House. He became Lamb's correspondent, as did probably his wife and certainly his daughters. He also became a translator of the *Inferno* (1812) and the author of *A Search into the Old Testament, in Order to Trace Its Claims of Being the Depository of Divine Communications* (1841). Aaron Burr, who dined with him at the Godwins' on March 10, 1812, claimed Hume had published "a translation, much esteemed, of Tasso" (*The Private Journal of Aaron Burr, during His Residence of Four Years in Europe; with Selections from His Correspondence*, ed. Matthew L. Davis [New York: Harper, 1838], II, 343). But the lack of a record of such a translation suggests Burr meant the Dante. I have not been able to determine the given and maiden names of Mrs. Hume. Her and her husband's daughters were Amelia, later Mrs. Bennett, or Bunnett; Augusta; Caroline; Julia,

later the wife of Vice Admiral George Davies (1800–1876), the mother of the poet Mrs. Augusta Webster (1837–1894), and the aunt and mother-in-law of the mathematician Isaac Todhunter (1820–1884); Louisa; and Mary, later the wife of the Reverend Mr. George Todhunter of Rye, Sussex, and the mother of Isaac.

8. *Letters from an American Farmer* (1782), by Michel-Guillaume-St. Jean de Crèvecoeur, called J. Hector St. John (1735–1813). Lamb condemns the book in Letter 188. Of what Charles Kemble, referred to below, entered into possession is not known. Number 109 Great Russell Street was the address of the John Hazlitts.

9. John Webster's *The White Devil*. The quotation, below, from III, i, 211–214, Lamb included in *Specimens of English Dramatic Poets* (*Works*, IV, 187).

10. Edward Search, the pseudonym under which the moralist Abraham Tucker (1705–1774) published the first four volumes of *The Light of Nature Pursued* (7 vols.; 1768–1778). Hazlitt at the suggestion of Coleridge in 1803 was presently working on *An Abridgment of the Light of Nature Pursued*, which Joseph Johnson would publish on the recommendation of Godwin in 1807. The "new art of colouring," mentioned following, may be an allusion to Pierre-François Tingry (1743–1821), *Traité théorique et pratique sur l'art de faire et appliquer les vernis sur les différents genres de peinture, les couleurs simples et composées* (1803), published in translation as *The Painter's and Varnisher's Guide* (1804). Lamb in Letter 196 writes of sending it to Hazlitt. The tickets noticed in the first postscript here and in the penultimate paragraph of Letter 193 are probably those to a lottery, which is mentioned in Vol. III, Letter 243, and eulogized in "The Illustrious Defunct" (*Works*, I, 259–264). A two-line postscript on the address leaf is canceled.

186. *C. L. to Manning*

[Friday, November 15, 1805]

Dear Manning

Certainly you could not have call'd at all hours from 2 till 10—for we have been only out of an evening Monday and Tuesday in this week. But if you think you have, your thought shall go for the deed.—

We did pray for you on Wednesday night. Oysters unusually luscious—pearls of extraordinary magnitude found in them—. I have made bracelets of them—given them in clusters to Ladies.— Last night we went out in despite, because you were not come at your hour. This night we shall be at home, so shall we certainly both Sunday, Monday, Tuesday, and Wednesday.— Take your choice, mind I do'nt say of **one**: but chuse which evening you will not, & come the other four. Doors open at five o Clock. Shells forced about nine. Every Gentleman smokes or not as he pleases. O! I forgot. bring the £10, for fear you should lose it.

C L

MS: Huntington Library. Pub.: Talfourd (1837), I, 260–261; Sala, I, 388–389; Purnell, I, 388–389; Fitzgerald, II, 221–222; Hazlitt, I, 354–355; Ainger (1888), I, 221–222; Ainger (1900), II, 122; Macdonald, I, 268–269; Ainger (1904), I, 271–272; Harper, III, 197; Lucas (1905), VI, 328–329; Lucas (1912), V, 342–343; Lucas (1935), I, 414–415. Address: Mr. Manning/14 Broad Street/ Golden Square. Postmark: November 15, 1805.

187. *M. A. L. to Mrs. Thomas Clarkson*

Dec. 25, 1805

My Dear Mrs. Clarkson,

I feel myself greatly obliged to you for your kind letter. The favorable account you give of your own health has afforded me the sincerest pleasure.

We wished ourselves with you at Grasmere. I rejoice to find both by yours, and Miss Wordsworth's last letter, that they have so wonderfully borne up under their sad affliction. We have heard no more of Coleridge. I will certainly write the instant I hear of him. I have not the most distant idea where it is probable he will land.

This is Christmas-day; it is a fine, cheerful morning, and I feel a kind of satisfaction that a sad, and dreary year, as this has been to me, and many of my best friends, is drawing to an end. In the usual compliments of this time of the year to you, and Mr. Clarkson, I include a wish and hope, that we shall meet in the course of the ensuing year, with you, together with our kind Grasmere friends, and Coleridge— How this happy meeting is to be brought about I know not; but I have a strong faith it will somehow happen.

My brother, who has been in an indifferent state of health lately, is tolerably well recovered and joins me in respects to Mr. Clarkson and yourself not forgetting our fellow-traveller Miss Buck, and our old friend Tom,[1] whom we do not like a bit the worse for being a little tall, a little awkward, and not over passionately addicted to literature.

Excuse this short return to your long, and interesting letter, but we have no common friends in town, to amuse you with particulars of in return. Whenever you shall feel yourself well enough to favor us with a line, we shall take it particularly kind.

Charles wants to hear about Mr. Clarkson's quaker book, in what state of forwardness it is.

<div align="right">
I remain, dear Mrs. C.—

Your affectionate friend,

M. Lamb
</div>

MS: unrecovered. Text: Lucas (1935), I, 415–416. Also pub.: Macdonald, I, 269–270. The original of this letter is listed and in part quoted in Harry B. Smith, *A Sentimental Library: Comprising Books Formerly Owned by Famous Writers, Presentation Copies, Manuscripts, and Drawings* (privately printed, 1914), pp. 151–152. There too it is shown to have been written on Christmas Day, 1805.

1. Thomas Clarkson (1797–1837), the Clarksons' only child, became a London magistrate. In about 1830 he was married to Mary, the daughter of his father's brother, naval Lieutenant John Clarkson (1764–1828), of Purfleet, Grays, Essex, and the former Miss Lee. The senior Thomas Clarkson's book mentioned in the concluding paragraph is *A Portraiture of Quakerism as Taken from a View of the Moral Education, Descriptions, Peculiar Customs, Religious Principles, Political and Civil Œconomy and Character of the Society of Friends* (3 vols.; 1806).

PART VI

Letters 188–231
16 Mitre Court Buildings, Inner Temple
January 7, 1806—February 25, 1809

[Tuesday,] 7th Jany. 18[06]

Dear Hazlitt

I have been a long time without writing to you, but I do'nt know that it has deprived you of any valuable communications. Nothing has occurrd to deserve a special dispatch. I have also had upon my mind to write a long letter to Malta, and whenever that duty came over me, I thought I must write to you, and how could I make out two letters? & which should I set about first? and in the same manner that occurr'd, when I thought of setting about one to you. So it is in contradictory duties, when one cannot reconcile interest to pleasure, or virtues to ease, or industry to indolence, which I take to be duties all pretty equally alike.— You know Lord Nelson is dead. He is also to be buried.[1] And the whole town is in a fever. Seats erecting, seats to be let, sold, lent &c—. Customers crowding in to every Shop between White-hall and St. Pauls, and the tradesman & the customer changing parts, the latter being willing to become the obliged person, and the former assuming new airs of choice & selection. "A favor to beg of you Mr. Tape.— to let my young Ladies come and see the funeral procession on Thursday—my girls are come home from school, and young folks love sights."— Mr. Tape very grave "how many, Maam?"— "O! there'll be only **me**, and my three daughters, and perhaps their cousin Betty, and two young men to escort them, unless my **Cousin Elbow-room** happens to come to town, then there'll be nine of us."— "I am afraid it will be impossible to accommodate so many, if one of the young ladies will come we perhaps shall be able to put her in the second floor." Exit Customer with thanks, & returns on Thursday with fourteen more than the number first begg'd for. Cold Edgebone of Beef and Small Beer suffer for it about three oClock.— The Streets are in a perfect fever. The whole town as unsettled as a young Lady the day before being married. St. Paul's virgers[2] making their hundred pounds a day in sixpences for letting people see the scaffolding inside, & the hole where he is to be let down; which money they under the Rose share with the Dean and Præcentors at night.— Great Aquatic bustle tomorrow. Body to come up from Greenwich with Lord Mayor & City

Barges. Fillets of Veal predestined to be demolished at The **Temple** in the afternoon. All Cheswick, Pimlico, & Pancras emptying out in the morning into the Temple. Templars do'nt pay for Militia men tho', so one tax to be set off against another. If you with your refinements were here, you would be as fidgety as a Scotchman's hand between the fingers, you could neither eat, sit, read nor paint, till the corpse were fairly laid. The ghost of the funeral will walk till over Sunday night I'm sure, & the streets be perturb'd. You ca'nt get along for People going about staring to see where it will come by, or asking when it will come by, and Have you got a Seat?— "I for my part am indifferent about it, only it looks foolish not to see it." And "I suppose it will be like all other shows, but the Croud and the Bustle is agreeable." "I for my part have no relish for spectacles, but my Husband is going to take the young Miss **Squeezes** out of the country, that are come up out 100 miles to see it, & he dont like to disappoint them." And then the eldest Miss **Squeeze** declares she dont know whether she shall like to see it or no, for she is afraid it will be too affecting. She is sure she shall turn her head away from the window **as it goes by.** O the immortal **Man!**— but when the time comes it is odds but the pressing & thrusting dont constrain her to turn her eyes into the street against her will, & who can help it?— —

Just to get the Buzzing out of my head let me remember something vastly different.— The American Farmer.[3] I thank you for lending it to us, and am a little sorry that I cannot say so much in its praise as the usual compliments in these cases require. To shame the Devil, then, at once, it does appear to me a very stupid uninteresting Book. In what kind mood you pick'd it up I ca'nt guess, or how Wordsworth also came to give his testimony for it; but to me it is perfectly disagreeable. Why should a book be pleasant to one, that if it were made into a man (the binding a coat, the leaves a shirt with a frill, the &c. &c. make out the rest of the metamorphosis yourself, I have no time,— Lord Nelson & one thing or other,—my head's dizzy) if the said book were a man & not a book, would be odious? A wretched purse-proud American Farmer with no virtue but industry & its ostentatious concomitant charity, no ideas but of clearing land & setting the poor to work (damn him for that if I was a lousy Beggar happy in the Sun) calling Ladies young Women & praising them for decent mirth & needle work & possibilities of being notable mothers: things too tradesman-quaker-like (quakers the worst of tradesmen) to come into that

agreeable book the young man's best companion or the Appr[e]ntices Guide:[4] cold and chill and barren as Dr. Franklin's Golden rules or Poor John's Thoughts in an American Almanac. Thou that hast read Romeo & Juliet & Midsummers Nights Dream, to feed on the garbage & husk of dried leaves of ledgers & journals & swallow ploughs & harrows! If I did'nt like it as you expected, it might be in part (principally, no doubt, its own stupidity) in part because we had just read thro' Bruce's Travels[5] with infinite delight where all is alive & **novel,** & about Kings & Queens & fabulous Heads of Rivers, & Abyssinia[n] wars & the Line of Solomon & he's a fine dashing fellow & intrigues with Empresses & gets into Harams of Black Women, & was himself descended from Kings of Scotland: rot farmers & mechanics & industry—

The above written in great precipitation, so ca'nt answer for the style & grammer, just to get rid of a vapour fit which comes often & clouds us over. Shall be more cool when Lord Nelson is buried, & one can walk the streets with less justling, & when the crowding & madness of the people is still. Believe me, dull or Giddy,

<div style="text-align:right">Yours as ever.
C Lamb</div>

MS: Harvard College Library. Pub.: M. A. de Wolfe Howe, "Lamb to Hazlitt: A New-found Letter," *The Spectator,* 161 (August 5, 1938), 237–238. Address: Mr. Wm. Hazlitt/Wem/Shropshire. Postmark: January 7, 1806.

1. On Thursday, January 9.
2. The spelling of "vergers" retained in St. Paul's and a few other English cathedrals.
3. See Letter 185, note 8.
4. A canceled line and three-quarters follow. "John's," below, is where "Richard's" should be. The allusions could be either to the "art of virtue" section of Benjamin Franklin's *Autobiography* and to the part of *Poor Richard's Almanac* published in 1774 and after as *The Way to Wealth* or to the latter work alone.
5. *Travels to Discover the Source of the Nile in the Years 1768, 1769, 1770, 1771, 1772, and 1773* (1790), by the Scottish explorer James Bruce (1730–1794). Its second (1805) edition, prepared by Bruce's biographer and editor the linguist Alexander Murray (1775–1813), includes a portion of Bruce's (unfinished) autobiography.

189. *C. L. to William Hazlitt*

<div style="text-align:right">Thursday 15 Jany 1806</div>

Dear Hazlitt,

Godwin went to Johnson's yesterday about your business.—[1] Johnson would not come down, or give any answer, but has promised to

open the manuscript & to give you an answer in one month. Godwin will punctually go again (Wednesday is Johnson's open day) yesterday four weeks next: i.e. in one lunar month from this time. Till when Johnson positively declines giving any answer.——

I wish you joy on ending your Search.— — Mrs. H.[2] was naming something about a **Life of Fawcett** to be by you undertaken:——— The Great Fawcett, as she explain'd to Manning when he ask'd *what Fawcett?* He innocently thought *Fawcett the player.* But Fawcett the Divine is known to many people albeit unknown to the Chinese Enquirer. I should think, if you liked it, & Johnson declined it, that Phillips is the man. He is perpetually bringing out Biographies, Richardson, Wilkes, Foot, Lee Lewis, without number: little trim things in two easy volumes price 12s the two, made up of letters to & from, scraps, posthumous trifles, anecdotes, & about forty pages of hard biography: you might dish up a **Fawcettiad** in 3 months & ask **60 or 80 Pounds** for it. I should dare say that Phillips would catch at it———

I wrote you the other day in a great hurry. Did you get it? *This* is merely a Letter of business at Godwin's request.

Lord Nelson is quiet at last. His ghost only keeps a slight fluttering in odes and elegies in newspapers, & impromptus which could not be got ready before the funeral. As for news.—— We have Miss Stoddart in our house, she has been with us a fortnight, & will stay a week or so longer. She is one of the few people who are not in the way when they are with you. No tidings of Coleridge.——

Fenwick is coming to town on Monday (if no kind angel intervene)[3] to surrender himself———to prison. He hopes to get the Rules of the Fleet. On the same or nearly the same day Fell my other quondam Co-friend & drinker will go to Newgate, & his wife & 4 children, I suppose, to the Parish. Plenty of reflection & motives of **gratitude** to the wise disposer of all things in *us* whose prudent conduct has hither to ensured us a warm fire & snug roof over our heads. Nullum numen abest si sit Prudentia. Alas! Prudentia is in the last quarter of her tutelary shining over me. A little time & I———

but may be I, may at last hit upon some mode of collecting some of the vast superfluities of this money-voiding town. Much is to be got, & I dont want much. All I ask is time & leisure; & I am cruelly off for them.——

When you have the inclination, I shall be very glad to have a letter from you.——— Your brother & Mrs. H. I am afraid, think hardly of us for not coming oftener to see them, but we are distracted beyond what they can conceive with visitors & visitings. I never have an hour for my head to work quietly its own workings; which you know is as necessary to the human system as **Sleep.**

Sleep too I can't get for these damn'd winds of a night: & without sleep & rest what should ensue? Lunacy. But I trust, it wont.

<div align="right">

Yours, dear H. mad or sober.

C Lamb

</div>

MS: Philip H. & A. S. W. Rosenbach Foundation, Philadelphia. Pub.: Talfourd (1837), I, 271–273; Sala, I, 422–424; Purnell, I, 422–424; Fitzgerald, II, 255–257; Hazlitt, I, 362–364; Ainger (1888), I, 222–223; Ainger (1900), II, 123–125; Macdonald, I, 270–272; Ainger (1904), I, 272–273; Harper, III, 197–200; Lucas (1905), VI, 329–331; Lucas (1912), V, 343–344; Lucas (1935), I, 416–418. Address: Mr. Wm. Hazlitt/Wem/Shropshire. Postmark: January 16, 18[06].

1. The publication of *An Abridgment of the Light of Nature Pursued.*

2. The seventh paragraph of the letter suggests Mrs. John Hazlitt. Lamb next writes of Hazlitt's (unfulfilled) intention of undertaking a biography of Joseph Fawcett (see Letter 185, note 5), whom Hazlitt had admired and come to know and whom Manning had confused with either the actor and dramatist John Fawcett (1768–1837) or his father, the actor John (d. 1793). Below that Lamb writes of what apparently are abridgments of Sir Richard Phillips' publications of *The Correspondence of Samuel Richardson,* edited by Anna Letitia Barbauld (6 vols.; 1804); the letters of the politician John Wilkes (1727–1797) edited by the bookseller and journalist John Almon (1737–1805) as *Correspondence of the Late John Wilkes with His Friends* (5 vols.; 1805); the biography of the actor and dramatist Samuel Foote (1720–1777) written by the barrister William Cook, or Cooke (d. 1824), and titled *Memoirs of Samuel Foote* (3 vols.; 1805); and the autobiography of the actor Charles Lee Lewes (1740–1803), edited by his son John Lee Lewes (the father of George Henry Lewes [1817–1878]), called *Memoirs of C. L. Lewes, Containing Anecdotes . . . of the English and Scottish Stages, During a Period of Forty Years* (4 vols.; 1805).

3. Cf. the Latin in Vol. I, Letter 18, near the reference to note 4, and translated in note 4. The Latin near the end of this paragraph translates, "No divinity is absent if Prudence is Present." It is taken from Juvenal's *Satires,* X, 365.

190. *C. L. to Mrs. William Godwin*

<div align="right">

[Late January or early February 1806?]

</div>

Dear Mrs. G—

Having observed with some concern that Mr. Godwin is a little fastidious in what he eats for supper, I herewith beg to present his palate with a piece of dried Salmon. I am assured it is the best that

swims in Trent. If you do not know how to dress it, allow me to add, that it should be cut in thin Slices and broil'd in Paper *previously prepared in Butter.* Wishing it exquisite, I remain,

much as before,

Some add *Mash'd Potatoes.* Yours Sincy

MS: Mr. W. Hugh Peal, Leesburg, Va. Pub.: Hazlitt, I, 313–314; Ainger (1888), I, 181; Ainger (1900), II, 64–65; Macdonald, I, 221; Ainger (1904), I, 229; Harper, III, 79; Lucas (1905), VI, 283; Lucas (1912), V, 234; Lucas (1935), I, 418–419. Address: Mrs. William Godwin. The date is conjectured from the fact that the Lambs were presently seeing much of the Godwins. Lamb had written *The King and Queen of Hearts: With the Rogueries of the Knave, Who Stole Away the Queen's Pies,* which is dated 1806 on its printed title page, but November 18, 1805, on its engraved title page. Lamb and Mary were writing *Tales from Shakespear. Designed for the Use of Young Persons* (2 vols.; 1807). Both books were published at the Juvenile Library, which Mrs. Godwin had conceived and with her husband had established in 1805 on Hanway Street. Having thought it best not to connect the political and moral associations of their name with books for children, they had chosen to use the name of Thomas Hodgkins, their manager until 1807, in the imprint of the Juvenile Library publications. In May 1807 they moved to 41 Skinner Street, where, under the name of M. J. Godwin except for the first of the following works, they published Lamb's *The Adventures of Ulysses* (1808), Lamb and Mary's *Mrs. Leicester's School: Or, the History of Several Young Ladies, Related by Themselves* and *Poetry for Children, Entirely Original* (both 1809), Lamb's *Prince Dorus: Or, Flattery Put out of Countenance. A Poetical Version of an Ancient Tale* (1811), and a work often attributed to Lamb, *Beauty and the Beast: Or a Rough Outside with a Gentle Heart. A Poetical Version of an Ancient Tale* [1811?]. All are in *Works,* Vol. III.

191. *M. A. L. to Richard Wordsworth, with enclosures written by others*

Thursday Morning [January ?30, 1806]

Miss Lamb's compliments, informs Mr Wordsworth these are the only Bills she has, as the fourteen shillings charged for Spenser, she *had* no Bill for, this sum together with three shillings and six pence for the Packing Case will amount to £6 . . — . . 6 ——

Miss Lamb will thank Mr Wordsworth to pay the money to Miss Stoddart the Bearer.

MS: Wordsworth Library. Unpublished. Address: R—— Wordsworth Esqr./No 11 Staples Inn. Endorsement, by Miss Stoddart:

Miss Wordsworth and Miss Lamb }	Receipts for Books for Miss Wordsworth 30th. Jany 1806 Paid £6:0:6. to Mr. Lamb by Mr. R Wordsworths dir[ection (?)]

S S

The first of three enclosures has the itemization by Lamb. The statement within the brace (in this note, below) and the address (on the verso of the enclosure) —"Mr. Lamb No. 6 Mitre Court/Buildings Temple"—are by Miss Stoddart:

⟨Shakespear	£2 . 2 . —⟩
⟨Chaucer	1 .16 —⟩
⟨Milton	1 . 5 —⟩
Spenser	—.14 . —
Packing Case	3 . 6
	⟨6 — 6 ⟩
	17 : 6

30th: Jany. 1806. Received
17/6. from Mr. Richd.
Wordsworth for Books for
Miss Wordsworth }

C Lamb

The second enclosure is by its signer:

Bought of J. White
[illegible word]
Jan. 25th 1806

Shakspear by Pope 6 vol. 4° ————————	2 . 2 . 0
Chaucer by Urry fo ————————	1 .16 . 0
	£3 .18 . 0

Recd. at same time
for J White
C Colman

The last enclosure is by its signer:

<div align="right">

London
Jany. 25th. 1805 [1806]

</div>

Bot. of Lackington Allen & co
Miltons Works 4 vol _____ £1 . 5 . 0

<div align="right">

Receivd
Wm Howorth

</div>

Pope's Shakespeare was published by Jacob Tonson from 1723 to 1725; the
Chaucer is that begun in 1711 by the nonjuror John Urry (1666–1715) and pub-
lished in 1721; the Milton would seem to be one of the four-volume editions of
the poetical works that follow the text of John Newton and that appeared in
1773, 1776, and 1782; and the Spenser, which Lamb identifies in the next letter
as a folio, is that of 1679. See Letter 211, note 1.

192. *C. L. to William Wordsworth*

<div align="right">

1 Feb 1806

</div>

Dear Wordsworth,

 I have seen the Books which you ordered booked at the White Horse
Inn Cripplegate by the Kendal Waggon this day 1st Feby 1806; you
will not fail to see after them in time. They are directed to you at
Grasmere. We have made some alteration in the editions since your
sister's directions. The handsome quarto Spencer which she authorized
Mary to buy for £2.12.6, when she brought it home in triumph proved
to be *only the Fairy Queen:*[1] so we got them to take it again and I
have procured in stead a **Folio** which luckily contains besides all the
Poems, The View of the State of Ireland, which is difficult to meet
with. The Spencer, & the Chaucer being noble old books, we did not
think Stockdale's modern volumes would look so well beside them;
added to which I dont know whether you are aware that the Print is
excessive small same as Eleg. Extracts, or smaller not calculated for
eyes in age; and Shakespear is one of the last books one should like to
give up, perhaps the one just before the Dying Service in a large Prayer
book. So we have used our own discretion in purchasing Pope's fine
Quarto in six volumes which may be read ad ultimam horam vitæ.[2] It
is bound like Law Books (rather, half bound) and the Law Robe I
have ever thought as comely & gentlemanly a garb as a Book would
wish to wear. The state of the purchase then stands thus,

Urry's Chaucer _____	£1.16.—.
Pope's Shakespeare _____	2. 2.—
Spenser _____	— .14.—
Milton _____	1. 5
Packing Case &c. _____	—. 3.6
	6.—.6

which your Brother immediately repaid us. He has the Bills for all (by his desire) except the Spenser which we took no bill with (not looking to have our accounts audited) : so for that & the Case he took a separate receipt for 17/6.— N. B. there is writing in the Shakespear: but it is only **variæ** lectiones which some careful Gentleman the former Owner was at the pains to insert in a very **neat** hand from 5 Commentators. It is no defacement. The fault of Pope's edition is, that he has comically & coxcombically marked the Beauties: which is vile, as if you were to chalk up the cheek & across the nose of a handsome woman in red chalk to shew where the comeliest parts lay. But I hope the noble **type** of Library-appearance of the Books will atone for that. With the Books come **certain** Books & Pamphlets of G. Dyer, Presents or rather Decoy-ducks of the Poet to take in his thus-far obliged friends to buy his other works; as he takes care to inform them in M: S: notes to the Title Pages, "G Dyer Author of Other Books printed for Longman &c—." The books have lain at your dispatchful brothers a 12 month, to the great staling of most of the subjects. The three Letters & what is else written at the beginning of the respective *Presents* will ascertain the division of the Property. If not; none of the **Donees,** I dare say, will grudge a Community of property in this case. We were constrained to pack 'em how we could, for room. Also there comes W. Hazlitt's book about Human Action[3] for Coleridge; a little song book for Sarah Coleridge; a **Box** for Hartley whi[c]h your Brother was to have sent, but now devolved on us. I dont know from whom it came, But the things altogether were too much for Mr (Iv'e forgot his name) to take charge of; a Paraphrase on the King & Queen of Hearts, of which I being the Author beg Mr. Johnny Wordsworth's acceptance & opinion. Liberal Criticism as G. Dyer declares, I am always ready to attend to!— And that's all, I believe. N. B. I must remain Debtor to Dorothy for 200 pens: but really Miss Stoddart (women are great gulfs of Stationery) **who is**

going home to Salisbury & has been with us some weeks, has drained us to the very last pen: by the time S. T. C. passes thro' London I reckon I shall be in **full feather.** No more news has transpired of that Wanderer. I suppose he has found his way to some of his German friends.

Apropos of Spencer (you will find him mentioned a page or two before, near enough for an a propos) I was discoursing on Poetry (as one's apt to deceive onesself & when a person is willing to *talk* of what one likes, to believe that he also likes the Same: as Lovers do) with a Young Gentleman of my office who is deep read in Anacreon Moore,[4] Lord Strongford, and the principal Modern Poets, and I happen'd to mention Epithalamiums & that I could shew him a very fine one of Spencer's. At the mention of this, my Gentleman, who is a very fine Gentleman & is brother to the Miss Evans which Coleridge so narrowly escaped marrying, pricked up his ears & exprest great pleasure, & begged that I would give him leave to copy it: he did not care how long it was (for I objected the length) he should be very happy to see *any thing by him.* Then pausing and looking sad, he ejaculated ***Poor Spenser!***[5] I begged to know the reason of his ejaculation, thinking that Time had by this time softened down any calamities which the Bard might have endured—. "Why, poor fellow!" said he "he has lost **his Wife!**" "Lost his Wife?" said I. Who are you talking of? "Why, Spencer"; said he. I've read the Monody he wrote on the occasion, **&** *a very pretty thing it is.* This led to an explanation (it could be delay'd no longer) that the sound **Spencer** which when Poetry is talk'd of generally excites an image of[6] an old Bard in a Ruff, and sometimes with it dim notions of Sir. P. Sydney & perhaps Lord Burleigh, had raised in my Gentleman a quite Contrary image of **The Honourable William Spencer,** who has translated some things from the German very prettily, which are publish'd with Lady Di Beauclerk's Designs.— Nothing like defining of Terms when we talk. What blunders might I have fallen into of quite inapplicable Criticism, but for this timely explanation.—

N. B. at the beginning of *Edm.* Spencer (to prevent mistakes) I have copied from my own copy, & primarily from a book of Chalmers on Shakespear,[7] a Sonnet of Spenser's never printed among his poems. It is curious as being Manly & rather Miltonic, & as a Sonnet of Spenser's with nothing in it about Love or Knighthood. I have no

room for remembrances; but I hope our doing your commission will prove we do not quite forget you.

C Lamb

MS: Huntington Library. Pub.: Talfourd (1837), I, 280–282; Sala, I, 248–250; Purnell, I, 248–250; Fitzgerald, II, 83–85; Hazlitt, I, 374–375; Ainger (1888), I, 232–233; Ainger (1900), II, 139–140; Macdonald, I, 273–274; Ainger (1904), I, 283–284; Harper, III, 201–205; Lucas (1905), VI, 332–335; Lucas (1912), V, 346–349; Lucas (1935), I, 419–421. Address: Mr. Wordsworth/Grasmere/near Kendal/Westmoreland. Postmark: February 1, 1806.

1. Which was published in quarto in three volumes by J. Brindley in 1751 and in two by Jacob and Richard (d. 1772) Tonson in 1758. Stockdale's, referred to below, was the bookselling firm established in the 1780s by the publisher and editor John Stockdale (1749?–1814).

2. "To the last hour of life."

3. *An Essay on the Principles of Human Action: Being an Argument in Favour of the Natural Disinterestedness of the Human Mind. To Which Are Added, Some Remarks on the Systems of Hartley and Helvetius* (1805).

4. The poet Thomas Moore (1779–1852), whose translation of the *Odes of Anacreon* appeared in 1800. Mentioned next is Moore's friend Percy Clinton Sydney Smythe, sixth Viscount Strangford and first Baron Penshurst (1780–1855), a diplomatist and the author of *Poems from the Portuguese of Camoëns* (1803). Lamb later developed this paragraph into "On the Ambiguities Arising from Proper Names" (*Works*, I, 69–70). For Mary Evans see my Vol. I, Introduction, p. xxxv, and Letter 3, note 29.

5. Underscored twice.

6. A canceled line and one-third follow. The statesman William Cecil, Baron Burghley (1520–1598), mentioned below, was the detractor of Spenser, whom Thomas Evans (see Vol. I, Letter 3, note 29) had confused with William Robert Spencer (1770–1834), the younger son of Lord Charles Spencer (1740–1820) and later the author of society verse that would attract the attention of Byron, Scott, and John Wilson (1785–1854), the "Christopher North" of *Blackwood's Edinburgh Magazine*. Spencer's monody of which Evans spoke may have been to Spencer's wife, Susan, who was the widow of a Count Spreti and the daughter of the diplomatist Francis Jenison, Count Jenison-Walworth (1764–1824), and the Countess Dowager of Jenison-Walworth (d. 1803) of Heidelberg. But if so, it seems not to have been published. The monody referred to is probably "The Year of Sorrow" (1804), which is in memory of Susan Spencer's mother and other women. Lady Diane Beauclerk (1734–1808), Spencer's great-aunt, an amateur artist, had furnished the illustrations for Spencer's translation (1796) of Gottfried August Bürger's "Lenore." See Vol. I, Letter 6, note 9.

7. The work by the Scottish antiquary George Chalmers (1742–1825) titled *A Supplemental Apology for the Believers in the Shakspeare-papers* (London: Thomas Egerton, 1799). On its page 94 is the sonnet of which Lamb writes, Spenser's "To the Right Worshipful, My Singular Good *Friend*, Mr. Gabriel Harvey [1545?–1630], Doctor of the Laws."

193. *C. L. to William Hazlitt*

Wednsday 19 Feb. 1806

Dear H———

Godwin has just been here in his way from Johnson's. Johnson has had a fire in his house, this happened about five weeks ago, it was in the daytime so it did not burn the house down, but did so much damage that the house must come down, to be repaired: his nephew[1] that we met on Hampstead Hill put it out: well, this fire has put him so back, that he craves one more month before he gives you an answer.

I will certainly goad Godwin (if necessary) to go again this very day four weeks; but I am confident he will want no goading—

Three or four most capital auctions of Pictures advertized.[2] In May *Wellbore Ellis Agar's*, the first private collection in England, so Holcroft says. In March Sir George Young's in Stratford Place (where Cosway lives), & a Mr. Halse's at Blackheath, both very capital collections, & have been announced for some months.— Also the Marquis of Lansdown's Pictures in March; & though inferior to mention, lastly, the Tructhsessian gallery.— Dont your mouth water to be here?

Tother night Loftus[3] called, whom we have not seen since you went before. We meditate a stroll next Wednesday, Fast day. He happened to light upon Mr. Holcroft, Wife & Daughter, their first visit at our house.—

Your brother called last night. We keep up our intimacy. He is going to begin a large Madona & Child from Mrs. H. & baby.[4] I fear he goes astray after ignes fatui. He is a clever man—by the bye I saw a miniature of his as far excelling any in his Shew cupboard (that of your sister not excepted) as that shewboard excells the shew things you see in windows—an old woman—damn her name—but most superlative—he has it to clean—I'll ask him the name—but the best miniature I ever saw, equal to Cooper[5] & them fellows.— But for **oil** pictures!—what has he to do with Madonas? If the Virgin Mary were alive & visitable, he would not hazard himself in a Covent-Garden-pit-door Croud, to see her. It a'nt his style of beauty, is it?— But he will go on painting things he ought not to paint, & not painting things he ought to paint—

Manning not gone to China, but talks of going this spring. God forbid.—

Coleridge not heard of——

I, going to leave off smoke. In mean time am so smoky with last nights' 10 Pipes, that I must leave off—

Mary begs her kind remembrances. **Pray, write to us.**—

This is no Letter, but I supposed you grew anxious about Johnson—

N. B. have taken a room[6] at 3/ — a week to be in between 5 and 8 at night, to avoid my *nocturnal* alias *knock-eternal* visitors. The first fruits of my retirement has been **a farce,** which goes to Manager to-morrow. *Wish my ticket luck.*—

God bless you, & do write.

<div align="right">

Yours, fumosissimus

C Lamb

</div>

MS: Courtesy of the Arents Collections, The New York Public Library, Astor, Lenox and Tilden Foundations. Pub.: Talfourd (1837), I, 273–276; Sala, I, 424–426; Purnell, I, 424–426; Fitzgerald, II, 257–259; Hazlitt, I, 365–366; Ainger (1888), I, 224–225; Ainger (1900), II, 126–128; Macdonald, I, 275–276; Ainger (1904), I, 274–275; Harper, III, 206–208; Lucas (1905), VI, 336–337; Lucas (1912), V, 350–351; Lucas (1935), I, 423–424. Address: Mr. Wm. Hazlitt/Wem/Shropshire. Postmark: February 19, 1806.

1. Possibly either Joseph Johnson of Liverpool, who with his uncle was a correspondent of Henry Fuseli (see John Knowles's *The Life and Writings of Henry Fuseli* [3 vols.; London: Henry Colburn and Richard Bentley, 1831], I, 286, 299–300, and 309–310), or Rowland Hunter (1774–1864), who was the senior Joseph Johnson's successor as the bookseller in St. Paul's Churchyard from 1815 to 1836, the publisher of Mary Matilda Betham's *The Lay of Marie* (1816) and, with Charles and James Ollier, of Hazlitt's *Characters of Shakespear's Plays* (1817), and the stepfather-in-law of Leigh Hunt. See *Hunt's Autobiography,* I, 231, note.

2. Those of Welbore Ellis Agar, second Earl of Normanton (1778–1868), on May 2 and 3; of Sir George Yonge, fifth baronet (1731–1812) and late governor of the Cape of Good Hope, at 20 Stratford Place (where the portrait and miniature painter Richard Cosway [1740–1821] lived from 1790 or 1791 to 1821) on March 24 and 25; of Richard Hulse (1727–1805) of Blackheath and Baldwin, Kent, late deputy governor of the Hudson's Bay Company, on March 21 and 22; and of William Petty, first Marquis of Lansdowne and second Earl of Shelburne (1737–1805), on March 19, 20, 25, and April 14–19. (See Frits Lugt, *Répertoire des catalogues de ventes publiques intéressant l'art ou la curiosité, . . . première période, vers 1600–1825* [The Hague: Nijhoff, 1938], which is arranged chronologically and without pagination.) The Truchsessian Picture Gallery, mentioned last, was located on The New Road opposite Portland Place.

3. Thomas Loftus, Hazlitt's cousin, the son of Thomas Loftus of Wisbech, Cambridgeshire, and the former Miss Coulson. The fast day referred to below is Ash Wednesday. The Thomas Holcrofts' daughter mentioned is probably Fanny. She was often her father's walking companion.

4. William, according to *The Hazlitts,* p. 331.

5. The miniature painter Samuel Cooper (1609–1672).

6. Where Lamb wrote "Mr. H——: A Farce in Two Acts" (*Works,* V, 180–211). It was performed at Drury Lane on December 10, 1806. Lamb never gives the location of the room. He gave it up within a month. The manager (Richard Wroughton) referred to below is identified in the next letter, note 3. The Latin in the complimentary close of this letter translates, "most smoky."

194. *M. A. L. to Sarah Stoddart*

[Thursday, February 20—
Saturday, February 22, 1806]

My dear Sarah

I am going to make a sort of a promise to myself and to you, that I will write you kind of journal-like letters, of the daily what-we-do-matters, as they occur. This day seems to me a kind of new æra in our time, it is not a birthday, nor a new-years-day, nor a leave-off-smoking-day; but it is about an hour after the time of leaving you our poor Phœnix, in the Salisbury Stage, and Charles has just left me for the first time alone to go to his lodging, and I am holding a solitary consultation with myself, as to the how I shall employ myself. Writing plays, novels, poems, and all manner of such-like vapouring and vapourish schemes are floating in my head, which at the same time aches with the thoughts of parting from you, and is perplext with the idea of I cannot tell what about notion that I have not made you half so comfortable as I ought to have done, and a melancholy sense of the dull prospect you have before you on your return home—then I think I will make my new gown, & now I consider the white peticoat will be better candle-light work, and then I look at the fire and think if the irons was but down I would iron my Gowns, you having put me out of conceit of mangling. So much for an account of my own confused head, and now for yours, returning home from the Inn we took that to pieces, and ca[n]vassed you as you know is our usual custom—we agreed we should miss you sadly, and that you had been, what you yourself discovered, *not at all in our way,* and although if the Post Master, should happen to open this, it would appear to him to be no great compliment, yet you who enter so warmly into the interior of our affairs will

understand and value it, as well as what we likewise asserted, that since you have been with us, you have done but one foolish thing, *vide* Pinkhorn.[1] (excuse my bad latin if it should chance to mean exactly contrary to what I intend.) We praised you for the very friendly way in which you regarded all our whimsies, & to use a phrase of Coleridge's, *understood us*. We had in short no drawback in our eulogy on your merit, except lamenting the want of respect you have to yourself—the want of a certain dignity of action you know what I mean, which though it only broke out in the acceptance of the old Justice's book, and was as it were smothered, & almost extinct while you were here, yet is it so native a feeling in your mind that you will do whatever the present moment prompts you to do, that I wish you would take that one slight offence seriously to heart, and make it a part of your daily consideration to drive this unlucky propensity, root, and branch, out of your character.— Then, Mercy on us, what a perfect little gentlewoman you will be! ! !—

You are not yet arrived at the first stage of your journey, yet have I the sense of your absense so strong upon me that I was really thinking what news I had to send you, and what had happened since you had left us, truly nothing, except that Martin Burney met us in Lincolns Inn Fields, and borrowed four-pence, of the repayment of which sum I will send you due notice.—

Friday

Last night I told Charles of your matrimonial overtures from Mr White,[2] and of the cause of that business being at a *stand-still.* Your generous conduct in acquainting Mr W. with the vexatious affair at Malta highly pleased him—he entirely approves of it—you would be quite comforted to hear all he said on the subject.

He wishes you success, and when Coleridge comes, will consult with him about what is best to be done. But I charge you, be most strictly cautious how you proceed yourself, do not give Mr W——— any reason to think you indiscreet, let him return of his own accord, and keep the probability of his doing so, full in your mind, so I mean as to regulate your whole conduct by that expectation. Do not allow yourself to see, or in any way renew your acquaintance with William, nor do not do any other silly thing of that kind, for you may depend upon it he will

be a kind of spy upon you, and if he observes nothing that he disapproves of, you will certainly hear of him again in time.

Charles is gone to finish the farce, & I am to hear it read this night, I am so uneasy between my hopes, & fears of how I shall like it, that I do not know what I am doing, I need not tell you so, for before I send this I shall be able to tell you all about it. If I think it will amuse you, I will send you a copy.

The bed was very cold last night.

Feby 21st [22nd]

I have received your letter, and am happy to hear that your Mother has been so well in your absence, which I wish had been prolonged a little, for you have been wanted to copy out the Farce—in the writing of which I made many an unlucky blunder. The said Farce I carried (after many consultations of who was the most proper person to perform so important an office) to Wroughton[3] the Manager of Drury Lane. He was very civil to me, said it did not depend upon himself, but that he would put it into the Proprietors hand, and that we should certainly have an answer from them.— I have been unable to finish this sheet before, for Charles has taken a weeks holliday from his lodging to rest himself after his labour, & we have talked and thought of nothing but the Farce night, and day, but yeste[r]d[ay][4] I carried it to Wroughton, & since it has been out of the [way] our minds have been a little easier. I wish you had be[en with] us to have given your opinion, I have half a mind to scr[ibble] another copy & send it you— I like it very much, and cannot help having great hopes of its success.

I would say I was very sorry for the death of Mr White's father, but not knowing the good old gentleman I cannot help being as well satisfied that he is gone, for his son will feel rather lonely, & so perhaps he may chance to visit a little of[tene]r at Winterslow.———— You so well describe your brother's grave lecturing letter that you make me ashamed of part of mine, I would fain rewrite it, leaving out my *"sage advice,"*[5] but if I begin another letter something may fall out to prevent me from finishing it. and therefore skip over it as well as you can, it shall be the last I ever send you,— It is well enough when one is talking to a friend to hedge in a odd word by way of counsel now, & then, but there is something mighty irksome, in its staring upon one in

a letter where one ought only to see kind words, & friendly remimbrances— —. I have heard a vague report from the *Dawes* (the pleasant looking young lady we called upon was Miss Daw) that Coleridge returned back to Naples—they are to make further enquiries & let me know the particulars.— We have seen little or nothing of Manning since you went,—your friend Burnett calls as usual, for Charles *to point out something*[6] *for him.* I miss you sadly, & but for the fidget I have been in about the Farce I should have missed you still more. I am sorry you cannot get your money, continue to tell us all your perplexities, & do not mind being called Widow Blackacre—

Say all in your mind too about your *Lover* now Charles knows of it; he will be as anxious to hear as me—. All the time we can spare from talking of the characters & plot of the Farce, we talk of you, I have got a fresh bottle of brandy today, if you were here you should have a glass *three parts brandy* so you *should,* I bought a pound of bacon today— not so good as yours. I wish the little caps were finished—. I am glad the Medicines, & the Cordials bore the fatigues of their journey so well. I promise you I will write often, & *"not mind the postage."* God bless you—Charles does *not* send his love because he is *not* here.

<div align="right">

Yours affectionately

M Lamb

</div>

Write as often as ever you can. do not work too hard.

I have heard that Coleridge was lately going through Scicilly to Rome with a party, but that being unwell, he returned back to Naples, We think there is some mistake in this account and that his intended journey to Rome was in his former jaunt to Naples, If you know that at that time, he had any such intention will you write instantly for I do not know whether I ought to write to Mrs Coleridge, or not—

MS: Pierpont Morgan Library. Pub.: Lucas (1905), VI, 338–341; Lucas (1912), V, 352–355; Lucas (1935), I, 425–428. Address: Miss Stoddart/Winterslow/near Salisbury. Postmark: February 22, 1806.
1. Unidentified except for what Mary writes of him later in this paragraph—that he was a justice, it seems, and had called on Miss Stoddart with a book.

2. Who appears (see below) to have been a neighbor of Miss Stoddart. He was not Lamb's friend James White.

3. The actor Richard Wroughton (1748–1822), who performed principally at Drury Lane, from 1787 to 1798, from 1800 to 1808, and in 1815. According to James Boaden's *Memoirs of the Life of John Philip Kemble, Esq. Including a History of the Stage, from the Time of Garrick to the Present Period* (London:

Longman *et al.,* 1825), II, 186, 271, and 429, Wroughton was a manager of Drury Lane from 1796 to 1800 and from 1805 through at least 1806.

4. The bracketed locutions here and below, supplied from Lucas (1935), I, 427, are obscured by the seal.

5. Burns, "Tam o' Shanter," line 35.

6. Perhaps regarding what in 1807 came to be George Burnett's *Specimens of English Prose-writers, from the Earliest Times to the Close of the Seventeenth Century.* Widow Blackacre, referred to below, is the busybody and habitual litigant in William Wycherley's *The Plain Dealer.*

195. *M. A. L. to Mrs. Coleridge*

[February 25, 1806]

"My Brother has received a letter from Stoddart" (Stoddart, you probably know, is at Malta) "dated December 26th in which he tells him that Coleridge was then at Naples. We have also heard from a Mr. Dawe that a friend of his had received a letter of the same date, which mentioned Coleridge having been lately travelling towards Rome with a party of gentlemen; but that he changed his mind, and returned back to Naples. Stoddart says nothing more than that he was driven back to Naples in consequence of the French having taken possession of Trieste."

MS: unrecovered. Text: *Wordsworths' Letters,* II, 9. Also pub.: Lucas (1905), VI, 341; Lucas (1935), I, 428. Dorothy Wordsworth wrote Mrs. Thomas Clarkson on March 2: "Last night we received a Note from Mrs. C., enclosing a letter to her from Miss Lamb, from which I will transcribe the whole that relates to Coleridge. It is dated Feb. 25th." This is that portion of Mary's letter, with Miss Wordsworth's parenthesis concerning Stoddart.

196. *C. L. to William Hazlitt*

[Saturday, March 8, 1806]

Dear H

I send you **Tingry**[1] (pr[omising you instruction] and [some] *entertainment*). I should not have delayed it [so] long, but have been waiting for **Loftus's** commission. I have made several graphical tours round & in t[he] metropolis without discovering any ⟨prints⟩ trees that I would ventu[re to] recommend: id est, I have gone no further than the shop [window,] for such is my modesty, that if I explored

internal sec[rets I] should be laying out complimentary shillings rather than give trouble without remuneration. I have sent you a pretty emblematical thing[2] which I happen to have in my possession: you may get some hints from it, though perhaps you may think it too tame: not sufficiently romantic,—the boughs not shooting fantastically enough &c—. But, to supply poetry & wildness, you may read the American Farmer over again. Nevertheless if you desire it, I will put my head *within* the shops—only speak your wants————

N. B. If I do not hear in *4 days* that you have received Tingry &c. **safe,** I shall put you to the expence of a Letter to ascertain whether this parcel have been deliver'd to you—

<div align="right">Yours ever

C L</div>

Johnson shall not be forgot at his month's end————

MS: Dr. D. G. Wilson, Bushey, Watford, Hertfordshire. Pub.: Macdonald, I, 274–275; Harper, III, 208–209; Lucas (1935), II, 4–5. Address: Mr W. Hazlitt. Watermark: 1804. Lamb provides the date for this letter in Letter 200. The ends of the first eight manuscript lines have been torn away. Most of the bracketed locutions are supplied from Lucas (1935), II, 4.
1. See Letter 185, note 10.
2. The print Lamb thought to be of a Titian mentioned in Letter 200, first paragraph.

197. *M. A. L. to Mrs. Clarkson*

<div align="right">March 13. 1806</div>

My dear Mrs Clarkson

Your kind letter would have given me great pleasure but for the concern I feel at the uneasiness you express at the unjust reports you have heard of John Wordsworth. It is upon your own account alone that I am distressed at it: for my own part I totally disbelieve it, and so does my brother and he desires me to tell you in the strongest terms I can think of, his full conviction that the injurious falsehood you have heard is intirely void of foundation. The report coming from an Underwriter Charles says makes it easy to be accounted for, because it is a well known fact that they always impute blame to the Captain whenever a Ship is lost.

My brother says that he never heard a whisper at the India House,

(or any where else) of poor John Wordsworth being drunk, which had
that been the case would certainly he says have been known and talked
of there. He is quite certain the India Directors were perfectly satisfied
with his conduct, and that no blame has ever been imputed to him.

We are very glad you have not told Wordsworth, and earnestly beg
you never will tell him, because it may not be easy to get at evidence
strong enough to make him perfectly satisfied. It was with great diffi-
culty that my brother got at the intelligence he sent to Wordsworth, the
survivors almost all being gone out to India in other ships. We think
we can trace the story of his being drunk to this slight foundation. A
gentleman of the name of Burgoyne, a Cornet in the Army, who was a
passenger in the Ship told at the India House that a few minutes before
the Ship sunk, he had opened a bottle of Cordial, and persuaded Capn
Wordsworth to take two glasses, and gave the remainder of the bottle
to those who happened to stand near him, and that while he was in the
act of opening another bottle to distribute more the Ship went down.
This Burgoyne we endeavoured to find out. We where[1] directed to him
from an Army Agent to the Prince of Wales Coffee House in Conduit
Street. I went there, but he had left town, the Master of the Coffee
house promised to forward a letter to him from my brother, Charles
requested Burgoyne to address his answer to William Wordsworth. I
mentioned this circumstance to Dorothy but as she took no notice of it
in her answer to my letter I am afraid he never wrote. I have been
again this morning to this Coffee House, to enquire for Burgoyne, and
find he is now in Ireland. The Master of the House with whom I had
a long conversation assured me that Burgoyne never imputed the least
blame to Captain Wordsworth, and that he had heard him speak very
handsomely of him and that he never heard the least word of his being
in liquor. You may place great confidence on this mans testimony be-
cause Burgoyne came to the Prince of Wales Coffee house immediately
on his arrival in town from Weymouth.

My brother says that this bad report coming from an Underwriter
he is the less surprized at it, because it is a well known fact that when-
ever a Ship is lost the Underwriters always blame the Captains, and he
has no doubt, no more have I, that the story of Burgoyne giving him
the cordial, was told from one to another, till at last the two glasses
became a bottle and then the Underwriters said he was drunk. We do

not even think it possible for any quantity of liquor to make a man drunk in the agony of feeling he must have been in at that time. But let me again beg you will not tell what you have heard to Wordsworth, because we are certain we can get no positive proof, without we see and talk ourselves with some of the survivors—and for that we must wait till they return from India.

You are very kind to interest yourself about our little affairs. When I writ last I was in great haste, and had not time to say more than that I had heard from Coleridge, and in my former letter my brother was unwell, which made me feel so uncomfortably, that I was glad to say anything or nothing rather than talk of ourselves. Thank God he is now perfectly well, and so am I. Charles has been lately very busily employed *writing a farce*. It is in the Manager's hand, but we have yet heard nothing of its fate, and we have many foolish hopes and fears about it, he has begun another farce,[2] he talks of writing three, and among them all he thinks he shall then have some chance of one succeeding. Wordsworth has advised him to write a Novel and I think he will soon begin one, for he often talks about it. Certainly he seems more disposed to write than I have known him for a very long time. If you have not had it from Wordsworth shall I send you a poem Charles wrote on tobacco? Wordsworth likes it very much.

Manning is going out to China, very soon, he is endeavouring to get a passage in a China Ship, he had intended to go through Russia but he found so many difficulties in the way that he gave up the idea. We shall miss him very much, for he has been very much with us lately, and we love him dearly.— You say nothing about yourself, & you give a very *cross* reason because I set you the example. You do not even say how you are in health, but it must have been your anxiety about poor John Wordsworth made you forget what you must know we were so very anxious to hear. Will you be so kind as to write soon for I shall be uneasy till I hear if you are more satisfied about this injurious report. I wish you would feel as I do that it is most certainly a *wicked & malicious falsehood*

My brother wishes to know if Mr Clarkson has finished his *Quaker book*,[3] and what he is doing. Are you settled at Purfleet? You gave us some hopes that you were coming to live near town have you given up that idea.

God bless you my dear Mrs Clarkson, my brother joins with me in friendly remembrances & affectionate wishes.

<div align="right">

Your affectionate friend

M Lamb

</div>

MS: Koopman Collection, Brown University Library, Providence, R.I. Pub.: Lucas (1935), I, 430–432. Address: Mrs Clarkson/J. Clarkson's Esqre/Purfleet/ Grays/Essex. Postmark: March 13, 1806.

1. For "were." See Letter 176, at the reference to note 5, for Mary's first mention of the letters mentioned below, to and requested from Burgoyne.

2. The only farce known by Lamb besides "Mr. H——" is "The Pawnbroker's Daughter: A Farce" (*Works*, V, 212–242). But Lamb did not write it until 1825. The only play known in addition to those already noticed is "The Wife's Trial; or, the Intruding Widow. A Dramatic Poem" (*Works*, V, 243–273). He wrote it in 1827. He once started but probably never completed and certainly never published a novel (mentioned below and in Vol. I, Introduction, p. lxxvi), unless one so denominates *Rosamund Gray*.

3. See Letter 187, note 1.

198. *M. A. L. to Sarah Stoddart*

<div align="right">

[Friday,] March 14 [1806]

</div>

My dear Sarah

No intention of forfeiting my promise but mere want of time has prevented me from continueing my *journal*, you seem pleased with the long stupid one I sent, and therefore I shall certainly continue to write at every opportunity. The reason why I have not had any time to spare is because Charles has given himself some hollidays after the hard labour of finishing his farce, and therefore I have had none of the evening leisure I promised myself. Next week he promises to go to work again. I wish he may happen to hit upon some new plan to *his* mind for another farce—when onece begun I do not fear his perseverance, but the hollidays he has allowed himself I fear will unsettle him. I look forward to next week with the same kind of anxiety I did to the first entrance at the new lodging. We have had as you know so many teazing anxieties of late, that I have got a kind of habit of foreboding that we shall never be comfortable, & that he will never settle to work which I know is wrong, and which I will try with all my might to overcome—for certainly if I could but see things as they really are, our prospects are considerably improved since the memorable day of

Mrs Fenwick's last visit. I have heard nothing of that good lady, or of the Fells since you left us, .

We have been visiting a little—to Norris's to Godwins and last night we did not come home from Captain Burneys till two O Clock, the *saturday night* was changed to *friday*[1] because Rickman could not be there tonight—. We had the best *tea things,* & the litter all cleared away, and every thing as handsome, as possible Mrs Rickman being of the party. Mrs Rickman is much *encreased in size,* since we saw her last, and the alteration in her strait shape wonderfully improves her. Phillips was there, and Charles had a long batch of Cribbage with him. & upon the whole we had the most chearful evening I have known there a long time. Tomorrow we dine at Holcrofts. These things rather fatigue me but I look for a quiet week, next week & hope for better times. We have had Mrs Brooks[2] & all the Martin's, and we have likewise been there so that I seem to have been in a continual bustle lately. I do not think Charles cares so much for the Martins as he did, which is a fact you will be glad to hear though you must not name them when you write. always remembe[r] when I tell you anything about them not to mention their names in return. We have had a letter from your brother by the same mail as yours I suppose. he says he does not mean to return till summer & that is all he says about himself, his letter being entirely filled with a long story about Lord Nelson—but nothing more than what the newspapers has been full of such as his last words &c. Why does he teaze you with so much *good advice,* is it merely to fill up his letters, as he he filled ours with Lord Nelsons exploits, or has any new thing come out against you? has he discovered Mr Curse a rats[3] correspondence? I hope you will not write to that *news-sending* gentleman any more—I promised never more to give my *advice* but one may be allowed to *hope* a little. and I also hope you will have something to tell me soon about Mr W—— have you seen him yet? I am sorry to hear your Mother is not better. , but I am in a hoping humour just now, & I cannot help hoping, that we shall all see happier days. The bells are just now ringing for the taking of the *Cape of good Hope*[4]

I have written to Mrs Coleridge to tell her that her husband is at Naples, your brother slightly named his being there, but he did not say that he had heard from him himself. . Charles is very busy at the Office, he will be kept there today till seven or eight o Clock, and he

came home very *smoky, & drinky* last night, so that I am afraid a hard days work will not agree very well with him.

O dear! what shall I say next. Why this I will say next, that I wish you was with me, I have been eating a mutton chop all alone, and I have been just looking in the pint porter pot which I find quite empty, and yet I am still very dry, if you was with me, we would have a glass of brandy & water, but it [is] quite impossible to drink brandy & water by oneself therefore I must wait with patience till the kettle boils. I hate to drink tea alone, it is worse than dining alone. We have got a fresh cargo of biscuits from Captain Burneys.—— I have——

Here I was interrupted, and a long tedious interval has intervened during which I have had neither time nor inclination to write a word.—— The Lodging—that pride and pleasure of your heart & mine, is given up—*and here he is again*—Charles I mean; as unsettled, and as undetermined as ever. When he went to the poor lodging after the hollidays I told you he had taken, he could not endure the solitariness of them, and I had no rest for the sole of my foot,[5] till I promised to believe his solemn protestations that he could, & would write as well at home as there——. Do you believe this?—— —— —— —— I have no power over Charles—he will do—what he will do. But I ought to have some little influence over myself—. And therefore I am most manfully resolving to turn over a new leaf with my own mind. Your visit to us, though not a very comfortable one to yourself, has been of great use to me; I set you up in my fancy, as a kind of *thing* that takes an interest in my concerns, and I hear you talk[i]ng to me, and argueing the matter very learnedly when I give way to despondency. You shall hear a good account of me, and of the progress I make in altering my fretful temper to a calm & quiet one. It is but being once thourowly convinced one is wrong, to make one resolve to do so no more, and I know my dismal faces have been almost as great a draw back upon Charles comfort, as his feverish teazing ways have been upon mine. Our love for each other has been the torment of our lives hitherto. I am most seriously intending to bend the whole force of my mind to counteract this, and I think I see some prospect of success.

Of Charles's ever bringing any work to pass at home, I am very doubtful—and of the farce succeeding I have little or no hope—but if I could once get into the way of being chearful myself I should see an easy remedy in leaving town & living cheaply almost wholly alone, but

till I do find we really are comfortable alone, and by ourselves, it seems a dangerous experiment. We shall certainly stay where we are till after next Christmas, and in the mean time, as I told you before all my whole thoughts shall be to *change* myself into just such a chearful soul as you would be in a lone House with no companion but your brother if you had nothing to vex you—nor no means of wandering after *Curse a rats*. Do write soon—though I write all about myself I am thinking all the while of you—and I am uneasy at the length of time it seems since I heard from you. Your Mother, and Mr White, is running continually in my head—and this *second winter* makes me think how cold, damp, and forlorn your solitary house will feel to you—I would your feet were perched up again on our fender—

Manning is not yet gone—Mrs Holcroft is brought to bed[6]—Mrs Reynolds has been confined at home with illness but is recovering. God bless you

<div style="text-align:right">

yours affectionately
M Lamb

</div>

MS: Courtesy of the Arents Collections, The New York Public Library, Astor, Lenox and Tilden Foundations. Pub.: Harper, III, 209–214; Lucas (1905), VI, 342–344; Lucas (1912), V, 356–359; Lucas (1935), II, 1–4. Address: Miss Stoddart/Winterslow/near Salisbury. Postmark: March 14, 1806.

1. Mary must have meant that the Friday night was changed to Thursday. Lamb's cribbage partner, mentioned below, was not, as has been surmised, marine Brevet Lieutenant Colonel Molesworth Phillips (1756–1832), who had served aboard the *Discovery* with James Burney on Cook's last voyage, in 1782 become James Burney's brother-in-law by his marriage to Susanna Elizabeth Burney (1755–1800), and in 1802 been seized by Napoleon and detained in France until 1814. The Phillips mentioned was, rather, Edward Phillips, who is frequently associated in these letters and once in *H. C. R. on Books and Writers* (I, 16) with cribbage and Lamb's cards parties generally. He had been a clerk for Thomas Poole, in 1805 had upon Poole's recommendation gone to work for Rickman, in 1810 was disappointed in his attempt to obtain some position with the Royal Society, and in 1814 succeeded Rickman as secretary to the speaker of the House of Commons. It is stated in *Rickman*, pp. 111–112, that he retained that post until at least 1833, when it was recorded that he returned his salary to the Committee on the Offices of the House of Commons. But any other House records that may have existed about him were destroyed in the fire of 1835.

2. Unidentified. The Martins are the members of Louisa Martin's family.

3. Unidentified. "Mr W——," below, is Mr. White. See Letter 194, at the reference to note 2.

4. Consequent to the surrender by the Dutch in January 1806 of the garrison of Cape Coast Castle, Cape of Good Hope, to the British forces led by Lieutenant General Sir David Baird (1757–1829).

5. Genesis 8:9.

6. Of a daughter, who was named Louisa. In 1828 or 1829 Louisa was married to Carlyle's friend John Badams (d. 1833), who in 1813 had left the University

of Edinburgh without completing his course of study in medicine, by 1818 had established himself in Birmingham as a manufacturing chemist, and from 1828 to 1831 additionally as a manufacturer of paints or dyes and of colored and marbled papers. After their marriage the Badamses became neighbors of the Lambs at Enfield. Louisa, according to *The Lambs,* p. 171, was married after Badams' death to Baron de Merger of Plessis la Barbe, near Tours, where William Carew Hazlitt called on them in about 1855.

199. C. L. to Godwin

14 March 1806

I repent. Can that God whom thy votaries say thou hast demolished expect more? I did endite a splenetic Letter[1]—but did the black Hypochondria never gripe *thy* heart till thou hast taken a friend for an enemy? The foul fiend **Flibbertigibbet** leads me over four inched bridges to course my own shadow for a traitor. There are certain positions of the Moon, under which I counsel thee not to take any thing written from this domicil as **serious**

I rank thee with **Alves,**[2] Latinè **Helvetius,** or any of his cursed crew? Thou art my friend and henceforth my philosopher—thou shalt teach **Distinction** to the junior branches of my household, and **Deception** to the grey hair'd Janitress at my door—

what! are there atonements—can **Arcadias**[3] be brought upon knees creeping & crouching—?

come, as Macbeth's drunken porter says, **Knock, knock, knock, Knock, knock, knock, Knock**—seven times in a day shalt thou batter at my peace and if I shut aught against thee **save the Temple of Janus,** may **Briareus** with his hundred hands, in each a brass knocker, lead me such a life—

C Lamb

MS: Lord Abinger. Pub.: Hazlitt, I, 383–384; Ainger (1888), I, 240–241; Ainger (1900), II, 150–151; Macdonald, I, 257–258; Ainger (1904), I, 291–292; Harper, III, 249–250; Lucas (1905), VI, 371; Lucas (1912), V, 388–389; Lucas (1935), II, 114.

1. Unrecovered, as is Godwin's to Lamb. The "foul fiend Flibbertigibbet," below, is from *King Lear,* III, iv, 115.

2. Lamb refers to the utilitarian philosopher and littérateur Claude Adrien Helvétius (1715–1771), whose surname had been Latinized from Schweitzer.

3. Either the feeble Roman emperor Arcadius (378–408) or the second-century Greek grammarian Arcadius of Antioch. The knocking of the drunken porter in

Macbeth, referred to below, is at II, iii, 1–21, and "batter'd at their peace" at IV, iii, 178. The gates of the temple of Janus were kept open in time of peace and closed in time of war. See Vol. I, Letter 59, note 4, for Briareus.

200. *C. L. to William Hazlitt*

[Saturday,] 15 Mar 1806

Dear H.

I am a little surprised at no letter from you. This day week, to wit Saturday the 8th Mar. 1806 I book'd off by the Wem Coach Bull & Mouth Inn directed to *you* at the Revd Mr Hazlitt's Wem Shropsh. a parcel containing besides a book &c—a rare print which I take to be a Titian: begging the said W. H. to acknowledge receipt thereof; which he not having done, I conclude the said parcel to be lying at the Inn & may be lost: for which reason lest you may [be] a Wales-hunting at this instant, I have authorized any of your family, who soever first gets this, to open it that so precious a parcel may not moulder away for want of looking after.——

What do you in Shropshire when so many fine pictures are a going a going every day in London? Monday I visit the Marq. Landsdown's in Berkeley Square. Catalogue 2/6. Leonardos in plenty. Some other day this week, I go to see Sir Wm. Young's in Stratford place— Hulse's of Blackheath are also to be sold this month; & in May the first private collection in Europe, Welbore Ellis Agar's. And there are you, perverting Nature in lying Landscapes filched from old rusty Titians such as I can scrape up here to send you, with an additament from Shropshire Nature thrown in to make the whole look unnatural.— I am afraid of your mouth watering when I tell you that Manning & I got into Anjersteins[1] on Wensday. **Mon dieu!—such Claudes!** four Claudes bought for more than £10000—those who talk of Wilson being equal to Claude are either mainly ignorant or stupid—. One of these was perfectly miraculous. What colours short of bonâ fide sun-beams it could be painted in, I am not earthly colourman enough to say. But I did not think it had been in the possibility of things. Then, a music-piece by Titian, a thousand pound picture—five figures standing behind [a][2] sixth playing—none of the heads, [as] M. observed indicating great men o[r] affecting it, but **so sweetly disposed,** all leaning separate ways but **so easy,**—like a flock of some divine shepherd—the

colouring, like the economy of the picture, so sweet & harmonious—as good as [Shakspeares] Twelfth night, *almost,* that is.— It will give you a love of **Order** & cure you of restless fidgety passions for a week after—more musical than the music it would, but cannot, yet in a manner *does* shew. I have no room for the rest. Let me say, Anjerstein[3] sits in a room, his study (only that & the library are shewn) when he writes a common letter, as I am doing, surrounded with 20 Pictures worth 60000! ! what a Luxury! **Apicius,** and Heliogabulus, hide your diminished heads.—

<div align="right">Yours, my dear Painter

[. . .]</div>

MS: Pierpont Morgan Library. Pub.: Talfourd (1848), I, 151–154; Sala, I, 426–428; Purnell, I, 426–428; Fitzgerald, II, 259–261; Hazlitt, I, 368–369; Ainger (1888), I, 227–228; Ainger (1900), II, 130–132; Macdonald, I, 277–279; Ainger (1904), I, 277–279; Harper, III, 216–217; Lucas (1905), VI, 346–347; Lucas (1912), V, 361–362; Lucas (1935), II, 5–6. Address: Mr. Wm. Hazlitt/Wem/ Shropshire/In his absence, to be opened immediately.

1. The Pall Mall residence of the merchant, philanthropist, and art collector John Julius Angerstein (1735–1823), whose acquisitions, purchased by the British nation in 1824 for £60,000, form the nucleus of the National Gallery. His (five) Claudes of Lorraine—"Landscape: Cephalus and Procris Reunited by Diana" (No. 2), "A Seaport" (No. 5), "Landscape: The Marriage of Isaac and Rebekah ('The Mill')" (No. 12), "Seaport: The Embarkation of the Queen of Sheba" (No. 14), and "Seaport: The Embarkation of S. Ursula" (No. 30)—are described in Martin Davis' *National Gallery Catalogues: French School* (2d ed., rev.; London: National Gallery, 1957), pp. 32–34, 35–42, and 44–45. Lamb below mentions the landscape painter Richard Wilson (1714–1782), who was somewhat influenced by Claude. Lamb then praises the "music-piece" called "A Concert" (No. 3), which was done by an imitator of Titian and is described in Cecil Gould's *National Gallery Catalogues: Sixteenth-Century Venetian School* (London: National Gallery, 1959), pp. 130–131.

2. A piece has been torn away from the manuscript and with it the last words at the end of this line and the next two lines. Previous editions have, without brackets, "a piano, the" where I have inserted "[a]": the size of the missing piece would not appear to have accommodated the longer locution. "Shakspeares," below, is placed in brackets because it was written on the manuscript presumably by the person who clipped the original word for Lamb's signature on its verso.

3. Angerstein's portrait (No. 129), by Sir Thomas Lawrence (1769–1830), is described in Martin Davis' *National Gallery Catalogues: The British School* (2d ed., rev.; London: National Gallery, 1959), pp. 72–74. Apicius, mentioned below, is the name of three Roman epicures, the most celebrated of whom was M. Gavius Apicius, who flourished under Tiberius (42 B.C.–A.D. 37) and figures in Seneca's moral essays "De vita beata" and "De consolatione ad Helviam." Varius Avitus, called Heliogabalus, or Elagabalus (205?–222), emperor of Rome from 218 to 222, was noted for his beauty, his ceremonies, and a profligacy that shocked even the Romans.

201. *C. L. to Manning*

10 May 1806

My dear Manning.

I did'nt know what your going was till I shook a last fist with you[1] & then twas just like having shaken hands with a **wretch** on the fatal scaffold & when you are down the ladder you can never strech out to him again. Mary says you are dead & there's nothing to do but to leave it to time to do for us in the end what it always does for those who mourn for people in such a case. But she'll see by your letter you are not quite dead. A little kicking and agony, & then—. Martin Burney *took me out* a walking that evening and we talked of Mister Manning and then I came home & smoked for you & at twelve oClock came home Mary & Monkey Louisa from the play & there was more talk & more smoking, and they all seemed first rate characters because they knew a certain person. But whats the use of talking about 'em. By the time you'll have made your escape from the **Kalmuks,** you'll have staid so long I shall never be able to bring to your mind **who Mary was,** who will have died about a year before, nor who the Holcrofts were; **me** perhaps you will mistake for Phillips, or confound me with Mr. **Daw** because you saw us together.

Mary (whom you seem to remember yet) is not quite easy that she had not a formal parting from you. I wish it had so happened. But you must bring her a token a shawl or something and remember a sprightly little Mandarin for our mantle piece as a companion to the Child I am going to purchase at the Museum. She says you saw her writings about the other day and she wishes you should know what they are. She is doing for Godwins Bookseller[2] 20 of Shakespears plays to be made into Childrens tales. Six are already done by her to wit The Tempest, Winters Tale, Midsummer Night, Much ado, Two Gentlemen of Verona & Cymbeline: & the Merchant of Venice is in forwardness: I have done Othello & Macbeth and mean to do all the Tragedies. I think it will be popular among the little people. Besides money. It's to bring in 60 guineas: Mary has done them capitally, I think you'd think. These are the humble amusements we propose while you are gone to plant the cross of Christ among barbar-

ous Pagan Anthropophagi. Quam homo homini præstat![3] but then perhaps you'll get murder'd & we shall die in our beds with a fair literary reputation. Besure if you see any of those people whose heads do grow beneath their shoulders that you make a draught of them. It will be very curious. O Manning I am serious to sinking almost when I think that all those evenings which you have made so pleasant are gone, perhaps for ever. Four years you talk of may be **ten** & you may come back & find such alterations. Some circumstance may grow up to you or to me that may be a bar to the return of any such intimacy. I dare say all this is **Hum!** & that all will come back—but indeed we die many deaths before we die & I am almost sick when I think that such a hold as I had of you is gone. I have friends but some of 'em are changed. Marriage or some circumstance rises up to make them not the same. But I felt sure of you. And that last token you gave me of expressing a wish to have my name joined with yours you know not how it affected me: like a Legacy. God bless you in every way you can form a wish. May he give you health & safety & the accomplishment of all your objects and return you again to us to gladden some fire side or other (I suppose we shall be moved from the Temple). I will nurse the remembrance of your steadiness & quiet which used to infuse something like itself into our nervous minds. Mary called you our ventilator. Farewell and take her best wishes & mine.— Good bye.

<div align="right">C L</div>

One thing more. When you get to Canton you will most likely see a young friend of mine, Inspector of Teas, named **Ball.**[4] He is a very good fellow & I should like to have my name talked of in **China.** Give my kind remembrances to the said Ball.

I have made strict enquiries thro' my friend Thompson as to your affairs with the Compy. If there had been a Committee yesterday an order would have been sent to the Captn. to draw on them for your passage money, but there was no Committee. But in the Secrrys. orders to receive you on board it was specified that the Compy would defray your passage. All the orders about you to the Supercargoes are certainly in your ship. He or I will manage any thing here you may want done. What can I add, but take care of yourself. We drink tea at the Holcrofts tomorrow.

MS: The Folger Shakespeare Library, Washington, D.C. Pub.: Talfourd (1837), I, 285–288; Sala, I, 389–391; Purnell, I, 389–391; Fitzgerald, II, 222–224; Hazlitt, I, 370–372; Ainger (1888), I, 228–230; Ainger (1900), II, 132–136 and 269; Macdonald, I, 279–281; Ainger (1904), I, 278–280 and 395; Harper, III, 218–221; Lucas (1905), VI, 348–349, and VII, 969; Lucas (1912), V, 362–364; Lucas (1935), II, 6–8. Address: Mr. Manning/Passenger/On board the Thames/ East India Man/Portsmouth.

1. On the afternoon of May 7, when Manning left London for Portsmouth and shortly after notified Lamb of his arrival. Manning replied to this letter on the twelfth (*Manning-Lamb Letters*, pp. 94–95) and perhaps on the same day sailed for China on board the East Indiaman *Thames*.

2. Thomas Hodgkins. See Letter 190, source note, for the identifications of him and Lamb and Mary's *Tales from Shakespear*. See also Letters 202–204 and 212.

3. "How one man differs from another!" (Terence, *Eunuchus*, II, ii, 1).

4. Samuel Ball, who was in receipt of salary from the accountant general's department of the East India House from 1797 to 1804, when he resigned upon his appointment as assistant inspector of teas in Canton. He and Manning did meet and according to Mrs. Gertrude Alison Anderson in the *Manning-Lamb Letters*, p. 99, returned to England at about the same time, visited Italy together over the period 1827–1829, and remained friends to the end. Referred to below is Joseph Thompson (d. 1854). He was appointed an established clerk in the accountant general's department of the East India House in 1790, transferred to the secret commercial office in 1821, made conductor of the correspondence with China and clerk to the secret commercial committee in 1822, and retired on pension in 1832.

202. *M. A. L. to Sarah Stoddart*

Friday [May 30—Monday, June 2, 1806]

My dear Sarah

You say truly that I have sent you too many make-believe letters. I do not mean to serve you so again if I can help it. I have been very ill for some days past with the toothache. Yesterday I had it drawn, and I find myself greatly relieved but far from easy, for my head & my jaws still ache, and being unable to do any business I would wish to write you a long letter to atone for my former offences, but I feel so languid that I am afraid wishing is all I can do.

I am sorry you are so worried with business & I am still more sorry for your sprained ancle—. you ought not to walk upon it. What is the matter between you & your goodnatured maid you used to boast of? & what the devil is the matter with your Aunt?[1] you say she is discontented—you must bear with them as well as you can for doubtless it is your poor Mothers teizing that puts you all out of sorts. I pity you from my heart.

We cannot come to see you this summer, Nor do I think it advisable to come & incommode you when you for the same expense could come to us. Whenever you feel yourself disposed to run away from your troubles, Come up to us again, I wish it was not such a long expensive journey then you could run backward & forwards every month or two.

I am very sorry you still hear nothing from Mr White, I am afraid that is all at an end, What do you intend to do about Mr Turner?[2]

I believe Mrs Rickman is well again, but I have not been able to get out lately to enquire because of my toothache. Louisa Martin is quite well again.

William Hazlitt the brother of him you know is in town, I believe you have heard us say we like him. He came in good time for the loss of Manning made Charles very dull. and he likes Hazlitt better than any body except Manning. My toothache has moped Charles to death, you know how he hates to see people ill.

Mrs Reynolds has been this month past in Deptford so that now I never know when Monday comes.—

I am glad you have got your Mothers pension.—

My Tales are to be puplished separate story books,[3] I mean in single stories like the childrens little shilling books, I cannot send you them in Manusc[r]ipt because they are all in the ⟨booksell[er's] han[ds]⟩ Godwins hands but one will be published very soon & then you shall have it *all in print*. I go on very well, & have no doubt but I shall alway be able to hit upon some such kind of job to keep going on. I think I shall get fifty pounds a year at the lowest calculation, but as I have not yet seen any *money* of my own earning for we do not expect to be paid till Christmas I do not feel the good fortune that has so unexpectedly befallen me half so much as I ought to do. But another year no doubt I shall perceive it.

When I write again you will hear tidings of the farce for Charles is to go in a few days to the Managers to enquire about it. But that must now be a next years business too even if it does succeed, so its all looking forward, and no prospect of present gain. But thats better than no hopes at all either for present or future times.

Charles has written Macbeth & Othello, King Lear & has begun Hamlet. you would like to see us as we often sit writing on one table

(but not on one cushion sitting) like Hermia & Helena in the Midsummer's Nights Dream. or rather like an old literary Darby and Joan.[4] I taking snuff & he groaning all the while & saying he can make nothing of it, which he always says till he has finished and then he finds out he has made something of it.

If I tell you, that you Widow Blackacreise you must tell me I **Taleise,** for my tales seem to be all the subject matter I write about, & when you see them you will think them poor little baby-stories to make such a talk about, but I have no news to send nor nothing in short to say that is worth paying two pence for, I wish I could get franks then I should not care how short or stupidly I wrote.

Charles smokes still, & will smoke to the end of the chapter.

Martin[5] has just been here. My Tales (*again*) and Charless Farce has made the boy mad to turn author & he has written a Farce & he has made the Winters Tale into a Story, but what Charles says of himself is really true of Martin for he *can make nothing at all of it* and I have been talking very eloquently this morning to convince him that nobody can write farces &c. under thirty years of age—and so I suppose he will go home & new model his Farce.

What is Mr Turner? & what is likely to come of him? and how do you like him? and what do you intend to do about it?— I almost wish you to remain single till your Mother dies, & then come & live with us and we would either get you a husband or teach you how to live comfortably without, I think I should like to have you always to the end of our lives living with us, and I do not know any reason why that should not be except for the great fancy you seem to have for marrying, which after all is but a hazardous kind of an affair, but however do as you like, every man knows best what pleases himself best

I have known many single men I should have liked in my life (if it had suited them) for a husband: but very few husbands have I ever wished was mine which is rather against the state in general that one never is disposed to envy wives their good husbands, So much for marrying—but however get married if you can.

I say we shall not come & see you, & I feel sure we shall not: but if some sudden freak was to come in to our wayward heads could you at all manage—you[r] mother we should not mind but I think still it would be so vastly inconvenient—I am certain we shall not come,

& yet you may tell me when you write if it would be horribly incon-
venient if we did, and do not tell me any lies, but say truly whether
you would rather we did or not.—

God bless you my dearest Sarah—I wish for your sake I could have
written a very amusing letter but do not scold for my head aches sadly.
Farewel.

<div style="text-align: right">yours affectionately
M Lamb</div>

Don't mind my head ach for before you get this it will be well being
only from the pain in my jaws & teeth

June 2d 1806

MS: Berg Collection, New York Public Library. Pub.: Harper, III, 222–226;
Lucas (1905), VI, 350–352; Lucas (1912), V, 365–367; Lucas (1935), II, 9–12.
Address: Miss Stoddart/Winterslow/near Salisbury. Postmark: June 2, 1806.
 1. Still, presumably, the senior Mrs. Stoddart's (unidentified) sister. See Letter
183, at the reference to note 1.
 2. See Letter 151, note 2.
 3. Some of them were so "puplished," with plates attributed to William Blake,
at sixpence each. See *Works,* III, 477, and J. C. Thomson, comp., *Bibliography
of the Writings of Charles and Mary Lamb: A Literary History* (Hull: Tutin,
1908), pp. 25–26.
 4. An expression used to typify an old married couple living contentedly a placid
domestic life. See Letter 194, note 6, for the Widow Blackacre, referred to in the
next paragraph.
 5. Martin Burney. I have not discovered any record of his writings.

203. *C. L. to William Wordsworth*

<div style="text-align: right">London June twentysix 1806
Office Brassington</div>

Dear Wordsworth

We got the sixpounds safe in your sisters letters—are pleased you
may be sure with the good news of Mrs. W[1]—hope all is well over by
this time. "**A fine boy!**—have you any more—one more & a girl—
poor copies of me" vide **Mr H** a farce which the Proprietors have
done me the honor—but I will set down Mr. Wroughton's own words.
N. B. the ensuing letter was sent in answer to one[2] which I wrote
begging to know if my **piece** had any chance, as I might make alter-

ations &c. I writing on the Monday, there comes this letter on the Wednesday. Attend.

[copy of a Letter from Mr. Rd. Wroughton]

Sir,

Your **Piece** of Mr. H—— I am desired to say, is accepted at Drury Lane Theatre by the Proprietors, and, if agreeable to you, will be brought forwards when the proper Opportunity serves—the **Piece** shall be sent to you for your Alterations in the course of a few days, as the same is not in my Hands but with the Proprietors.

[dated]

66 Gower St.	I am Sir
Wednesday	Your obedient Sert.
June 11 1806	Rd. Wroughton

On the following Sunday Mr. Tobin[3] comes. The scent of a managers letter brought him. He would have gone further any day on such a business. I read the letter to him. He deems it authentic & peremptory. Our conversation naturally fell upon **pieces**—different sorts of **pieces**—what is the best way of offering a **piece**—how far the caprice of managers is an obstacle in the way of a **piece**—how to judge of the merits of a **piece**—how long a **piece** may remain in the hands of the managers before it is acted—and my **piece**—and your **piece**—and my poor brother's **piece**—my poor brother was all his life endeavouring to get a **piece** accepted—

I am not sure that when *my poor Brother* bequeathed the care of his **pieces** to Mr. James Tobin he did not therein convey a legacy which in some measure **mollified** the otherwise first stupefactions of grief. It ca'nt be expected that the present Earl Nelson[4] passes all his time in watering the laurels of the Admiral with Right Reverend Tears. Certainly he steals a fine day now & then to plot how to lay out the grounds & mansion at Burnham **most suitably** to the late Earl's taste, if he had lived, and how to spend the hundred thousand pound parliament has given him in erecting some little neat monument to his memory.

Mr. H.[5] I wrote that in mere wantonness of triumph. Have nothing more to say about it. The Managers I thank my stars have decided its merits for ever. They are the best judges of **pieces**, and it would be

insensible in me to affect a false modesty after the very flattering
letter which I have received & the ample————

I think this will be as good a pattern for Orders as I can think on.
A little thin flowery border round, neat not gaudy, and the Drury
Lane Apollo with the harp at the top. Or shall I have no apollo?—
simply nothing?— Or perhaps the Comic Muse? the same form, only
I think without the Apollo, will serve for the pit & galleries. I think it
will be best to write my name at full length. But then if I give away a
great many, that will be tedious. Perhaps *Ch. Lamb* will do. *BOXES*
Now I think on it I'll have in Capitals. The rest in a neat Italian *hand*.
Or better perhaps, 𝕭𝖔𝖝𝖊𝖘 in old English characters like Madoc or
Thalaba?—[6]

I suppose you know poor Mountague has lost his wife. That has
been the reason for my sending off all we have got of yours separately.
I thought it a bad time to trouble him. The **Tea** 25 lb in 5 5[-]lb
Papers, two sheets to each, with the chocolate which we were afraid
Mrs. W. would want, comes in one Box & the Hats in a small one.
I booked them off last night by the Kendal waggon. There comes

with this letter (no, it comes a day or two earlier) a Letter for you from the Doctor at Malta about Coleridge, just received. Nothing of certainty, you see, only that he is not at Malta.— We supt with the Clarksons one night—Mrs. Clarkson pretty well—Mr. C. somewhat fidgety, but a good man. The **Baby**[7] has been on a visit to Mrs. Charlotte Smith Novellist & morals-tainter, but is returned. A Ludicrous thought struck me. These two Ladies have both as you may have *seen* **great b*tt*ms**. I fancied upon their first meeting & salutation, while the Ladies were bowing & kissing, the two b*tt*ms saluting and doing the honours of a first meeting independently; as I have seen or fancy to have seen, when two Great Ladies have met on a Country Visit, their two **House-keepers** at the same instant in the store-room saluting & doing equal courtesies in separate formality.

Mary[8] is just stuck fast in All's Well that Ends Well. She complains of having to set forth so many female characters in boy's clothes. She begins to think Shakspear must have wanted Imagination.— I to encourage her, for she often faints in the prosecution of her great work, flatter her with telling her how well such a play & such a play is done. But she is stuck fast & I have been obliged to promise to assist her. To do this it will be necessary to leave off Tobacco. But I had some thoughts of doing that before, for I sometimes think it does not agree with me. W. Hazlitt is in Town. I took him to see a very pretty girl professedly, where there were two young girls[9]—the very head & sum of the **Girlery** was two young girls— they neither laughed nor sneered nor giggled nor whispered—but they were young girls—and he sat and frowned blacker & blacker indignant that there should be such a thing as Youth & Beauty, till he tore me away before supper in perfect misery & owned he could not **bear** young girls. They drove him mad. So I took him home to my **old Nurse** where he recover'd perfect tranquillity. Independent of this & as I am not a young girl myself, he is a **great acquisition to us.** He is rather imprudently, I think, printing a political pamphlet[10] on his own account & will have to pay for the paper &c. The first duty of an Author, I take it, **is never to pay anything.**— But non cuivis attigit adire Corinthum. The Managers I thank my stars have settled that question for me. Yours truly.

C Lamb

MS: University of Texas Library. Pub. Talfourd (1837), I, 277–280; Talfourd (1848), I, 168–170; Sala, I, 242–243 and 246–248; Purnell, I, 242–243 and 246–248; Fitzgerald, II, 77–78 and 81–83; Hazlitt, I, 352–353 and 373–374; Ainger (1888), I, 215 and 230–232; Ainger (1900), II, 135–139; Macdonald, I, 281–284; Ainger (1904), I, 280–283; Harper, III, 227–231; Lucas (1905), VI, 353–355 (with a facsimile of a portion); Lucas (1912), V, 368–371; Lucas (1935), II, 12–15. Address: Mr. Wordsworth/Grasmere/Kendal. Postmark: June 26, 1806. The heading and address are by James Brassington, a porter in the accountant general's department of the East India House from 1783 to two or three months before September 1807.

1. Who had given birth to Thomas on June 15. He died, probably from pneumonia, after an attack of the measles on December 1, 1812. The quotation from "Mr. H——," in the next sentence, is from Mr. H.'s soliloquy in the second act (*Works*, V, 205).

2. Unrecovered. The brackets, below, are Lamb's.

3. James Webbe Tobin. His brother John, mentioned below, had submitted thirteen stage pieces to the managers of various theaters, but had received only rejections. At the last the management of Drury Lane accepted his fourteenth, *The Honey Moon*, but John Tobin died seven weeks before it was performed, on January 31, 1805. See Vol. I, Letter 90, note 3.

4. William Nelson, first Earl Nelson (1757–1835), who on the death of his brother, on October 21, 1805, had succeeded him as second Baron Nelson of the Nile and Burnham-Thorpe. On November 10, 1805, he was created Viscount Merton and Earl Nelson of Trafalgar and Merton and in the next year succeeded also as Duke of Bronté in Sicily. Parliament granted him an annual pension of £5,000 and the sum of £90,000, which in 1814 he used to purchase Stanlynch Park, Downton, Wiltshire. Burnham-Thorpe, Norfolk, was the birthplace of the brothers and where their father, Edmund (1722–1802), had served as rector.

5. Underscored twice.

6. Each "Boxes" is underscored once. Black letter is used on the title pages and for the book or part designations in Southey's *Madoc* (1805) and *Thalaba the Destroyer* (1801). Mrs. Basil Montagu, the former Laura Rush, had died on June 17, 1806, from complications resulting from the birth of her third child.

7. Mrs. Godwin, as is clear from Letter 212. Mrs. Smith was living at Tilford, near Farnham, Surrey, where she died on October 28, 1806.

8. Three canceled lines precede. Two others follow the third sentence in this paragraph.

9. Unidentified. There is more on the subject introduced here in Vol. III, Letter 286 and its notes.

10. *Free Thoughts on Public Affairs: Or Advice to a Patriot; in a Letter Addressed to a Member of the Old Opposition* (1806). The Latin, below, is from Horace's *Epistles*, I, xvii, 36, and translates, "it is not given to every man to visit Corinth."

204. *M. A. L. to Sarah Stoddart*

Friday evening [June 27—
Wednesday, July 2, 1806]

My dear Sarah

Charles and Hazlitt are going to Sadlers Wells and I am amusing myself in their absence with reading a Manusc[r]ipt of Haslitts, but

have laid it down to write a few lines to tell you how we are going on. Charles has begged a months hollidays of which this is the first day, and they are all to be spent at home. We thank you for your kind invitations and were half inclined to come down to you, but after mature deliberation and many wise consultations such as you know we often hold, we came to the resolution of staying quietly at home, and during the hollidays we are both of us to set stoutly to work & finish the Tales, six of them being yet to do, we thought if we went any where and left them undone, they would lay upon our minds, and that when we returned we should feel unsettled, and our money all spent besides, and next summer we are to be very rich and then we can afford a long journey somewhere, I will not say to Salisbury because I really think [i]t is better for you to come to us, but of that we will talk another ti[m]e.

The best news I have to send you is that the Farce is accepted. That is to say the manager has written to say it shall be brought out when an opportunity serves. I hope that it may come out by next Christmas. You must come & see it the first night, for if it succeeds it will be a great pleasure to you, and if it should not we shall want your consolation. So you must come.

I shall soon have done my work and know not what to begin next. Now will you set your brains to work and invent a story either for a short childs story or a long one that would make a kind of Novel or a Story that would make a play. Charles wants me to write a play but I am not over anxious to set about it, but seriously will you draw me out a skeleton of a story either from memory of any thing that you have read or from your own invention and I will fill it up in some way or other.

The reason I have not written so long is that I worked, and worked in hopes to get through my task before the hollidays began, but at last I was not able for Charles was forced to get them now or he could not have had any at all, and having picked out the best stories first these latter ones take more time being more perplext and unmanageable. But however I hope soon to tell you that they are quite completed. I have finished one today which teazed me more than all the rest put together. They sometimes plague me as bad as your *Lovers* do you. How do you go on and how many new ones have you had lately?

I met Mrs Fenwick at Mrs Holcrofts the other day. she loo[ked] placid and smiling but I was so disconcerted that I hardly knew how to sit on my chair. She invited us to come and see her but we did not invite her in return, and nothing at all was said in an explanatory sort. So that matter rests at present.[1] Mrs Rickman continues very ill, so ill that there are no hopes of her recovery, for which I am very sorry indeed.

I am sorry you are altogether so uncomfortable, I shall be glad to hear you are settled at Salisbury, that must be better than living in a lone house companionless as you are, I wish you could afford to bring your Mother up to London, but that is quite impossible.

Your brother wrote a letter a week ago (which passed through our hands) to Wordsworth to tell him all he knew of Coleridge but as he had not heard from C. for some time there was nothing in the letter we did not know before.

Thank you for your brothers letters. I preserve them very carefully and you shall have them (as the Manager says) when opportunity serves.

Mrs Wordsworth is brought to bed, and I ought to write to Miss Wordsworth to thank her for the information but I suppose I shall defer it till another child is coming. I do so hate writing letters, I wish all my friends would co[me][2] and live in town. Charles has been telling me even[. . .] two months that he ought to write to your [. . .] my dislike to writing letters that prevents my [. . .] to you but sheer want of time I assure you, because [. . .] you care not how stupidly I write so as you do but [. . .] time what we are about.

Let me hear from you soon, and do let me hear some [. . .] and dont let me hear of your walking with sprained ancles again. no business is an excuse for making yourself lame.

I hope your poor Mother is better, and Aunty and Maid jog on pretty well, remember me to them all in due form and order. Charles's love and our best wishes that all your little busy affairs may come to a prosperous conclusion

<div align="right">

yours affectionately
M Lamb

</div>

<div align="right">

Sunday morning

</div>

I did not put this in the post hoping to be able to write a less dull

letter to you this morning but I have been prevented so it shall go as it is—I am in good spirits just at this present time for Charles has been reading over the *Tale* I told you plagued me so much and he thinks it one of the very best. It is "All's Well that Ends Well." You must not mind the many wretchedly dull letters I have sent you for indeed I cannot help it, my mind is so *dry* always after poring over my work all day. But it will soon be over.

I am cooking a shoulder of Lamb (Hazlitt dines with us.) it will be ready at two OClock if you can pop in and eat a bit with us.

They (Hazlitt & Charles) came home from Sadlers Wells so dismal & dreary dull on friday that I gave them both a good scolding—*quite a setting to rights,* and I think it has done some good for Charles has been very chearful ever since. I begin to hope the *home holidays* will go on very well. Mrs Rickman is better. Rickman we saw at Captain Burneys for the first time since her illness last night.

Write directly for I am uneasy about your *Lovers*. I wish something was settled. God bless you once more

<div style="text-align:right">

yours affectionately

M Lamb

</div>

2d July 1806

MS: Berg Collection, New York Public Library. Pub.: Lucas (1905), VI, 356–358; Lucas (1912), V, 372–374; Lucas (1935), II, 16–18. Address: Miss Stoddart/Winterslow/near Salisbury. Postmark: 18[0]6.

1. The cause of the estrangement is not known, but it had ended by December 23, when Mrs. Fenwick wrote Mary Hays: "yesterday evening Mr and Miss Lamb called and left an invitation for Wednesday evening which I wrote an assent to. Were it anywhere else I wd send an apology . . . but with them the case is peculiar. You may remember there had been a disagreement between us. It so happened that they one evening saw Eliza play, and were so much pleased with her that they immediately solicited a renewal of intimacy. I had too strong a sense of former kindness, and too much moved by the cause of their return, to withstand the offer" (*The Fate of the Fenwicks*, p. 18). Mrs. Rickman, mentioned next, did not die until 1836.

2. Two or three words or parts of words were torn away at this point when the seal was broken. Two or three more at the ends of this line, each of the next three lines, and the first line in the next paragraph went with the portion that is gone from the edge of the leaf.

205. *M. A. L. to Dorothy Wordsworth*

Friday [August 29, 1806]

My dear Miss Wordsworth

After I had put my letter[1] in the post yesterday I was uneasy all the night because of some few expressions relative to poor Coleridge, I mean in saying I wished you[r] brother would come to town & that I wished your brother would consult Mr Southey. I am very sure your brother will take no step in consequence of any foolish advice that I can give him, so far I am easy, but the painful reflections I have had during a sleepless night has induced me to write merely to quiet myself, because I have felt ever since, that in the present situation of Coleridge, returned after an absence of two years, and feeling a reluctance to return to his family I ought not to throw in the weight of a hair in advising you or your Brother, and that I ought not to have so much as named to you his reluctance to return to Keswick, for so little is it in my power to calculate on his actions that perhaps in a few days he may be on his return home.

You my dear friend will perfectly understand me that I do not mean that I might not freely say to you anything that is upon my mind— but [the] truth is my poor mind is so weak that I never dare trust my own judgement in anything, What I think one hour a fit of low spirits makes me unthink the next. Yesterday I wrote anxiously longing for Mr Wordsworth & Mr Southey to endeavour to bring Mrs C. to consent to a separation & today I think of the letter I received from Mrs Coleridge, telling me as joyful news, that her husband is arrived, and I feel it very wrong in me even in the remotest degree to do anything to prevent her seeing that husband—she and her husband being the only people who ought to be concerned in the affair.

All that I have said, or meant to say, you will perfectly understand, it being nothing more than to beg you will consider both my letter today and yesterday as if you had not read either, they being both equally the effect of low spirits, brought on by the fatigue of Coleridge's conversation and the anxious care even to misery which I have felt since he has been here that something could be done to

make such an admirable creature happy. Nor has I assure you Mrs Coleridge been without her full share in adding to my uneasiness. They say she grows fat & is very happy—and people say I grow fat & look happy—

It is foolish to teize you about my anxieties, you will feel quite enough on the subject yourself, and your little ones are all ill, and no doubt you are fatigued with nursing, but I could not help writing today, to tell you how what I said yesterday ha[s] vext & worried me. Burn both these foolish letters and do not name the subject of them because Charles will either blame me for having written something improper or he will laugh at me for my foolish fears about nothing.

Though I wish you not to take notice of what I have said yet I shall rejoice to see a letter from you, and I hope when you have half an hours leisure to see a line from you

We have not heard from Coleridge since he went out of town but I dare say you have heard either from him or Mrs Clarkson—

I remain my dear friend

<div style="text-align: right">

yours most affectionately

M Lamb

</div>

MS: University of Texas Library. Pub.: Harper, III, 231–233; Lucas (1905), VI, 359–360; Lucas (1912), V, 375–376; Lucas (1935), II, 19–20. Address: Miss Wordsworth/Grasmere/near Kendal/Westmorland. Postmark: August 29, 1806.

1. Unrecovered. Coleridge, mentioned below, had landed at Stangate Creek, Lower Halstow, Kent, on August 17 after a bad voyage of fifty-five days. His Malta earnings were almost gone and the Wedgwood annuity seemed to be going. He was ill and depressed and more dependent on laudanum than ever. And he was dreading his home-coming at Keswick. That night he reached The Bell inn, London, and the next morning wrote of his condition to Daniel Stuart, who was then staying at a Mrs. Humble's boarding house in Margate and whom Coleridge soon rejoined as a contributor to *The Courier*. On the twentieth he wrote Southey he was moving in with the Lambs. He left them before the end of the month to spend a few days with the Clarksons at the Parndon, Essex, home of William Smith (1756–1835), M.P. for Norwich, and his wife, the former Frances Coape. Coleridge apparently returned to London during the first week of September and journeyed between there and Margate on business with Stuart. By September 13 he had taken quarters in the office of *The Courier*, at 348 Strand, London. On September 16 he wrote his first letter to Mrs. Coleridge since his landing. On October 9 he wrote his sixth. In each he promised to come to her and in each gave excuses for not having done so earlier or for breaking his promise. He finally set out. After stops at Parndon, Bury St. Edmunds, Cambridge, Penrith, and Kendal he reached Keswick on October 30. By about mid-November he had made up his mind that he and his wife were hopelessly incompatible and they determined on a last separation. They first agreed he should take David Hartley and Derwent—"If

I go away without them," he wrote Wordsworth early in December (*Coleridge's Letters*, II, 1203), "I am a Bird who has struggled himself from off a Bird-lime twig, & then finds a string round his leg pulling him back. . . ." But he went away with only David Hartley. On December 21 father and son joined the Wordsworths at their winter residence, lent them by Sir George Howland Beaumont, at Hall Farm, Coleorton, Leicestershire.

206. *M. A. L. to Coleridge*

[Early to mid-September 1806]

Dear Coleridge

I have read your silly very silly letter & between laughing & crying I hardly know how to answer it. You are too serious & too kind a vast deal, for we are not much used to either seriousness or kindness from our present friends and therefore your letter has put me into a greater hurry of spirits that[1] your pleasant Segar did last night for believe me your two odd faces amused me much more than the mighty transgression vexed me. If Charles had not smoked last night his virtue would have not lasted longer than tonight, and now perhaps with a little of your good counsel he will refrain. But be not too serious if he smokes all the time you are with us——. A few chearful evenings spent with you serves to bear up our spirits many a long & weary year. And the very being led unto the crime by your Segar that you thought so harmless, will serve for our amusement many a dreary time when we can get no letter nor hear no tidings of you.— —

You must positively must write to Mrs Coleridge this day, and you must write here that I may know you write or you must come and dictate a letter for me to write to her. I know all that you would say in defence of not writing & I allow in full force every thing that [you] can say or think, but yet a letter from me or you *shall go today*.

I wanted to tell you but feared to begin the subject how well your children are how Pypos thrives & what a nice child Sara is and above all I hear such favorable accounts from Southy from Wordsworth & Hazlitt of Hartley.

I have got Wordsworths letters out for you to look at but you shall not see them or talk of them without you like——. Only come here as soon as you receive this, and I will not teize you about writing, but

will manage a few lines Charles and I between us, but something like
a letter shall go today.

Come directly

<div align="right">Yours affectionately

M Lamb</div>

MS: Mr. W. Hugh Peal. Pub.: Harper, III, 235–236; Lucas (1905), VI, 361–362; Lucas (1912), V, 377–378; Lucas (1935), II, 21–22. Address: Mr Coleridge. The date is established (considering the information in Letter 205, note 1) in the second paragraph.
1. For "than."

207. *M. A. L. to Sarah Stoddart*

<div align="right">Thursday [October 23, 1806]</div>

My dear Sarah

I thank you a thousand times for the beautiful work you have sent
me, I received the parcel from a strange gentleman yesterday. I like
the patterns very much, you have quite set me up in finery, but you
should have sent the silk handkerchief too. Will you make a parcel of
that & send it by the Salisbury coach, I should like to have it in a few
days because we have not yet been to Mr Babbs[1] and that handkerchief would suit this time of year nicely——

I have received a long letter from your brother on the subject of
your intended marriage. I have no doubt but you also have one on
this business therefore it is needless to repeat what he says. I am well
pleased to find that upon the whole he does not seem to see it in an unfavorable light. He says that if Mr D. is a worthy man he shall have
no objection to become the brother of a farmer, and he makes an odd
request to me that I shall set out to Salisbury to look at & examine
into the merits of the said Mr D—— & speaks very confidently as if
you would abide by my dete[r]mination. A pretty sort of an office
truly.— shall I come?

The objections he starts are only such as you & I have already
talked over such as the difference in age, education, habit of life &c.

You have gone too far in this affair for any interference to be at all
desirable, and if you had not, I really do not know what my wishes
would be. When you bring Mr Dowling at Christmas I suppose it will

be quite time enough for me to sit in judgement upon him, but my examination will not be a very severe one. If you fancy a very young man, and he likes an elderly gentlewoman, if he likes a learned & accomplished lady, and you like a not very learned youth who may need a little polishing which probably he will never acquire; it is all very well & God bless you both together & may you be both very long in the same mind.

I am to assist you too your brothers says in drawing up the marriage settlements, another thankful office! I am not it seems to suffer you to keep too much money in your own power, and yet I am to take care of you in case of bankruptcy &c., and I am to recommend to you for the better management of this point, the serious perusal of *Jeremy Taylor* his opinion on the marriage state, especially his advice against *separate interests*[2] in that happy state, and I am also to tell you how desirable it is that the husband should have the entire direction of all money concerns, except as your good brother adds, in the case of his own family, where the money he observes, is very properly deposited in Mrs Stoddarts hands she being better suited to enjoy such a trust than any other woman, and therefore it is fit that the general rule should not be extended to her.

We will talk over these things when you come to town, and as to settlements, which are matters of which I never having had a penny in my own disposal I never in my life thought of, and if I had been blessed with a good fortune, & that marvellous blessing to boot a husband I verily believe I should have crammed it all uncounted into his pocket—. But thou hast a cooler head of thy own & I dare say will do exactly what is expedient & proper, but your brothers opinion seems somewhat like Mr Barwis:[3] & I dare say you will take it into due consideration, yet perhaps an offer of your own money to take a farm may make *uncle* do less for his nephew & in that case Mr D might be a loser by your generosity———. weigh all these things well & if you can so contrive it let your brother *settle* the *settlements* himself when he returns which will most probably be long before you want them.———

You are settled it seems in the very house which your brother most dislikes—. If you find this house very inconvenient get out of it as fast as you can, for you[r] brother says he sent you the fifty pound to make you comfortable, and by the general tone of his letter I am sure he

wishes to make you easy in money matters, therefore why straiten yourself to pay the debt you owe him which I am well assured he never means to take. Thank you for the letter and for the picture of pretty little chubby nephew John.[4]

I have been busy making waistcoats and plotting new work to succeed the Tales, as yet I have not hit upon any thing to my mind—

Charles took an amended copy of his farce to Mr Wroughton the Manager yesterday. Mr Wroughto[n] was very friendly to him and expressed high approbation of the farce, but there are two he tells him to come out before it, yet he gave him hopes that it will come out this season, but I am afraid you will not see it by Christmas. It will do for another jaunt for you in the spring—. We are pretty well & in fresh spirits about this farce. Charles has been very good lately in the matter of *Smoking*.

When you come bring the gown you wish to sell. Mrs Coleridge will be in town then, & if she happens not to fancy it, perhaps some other person may.

Coleridge I believe is gone home, he left us with that design but we have not heard from him this fortnight

Louisa sends her love, she has been very unwell lately

My respects to Coridon, Mother, and Aunty.

Farewel, My best wishes are with you.

<div style="text-align:right">yours affectionately.</div>

<div style="text-align:right">M Lamb</div>

When I saw what a prodigious quantity of work you had put into the finery I was quite ashamed of my unreasonable request, I will never serve you so again, but I do dearly love worked muslin.——

MS: Pierpont Morgan Library. Pub.: Lucas (1905), VI, 362–364; Lucas (1912), V, 378–381; Lucas (1935), II, 22–25. Address: Miss Stoddart/Salisbury. Postmark: October 23, 1806.

1. The friend and admirer of the late Mrs. Lamb mentioned in Letter 144, note 1. Sarah Stoddart's intended marriage to the farmer Mr. Dowling named, and nicknamed Coridon (later spelled "Corydon"), below, never came about.

2. In *The Rule and Exercises of Holy Living*, ch. 3, sect. 2, "Rules for Married Persons."

3. Dowling's uncle, according to what follows.

4. John Frederick Stoddart. See Vol. I, Letter 3, note 28.

208. *C. L. to Manning*

5th decem. 1806

Manning,

Your Letter dated Hottentots August the what-was-it came to hand. I can scarce hope that mine will have the same luck. China—Canton—bless us—how it strains the imagination and makes it ache! I write under another uncertainty whether it can go tomorrow by a ship which I have just learned is going off direct to your part of the world, or whether the dispatches may not be sealed up & this have to wait—for if it is detained here, it will grow staler in a fortnight than in a five months voyage coming to you. It will be a point of conscience to send you none but bran new news (the latest edition) which will but grow the better like oranges for a sea voyage. O that you should be so many hemispheres off—if I speak incorrectly you can correct me—why the simplest death or marriage that takes place here must be important to you as news in the old Bastille.[1] There's your friend **Tuthill** has got away from France—you remember France? & Tuthill?—ten to one but he writes by this post. If he do'nt get my note in time, apprizing him of the vessel sailing, **Know then** that he has found means to obtain leave from Bonaparte, without making use of any *incredible romantic pretences* as some have done, who never meant to fulfill them, to come home & I have seen him here & at Holcrofts—. I have likewise seen his Wife & his elegant little French Woman whose hair reaches to her heels—by the same token that Tom—(Tommy H.)[2] took the comb out of her head, not expecting the issue, & it fell down to the ground to his utter consternation two ells long.— An't you glad about Tuthill? Now then be sorry for Holcroft whose new play, called the Vindictive Man, was damned about a fortnight since. It died in part of its own weakness, & in part for being choked up with bad actors. The two principal parts were destin'd to Mrs. Jordan[3] & Mr. Bannister, but Mrs. J. has not come to terms with the Managers, they have had some squabble, & Bannister shot some of his fingers off by the going off of a gun. So Miss Duncan had her part, & Mr. DeCamp (a vulgar Brother of Miss DeCamp) took his. He is a fellow with the make of a Jockey & the air

of a Lamplighter. His part, the principal comic hope of the play, was most unluckily Goldfinch taken out of the Road to Ruin,[4] not only the same character but the identical Goldfinch—the same as Falstaff is in two plays of Shakespear—as the devil of ill luck would have it, half the audience did not know that H. had written it, but were displeased at his stealing from the Road to Ruin; & those who might have borne a Gentlemanly Coxcomb with his "That's your sort" "go it"—such as **Lewis** is—did not relish the intolerable vulgarity & inanity of the idea stript of its manner. DeCamp was hooted, more than hist, hooted & bellow'd off the stage, before the second act was finished, so that the remainder of his part was forced to be with some violence to the play omitted. In addition to this, a whore was another principal character, a most unfortunate choice in this moral day. The audience were as scandalized as if you were to introduce such a personage to their private tea tables. Besides, her action in the play was gross— wheedling an old man into marriage—. But the mortal blunder of the play was that which oddly enough H. took pride in & exultingly told me of the night before it came out, that there were no less than **Eleven** principal characters in it, & I believe he meant of the men only, for the playbill exprest as much, not reckoning one woman & one whore—and true it was, for Mr. Powell, Mr. Raymond,[5] Mr. Bartlett, Mr. H. Siddons, Mr. Barrymore &c. &c—to the number of 11 had all parts equally prominent, & there was as much of them in quantity & rank as of the Hero & Heroine—& most of them Gentlemen who seldom appear but as the Hero's friend in a farce—for a minute or two—& here they all had their ten minute speeches, & one of them gave the audience a serious account how he was now a Lawyer but had been a Poet & then a long enumeration of the inconveniences of authorship, rascally booksellers, Reviewers &c. which first set the audience a gaping—but I have said enough—you will be so sorry that you w[ill] not think the best of me for my detail, but **news is news** at Canton—. [Poor][6] H. I fear will feel the disappointment very seriously in a pecuniary light—from what I can learn, he has saved nothing—you & I were hoping one day that he had, but I fear he has nothing but his pictures & books—no very flourishing business—and to be obliged to part with his lo[ng] neck'd **Guido** that hangs opposite as you enter, & the game piece that hangs in the back drawing room & all those Vandykes &c—God should temper the wind to the shorn con-

noisseur—I hope I need not say to you, that I feel for the weather-
beaten Author, & for all his Household. I assure you his fate has soured
a good deal the pleasure I should have otherwise taken in my own
little Farce being accepted & I hope about to be acted—it is in re-
hearsal actually, & I expect it to come out next week. It is kept a sort
of secret & the rehearsals have gone on privately, lest by many folks
knowing it, the story should come out, which would infallibly damn it.
You remember I had sent it before you went. Wroughton read it &
was much pleased with it. I speedily got an answer. I took it to make
alterations & lazily kept it some months, then took courage & furbish'd
it up in a day or two & took it. In less than a fortnight I heard the
principal part was given to **Elliston**[7] who liked it & only wanted a
prologue, which I have since done & sent, & I had a note the day
before yesterday from the manager **Wroughton** (bless his fat face—
he is not a bad Actor in some things) to say that I should be sum-
moned to the Rehearsal after the next, which next was to be yester-
day. I had no idea it was so forward. I have had no trouble, attended
no **reading** or rehearsal, made no interest, what a contrast to the
usual **parade** of Authors. But **it is peculiar to modesty to do all things
without noise or pomp!** I have some suspicion it will appear i[n]
public on Wednesday next, for W. says in his note, it is so forward
that if wanted it may come out **next week,** & a new melodram is an-
nounced for every day till then; and a "new farce is in rehearsal"
is put up in the bills. Now you'd like to know the subject. **The Title
is "Mr. H."**[8]—no more, how simple, how taking! a great *H.* sprawl-
ing over the play bill & attracting eyes at every corner. The story is,
a coxcomb appearing at Bath vastly rich—all the Ladies dying for
him—all bursting to know who he is—but he goes by no other name
than Mr. H.—a curiosity like that of the dames of Strasburg about
the man with the great nose—. But I wont tell you any more about
it—yes I will—but I cant give you an idea **how** I have done it—.
I'll just tell you that after much vehement admiration, when his
true name comes out, *Hogsflesh,*[9] all the women shun him, [av]oid
him & not one can be found to change their name for him—that's
the idea—how flat it is here—but how whimsical in the farce. And
only think how hard upon me it is that the ship is dispatch'd to-
morrow, & my triumph cannot be ascertain'd till the Wednesday
after—but all China will ring of it by & by. **N. B.** (but this is a

secret) [The Pr]ofessor has got a tragedy[10] coming out with the young Rosciu[s i]n it in January next, as we say, January last [i]t will be with you—& though tis a profound [secre]t now, as all his affairs are, it cannot be much [of one b]y the time you read this. However, do'nt let it go any farther. I understand there are dramatic Exhibitions in China. One would not like to be forestalled. Do you find in all this stuff I have written any thing like those feelings which one should send my old adventuring friend, that is gone to wander among Tartars and may never come again? I dont—but your going away & all about you is a thread-bare topic—I have worn it out with thinking—it has come to me when I have been **dull** with any thing, till my sadness has seemed more to have come from it than to have introduced it—. I want you, you dont know how m[u]ch—but if I had you here in my European garret we should but talk over such stuff as I have written—so—Those Tales from Shakespear are near coming out—& Mary has begun a new work—.[11] **Mr. Daw** is turn'd Author—he has been in such a way lately—**Daw** the Painter, I mean—he sits & stands about at Holcrofts, & says nothing —then sighs & leans his head on his hand—I took him to be in Love—but it seems he was only meditating a work, the Life of Morland—the young man is not used to composition—. Rickman & Capt. Burney are well—they assemble at my house pretty regularly of a Wednesday, a new institution, like other great men, I have a public day; cribbage & pipes, with Phillips & noisy Ma[rtin.]

Good God what a bit only I've got left. How shall I squeeze all I know into this morsel! Coleridge is come home, & is going to turn Lecturer on Taste[12] at the Royal Institution. I shall get £200 from the theatre if Mr. H. has a good run & I hope £100 for the copyright. Nothing, if it fails; & there never was a more ticklish thing. The whole depends on the manner in which the name is brought out, which I value myself on, as a Chef d'ouvre. How the paper grows less & less! In less than two minutes I shall cease to talk to you, & you may rave to the great Wall of China. N. B. Is there such a Wall. Is it as big as Old London Wall by Bedlam?— Have you met with a friend of mine named Ball at Canton? if you are acquainted, re-member me kindly to him. Amongst many queer cattle I have & do meet with at the India Ho. I always liked h[i]s behavior. Tell him his friend Evans[13] &c are well. Woodruff not dead yet. (May be

you'll think I have not said enough of Tuthill & the Holcrofts. Tuthill is a noble fellow, as far as I can judge. The H's bear their disappointment pretty well; but indeed they are sadly mortify'd. Mrs. H. is cast down. It was well, if it were but on this account, that T. is come home.—) N. B. if my little thing dont succeed, I shall easily survive, having, as it were, compared to H's venture, but a sixteenth in the Lottery. Mary & I are to sit next the orchestra in the pit, next the Tweedle-Dees.— She remembers you. You are more to us than five hundred farces, clappings &c. Come back one day.

<div align="right">C. Lamb</div>

Holcroft has just writ to me as follows. "Dear Sir, Miss L. has informed us you are writing to Manning. Will you be kind enough to tell him directly from me, that I & my family are most truly anxious for his safety; that if praying could bring down blessings on him we should pray morning noon & night; that his & our dear friends, the Tuthills, are most happily once more safe in England, & that I earnestly entreat not only a single Letter but a correspondence with him whenever the thing is practicable with such an address as may make letters from me likely to find him. In short, dear Sir, if you will be kind enough to speak of me to Manning you cannot speak with greater friendship & respect than I feel.

<div align="right">Yours
with true friendship & kindness"</div>

Tuthill is at crabtree's, who has married Tuthill's sister.

MS: Folger Shakespeare Library. Pub.: Talfourd (1837), I, 289–296; Sala, I, 391–397; Purnell, I, 391–397; Fitzgerald, II, 224–230; Hazlitt, I, 376–380; Ainger (1888), I, 234–238; Ainger (1900), II, 141–148; Macdonald, I, 285–290; Ainger (1904), I, 285–289; Harper, III, 237–244; Lucas (1905), VI, 364–368, and VII, 970; Lucas (1912), V, 381–386; Lucas (1935), II, 25–30. Address: T. Manning Esqr./Canton.

1. The passage is another foreshadowing of "Distant Correspondents" (*Works*, II, 104–108). The physician, mentioned next, George, later Sir George, Leman Tuthill (1772–1835), who had spent 1790 to 1796 at Caius College, Cambridge, and there come to know Manning, had with his wife, the former Maria Smith of Halesworth, Suffolk, been in France since about 1801, been detained as a political prisoner at Verdun since the breakdown of the Treaty of Amiens in May 1803, and been recently allowed to leave for England upon Mrs. Tuthill's petition to Napoleon for release. (See James Henry Lawrence's *A Picture of Verdun, or the English Detained in France* [London: Hookham, 1810], II, 82–83.) Tuthill returned to Caius College, earned his M.A. in 1809, was granted a license to practice medicine in 1812, and received his M.D. in 1816. He thereafter served the Westminster, Bridewell, and Bethlehem hospitals, assisted significantly in the preparation of the *Pharmacopœia Londinensis* of 1824 and 1836, and wrote

Vindiciæ Medicæ, or a Defence of the College of Physicians (1834). His and Mrs. Tuthill's only child, Laura Maria, to whom Lamb presently refers as Tuthill's "elegant little French Woman," became the wife of Thomas Bowett, a London solicitor. Tuthill's sister and her husband, one Crabtree, both of whom Lamb mentions in his postscript, have not been identified except for the fact that Manning gave the residence of the latter in May 1806 as 13 Newgate Street (*Manning-Lamb Letters*, p. 95) and the possibility that he could still have been one of the two Crabtrees listed in the London postal directory for 1806—either Joseph, who operated a shalloon and serge warehouse at 49 Aldermanbury, or Richard, a tithe-land and timber surveyor whose office was at 11 Thayer Street, Manchester Square. Lamb's note to Tuthill has not been recovered.

2. Thomas Holcroft (d. 1852), Holcroft's son by his wife Louisa. He later worked as a clerk for Rickman, was dismissed by him in 1819, and by means of passage money raised for him by Lamb, Henry Crabb Robinson, and Robinson's friend the Unitarian Anthony Robinson (1762–1827) was able to join a brother in India. He became the editor of an East Indian newspaper, by 1822 a journalist in London, and sometime after its establishment in 1823 a secretary to the Royal Asiatic Society. By 1838 he had become a correspondent, translator, and leader writer for the *Morning Herald* in Paris, where on October 4 of that year Crabb Robinson found him "comfortably situated" (*H. C. R. on Books and Writers*, II, 553) with a pleasant wife. He returned to London only a week or two before his death. His father's comedy *The Vindictive Man* (1806), discussed below, had been produced at Drury Lane on November 20 and failed utterly. Lamb recalled the performance and some of the language he uses in this letter to condemn it in "New Pieces at the Lyceum" (*Works*, I, 189).

3. Dorothea, or Dorothy, Jordan (1762–1816), who was born Bland but had adopted the stage name Mrs. Jordan when she played the York circuit from 1782 to 1785. She made her debut at Drury Lane in 1785, performed there and at the Haymarket until 1809, and at Covent Garden from 1811 to 1814. Lamb praised her in "On Some of the Old Actors" (*Works*, II, 132–133). See Vol. I, Letter 90, note 4, for John Bannister. Maria Rebecca Duncan Davison (1783–1858), mentioned below—she was married to James Davison (d. 1858) in 1812—played at Drury Lane from 1804 to 1818 and at Drury Lane, Covent Garden, and the Haymarket from 1819 to 1829. Vincent de Camp (1777–1839), a son of George de Camp and a member of a family of singers and dancers, occasionally performed in minor roles at Drury Lane and the Haymarket and later became an actor and a cattle dealer or breeder in America. His sister Maria Theresa, or Marie Thérèse, de Camp Kemble (1774–1838) was born in Vienna, acted at Drury Lane and the Haymarket from 1786 to 1806, was then married to Charles Kemble and transferred to Covent Garden, where she played from 1806 to 1815, from 1818 to 1819, and in 1829.

4. *The Road to Ruin* was Holcroft's most successful play. It had opened at Covent Garden on February 18, 1792, with William Thomas, "Gentleman," Lewis (1748?–1811) in the role of Goldfinch, and was published in the same year.

5. Probably Snelling Powell (d. 1821) and James Grant Raymond (1771–1817). By Bartlett, named next, Lamb means the comedian George Bartley (1782?–1858), who appeared at Drury Lane from about 1802 to 1808 and from 1814 to 1815. He was married in 1814 to the actress Sarah Smith (1783–1850), was engaged at Covent Garden after he and his wife returned from America in 1818 to perhaps 1843, and last performed in 1852 at the Princess Theatre. Henry Siddons (1774–1815), the son of Sarah Siddons, played at Covent Garden from 1801 to 1805 and at Drury Lane from 1805 to 1809. He managed the Edinburgh from 1809 to 1815. Barrymore was possibly William Barrymore (d. 1845), born Blewitt, the husband of the dancer and pantomimist the former Miss Adams (1783–1863).

She performed at the Royal Circus (after 1809 renamed the Surrey) and Drury Lane between 1803 and 1829 and opened in New York City in 1831.

6. Torn away and supplied from Lucas (1935), II, 27. The Guido referred to below is presumably a work by the Bolognese artist Guido Reni (1575-1642).

7. Robert William Elliston (1774-1831), who spoke the Prologue and took the part of Mr. H. and of whom Lamb wrote grandly in "To the Shade of Elliston" and "Ellistoniana" (*Works*, II, 166-167 and 168-172). He appeared at the Bath and Haymarket, and at Covent Garden and Drury Lane from 1791 to 1812, functioned in administrative capacities at the Surrey, Leicester, and Olympic from 1809 to about 1814, was a lessee and manager of Drury Lane from 1819 to 1826, and a lessee of the Surrey from 1827 to 1831.

8. Underscored twice, as is the next "*H.*" The dames of Strasburg, mentioned below, to whom Lamb also refers in the first act of "Mr. H——" (*Works*, V, 185), are in Laurence Sterne's *Tristram Shandy*, Vol. IV, "Slawkenbergius's Tale."

9. Underscored twice.

10. Godwin's "Faulkener, a Tragedy in Prose," whose opening was delayed until December 16, 1807, by the vacillations of the boy actor William Henry West Betty (1791-1874), called the Young Roscius after the handsome and graceful Roman actor Quintus Roscius Gallus (ca. 126-62 B.C.). In the end Betty refused its title role. The part went to Elliston.

11. Presumably *Mrs. Leicester's School*. George Dawe, mentioned next, was at work on the biography of his godfather, the painter George Morland (1763-1804), titled *Life of George Morland, with Remarks on His Works* (1807). The cribbage players are Edward Phillips (see Letter 198, note 1) and Martin Burney.

12. More specifically, on the "Principles common to all the Fine Arts" (*Coleridge's Letters*, II, 1181). But Coleridge abandoned the notion and did not speak at the Royal Institution until 1808. See Letter 222, note 10.

13. Which Evans I cannot say. Thomas Woodruff (d. 1816), next mentioned, was appointed to the accountant general's office of the East India House in 1762, in receipt of salary from 1767, promoted to chief clerk in 1778, and retired in 1815.

209. *C. L. to William Wordsworth*

11 Dec. [1806]

Dear Wordsworth,

Mr. H.—— came out last night & failed. I had many fears; the subject was not substantial enough. John Bull must have solider fare than a *Letter*. We are pretty stout about it, have had plenty of condoling friends, but after all, **we** had rather it should have succeeded. You will see the Prologue in most of the Morning Papers. It was received with such shouts as I never witness'd to a Prologue. It was attempted to be **encored**. How hard! a thing I did merely as a task, because it was wanted——& set no great store by; & Mr. H.——! !——

The quantity of friends we had in the house my brother & I being

in Public Offices &c. was astonishing——but they yielded at length
to a few hissers— —. A hundred hisses——damn the word, I write
it like **kisses**—how different—a hundred hisses outweigh a 1000
Claps. The former come more directly from the Heart.— Well, tis
withdrawn & there is an end.[1]

Better Luck to us——

<div align="right">C L</div>

(turn over)

P. S. Pray when any of you write to the Clarksons, give our kind
Loves, & say we shall not be able to come & see them at Xmas——
as I shall have but a day or two,——& tell them we bear our mortifica-
tion pretty well——

Mary's Love to all of you——I wouldn't let her write——

MS: University of Texas Library. Pub.: Talfourd (1848), I, 155–156; Sala, I,
250–251; Purnell, I, 250–251; Fitzgerald, II, 85–86; Hazlitt, I, 382–383; Ainger
(1888), I, 239–240; Ainger (1900), II, 149–150; Macdonald, I, 290–291; Ainger
(1904), I, 290–291; Harper, III, 244–245; Lucas (1905), VI, 369–370; Lucas
(1912), V, 387; Lucas (1935), II, 31.

1. Crabb Robinson, who had accompanied the Lambs and Hazlitt to the per-
formance and wrote highly of the Prologue and its fine reception, recollected that
when "the squeamishness of the vulgar taste in the pit on the disclosure of the
name showed itself in hisses, Lamb joined and was probably the loudest hisser in
the house" (*H. C. R. on Books and Writers*, I, 9). The reviewer for *Monthly
Literary Recreations,* 1 (December 1806), 488, commented that when the secret
of the name was made public "all the interest vanished, the audience were dis-
gusted, and the farce went on to its very conclusion almost unheard, amidst the
contending clamours of Silence! Hear! hear! and off! off! off!" And Hazlitt
remembered in "On Great and Little Things" that after the damning of the play
he dreamt "every night for a month . . . that it was revived at one of the
Minor or provincial theatres with great success" (*Hazlitt's Works*, VIII, 232). Its
earliest American and English revivals, both successful, appear to have been at
the Park Theatre, New York, on March 16, 1807; and at the Theatre Royal,
Worthing, Sussex, on July 27, 1822. (See [the unsigned] "Mr. H. in America, or,
Anonymous Redivivus. By W. R. Nethery," in the *CLSB* of May 1956, p. 106; and
R. Meadows White, "1806 and 'Mr. H.,' " in the *CLSB* of November 1957, esp.
p. 179. The former of those titles is a review of one of the booklets Wallace
Nethery wrote, printed, and, with some of his other writings, formed into *Charles
Lamb in America to 1848* [Worcester, Mass.: Achille J. St. Onge, 1963]. He is also
the author of its sequel, *Eliana Americana: Charles Lamb in the United States,
1849–1866* [Los Angeles: Plantin Press, 1971].) Lamb's play was first published
as *Mr. H. Or Beware a Bad Name. A Farce in Two Acts: As Performed at the
Philadelphia Theatre* (Philadelphia: Carey, 1813).

210. *C. L. to Sarah Stoddart*

11 Dec [1806]

Dear Sarah,

Mary is a little cut at the ill success of Mr. H. which came out last night and *failed*. I know you'll be sorry, but never mind. We are determin'd not to be cast down.— I am going to leave off Tobacco, & then we must thrive. A smoking man must write smoky farces.——

Mary is pretty well, but I persuaded her to let me write. We did not apprize you of the coming out of Mr. H. for fear of ill Luck. You were much better out of the honor. If it had taken, your partaking of our good luck would have been one of our greatest joys. As it is, we shall expect you at the time you mentioned. But whenever you come, you shall be **most welcome**——

God bless you, **dear** Sarah,

Yours must truly

C L

Mary is by no means unwell, but I made her let me write——

Dont mind this being a queer letter. I am in haste, & taken up by **visitors,** condolers &c.— God bless you

MS: Montague Collection, Manuscripts & Archives Division, The New York Public Library, Astor, Lenox and Tilden Foundations. Pub.: Talfourd (1848), I, 154–155; Sala, I, 428; Purnell, I, 428; Fitzgerald, II, 261; Hazlitt, I, 382; Ainger (1888), I, 239; Ainger (1900), II, 148–149; Macdonald, I, 291; Ainger (1904), I, 290; Harper, III, 245–246; Lucas (1905), VI, 370; Lucas (1912), V, 388; Lucas (1935), II, 32.

211. *M. A. L. to Mrs. Clarkson*

Tuesday Decr 23. 1806

My dear Mrs Clarkson

You are very kind to say you are out of humour with yourself for not writing before, but I beg you will never be so again; I know so well, and often feel so sadly, how irksome writing sometimes is, that I entreat you never will write but when you feel yourself quite in-

clined———. I tried the morning after the failure of our little farce to
write a line to let you know its ill success, and how stoutly we meant
to bear it, but I found myself utterly incapable of writing one con-
nected sentence, so stout was the phylosophy I wished to boast of.

I do not love to throw the blame of the ill success of a piece upon
the actors—it is a common trick with unsuccessful dramatists. The
blame rested chiefly with Charles & yet should not be called blame
for it was mere ignorance of stage effect—. And I am mistaken if he
has not gained much useful knowledge, more than he could have
learned from a constant attendance on the representation of other
peoples pieces, by seeing his own fail, he seems perfectly aware why, &
from what cause it failed. He intends to write one more, with all his
dear bought experience in his head, and should that share the same
fate, he will then turn his mind to some other pursuit.

I am happy to hear so good an account of your health, go on im-
proving as fast as you can, that I may find you quite well. At Easter
or a few weeks after I hope to spend a delightful holliday with you
at Bury: if we come at Easter we cannot stay longer than one week;
if we defer our journey we can make a much longer visit, but at
present I know not how it will be settled for my brother sometimes
threatens to pass his hollidays in town hunting over old plays at the
Museum to extract passages for a work (a collection of poetry)[1] Mr
Wordsworth intends to publish. however I hope before that time
arrives he will be able to borrow the books of some good old collector
of those hidden treasures, and then they can be copied at home &
much of Charles labour & time saved. The Museum is only open
during his office hours.

I am much pleased with your friend Henry Robinson. He has been
truly kind & friendly about the farce. That disappointment is wearing
out of our heads very fast. My brother means to keep at home very
much this winter, and work very hard. When he is at work he is alway
happier & in better health.

I am glad Miss Smith[2] is with you, because Coleridge has told me
she is the best good girl in the world———

I am pleased to hear again the name of your old neigbour Mr
Smith. I well remember him the first season of the School for
Scandel; he was, ("I being a young thing then") a prodigious
favorite with me. I cannot for the life of me conceive of him as an

old man.— *O what Actors there were then!* but as I said before disappointed authors must not complain of actors——(You shall see the farce when I can spare time to write a copy, or can spare the only one we have) No matter for the *brains* of your good towns-people. Go amongst them as much as you can, I am sure company is a certain cure for your malady.

I am glad to hear of my friend Tom's improvement, never mind his learning that will come in due time. Indeed I have reasons for wishing him a little backward in that respect, for I have a little book I mean to send him & the printer has been so long bringing it out I began to fear Tom would attain so much knowledge as to outgrow the use there of, & Toms approbation of my first production, was one of the things I built upon.— I suppose I may send a parcel by the Bury stage? That is a foolish question to ask, for no doubt I may.

I rejoice to hear Mr Clarkson has begun his history o[f th]e Abolition—.[3] May we not expect to see him now in a few days—how I wish he would bring you too.

We are to stay at home & work and forget it is Christmas, but we sincerely wish you a *merry* happy Christmas & many many happy *healthy* new years.

Charles's kindest respects to you & Mr Clarkson & young Tom & Miss Buck; is she not at Bury.

I remain your affectionate friend.

M Lamb

No news of Coleridge lately

I shall rejoice to hear from you whenever you feel writing quite pleasant to you. (*Did you ever see such a queer scrawl as mine?*)

MS: Huntington Library. Pub.: Macdonald, I, 292–294; Harper, III, 246–249; Lucas (1935), II, 32–34. Address: Mrs Clarkson/Bury St Edmonds/Suffolk. Postmark: December 23, 1806.

1. Which became Lamb's *Specimens of English Dramatic Poets, Who Lived about the Time of Shakspeare: With Notes* (*Works*, IV, xi–xii and 1–393). It is surmised in Lucas (1935), II, 34, that Mary accidentally wrote "Wordsworth" (next) for "Longman," Wordsworth's publisher. But her use here of Wordsworth's name and especially the assurance of Lamb on October 13, 1804 (Letter 167), that he would furnish Wordsworth with "as complete a library of old Poets & Dramatists as will be prudent to buy" suggest that Wordsworth first intended to construct the work that came to be Lamb's or one similar to it. Wordsworth may have been prompted to do so as a result of Southey's proposal to Longman and Rees on January 26, 1804, to prepare and their agreement, presumably in the fall of 1804, to publish what developed into Southey's *Specimens of the Later*

English Poets, with Preliminary Notices. Southey planned it to be a sequel to George Ellis' *Specimens of the Early English Poets* (1790; republished in an expanded edition by Longman in 1803) and, together with Ellis' work, to include all the English poets except those still living and the dramatic poets. In May 1804 Southey wrote his wife that he thought it would be "the fittest thing in the world for Lamb to manage, if he like it; or, perhaps, to manage with my co-operation." (It is perhaps more than coincidental that Lamb applied for a reader's ticket at the British Museum on May 12, 1804.) On June 11, 1804, Southey wrote Coleridge that should Longman agree "to publish a collection of the scarcer and better old poets . . . my name must stand to the prospectus, and Lamb shall take the job and the emolument, for whom, in fact, I invented it, being a fit thing to be done, and he the fit man to do it." (See *Southey's Correspondence,* II, 253, 259–260, 287, 293–294, and 303.) If Southey did offer the job to Lamb, Lamb did not accept it. Lamb instead—it seems from Letter 167, possibly from Letters 191 and 192, and from this letter—started, stopped, and in fifteen to twenty-six months started again to help Wordsworth collect the material for an anthology that would include the dramatic poets. Southey and his lifelong friend Grosvenor C. Bedford (mentioned in Lamb's letter to Southey of October 20, 1814, Vol. III) proceeded with Southey's anthology, though Southey's letters to Rickman of December 18, 1804, and January 23, 1805, show that Southey called on Lamb to supply extracts at least from the poems of Charles Cotton. Southey's letters to Henry Herbert Southey of December 10, 1805, and January 11, 1806, show that Robert Southey started George Burnett on what came to be *Specimens of English Prose-writers, from the Earliest Times to the Close of the Seventeenth Century, with Sketches Biographical and Literary,* to which Lamb may have also contributed. (See *New Southey Letters,* I, 372, 375–376, 410–411, and 416; see also I, 363, note 4.) Longman's firm published Southey's *Specimens* and Burnett's *Specimens* in 1807. In 1808 Longman's firm published Lamb's *Specimens,* whose preparation Lamb may have assumed from Wordsworth by June 1807. (See Letters 213 and 214; see also Letter 222 and *Coleridge's Letters,* III, 59.) The firm's ledgers indicate that the month of its publication was September, for it is recorded that on September 7 twelve of the one thousand copies originally printed were sent to Lamb. A notice in the *Monthly Literary Advertiser* for July 1808, p. 50, indicates that the book was published in the week ending July 9. But that notice, especially in light of Lamb's remarks in Letter 227, seems to have been a premature one. For additional information see *Works,* IV 597–603. Information about two reviews of the work is given in Vol. III, Letter 236 and its notes. Vera Watson assisted considerably with the preparation of this note.

2. A daughter, probably Patty, of the William Smiths of Parndon. Patty is mentioned in Dorothy Wordsworth's letter to Catherine Clarkson of November 6, 1806, and as staying with Mrs. Clarkson in Miss Wordsworth's letter to her of May 12, 1811. (See *Wordsworths' Letters,* II, 87 and 485.) William, "Gentleman," Smith (1730?–1819), referred to below, who had retired to Bury St. Edmunds after a career at Covent Garden from 1753 to 1774 and at Drury Lane from 1774 to 1788, first took the part of Charles Surface in Sheridan's *School for Scandal* on May 8, 1777, when Mary was twelve. It was a remarkable performance. He repeated it in his last professional appearance, on June 9, 1788, and a final time, on May 18, 1798, when he returned to Drury Lane to play before the king. The quotation in parentheses has not been identified.

3. *The History of the Rise, Progress, and Accomplishment of the Abolition of the African Slave-trade by the British Parliament* (2 vols.; 1808).

212. *C. L. to William Wordsworth*

<div align="right">Thursday 29 Jan. 1807</div>

Dear Wordsworth—

We have book'd off from Swan & Two Necks Lad Lane this day (per Coach) the Tales from Shakespear.— You will forgive the plates,[1] when I tell you that they were left to the direction of Godwin, who left the choice of subjects to the **bad baby,** who from mischief— (I suppose) has chosen one from damn'd beastly vulgarity (vide Merch. Venice) where no atom of authority was in the tale to justify it—to another has given a name which exists not in the tale, **Nic. Bottom,** & which she thought would be funny, though in this I suspect *his* hand, for I guess her reading does not reach far enough to know Bottom's Xtian name—— ——& one of Hamlet, & Grave diggg., a scene which is not hinted at in the story, & you might as well have put King Canute the Great[2] reproving his courtiers—the rest are Giants & Giantesses——. suffice it, to save our taste & damn our folly, that we left it all to a friend W. G.—who in the first place cheated me into putting a name to them, which I did not mean, but do not repent, & then wrote a **puff** about their *simplicity* &c. to go with the advertisemt. as in my name!— Enough of this egregious **dupery.**— I will try to abstract the load of teazing circumstances from the **Stories & tell you** that I am answerable for Lear, Macbeth, Timon, Romeo, Hamlet, Othello, for occasionaly a tail piece or correction of grammar, for **none** of the cuts and **all** of the spelling. The rest is my Sister's——. We think Pericles of hers the best, & Othello of mine—but I hope all have some good. As You Like It we like least—

So much, only begging you to tear out the cuts & give them to Johnny, as "Mrs Godwin's fancy."—

<div align="right">C L</div>

Our Love *to all*

⟨God bless me⟩, I had almost forgot, My part of the Preface begins in the middle of a sentence, in last but one page after a colon thus

<div align="center">:—*which if they be happily*[3] *so done &c.*</div>

the former part hath a more **feminine** turn and does hold me up

something as an instructor to young Ladies: but upon my modesty's honour I wrote it not—

Godwin told My Sister that the Baby chose the subjects. A fact in Taste.—

MS: Dr. Williams's Library, London. Pub.: Sala, I, 251–252; Purnell, I, 251–252; Fitzgerald, II, 86–87; Hazlitt, I, 384–386; Ainger (1888), I, 241–242; Ainger (1900), II, 151–153; Macdonald, I, 294–295; Ainger (1904), I, 292–293; Harper, III, 250–252; Lucas (1905), VI, 372–373; Lucas (1912), V, 389–390; Lucas (1935), II, 35–36.

1. Whose designs have been attributed to the genre painter William Mulready (1786–1863) and engravings to William Blake. All are reproduced in *Works*, III, facing pp. 2–194, *passim*. Lamb refers below to those facing pp. 60, 10 (where Nick Bottom, of *A Midsummer Night's Dream*, is named Nic), and 172.

2. Canute, or Cnut (994?–1035), called the Great, king of the English, Danes, and Norwegians.

3. Which Lamb changed to "fortunately" (*Works*, III, 2) in the second (1809) edition.

213. *C. L. to Mr. and Mrs. Thomas Clarkson*

[June 1807]

Dear Mr. and Mrs. Clarkson,

you will wish to know how we performed our journey.— My sister was tolerably quiet until we got to Chelmsford, where she began to be very bad indeed, as your friends William Knight[1] and his family can tell you when you see them. What I should have done without their kindness I do'nt know, but among other acts of great attention, they provided me with a waistcoat to confine her arms, by the help of which we went through the rest of our journey. But sadly tired and miserably depressed she was before we arrived at Hoxton. We got there about half past eight; and now 'tis all over, I have great satisfaction that she is among people who have been used to her. In all probability a few months or even weeks will restore her (her last illness confined her ten weeks) but if she does recover I shall be very careful how I take her so far from home again.[2] I am so fatigued, for she talked in the most wretched desponding way conceivable, particularly the last three stages, she talked all the way,—so that you wont expect me to say much, or even to express myself as I should do in thanks for your kindnesses. My sister will acknowledge them when she can.—

I shall not have heard how she is to day until too late for the Post,

but if any great change takes place for better or worse, I shall certainly let you know.

She tells me something about having given away one of my coats to your servant. It is a new one, and perhaps may be of small use to him. If you can get it me again, I shall very willingly give him a compensation. I shall also be much obliged by your sending in a parcel all the manuscripts books &c. she left behind. I want in particular the Dramatic Extracts, as my purpose is to make use of the remainder of my holydays in completing them at the British Museum, which will be employment & money in the end.

I am exceedingly harrassed with the journey, but that will go off in a day or two, and I will set to work. I know you will grieve for us, but I hope my sister's illness is not worse than many she has got through before. Only I am afraid the fatigue of the journey may affect her general health. You shall have notice how she goes on. In the meantime, accept our kindest thanks—[3]

MS: Huntington Library. Pub.: Macdonald, I, 326–327; Harper, III, 252–254; Lucas (1905), VI, 373–374; Lucas (1912), V, 391–392; Lucas (1935), II, 36–37. Address: T. Clarkson Esq./Bury/Suffolk. Postmark: June [1807]. The next letter and the third paragraph in this one establish its date.

1. William Knight (1757?–1814) was a grocer of Chelmsford, Essex. His wife, Priscilla (1754?–1829), who participated with him in various charities, resided after his death in Springfield, Essex. Their eldest son, William (1785–1838), became a grocer in High Street, Chelmsford, had scientific and philanthropic interests, and with his father was a subscriber of *The Friend*. He moved in 1836 for medical attention to Stoke Newington, London. A daughter became the wife of one John Chandler. Mr. K. C. Newton, County Archivist of Chelmsford, supplied most of the information in this note from his copy of the pamphlet *A Brief Memorial of William Knight of Chelmsford* (2d ed. [1840]) and from the records of the Witham Monthly Meeting of the Society of Friends, the *Universal British Directory* for 1793, and Pigot's directories for 1823–1824 and 1826–1827. See *The Friend*, ed. Barbara Rooke, II, 439–440.

2. The experience left Mary with the same concern. For Dorothy Wordsworth wrote Catherine Clarkson on December 28 (*Wordsworths' Letters*, II, 185) that she had received a letter (unrecovered) from Mary "about a month ago, in which she spoke feelingly of the distress she had given you, and the damping of her own hopes of going from home again to any Friends house, or coming to see us."

3. The signature has not been cut off, as is stated in Lucas (1935), II, 37, and the other editions. Lamb simply neglected to provide one.

214. *C. L. to Mrs. Clarkson*

Monday [July ?20, 1807]

Dear Mrs. Clarkson,

I ought to have written to you before, but I expected to see Mr. Clarkson. By your letter, I must suppose that he has been in town; but I have been so much out, since I have been alone, that I am afraid he may have call'd & not found me.—

Mary still keeps very bad. I have not seen her, **Nor** do they let me see her till she is getting pretty well. She was a little mending when I enquired last, on Saturday.— You shall have the earliest intelligence of her restoration.—

Thank you for wishing me at Bury. But I have made good use of my holydays in town. I still go to the Museum, and shall to the end of this week, which closes my vacation. Sometimes I can hardly think I have been at Bury, it passed away so like a dream. But I have some recollections of a great deal of kindness & hospitality, abruptly terminating.

I have not heard of Coleridge or the Wordsworths.——— I hope H. Robinson will get safe back.[1]

Believe me ever

Yours affectionately
C Lamb

I got the Parcels safe. Thank you.—— By looking to the date of yours, I see I should have received it on Saturday. But not being at office, it was only brought to day. I am answering it the minute I received it.—

I can give no guess when my sister will be well. She has been confined 5. 6. 7. & even 10 weeks at a time. If she goes on mending, & has no relapse, a few weeks may bring her about.—

God bless you—

MS: Wordsworth Collection, Cornell University Library, Ithaca, N.Y. Pub.: Basil Willey and Paul Zall, "Another Unpublished Letter of Charles Lamb," *CLSB* of March 1954. Address: Mrs. Clarkson/Bury/Suffolk. Postmark: July [20?], 1807.
1. In January 1807 Robinson had left England for Altoona, Germany, as a

foreign correspondent for the *Times*. On June 16, two days before the British bombardment of Copenhagen, he had been forced to flee, first to Hamburg and then to Mecklenburg. On September 8 he obtained passage to Stockholm and on September 30 left Gothenburg for Harwich, Essex, where he landed on October 7.

215. *C. L. to Rickman*

Monday [late summer 1807?]

Dear Rickman,

I send you some papers[1] about a Salt water soap for which the Inventor is desirous of getting a parliamentary reward, like Dr. Jenner. Whether such a prospect be feasable I mainly doubt, taking for granted the equal utility. I should suppose the usual way of paying such projectors is by patent & contracts. The patent you see, he has got. A contract he is about with the Navy board. Meantime the Projector is hungry.— Will you answer me two questions, & return them with the papers as soon as you can? Imprimis, is there any chance of success in application to parliament for a reward? did you ever hear of the invention? you see its benefits & saving to the nation (always the first motive with a true projector) are feelingly set forth: the last paragraph but one of the Estimate, in enumerating the shifts poor seamen are put to, even approaches to the pathetic. But agreeing to all he says, is there the remotest chance of parliament giving the projector any thing; & *when* should application be made, **now** or after a report (if he can get it) from the Navy board? Secondly, let the infeasability be as great as you will, you will oblige me by telling me the **way of introducing** such an application in parliament—without buying over a majority of members, which is totally out of projector's power. I vouch nothing for the soap myself; for I always was[h (?)] in *fresh water* & find it answer tolerably well for all purposes of cleanliness; nor do I know the projector; but a relation of mine[2] has put me on writing to you, for whose parliamentary knowledge he has great veneration—

P. S. The Capt. & Mrs. Burney &, Phillips take their chance at cribbage here on Wednesday. Will you and Mrs. R. join the party? Mary desires her compliments to Mrs. R. & joins in the invitation

yours truly

C L

MS: Huntington Library. Pub.: Talfourd (1837), I, 283–285; Purnell, II, 89–91; Fitzgerald, III, 10–12; Hazlitt, I, 366–367; Ainger (1888), I, 226; Ainger (1900), II, 128–129; Macdonald, I, 276–277; Ainger (1904), I, 276; Harper, III, 214–215; Lucas (1905), VI, 345–346; Lucas (1912), V, 360–361; Lucas (1935), I, 429–430. Address: Jno. Rickman Esqr/New Palace Yard/Westminster. Watermark: 1804. Other editors erroneously show the letter to bear the date of March 1806. The date now assigned is conjectured from Lamb's comment on the rewards by Parliament to Edward Jenner (1749–1823) for his discovery and further investigations of vaccination. The first, for £10,000, was voted in 1802. The second, for £20,000, was, according to John Baron's *The Life of Edward Jenner* (London: Colburn, 1838), II, 66–70, voted on or shortly after July 29, 1807.

1. Unrecovered. The "Inventor" of whom Lamb writes has not been identified.

2. Possibly Charles Lovekin (1780?–1827), a cousin of the Lambs mentioned, presumably with his wife, in later letters. He was a descendant of the Fields of Hertfordshire and one of four sons born to Joseph Lovekin, a bridle cutter of Baldwin's Gardens, Leather Lane, and the former Sarah Ann Dappee. In 1808 he acquired the business of a bookbinder who had committed suicide. In 1821 he was operating at 10 Pemberton Row, Gough Square, Fleet Street. He died at Windsor Place, Islington. See Major S. Butterworth's "Charles Lamb: Some New Biographical and Other Details," *The Bookman,* 60 (July 1921), 167, and Phyllis G. Mann's "Notes by the Way" and "Adventures in Research," in the *CLSB* of January 1959 and April 1968.

216. *M. A. L. to Sarah Stoddart*

Saturday morning [November 28, 1807]

My dear Sarah

I am two letters in your debt, but it is has not been so much from idleness, as a wish first to see how your comical love affair would turn out. You know I make a pretence not to interfere, but like all old maids I feel a mighty solicitude about the event of love stories. I learn from The Lover[1] that he has not been so remiss in his duty as you supposed. His Effusion, and your Complaints of his Inconstancy crossed each other on the road. He tells me his was a very strange letter and that probably it has affronted you.— That it was a strange letter I can readily believe, but that you were affronted by a strange letter is not so easy for me to conceive, that not being your way of taking things. But however it be, let some answer come, either to him, or else to me, shewing cause why you do not answer him—. And pray, by all means, preserve the said letter, that I may one day have the pleasure of seeing how Mr Hazlitt treats of love

I was at your brother's on thursday.[2] Mrs S. tells me she has not

written because she does not like to put you to the expense of postage. They are very well, little Missy thrives amazingly. Mrs Stoddart conjectures she is in the family way again, and those kind of conjectures generally prove too true. Your other sister-in-law, Mrs Hazlitt, was brought to bed last week of a boy. you are likely to have plenty of Nephews and neices.— Yesterday evening we were at Rickmans and who should we find there but Hazlitt; though if you do not know it[3] was his first invitation there it will not surprize you so much as it did us. We were very much pleased because we dearly love our friends to be respected by our friends.— The most remarkable events of the evening were that we had a very fine pine-apple—that Mr Phillips, Mr Lamb, and Mr Hazlitt played at Cribbage in the most polite and gentlemanly manner possible—and that I won two rubbers of whist.

I am glad Aunty left you some business to do. Our compliments to her and your Mother. Is it as cold at Winterslow as it is here? How do the **Lions** go on?[4] I am better and Charles is tolerably well. Godwin's new Tragedy will probably be damned the latter end of next week. Charles has written the Prologue. Prologues and Epilogues will be his death. If you know the extent of Mrs Reynolds's poverty, you will be glad to hear that Mr Norris has got ten pounds a year for her from the Temple Society. She will be able to make out pretty well now.

Farewell—. Determine as wisely as you can in regard to Hazlitt, and if your determ[in]ation be to have him, Heaven send you ma[ny] happy years together. If I am not mis[tak]en I have concluded letters on the Corydon Cour[t]ship with this same wish, I hope it is not ominous of change, for if I were sure you would not be quite starved to death, nor beaten to a mummy I confess I should like to see Hazlitt and you come together if (as Charles observes) it were only for the joke sake.

Write instantly to me.

<div align="right">yours most affectionately
M Lamb</div>

MS: Lockwood Library, State University of New York at Buffalo. Pub.: Harper, III, 254–256; Lucas (1905), VI, 374–375; Lucas (1912), V, 392–393; Lucas (1935), II, 37–39. Address: Miss Stoddart/Winterslow/near Salisbury. Postmark: November 28, 1807.
1. Now William Hazlitt. One of his love letters to Miss Stoddart is in W. C.

Hazlitt's *Memoirs of William Hazlitt. With Portions of His Correspondence* (2 vols.; London: Bentley, 1867), I, 153–155.

2. Stoddart had brought his family back to London this year and was practicing law at Doctors' Commons. Neither the formal name of the Stoddarts' daughter, called "little Missy" below, nor the given name of the John Hazlitts' new son has been determined.

3. A canceled line follows.

4. I cannot explain this. "Faulkener, a Tragedy in Prose," referred to below, ran only for five nights beyond its December 16 opening at Drury Lane. Godwin blamed its poor showing on Holcroft, to whom Godwin had sent the play for perfecting before its opening and who, probably through some misunderstanding, greatly revised it. The two men became estranged because of it and were not reconciled until Holcroft lay dying in March 1809. See Vol. I, Letter 96, note 2. See also Letter 110, note 1, and Letter 208, note 10.

217. *M. A. L. to Sarah Stoddart*

Monday morning [December ?21, 1807]

My dear Sarah

I have deferred answering your last letter in hopes of being able to give you some intelligence that might be useful to you, for I every day expected that Hazlitt, or you, would communicate the affair[1] to your brother, but as the Doctor is silent on the subject I conclude he yet knows nothing of the matter. You desire my advice and therefore I tell you I think you ought to tell your brother as soon as possible, for at present he is on very friendly visiting terms with Hazlitt, and if he is not offended by a too long concealment will do everything in his power to serve you. If you chuse that I should tell him I will but I think it would come better from you——if you can persuade Hazlitt to mention it that would be still better, for I know your brother would be unwilling to give credit to you because you deceived yourself in regard to Corydon. Hazlitt I know is shy of speaking first but I think it of such great importance to you to have your brother friendly in the business that if you can overcome his reluctance it would be a great point gained: for you must begin the world with ready money —at least an hundred pound; for if you once go into furnished lodgings you will never be able to lay by money to buy furniture.

If you obtain your brothers approbation he might assist you, either by lending or otherwise—I have a great opinion of his generosity, where he thinks it will be useful.

Hazlitts brother is mightily pleased with the match but he says

that you must have furniture & be clear in the world at first setting out, or you will be always behindhand——he also said he would give you what furniture he could spare. I am afraid you can bring but few things away from your own house——. What a pity that you have laid out so much money on your cottage; that money would have just done.— I most heartily congratulate you on having so well got over your first difficulties, and now that it is quite settled, let us have no more fears. I now mean not only to hope, & wish, but to persuade myself that you will be very happy together. Endeavour to keep your mind as easy as you can. You ought to begin the world with a good stock of health & spirits; it is quite as necessary as ready money at first setting out. Do not teize yourself about coming to town——. When your brother learns how things are going we will consult him about meetings & so forth but at present any hasty step of that kind would not answer I know. If Hazlitt were to go down to Salisbury ⟨without your brothers knowledge⟩, or you were to come up here without consulting your brother you know it would never do—

Charles is just come in to dinner, he desires his love & best wishes.

<div align="right">Yours affectionately
M Lamb</div>

MS: Mrs. Donald F. Hyde, Somerville, N.J. Pub.: Lucas (1905), VI, 376–377; Lucas (1912), V, 394–395; Lucas (1935), II, 39–40. Address: Miss Stoddart/Winterslow/near Salisbury/Wilts. Postmark: 1807. This letter was certainly written after the preceding one, and from what remains of the postmark must have been written in December. Lucas presented it improperly as carrying the date of December 21, 1807, which, however, did fall on a Monday. Perhaps in Lucas' time the postmark showed that date.

1. Of Sarah Stoddart's engagement to William Hazlitt.

218. *C. L. to Joseph Hume*

<div align="right">29 Dec 1807</div>

Alas! Sir,

I cannot be among you—my fate is still not to know on which side my bread is butter'd—. I hang between two Engagements perpetually, and the worst always comes first—the Devil always takes care to clap in with a retainer where he sees God about to offer a fee—cold bones of mutton and leather-roasted potatoes at Pimlico at ten

must carry it away from a certain Turkey and a contingent **plumb-pudding** at Montpelier[1] at four—(I always spell plumb-pudding with a *b* p-l-u-m-*b*—I think it reads fatter and more suetty)

I suppose you know what has happen'd to our poor friend Hazlitt. If not, take it as I read it in the Morning Post or Fashionable World of this morning—"Last night Mr. H. a portrait painter in Southampton Buildings Holborn put an end to his existence by cutting his throat in a shocking manner. It is supposed that he must have accomplished his purpose with a pallet-knife as the edges of the cicatrice or wound were found besmeared with a yellow consistence, but the knife could not be found. The reasons of this rash act are not assigned, an unfortunate passion has been mentioned, but nothing certain is known. The deceased was subject to hypochondria, low spirits, but he had lately seemed better, having paid more than usual attention to his dress and person. Besides being a painter, he had written some pretty things in prose & verse——"

God bless me, **ten oClock**—I have cut out the paragraph, and will shew it you entire, I have not time to transcribe more

<div style="text-align:right">

Yours &

C Lamb

</div>

MS: Lockwood Library, State University of New York at Buffalo. Pub.: Macdonald, I, 296; Harper, III, 257–258; Lucas (1935), II, 41.

1. The Humes's residence, Montpelier House, Notting Hill, Kensington. The concluding two *b*'s within the parentheses are underscored twice. The next paragraph, with its fiction of a report in the *Morning Post* of William Hazlitt's suicide, is the start of an elaborate joke conducted by Lamb, Hazlitt, and Hume, in documents that may be read in *Lamb and Hazlitt*, pp. 66–102. Hume responds on January 11, 1808, by apprising Lamb of an eight-page petition signed "W. Hazlitt" and written in his manner that "ridiculously assumes him to be alive" (p. 67) and cautioning Lamb, because of its "whacking sentences" against him, not to approach Hazlitt's lodgings for fear of attack by the impostor. Then comes the "humble petition & remonstrance of William Hazlitt, ———— [the blank is left for the reader to fill, with 'the class of *non-descripts*,' 'gentleman,' 'low fellow,' 'author,' or 'pourtrait-painter'] now residing at No. 34, Southhampton Buildings, in the parish of St. Ann's, Holborn" (p. 69). The petition (its original is in the Lockwood Library) is dated January 10, postmarked January 11, addressed to Hume, and seeks to convince that its author is not dead by itemizing his ways of living while also itemizing his effects and valuables in the event that the petition is unconvincing and its author is buried against his will. Following it are Lamb's letter to Hume of January 12 (pp. 83–87: Letter 219 of the present edition); Hume's to Lamb of January 12–13 (pp. 88–101), in which Hume remarks on several points in the petition that call its authorship into question and proposes a scheme to uncover the forger; and Hume's undated note to Hazlitt (pp. 101–102). That note ends the joke:

Dear Sir,—I don't know what a parcel of your Friends, or rather foes, are about, but I the other day received in the form of a Petition some stuff and farrago about your death: and I have had sent me this morning by a very mysterious conveyance a Letter not signed (I enclose it), but which I would swear is Mr. Lamb's writing. I don't like that Lamb; Look to him; I hate snakes in the grass. I say let a man, if he has a grudge against a friend, out with it; and not be scribbling and scrawling backwards & forwards every day or two, and secretly abusing one. For God's sake come down here, and convince those silly fellows, to say the least of it, that talk about your death, that you are alive.

<div align="right">

Yours until death,
Joseph Hume

</div>

P.S.—"A living dog is better than a dead Lion."—*Solomon.* [The saying is in Ecclesiastes 9:4.—Ed.]

219. *C. L. to Hume*

<div align="right">

12 January 1808

</div>

Dear Sir,

The strange rumours which have been spread about since the death of our respected friend, as well as some things which have come under my own observation, which I do not care to trust to the ordinary communication of a Post, but reserve them for the especial confidence of your most valued ear in private,—these things, without much help from a rainy day or a time of year which usually disposes men to sadness, have contributed to make me not a little serious and thoughtful of late. I have run over in my mind the various treatises which I have perused in the course of a studious, and, I hope, innocently employed life, on the nature of disembodied Spirits & the causes of their revisiting the earth. The fact I will take for granted; presuming that I am not addressing an Atheist. I find the most commonly assigned reason to be, *for the revealing of hidden Treasures which the Deceased had hoarded up in his or her Lifetime.* Now though I cannot sufficiently admire the providence of God who by this means has ofttimes restored great heaps of Gold & Silver to the circulation of the Living, thereby sparing the iterately plowed and now almost effoete wombs of Peru & Mexico, which would need another Sarah's miracle[1] to replenish, yet in the particular case of the Defunct I cannot but suspect some other cause, and not this, to have called him from his six foot bed of earth. For it is highly improbable that He should have accumulated any such vast treasures, for the revealing

of which a miracle was needed, without some suspicion of the fact among his friends during his Life time. I for my part always looked upon our dear friend as a man rich rather in the gifts of his mind than in earthly treasures. He had few rents or comings in, that I was ever aware of, small (if any) landed property, and by all that I could witness he subsisted more upon the well timed contributions of a few chosen friends who knew his worth, than upon any Estate which could properly be called his own. I myself have contributed my part. God knows, I speak not this in reproach. I have never taken, nor indeed did the Deceased offer, any *written acknowledgments* of the various sums which he has had of me, by which I could make the fact manifest to the legal eye of an Executor or Administrator. He was not a Man to affect these niceties in his transactions with his friends. He would often say, Money was nothing between intimate acquaintances, that Golden Streams had no Ebb, that a Purse mouth never regorged, that God loved a chearful giver but the Devil hated a free taker, that a paid Loan makes angels groan, with many such like sayings: he had always free and generous notions about money. His nearest friends know this best. Induced by these considerations I give up that commonly received notion of Revealable Treasures in our friend's case. Neither am I too forward to adopt that vulgar superstition of some hidden **Murder** to be brought to light; which yet I do not universally reject: for when I revolve, that the Defunct was naturally of a discoursible and communicative temper, (though of a gloomy and close aspect, as born under Saturn) a great repeater of conversations which he generally carried away verbatim & would repeat with syllabic exactness in the next company where he was received, (by which means I that have staid at home have often reaped the profit of his travels without stirring from my elbow chair) I cannot think that if He had been present at so remarkable circumstance as a murder he would so soon have forgotten it as to make no mention of it at the next place where he dined or supt, or that he could have restrained himself from giving the particulars of a matter of fact like that in his life time. I am sure I have often heard him dilate upon occurrences of a much less interesting sort than that in question. I am most inclined to support that opinion which favors the Establishing of some Speculative Point in Religion: a frequent cause, says **Wierus**,[2] for Spirits returning to the Earth, to confute **Atheists &c.**—

When I consider the Education which our friend received from a
venerable Parent, his religious destination, his nurture at a Seminary
appropriated to young Ministers: but whatever the cause of this re-
appearance may prove to be, we may now with truth assert that our
deceased friend has attained to one object of his pursuits, **one** hours
separate existence gives a dead man clearer notions of metaphysics
than all the treatises which in this state of carnal entanglement the
least-immersed Spirit can out-spin. It is good to leave such subjects to
that period when we shall have no Heads to ache, no brains to distort,
no faces to lengthen, no clothes to neglect. Had our dear friend
attended to this, he might have shewn his airy form in courts & all
rooms, whispered the fair, ogled, sung, danced, and known just as
much of those subjects as it is probable he ever knew previous to his
death: for I always take it, that a disposition to such sort of enquiries
* * * * * * * * * * * * * * * * * * * and ends in Lunacy and dirty linen.
You have *my* opinions.[3]

MS: Lockwood Library, State University of New York at Buffalo. Pub.: Mac-
donald, I, 297–299; Harper, III, 258–261; Lucas (1935), II, 42–44. Address: J.
Hume Esqr/Victualling Office/Somerset House. Postmark: January 12, 1808.

1. Told in Genesis 17:15–19 and 21:1–3, of the divine promise and miraculous
birth of a son, Isaac, to the ancients Abraham and Sarah, his wife.

2. Johann Weier, or Wier (1516–1588), a Belgian physician, one of the early
opponents of witchcraft, and the author among other works of *De præstigiis
dæmonum* (1563) and *Pseudomonarchiâ dæmonis* (1577). The seminary men-
tioned below was the Unitarian New College at Hackney, closed in 1796, which
Hazlitt had attended from 1793 to 1795 or 1796.

3. The paragraph subjoined in Lucas (1935), II, 44, concludes not this letter
but Hume's to Lamb of January 12–13, in *Lamb and Hazlitt*, p. 101.

220. *M. A. L. to Sarah Stoddart*

[Friday, February 12, 1808]

My Dear Sarah,

I have sent your letter and drawing off to Wem, Hazlitt's father's in
Shropshire, where I conjecture Hazlitt is.[1] He left town on Saturday
afternoon, without telling us where he was going. He seemed very im-
patient at not hearing from you. He was very ill and I suppose is gone
home to his father's to be nursed.

I find Hazlitt has mentioned to you an intention which we had of

asking you up to town, which we were bent on doing, but having named it since to your brother, the Doctor expressed a strong desire that you should not come to town to be at any other house than his own, for he said that it would have a very strange appearance. His wife's father[2] is coming to be with them till near the end of April, after which time he shall have full room for you. And if you are to be married, he wishes that you should be married with all the proper decorums, *from his house.* Now though we should be willing to run any hazards of disobliging him, if there were no other means of your and Hazlitt's meeting, yet as he seems so friendly to the match, it would not be worth while to alienate him from you and ourselves too, for the slight accommodation which the difference of a few weeks would make, provided always, and be it understood, that if you and H. made up your minds to be married before the time in which you can be at your brother's, our house stands open and most ready at a moment's notice to receive you. Only we would not quarrel unnecessarily with your brother. Let there be a clear necessity shewn, and we will quarrel with any body's brother. Now though I have written to the above effect, I hope you will not conceive, but that both my brother & I had looked forward to your coming with unmixed pleasure, and we are really disappointed at your brother's declaration, for next to the pleasure of being married, is the pleasure of making, or helping marriages forward.

We wish to hear from you, that you do not take the *seeming change* of purpose in ill part; for it is but *seeming* on our part; for it was my brother's suggestion, by him first mentioned to Hazlitt, and cordially approved by me; but your brother has set his face against it, and it is better to take him along with us, in our plans, if he will good-naturedly go along with us, than not.

The reason I have not written lately has been that I thought it better to leave you all to the workings of your own minds in this momentous affair, in which the inclinations of a bye-stander have a right to form a wish, but not to give a vote.

Being, with the help of wide lines, at the end of my last page, I conclude with our kind wishes, and prayers for the best.

<div align="right">Yours affectionately,
M. Lamb</div>

H.'s direction is (if he is there) at Wem in Shropshire. I suppose as letters must come to London first, you had better inclose them, while he is there, for my brother in London.

MS: unrecovered. Text: Lucas (1935), II, 44–46. Also pub.: Lucas (1905), VI, 379–380; Lucas (1912), V, 396–398. Address, from *Mary and Charles Lamb,* p. 71: Miss Stoddart/Winterslow/near Salisbury/Wilts. Postmark, from Lucas: February 12, 1808.

1. The drawing, or cartoon, in pencil by Hazlitt was of Middleton, or Midleton, Cottage, Winterslow (see *The Hazlitts,* p. xiii), a property that belonged to Miss Stoddart. Hazlitt had gone there, as the next letter tells.

2. See Vol. I, Letter 3, note 28.

221. *C. L. to the Reverend Mr. William Hazlitt*

Temple
18 febr. 1808

Sir,

I am truly concerned that any mistake of mine should have caused you uneasiness, but I hope we have got a clue to William's absence, which may clear up all apprehensions. The people where he lodges in town have received direction from him to forward one or two of his shirts to a place called Winterslow in the County of Hants (not far from Salisbury) where the Lady lives whose Cottage pictured upon a card, if you opened my letter, you have doubtless seen; and though we have had no explanation of the mystery since, we shrewdly suspect that at the time of writing that Letter which has given you all this trouble, a certain son of yours (who is both Painter & Author) was at her elbow, and did assist in framing that very Cartoon which was sent to amuse and mislead us in town as to the real place of his destination. And some words at the back of the said Cartoon, which we had not marked so narrowly before, by the similarity of the hand writing to William's, do very much confirm the suspicion. If our theory be right, they have had the pleasure of their jest, and I am afraid you have paid for it in anxiety.[1] But I hope your uneasiness will now be removed, and you will pardon a suspense occasioned by *Love,* who does so many worse mischiefs every day.—

The Letter to the people where William lodges says moreover, that he shall be in town in a fortnight.———

My Sister joins in respect to you and Mrs. Hazlitt, and in our kindest remembrances & wishes for the restoration of Peggy's health.[2]

I am, Sir, your humble Servt.

Ch Lamb

MS: Lockwood Library, State University of New York at Buffalo. Pub.: Talfourd (1848), I, 157–158; Sala, I, 429–430; Purnell, I, 429–430; Fitzgerald, II, 262–263; Hazlitt, I, 386–387; Ainger (1888), I, 242–243; Ainger (1900), II, 153–154; Macdonald, I, 299–300; Ainger (1904), I, 293–294; Harper, III, 262–263; Lucas (1905), VI, 380–381; Lucas (1912), V, 398; Lucas (1935), II, 46–47. Address: Revd. W. Hazlitt/Wem/Shropshire. Postmark: February 18, 1808.
1. A canceled line follows. *"Love,"* in the next sentence, is underscored twice.
2. That of the senior William Hazlitts' surviving daughter, Margaret Hazlitt. See Letter 167, note 8.

222. *C. L. to Manning*

26 febr. 1808

Dear Missionary,

Your letters[1] from the farthest ends of the world have arrived safe. Mary is very thankful for your remembrance of her; and with the less suspicion of mercenariness, as the silk, the symbolum materiale of your friendship, has not yet appeared. I think Horace says somewhere *Knox Longa.* I would not impute negligence or unhandsome delays to a person whom you have honour'd with your confidence. But I have not heard of the Silk or of Mr. Knox save by your letter. May be he expects the first advances! or it may be that he has not succeeded in getting the Article on shore, for [it] is among the **Res Prohibitæ** et non nisi smuggle-ationis viâ fruendæ.[2] But so it is, in the friendships between *wicked men,* the very expressions of their good will cannot but be sinful. Splendida vitia at best.— Stay, while I remember it— Mrs. Holcroft was safely delivered of a girl some day in last week. Mother and child doing well. Mr. Holcroft has been attack'd with a severe rheumatism. They have moved to Clipstone Street. I suppose you know my farce was damn'd. The noise still rings in my ears. Was you ever in the pillory? ? *being damn'd* is something like that. Godwin keeps a shop in Skinner Street Snow Hill, he is turned children's bookseller and sells penny, two penny, threepenny, and fourpenny books. Sometimes he gets an order for the dearer sort of Books. (**Mind,** all

that I tell you in this letter is **true**.) A treaty of marriage is on foot
between William Hazlitt and Miss Stoddart. Something about settle-
ments only retards it. She has somewhere about £80 a year, to be
£120 when her mother dies: he has no settlement, except what he
can claim from the parish. Pauper est Cinna, sed amat.³ The thing is
therefore in abeyance. But there is love a-both sides. Little Fenwick
(you do'nt see the connexion of ideas here. How the devil should
you?) is in the rules of the Fleet. Cruel Creditors! operation of iniqui-
tous laws! is Magna Charta then a mockery?— Why, in general (here
I suppose you to ask a question) my spirits are pretty good, but I have
my depressions, black as a Smith's beard, vulcanic, stygian. At such
times I have recourse to a pipe. Which is like not being at home to a
Dun. He comes again with tenfold bitterness the next day. (Mind, I
am not in debt. I only borrow a similitude from others. It shews
imagination.) I have done two books since the failure of my farce,
they will both be out this summer. The one is a Juvenile Book, The
Adventures of Ulysses, intended to be an introduction to the Reading
of Telemachus!⁴—it is done out of the Odyssey, not from the Greek—
I would not mislead you—nor yet from Pope's Odyssey, but from an
older translation of one Chapman. The Shakspeare Tales suggested
the doing it. Godwin is in both those cases my bookseller. The other is
done for Longman, and is Specimens of English Dramatic Poets con-
temporary with Shakspeare. Specimens are becoming fashionable. We
have Specimens of Ancient English Poets. Specimens of Modern
English Poets. Specimens of Ancient English Prose Writers, without
end. They used to be called Beauties. You have seen Beauties of
Shakspeare?—so have many people, that never saw any Beauties in
Shakspeare.— Longman is to print it & be at all the expence and risk,
& I am to share the profits after all deductions **i.e.** a year or two hence
I must pocket what they please to tell me is due to me. But the Book
is such as I am glad there should be. It is done out of old plays at the
Museum & out of Dodsley's collection &c. It is to have Notes. So I go
creeping on since I was lamed with that cursed fall from off the top of
Drury Lane Theatre into the Pit something more than a year ago.
However I have been free of the House ever since, and the House was
pretty free with me upon that occasion—. Damn 'em how they hiss'd!⁵
it was not a hiss neither but a sort of a frantic yell like a congregation
of mad geese, with roaring sometimes like bears, mows & mops like

ap[e]s, sometimes snakes that hiss'd me into madness. Twas like St. Anthony's temptations. Mercy on us that God should give his favorite children **men,** mouths to speak with, to discourse rationally, to promise smoothly, to flatter agreeably, to encourage warmly, to counsel wisely, to sing with, to drink with, and to kiss with, and that they should turn them into mouths of adders, bears, wolves, hyenas, and whistle like tempests and emit breath thro' them like distillations of aspic poison, to asperse and vilify the innocent labours of their fellow creatures who are desirous to please them! God be pleased to make the breaths stink and the teeth rot out of them all therefore. Make them a reproach and all that pass by them to loll out their tongue at them.— **Blind mouths!** as Milton somewhere calls them.

Do you like Braham's singing.[6] The little Jew has bewitched me. I follow him like as the Boys follow'd Tom the Piper. He cures me of Melancholy as David cured Saul, but I do'nt throw stones at him as Saul did in payment. I was insensible to Music till he gave me a new sense. O that you could go to the new opera of Kais tonight! Tis all about Eastern manners it would just suit you. It describes the wild Arabs, wandering Egyptians, lying dervises, and all that sort of people, to a Hair. You need'nt ha' gone so far to see what you see if you saw it as I do every night at Drury Lane Theatre. Braham's singing when it is impassion'd is finer than Mrs. Siddons or Mr Kemble's acting & when it is not impassion'd it [is] as good as hearing a person of fine sense talking. The brave little Jew!— Old Sarjeant Hill[7] is dead. Mrs Rickman is in a family way. It is thought that Hazlitt will have children if he marries Miss Stoddart. I made a pun the other day & palm'd it upon Holcroft who grinned like a cheshire cat (why do cats grin in Cheshire? because it was once a County Palatine, & the cats cannot help laughing whenever they think of it, though I see no great joke in it.) I said that Holcroft said, being ask'd who were the best dramatic writers of the day, *"Hook and I."*[8] Mr. Hook is author of several pieces, Tekeli &cc.—you know what *hooks* & *eyes* are, dont you? they are what little boys do up their breeches with.— Your letter had many things in it hard to be understood, the puns were ready and swiftlike. But dont you begin to be melancholy in the midst of Eastern Customs? "the mind does not easily conform to foreign usages even in trifles. It requires something that it has been familiar with." That begins one of Dr. Hawksworth's papers in the Adventurer,[9] and is I

think as sensible a remark as ever fell from the Doctor's mouth. Do you know Watford in Hertfordshire? it is a pretty village. Louisa goes to school there. They say the Governess is a very intelligent managing person, takes care of the morals of the pupils, teaches them something beyond exteriors. Poor Mrs. Beaumont! Rickman's aunt, she might have been a governess (as both her neices are) if she had had any ability or any education, but I never thought she was good for any thing; she is dead and so is her nephew. He was shot in half at Monte Video; that is, not exactly in half, but as as you have seen a 3 quarter Picture. Stoddart is in England. White is at Xts hospital, a **Wit** of the first magnitude, but had rather be thought a gentleman, like Congreve. You know Congreve's repulse which he gave to Voltaire when he came to visit him as a *literary man,* that he wished to be consider'd only in the light of a private gentleman. I think the impertinent Frenchman was properly answer'd.[10] I should just serve any Member of the French Institute in the same manner, that wished to be introduced to **me.** Bonaparte has voted 5000 livres to Davy the great young English Chemist! but it has not arrived. Coleridge has deliver'd two Lectures at the Royal Institution; two more were attended, but he did not come. It is thought he has gone sick upon them. He a'nt well thats certain—Wordsworth is coming to see him. He sits up in a two pair of stairs room at the Courier Office, & receives visitors on his close-stool. How is Mr. Ball? he has sent for a prospectus of the London Library. Does any one read at Canton? Lord Moira[11] is president of the Westminister Library. I suppose you might have interest with Sir Joseph Banks to get to be president of any similar institution that should be set up at Canton. I think public reading rooms the best mode of educating young men. Solitary reading is apt to give the headach. Besides who knows that you *do* read? There are ten thousand institutions similar to the Royal Institution which have sprung up from it. There is the London Institution, The Southwark Institution, The Russell Square Rooms Institution &c—**College** quasi **Con-lege,** a place where people read together. Wordsworth the great poet is coming to town. He is to have apartments in the Mansion House.[12] He says he does not see much difficulty in writing like Shakspeare, if he had a mind to try it. It is clear then nothing is wanting but the mind. Even Coleridge a little checked at this hardihood of asser-

tion. Jones of Trinity I suppose you know is dead. A proposal for erecting a monument to him by his friends is advertized in this day's newspapers. Was not he your friend? or was your friend of Caius' College?— Dyer came to me the other evening at eleven oClock, when there was a large room full of company, which I usually get together on a Wednesday Evening (all great men have public days) to propose to me to have my face done by a Miss Beetham,[13] a miniature painter, some relation to Mrs. Beetham the Profilist & Patern Mangle woman opposite St. Dunstan's, to put before my book of Extracts. I declined it. Well, my dear Manning, talking cannot be infinite, I have said all I have to say, the rest is but remembrances which we shall bear in our heads of you while we have heads. Here is a packet of trifles nothing worth, but it is a trifling part of the world where I live. Emptyness abounds. But in fullness of affection we remain yours.

<div style="text-align: right">C L</div>

MS: Folger Shakespeare Library. Pub.: Talfourd (1837), I, 300–306; Sala, I, 397–403; Purnell, I, 397–403; Fitzgerald, II, 230–236; Hazlitt, I, 388–392; Ainger (1888), I, 243–247; Ainger (1900), II, 154–161 and 270; Macdonald, I, 300–305; Ainger (1904), I, 294–298 and 396; Harper, III, 263–270; Lucas (1905), VI, 381–384, and VII, 970; Lucas (1912), V, 399–403; Lucas (1935), II, 47–51.

1. Written in Canton on April 21 and November 20, 1807, and January 6–7, 1808 (*Manning-Lamb Letters,* pp. 96–105), in the first of which Manning remarks on the roll of silk and the letter he has sent Mary. That letter has not been recovered and was presumably the one in which he named (the unidentified) Knox, the bearer of the silk, mentioned below. *"Nox longa"*—"long night"—is from Horace's *Epistles,* I, i, 20.

2. "Things forbidden and only to be enjoyed through smuggling." The Latin below translates, "Brilliant blemishes." The Holcrofts' new daughter would be either Betsy or Ellen, according to *The Lambs,* p. 170. (Sophy [b. 1775] is listed there with them as a daughter of the present Mrs. Holcroft. But she had been born to Holcroft's second wife, the former Maria Tipler of Nottingham, and in 1796 had been married to Lieutenant Colonel William Tooke Harwood. He had been an acquaintance of Godwin since 1793 and retired on half pay since 1804. See *Holcroft,* I, 157, and II, 107, and *Shelley and His Circle,* I, 183 and 309–310.)

3. "Cinna is poor, but he loves," an adaptation of Martial's *Epigrams,* VIII, 19.

4. One of the many translations, usually titled *The Adventures of Telemachus,* of Archbishop Fénelon's (see Vol. I, Letter 96, note 3) *Les avantures de Télémaque fils d'Ulysse, ou suite du quatrième livre de l'Odyssée d'Homère* (3 vols.; 1699). See Letter 136, note 6, for the translations by George Chapman, one of which is referred to below, and Vol. I, Letter 80, note 5, for Robert Dodsley's collection of plays.

5. This and what follows to the end of the paragraph, where is the borrowing from Milton, "Lycidas," line 119, Lamb expanded into "On the Custom of Hissing at the Theatres, with Some Account of a Club of Damned Authors" (*Works,* I, 87–92). See my Vol. I, Letter 65, note 3, about the temptations of St. Anthony of Egypt.

6. That of the tenor and composer John Braham (1774?–1856), which Lamb compares below to the acting of Kemble—John Philip Kemble, one assumes from "The Old Actors" (*Works*, II, 291)—and again in "Imperfect Sympathies." Lamb commented on Braham's recantation of Judaism in the latter essay and also in "The Religion of Actors" (*Works*, II, 62, and I, 288). Braham had begun his career at Covent Garden in 1787, had been engaged at the Royalty from 1787 to 1789 and at Bath from 1794 to 1796, and had been appearing since then at Drury Lane, where his opera *Kais*, written in collaboration with the actor and composer William Reeve (1757–1815), had opened on February 11, 1808. Tom the Piper and his followers are in William Browne's *Britannia's Pastorals*, Book II (1616), Song 2, esp. lines 85–146, as FitzGerald, the poet and translator, observed in a letter to the Shakespearean and Biblical scholar William Aldis Wright (1831–1914) of March 21, 1878. (See Wright, ed., *Letters and Literary Remains of Edward FitzGerald* [1902–1903; rpt. New York: AMS Press, 1966], III, 317–318.) For the references to David and Saul see 1 Samuel 16:14–23, 18:11, 19:10, and 20:33.

7. George Hill (1716–1808) of Lincoln's Inn, who had been made serjeant-at-law and king's serjeant in 1772 and was a scholar of mathematics as well as the law. He had become known as Serjeant Labyrinth because of his abstractions about impractical points of law and the subject of stories about his absence of mind. He had died on February 21, at his home in Bedford Square. Mrs. Rickman, mentioned next, gave birth to Ann this year.

8. The pun is underscored twice. Theodore Edward Hook (1788–1841), a novelist, a wit, an editor, and the model for Lucian Gay of Benjamin Disraeli's *Coningsby* and Mr. Wagg of Thackeray's *Vanity Fair*, wrote only the words for *Tekeli* (1806) and other comic operas and melodramas of his father, the organist and composer James Hook (1746–1827).

9. Cf. Nos. 75, 80, and 83 of *The Adventurer* (in *The British Essayists*, ed. Alexander Chalmers [London: Johnson, 1808], XXIV, 205–211, 244–250, and 261–265). They are by Joseph Warton (1722–1800) rather than by John Hawkesworth (1715?–1773), but they appear to be the only papers in *The Adventurer* that contain even the substance of the quotation. Louisa, referred to below, is Louisa Martin. (See Letter 185, note 2.) Mrs. Beaumont is presumably *Miss* Beaumont, the "maiden Aunt Beaumont" (*Rickman*, p. 77) whom Rickman took into his home upon his return from Dublin to London in 1802 and whose nephew Lamb mentioned in Letter 126, near the reference to note 1. Her nieces have not been identified except for what Lamb writes of them here. See Vol. I, Introduction, pp. xxxv–xxxvi, about James White.

10. But it was Voltaire who answered Congreve's "despicable foppery of desiring to be considered not as an author but a gentleman" with the riposte that had Congreve been "only a gentleman, he should not have come to visit him" (*Lives of the English Poets*, II, 226). The French Institute had in 1807 awarded the natural philosopher Humphry, later Sir Humphry, Davy (1778–1829), mentioned below, the Napoleon prize of a medal and three thousand francs for the best experiment conducted that year on galvanism. It was Davy, Coleridge's acquaintance since 1799 and correspondent since 1800, who had secured for Coleridge an invitation to speak this year at the Royal Institution. (For some account of Coleridge's condition, performance, and lectures—perhaps eighteen on the "Principles of Poetry" [*Coleridge's Letters*, III, 29] given from January 15 to circa June 13—see the sections of *Coleridge's Letters* for the period, *Coleridge's Shakespearean Criticism*, II, 3–19, and *De Quincey's Writings*, II, 188–190. Coleridge and De Quincey had met in 1807.) Wordsworth had left Grasmere on February 23 to see to Coleridge and the publication, deferred to 1815, of his own *The White Doe of Rylstone*. He attended Coleridge every evening until March 16, then visited the

Clarksons in Bury St. Edmunds and the George Howland Beaumonts in Dunmow, returned to London, and left for Grasmere on April 3.

11. The soldier and statesman Francis Rawdon-Hastings, first Marquis of Hastings and second Earl of Moira (1754–1826), who according to the Royal Kalendar (in the City of Westminster Central Reference Library) served as president of the Westminster Library from 1801 to 1821. The traveler and natural historian Sir Joseph Banks (1743–1820), referred to in the following sentence, had in his capacity as president of the Royal Society from 1778 to 1820 influenced the East India Company to provide Manning with passage to China. Those institutions next mentioned that were imitative of the Royal Institution have disappeared.

12. The official residence of the lord mayor of London. Thomas Jones (1756–1807), referred to below, had been since 1781 a fellow of, and from 1787 to his death a tutor in mathematics at, Trinity College, Cambridge. A bust and tablet were fashioned in his memory for the antechapel of Trinity. No other Jones (see below) occurs in the correspondence between Lamb and Manning.

13. Mary Matilda Betham (1776–1852), to whom Coleridge in 1802 had written "To Matilda Betham from a Stranger" and with whom Lamb in 1811 began a correspondence. He and his sister also came to know Anne (d. 1833), later Mrs. Norman; Barbara (b. 1800?), later Mrs. Edward Edwards of Westerfield, Suffolk; Louisa; Mary; perhaps Charles (b. 1780), who after serving as an officer for the East India Company became in 1812 the tenant farmer of Walter Savage Landor at Llanthony, Monmouth, and involved him in an extended lawsuit; Captain John of the East India service; Sir William (1779–1853), Ulster king of arms and the author of works on Irish archaeology; and others of the fifteen children of the Reverend Mr. William Betham (1749–1839), antiquary, of Stonham Aspall, Suffolk, and of Stoke Lacy, Herefordshire, and the former Mary Damant, or Dammant (b. 1753?), of Eye, Suffolk. Lamb characterized them for their tallness in "Many Friends" (*Works,* I, 271–272). Mary Matilda Betham acquired her education and love of literature and history largely from her father and in his extensive library, taught herself miniature painting, in 1797 had published *Elegies, and Other Smaller Poems,* and by 1804 had given readings from Shakespeare in London and exhibited her portraits at the Royal Academy. Her *A Biographical Dictionary of the Celebrated Women of Every Age and Country* appeared in 1804, *Poems* in 1808, the (successful) *Lay of Marie* in 1816, and *Vignettes: In Verse* in 1818. Family difficulties and a breakdown in her health necessitated her retirement to the country in about 1818. Sometime after 1830 she settled once more in London and resumed some of her old friendships. Although she seems never to have done a portrait of Lamb, she did do at least one each of George Dyer, the Southeys, the Coleridges, and Randal Norris. (For a reproduction of the last see Lucas' *At the Shrine of St. Charles: Stray Papers on Lamb Brought Together for the Centenary of His Death in 1834* [London: Methuen, 1934], facing p. 14. For further information on her see M. Betham-Edwards, *Six Life Studies of Famous Women* [London: Griffith and Farran, 1880], pp. 231–303, and *A House of Letters,* ed. Ernest Betham [London: Jarrolds, 1905].) The Mrs. Beetham next mentioned, to whom Lamb imagines her related, was probably the wife of Edward Beetham. He is listed in the London directories of 1808 and 1809 as a patent washing-mill maker and mangle manufacturer of 26 and 27 Fleet Street.

223. *C. L. to Godwin, written on the following letter from Godwin to C. L.*

<div align="right">

Skinner Street
Mar. 10, 1808
</div>

Dear Lamb

I address you with all humility, because I know you to be tenax propositi.[1] Hear me I intreat you with patience.

It is strange with what different feelings an author & a bookseller looks at the sam[e] manuscript. I know this by experience: I was an author—I am a bookseller. The author thinks what will conduce to his honour: the bookseller what will cause his commodities to sell.

You or some other wise man I have heard to say, It is children that read children's books (when they are read); but it is parents that choose them. The critical thought of the tradesman puts itself therefore into the place of the parent, & enquires what will please the parent, & what the parent will condemn.

We live in squeamish days. Amidst the beauties of your manuscript, of which no man can think more highly than I do, what will the squeamish say to such expressions as these? "devoured their limbs, yet warm & trembling, lapping the blood."[2] p. 10, or to the giant's vomit, p. 14, or to the minute & shocking description of the extinguishing the giant's eye, in the page following. You I dare say have no formed plan of excluding the female sex from among your readers, & I, as a bookseller, must consider that, if you have, you exclude one half of the human species.

Nothing is more easy than to modify these things, if you please; & nothing, I think, is more indispensible.

Give me, as soon as possible, your thoughts on the matter.

I should also like a preface. Half our customers know not Homer, or know him only as you & I know the lost authors of antiquity. What can be more proper, than to mention one or two of those obvious recommendations of his works, which must lead every human creature to desire a nearer acquaintance?

<div align="right">

Believe me ever
faithfully yours
W Godwin
</div>

I inclose the pages, 9–15.

[16 Mitre Court Buildings
March ?10]

Dear Godwin,

The Giant's vomit was perfectly nauseous, and I am glad that you pointed it out. I have removed the objection.— To the other passages I can find no other objection but what you may bring to numberless passages besides, such as **Scylla** snatching up the six men &c—that is to say, they are lively images of *shocking* things. If you want a book which is not occasionally to *shock,* you should not have thought of a Tale which was so full of Anthropophagi & monsters. I cannot alter those things without enervating the Book, I will not alter them if the penalty should be that you & all the London Booksellers should refuse it.— But speaking as author to author, I must say, that I think *the terrible* in those two passages seems to me so much to preponderate over *the nauseous* as to make them rather *fine* than *disgusting.* Who is to read them I do'nt know—who is it reads Tales of Terror & Mysteries of Udolpho?³ such things **sell.**— I only say that I will not consent to alter such passages which I know to be some of the best in the Book. As an author I say to you, an Author, Touch not my Work. As to a booksolle[r] I say, Take the work such as it is, or refuse it. you are as *free* to refuse it as when we first talk'd of it. As to a friend, *I say,* dont plague yourself or me with nonsensical objections. I assure you I will not alter one more word.

MS: Lord Abinger. Pub.: Hazlitt, I, 393–394; Ainger (1888), I, 247–248; Ainger (1900), II, 161–162; Macdonald, I, 306; Ainger (1904), I, 298–299; Harper, III, 270–271; Lucas (1905), VI, 386–387; Lucas (1912), V, 405–406; Lucas (1935), II, 53–54. Address: Mr. Lamb/16/Mitre Court Buildings/Temple. There is no address by Lamb.

1. "Tenacious in your proposals" (Horace, *Odes,* III, iii, 1). The subject is Lamb's manuscript of *The Adventures of Ulysses.*
2. Ch. i (*Works,* III, 211). The passage descriptive of the extinguishing of Cyclops' eye, mentioned below, also remains, on p. 212. Lamb supplied a preface (*Works,* III, 207), as Godwin shortly requests, but not one biographical or recommending the works of Homer.
3. *Tales of Terror* (1801), by Matthew Gregory Lewis, and *The Mysteries of Udolpho* (1794), by Mrs. Ann Radcliffe.

224. C. L. to Henry Crabb Robinson

Saturday 12 Mar 1808

Dear Sir,

Wordsworth breakfasts with me on **Tuesday** morning next, he goes
to Mrs. Clarkson the next day, and will be glad to meet you before
he goes.— Can you come to us before nine or at nine that morn-
ing?—[1] I am afraid, W is so engaged with Coleridge who is ill,
we cannot have him in an evening. If I do not hear from you, I will
expect you to breakfast on Tuesday—

Yours truly

C Lamb

MS: Dr. Williams's Library. Pub.: Harper, III, 271; Lucas (1905), VI, 388;
Lucas (1912), V, 407; Lucas (1935), II, 55. Address: Mr. H. Robinson/Mr Col-
lier's/56 Hatton Garden. Postmark: March 1808. Robinson resided for several
years with the journalist John Dyer Collier (1762–1825) and his wife, the former
Jane Payne (d. 1833), both of whom became correspondents of Lamb. Collier, the
son of a London physician, was educated at the Charterhouse from 1771 to 1776,
was for a time in the Spanish wool trade, and had turned to journalism after
suffering business losses in 1793–1794. He first edited the *Monthly Register* and
the *Critical Review*, in 1804 joined the staff of the *Times* and later that of the
Morning Chronicle, and with his son the Shakespearean critic John Payne
Collier (1789–1883), who also became Lamb's correspondent, came to establish a
system of newspapers for the provinces. In 1803 John Dyer Collier published an
Essay on the Patent Laws. In 1808 he published a biography of Abraham New-
land (1730–1807), the chief cashier of the Bank of England from 1782 to 1807.
 1. Robinson did go to the Lambs' and there met Wordsworth. See *H. C. R. on
Books and Writers*, I, 10.

225. M. A. L. to Sarah Stoddart

[March 16, 1808]

My dear Sarah

Do not be very angry that I have not written to you. I have
promised your brother to be at your wedding,[1] and that favor you
must accept as an atonement for my offences—you have been in no
want of correspondence lately, and I wished to leave you both to
your own inventions.

The border you are working for me I prize at a very high rate because I consider it as the last work you can do for me, the time so fast approaching when you must no longer work for your friends. Yet my old fault of giving away presents has not left me and I am desirous of even giving away this your last gift. I had intended to have given it away without your knowledge but I have intrusted my secret to Hazlitt, and I suppose it will not remain a secret long, so I condescend to consult you. It is to Miss Hazlitt to whose superior claim I wish to give up my right to this precious worked border. Her brother William is her great favorite, and she would be pleased to possess his bride's last work. Are you not to give the fellow-border to one sister-in-law, and therefore has she not a just claim to it?—— I never heard in the annals of weddings (since the days of Nausicaa, and she only washed her old gowns for that purpose)² that the bride's ever furnished the apparel of their maids. Besides, I can be completely clad in your work without it, for the spotted muslin will serve both for cap & hat (Nota bene, my hat is the same as yours) and the gown you sprigged for me has never been made up, therefore I can wear that.—— Or, if you like better, I will make up a new silk which Manning has sent me from China. Manning would like to hear I wore it for the first time at your wedding. It is a very pretty light colour, but there is one objection (besides not being your work & that is a very serious objection) and that is, Mrs Hazlitt tells me that all Winterslow would be in an uproar if the bride-maid was to be dressed in anything but white, and although it is a very light colour I confess we cannot call it white, being a sort of a dead-white-ish-bloom colour; then silk, perhaps, in a morning is not so proper, though the occasion, so joyful, might justify a full dress. Determine for me in this perplexity between the sprig and the China-Manning-silk, But do not contradict my whim about Miss Hazlitt having the border, for I have set my heart upon the matter: if you agree wih me in this I shall think you have forgiven me for giving away your pin; that was a *mad* trick, but I had many obligations and no money. I repent me of the deed wishing I had it now to send to Miss H. with the border, & I cannot, will not, give her the Doctor's pin for having never had any presents from gentlemen in my young days, I highly prize all they now give me, thinking my latter days are better than my former.

You must send this same border in your own name to Miss Hazlitt,

which will save me the disgrace of giving away your gift, and make it amount merely to a civil refusal.

I shall have no present to give you on your marriage, nor do I expect I shall be rich enough to give anything to baby at the first christening, but at the second, or third child's I hope to have a coral or so to spare out of my own earnings. Do not ask me to be Godmother for I have an objection to that—but there is I believe no serious duties attached to a bride's maid, therefore I come with a willing mind, bringing nothing with me but many wishes, and not a few hopes, an[d] a very little of fears—of happy years to come.

<div align="right">

I am dear Sarah

Yours ever most affectionately

M Lamb
</div>

What has Charles done that nobody invites him to the wedding?

MS: Harvard College Library. Pub.: Lucas (1905), VI, 389–390; Lucas (1912), V, 408–409; Lucas (1935), II, 55–57. Address: Miss Stoddart/Winterslow/near Salisbury. Postmark: March 16, 1808.

1. Which took place not at Winterslow, as was planned, but in St. Andrew's, Holborn, on May 1, with Mary as a bridesmaid and Lamb as a guest who, as he told Southey in a letter of August 9, 1815 (in Vol. III), "had like to have been turned out several times during the ceremony. Any thing awful makes me laugh."

2. In *The Adventures of Ulysses*, ch. vi (*Works*, III, 240–241).

226. *C. L. to Godwin, written on the following letter from Godwin to C. L.*

<div align="right">

[41 Skinner Street]

Apr. 11 [1808]
</div>

Dear Lamb

I tremble to speak my mind respecting whatever flows from your pen or your tongue, when I have to express any thing but satisfaction. I can only say to you, like Themistocles[1] in Grecian story, *Strike, but hear me!* If you would only let my remarks lie upon the surface of your mind, like manure on the bosom of the fruitful earth, & not indignantly cast them away by the vehicle that brought them, they might sometimes produce a goodly crop.

It is not every one that knows Homer, & those that have heard of him, do not always call him to mind on the spur of the occasion in his

most alluring form. The Preface ought I think to tell what Homer was—the Father of poetry, the eldest of historians, the collector & recorder of all that was then known, the parent of continuous narration, of imagery, of dramatic character, of dramatic dialogue, of a whole having beginning, middle & end. What book can be better adapted to be put into the hands of children, or of the majority of adults, than a simple unfolding of the tale of the simplest, yet the most famous & venerable of poets, especially when that tale contains the oldest adventures, & the oldest, beautiful manners, now known in the world?

Your Preface is too naked, & wants some such introduction given in the style which no one professes so completely as you. All that you have said is well, & would form an admirable sequel to such an introduction.

> very truly yours
> W Godwin

> [16 Mitre Court Buildings
> April 11]

Dr. G—

I have read your letter and am fully of opinion that such a drawling biography as you have chalk'd out is not my forte to write. I totally disagree with you; and prefer my own preface (as I am always likely to do) to any preface a man tells me I am qualified to write. You must take that, or none. I am *sick* absolutely sick of that spirit of objection which you constantly shew, as if it were only to **teaze one,** or to warn one against having any more dealings with you in the way of trade. My preface is just such a one as I approve, & there is enough of it, but I had quite as lieve have *no preface* if you prefer it. I shall remember Ulysses as long as I live to write.——

> Yours in the way of friendship
> still Ever
> C L²

MS: Lord Abinger. Unpublished. Address, by Godwin: ⟨Mr. Lamb/16/Mitre Court Building[s]/Temple⟩; by Lamb: Mr. Godwin/41 Skinner Street/Snow hill. Postmark: April 11, 1808.

1. Themistocles (ca. 514–449 B.C.) was the Athenian soldier and statesman to whom Plutarch in his *Lives of the Noble Grecians and Romans* attributed the admonition following. See, for example, the translation by Thomas North (New York: AMS Press, 1967), I, 295.

2. Godwin answered, on the twelfth:

What I wanted was a Preface exactly on the model of the Preface to the Tales, where you should express yourself with the same kindness of Homer, that you had there done of Shakespear.

But I am rightly served for having wanted any thing, In particularly for having expresse[d] my wants in so diffident a manner.

God bless you!

[MS: Lord Abinger]

227. *C. L. to George Dyer*

from my Desk in Leadenhall Street
5 July, 1808

Dear Dyer,—

Coleridge is not so bad as your fears have represented him; it is true that he is Bury'd, although he is not dead: to understand this quibble, you must know that he is at Bury St. Edmund's,[1] relaxing, after the fatigues of lecturing and Londonizing. The little Rickmaness, whom you inquire after so kindly, thrives and grows apace; she is already a prattler, and 'tis thought that on some future day she may be a speaker! We hold our weekly meetings still at No. 16, where, although we are not so high as the top of Malvern, we are involved in almost as much mist. Miss B.'s merit,[2] "in every point of view," I am not disposed to question, although *I have not been indulged with any view of that lady, back, side, or front—fie! Dyer, to praise a female in such common market phrases,*—you, who are held so courtly and so attentive. My book is not yet out, that is, not my 'Extracts'; my 'Ulysses' is, and waits your acceptance. When you shall come to town, I hope to present you both together, never thinking of buying the 'Extracts'—half-a-guinea books were never calculated for my friends. More poets have started up since your departure; William Hazlitt, your friend and mine, is putting to press a collection of verses, chiefly amatory, some of them pretty enough.[3] How these painters encroach on our province! There's Hopner, Shee, Westall, and I dont know who besides, and Tresham. *It seems, on confession, that they are not at the top of their own art, when they seek to eke out their fame with the assistance of another's; no large tea-dealer sells cheeses, no great silversmith deals in razor-straps:* it is only your petty dealers who mix commodities. *If Nero had been a great emperor he would never have*

played the violoncello! Who ever caught you, Dyer, designing a land-scape, or taking a likeness? I have no more to add, who am the friend of virtue, poetry, and painting, therefore, in an especial manner,

Unalterably thine,

C. Lamb

MS: unavailable, but purchased by Maggs Bros., Ltd., from Sotheby's on April 29, 1969. Text: E. S., "Recollections of George Dyer," *Mirror of Literature, Amusement, and Instruction*, 38 (December 1841), 310–311. Also pub.: Ainger (1900), II, 162–163; Macdonald, I, 306–307; Ainger (1904), I, 299–300; Harper, III, 272–273; Lucas (1905), VII, 970–971; Lucas (1912), V, 410–411; Lucas (1935), II, 57–58. Address: To G. Dyer, Esq.,/Jas. Martin's, M. P.,/Overbury, Worcestershire. The heading is taken from the description of the letter in Sotheby's catalogue for April 29, 1969, p. 130, item 378, which includes the statement that the "full and authentic text of this delightful letter is UNPUBLISHED, for the version printed in the *Letters*, ed. E. V. Lucas (1935) . . . is quite remarkably inaccurate. Lucas does not cite his source for this letter, but it seems clear that he relied on a badly garbled copy for his text (the original is clearly dated: Lucas supplies the date conjecturally, describing the letter as undated)." In Lucas (1905), VII, 970, the source of the letter is given as "*The Mirror*, 1841." James Martin (1738–1810) was a member of Parliament for Tewkesbury, Gloucestershire, from 1776 to 1807.

1. With the Clarksons. Coleridge was with them from about July 3 to perhaps the end of the month. Then he went to the home of John Broadhead of Leeds, a friend of the Clarksons, where illness detained him until August 24. (See *The Friend*, ed. Barbara Rooke, II, 471–472.) On September 1 Coleridge went to the Wordsworths' home since June—Allan Bank, Grasmere—where he remained off and on for the next eighteen months. The "little Rickmaness," mentioned below, is presumably Ann.

2. That of Mary Matilda Betham. The expression quoted, following, is conjecturally from Dyer's letter to Lamb. About the publication of *Specimens of English Dramatic Poets*, referred to as "Extracts" below, see Letter 211, note 1. The frontispiece of *The Adventures of Ulysses*, which is reproduced in *Works*, III, facing p. 206, carries the notation "Published at Skinner Street June 6 1808."

3. But not published. Next mentioned are the portrait painters John Hoppner (1758–1810), whose *Oriental Tales Translated into Verse* had appeared in 1805, and Sir Martin Archer Shee (1769–1850), whose *Rhymes on Art, or the Remonstrance of a Painter* had appeared also in 1805; and the historical painters Richard Westall (1765–1836), who wrote and illustrated *A Day in Spring* (1808), and Henry Tresham (1749?–1814), the author of *The Sea-sick Minstrel* (1796), *Rome at the Close of the Eighteenth Century* (1799), *Britannicus to Buonaparte: An Heroic Epistle* (1803), and *Recreation at Ramsgate* [1805?].

228. *M. A. L. to Sarah Stoddart Hazlitt, with a postscript from C. L.*

[Friday, December 9—
Saturday, December 10, 1808]

My dear Sarah,

I hear of you from your brother but you do not write yourself, nor does Hazlitt, I beg that one or both of you will amend this fault as speedily as possible, for I am very anxious to hear of your health. I hope, as you say nothing about your fall to your brother, you are perfectly recovered from the effects of it.

You cannot think how very much we miss you and H. of a wednesday evening—all the glory of the night, I may say, is at an end. Phillips makes his jokes and there is no one to applaud him. Rickman argues & there is no one to oppose him.

The worst miss of all to me is that when we are in the dismals there is now no hope of relief from any quarter whatsoever. . Hazlitt was most brilliant, most ornamental as a wednesday-man, but he was a more useful one on common day, when he dropt in after a quarrel or a fit of the glooms. The Skeffington[1] is quite out now, my brother having got drunk with claret & Tom Sheridan—. This visit, and the occasion of it, is a profound secret & therefore I tell it to nobody but you & Mrs Reynolds. Through the medium of Wroughton there came an invitation & proposal from T. S. that C. L. should write some scenes in a speaking Pantomime the other parts of which Tom, now, and his father formerly, have manufactured between them. So in the Christmas holydays my brother & his two great associates we expect will be all three damned together, that is I mean if Charles's share, which is done & sent in, is accepted.

Saturday

I left this unfinished yesterday in the hope that my brother would have done it for me, his reason for refusing me was "no exquisite reason"[2] for it was because he must write a letter to Manning in three or four weeks, and therefore he could not be always writing letters he said. I wanted him to tell your husband about a great work which

Godwin is going to publish to enlighten the world once more, and I shall not be able to make out what it is. He (Godwin) took his usual walk one evening, a fortnight since, to the end of Hatton Garden & back again, during that walk a thought came into his mind, which he instantly sate down & improved upon till he brought it, in seven or eight days, into the compass of a reasonable sized pamphet. To propose a subscription to all well-disposed people to raise a certain sum of money to be expended in the care of a cheap monument for the former & the future Great dead **men,** the monument to be a white cross with a wooden slab at the end, telling their name & qualifications,— This wooden slab & white cross, to be perpetuated to the end of time. To survive the fall of empires & the destruction of cities by means of a map, which was in case of an insurrection among the people, or any other cause by which a city or country may be destroyed, was to be carefully preserved & then when things got again into their usual order, the White-cross-wooden slab makers were to go to work again and set them in their former places. This as nearly as I can tell you is the sum & substance of it, but it is written remarkably well. In his very best manner, for the proposal (which seems to me very like throwing salt on a sparrows tail to catch him) occupies but half a page which is followed by very fine writing on the benefits he conjectures would follow if it were done. Very excellent thoughts on death, and our feelings concerning dead friends. And the advantages an old country has over a new one, even in the slender memorials we have of great men who once flourished:

Charles is come home & wants his dinner, and so the dead men must be no more thought on: Tell us how you go on & how you like Winterslow and winter evenings.

Noales[3] has not yet got back again, but he i[s] in better spirits. John Hazlitt was here on wednesday very sober.

Our love to Hazlitt

<div align="right">

Yours affectionately
M Lamb

</div>

There came this morning a printed **Prospectus**[4] **from** S T Coleridge Grasmere of a Weekly Paper to be called *The Friend.* A flaming Prospectus, I have no time to give the heads of it. To commence first Saturdy. in Jany. There came also Notice of a Turkey from Mr

Clarkson, which I am more sanguine in expecting the accomplish-
ment of than I am of Coleridge's prophecy.

C Lamb

MS: Huntington Library. Pub.: Talfourd (1848), I, 159–163; Sala, I, 430–
433; Purnell, I, 430–433; Fitzgerald, II, 263; Ainger (1888), I, 248; Ainger
(1900), II, 164; Macdonald, I, 305; Ainger (1904), I, 300; Harper, I, facsimile,
and III, 273–274; Lucas (1905), VI, 391–392; Lucas (1912), V, 411–413;
Lucas (1935), II, 59–61. Address: Mrs. Hazlitt/Winterslow/near Sarum/Wilts.
Postmark: December 10, 1808.

1. Seemingly an illusion to some plan for a drama proposed to Lamb by the
fop and playwright Sir Lumley St. George Skeffington (1771–1850). The plan
for which it was dropped, referred to below as having been proposed by Tom
Sheridan (1775–1817)—he was the only son of Richard Brinsley Sheridan by his
first wife, the former Elizabeth Ann Linley (1754–1792), and after 1813 the
colonial treasurer of the Cape of Good Hope—may have resulted in the manuscript
of an untitled comic opera once owned by the author and Lamb's later correspon-
dent Peter George Patmore (1786–1855). It is now in the British Museum (Add.
MSS. 25,924) and is published in The Works of Charles Lamb: Poetical and
Dramatic Tales, Essays and Criticisms, ed. Charles Kent (London: Routledge
[1876]), pp. 171–195. Kent followed Patmore in ascribing it to Lamb primarily
on the basis that "nobody else claiming it, it is undoubtedly every bit of it in his
own handwriting." Lucas noted that Edmund Blunden, though not persuaded as
much as Patmore and Kent, thought that some of the names in the manuscript
looked as though they were in Lamb's handwriting. But Lucas was convinced
(as I am) that "the writing is not Lamb's, while the matter has nothing char-
acteristic in it" (Lucas [1935], II, 61).

2. Twelfth Night, II, iii, 145. Godwin's "pamphet," discussed below, is An Essay
on Sepulchres: Of a Proposal for Erecting Some Memorial of the Illustrious Dead
in All Ages on the Spot Where Their Remains Have Been Interred (1809).

3. The dramatists James Sheridan Knowles (1784–1862), whose family was
acquainted with the Hazlitts of Wem and whom the Reverend Mr. Hazlitt had
introduced to Lamb this year. Knowles too became Lamb's correspondent, and Lamb
wrote to him the poem "To R [J.]. S. Knowles, Esq., on His Tragedy of Virginius"
and for him the Prologue and Epilogue to his comedy The Wife (Works, V, 58,
129, 130, and 349).

4. Its first and revised issues were printed by W. Pennington of Kendal. A third
issue, dated February 2, 1809, was printed by C. and R. Baldwin of New Bridge
Street, London. (See The Friend, ed. Barbara Rooke, I, esp. xxxvii–xliv.) The
twenty-seven numbers of the first edition of the periodical itself extend from
Thursday, June 1 (not Saturday January 7, as originally announced), 1809, to
Thursday, March 15, 1810.

229. *M. A. L. to Mrs. Clarkson, with a postscript from C. L.*

No 16 Mitre Court Buildings
Inner Temple
Saturday Morning [December 10, 1808]

My dear Mrs Clarkson

I feel myself greatly indebted to Mr Clarkson for his care about our direction since it has procured us the pleasure of a line from you. Why are we all, my dear friend, so unwilling to sit down and write a letter when we all so well know the grea[t] satisfaction it is to hear of the welfare of an absent friend? I began to think that you and all I connect i[n] my mind with you were gone from us for ever——Coleridge in a manner gave us up when he was in town, and we have now lost all traces of him. At the time he was in town I received two letters from Miss Wordsworth which I never answered because I would not complain to her of our old friend. As this has never been explained to her it must seem very strange, more particularly so, as Miss Hutchinson[1] & Mrs Wordsworth were in an ill state of health at the time. Will you some day soon write a few words just to tell me how they all are and all you know concerning them?

Do not imagine that I am now *complaining* to you of Coleridge, perhaps we are both in fault. We expect *too much,* and he gives *too little.* We ought many years ago to have understood each other better. Nor is it quite all over with us yet, for he will some day or other come in with the same old face, and receive (after a few spiteful words from me) the same warm welcome as ever. But we could not submit to sit as hearers at his lectures and not be permitted to see our old friend when *school-hours* were over. I beg you will not let what I have said give you a moments thought, nor pray do not mention it to the Wordsworths nor to Coleridge, for I know he thinks I am apt to speak unkindly of him: I am not good tempered, and I have two or three times given him proofs that I am not. You say you are all in your "better way" which is a very chearful hearing, for I trust you mean to include that your health is *bettering* too.

I look forward with great pleasure to the near approach of Christmas and Mr Clarkson, And now the turkey you are so kind as to

promise us comes into my head & tells me it is so very near that if writing before then should happen to be the least irksome to you, I will be content to wait for intelligence of our old friends till I have the pleasure of seeing Mr Clarkson in town. I ought to say this because I know at times how dreadfully irksome writing a letter is to me, even when I have no reason in the world to give why it is so, and I remember I have heard you express something of the same kind of feelings.

I try to remember something to enquire after at Bury—. The lady[2] we visited, the cherry tree Tom and I robbed, Tom my partner in the robbery (Mr Thomas C—I suppose now) and your Cook maid that was so kind to me, are all at present I can recollect. Of all the places I ever saw Bury has made the liveliest impression on my memory. I have a very indistinct recollection of the Lakes.

Charles joins with me in affectionate remembrances to you all, and he is more warm in his expressions of gratitude for the turky because he is fonder of good eating than I am, though I am not amiss in that way.

<div align="right">

God bless you my kind friends
I remain yours affectionately.
M Lamb
</div>

Excuse this slovenly letter, if I were to write it over again I should abridge it one half.

We have this moment receivd a very chearful letter from Coleridge who is now at Grasmere. It contains a prospectus for a new weekly publication to be called *the friend*. He says they are well there, and in good spirits & that he has not been so well for a long time.

The[3] Prospectus is of a weekly paper of a miscellaneous nature to be call'd the Friend & to come out the first number the first Saturday in January. Those who remember *the Watchman* will not be very sanguine in expecting a regular fulfillment of this Prophecy. But C. writes in delightful spirits & *if ever*, he may *now* do this thing. I suppose he will send you a Prospectus. I had some thought of inclosing mine. But I want to shew it about. My kindest remembre. to Mr C & thanks for the turkey.

<div align="right">

C Lamb
</div>

MS: Berg Collection, New York Public Library. Pub.: Macdonald, I, 308–310; Harper, III, 274–277; Lucas (1905), VI, 393–395; Lucas (1912), V, 413–415; Lucas (1935), II, 61–63. Address: Mrs. Clarkson/Bury/Suffolk. Postmark: December 10, 1808.

1. Sara Hutchinson. See *Wordsworths' Letters*, II, 254–255, for an account of her illness.
2. Perhaps Sarah Jane Maling, who became Mrs. Wimbridge. Robinson, who was her friend, described her as an "intimate friend" of Mrs. Clarkson and "a person rather older than herself and of much originality of mind and character" (*H. C. R.'s Diary*, I, 20; Mr. Wimbridge, a civil servant in London in 1839, is mentioned in *H. C. R. on Books and Writers*, II, 574, as having advised Richard Wordsworth's son, John [1815–1846], about employment he was seeking in Wimbridge's office). Referred to after the son of the Clarksons is probably Betsy, their maid, but possibly Mrs. Kitchener, their housekeeper.
3. From Lamb.

230. *C. L. to George Dawe*

Saturday

I dont know what day [21] of Jany. 09

Dear D—

I think that I should not find much entertainmt. in an Anatomical Lecture, therefore if you will excuse me, I will decline your kind offer of a ticket. It would not be convenient for me to go on Monday, & I think that it would not amuse me any other night. Therefore I resign my interest in said Ticket or Tickets to some more scientific wight—

& am

(as they say)

equally obliged

C L

P. S. When did you see Mrs. Godwin?

MS: Huntington Library. Pub.: Lucas (1935), II, 64. Address: Mr Dawe/ Wells Street/Oxford Road. Postmark: January 21, 1809.

231. *C. L. to Robert Lloyd*

Saty 25 feb 1809

Dear Robert,

A great gap has been filled up since our intercourse was broken off.

We shall at least have some things to talk over, when we meet. That you should never have been in London since I saw you last is a fact which I cannot account for on the principles of my own mental formation. You are worthy to be mentioned with Claudian's old Man of Verona.[1] I forbear to ask you any questions concerning your family, *who* are dead, and *who* married; I will not anticipate our meeting. I have been in total darkness respecting you all these years. I am just up; & have heard, without being able to confirm the fact, that Drury Lane Theatre is burnt to the ground.[2] Of Walton's Angler a new edition is just published with the original plates revived, I think of buying it. The old editions are two guineas, & two guineas & a half.— I have not forgotten our ride from Saffron Waldon, and the madness of young parson Thomson of Cambridge that I took your brother to see. He is gone as a missionary to the East.——

I live at present at Number 16 Mitre Court Buildings Inner Temple. I shall move at ladyday,[3] or a little later: if you dont find me in M. C. B. I shall be at No. *2. or 4* **Inner Temple Lane.**— At either of which places I shall be happy to shake my old friend Robert by the hand.

<div align="right">C L</div>

MS: Huntington Library. Pub.: Ainger (1900), II, 165–166; Macdonald, I, 310–311; Ainger (1904), I, 301–302; Harper, III, 277–278; Lucas (1935), II, 64–65. Address: Mr Robert Lloyd/Birmingham. Postmark: February 25, 1809.

1. "De sene Veronensi, qui suburbium nunquam egressus est," with which Abraham Cowley concluded his essay "The Dangers of an Honest Man in Much Company" and whose translation of its opening lines reads so:

Happy the man, who his whole time doth bound
Within th' inclosure of his little ground.
Happy the man, whom the same humble place
(Th' hereditary cottage of his race)
From his first rising infancy has known,
And by degrees sees gently bending down,
With natural propension, to that earth
Which both preserv'd his life, and gave him birth.

2. The fire had occurred on February 24. The new theater was opened on October 10, 1812. The seventh (1808) edition of *The Compleat Angler,* to which Lamb refers next, is the revision by the bookseller Samuel Bagster (1772–1851) of Sir John Hawkins' edition of 1797. (See Vol. I, Letter 100, note 1.) Thomson is Marmaduke Thompson. See Vol. I, Introduction, p. xxxii.

3. Lady Day is March 25. The Lambs were settled in Hazlitt's former lodgings at 34 Southampton Buildings by March 28 and moved to 4 Inner Temple Lane on June 3. Robert Lloyd came to London in late March and stayed through mid-April. On April 3 he wrote home to his wife that the Lambs' "Union of affection is what we conceive of marriage in Heaven. They are the World *one* to the *other*" (*Lamb and the Lloyds*, p. 159).

INDEX OF NAMES

Boldface numbers refer to key pages.